POLITICAL PARTIES

AN INTRODUCTION

Robert H. Blank

University of Idaho

PRENTICE-HALL, INC., Englewood Cliffs, N.J. 07632

Library of Congress Cataloging in Publication Data

Blank, Robert H.
    Political parties.

    Includes bibliographical references and index.
    1. Political parties—United States.   I. Title.
JK2261.B64   329'.02   79-10685
ISBN   0-13-684761-7

TO MALLORY

Printed in the United States of America

10   9   8   7   6   5   4   3   2   1

Editorial/production supervision
and interior design by Scott Amerman
Cover design by Jim Wall
Manufacturing buyer: Harry P. Baisley

PRENTICE-HALL INTERNATIONAL, INC., *London*
PRENTICE-HALL OF AUSTRALIA PTY. LIMITED, *Sydney*
PRENTICE-HALL OF CANADA, LTD., *Toronto*
PRENTICE-HALL OF INDIA PRIVATE LIMITED, *New Delhi*
PRENTICE-HALL OF JAPAN, INC., *Tokyo*
PRENTICE-HALL OF SOUTHEAST ASIA PTE. LTD., *Singapore*
WHITEHALL BOOKS LIMITED, *Wellington, New Zealand*

Contents

SECTION VII
THE PARTIES:
HOPE OR DESPAIR?   445

Preface

This book provides a comprehensive coverage of American political parties and elections that can be understood by undergraduate students. While it includes summaries of the most recent political research and offers a variety of models for anlayzing the role of parties, an attempt has been made to limit political science jargon to a minimum. In subject areas where there is disagreement among political observers over the meaning of particular phenomena, the reader is given the pertinent facts, the alternative explanations, and a framework for independent analysis.

Throughout the book, the complexity of social reality and the constant interaction between political parties and other political and nonpolitical elements is demonstrated. It is stressed that parties do not operate in isolation and that changes in society affect alterations in parties as electoral organizations, governing organizations, and psychological affiliation. Recent trends in American politics and political behavior are traced in each section of the book.

Section I introduces the concept of political party and defines the role of parties in a democratic society. Section II illustrates the uniqueness of the American party system by describing its characteristics and the context within which it has evolved.

The next three sections describe each of the elements of a political party presented in the first chapter. Section III emphasizes the decentralized nature of parties as electoral organizations at the national, state, and substate levels. Section IV analyzes parties as governing organizations and demonstrates their relative ineffectiveness in organizing Congress, the Presidency, and the Courts. Section V discusses parties as psychological affiliations. First, the source and degree of party identification is summarized. Then, two models of voting behavior are presented along with a description of recent voting trends and alternatives for the future of the party system.

Section VI links the first five sections together by examining the role of political parties in nominating candidates and contesting elections. Throughout chapters on presidential and nonpresidential nominations, campaign strategy, and campaign finance, the weakening of the traditional role of political parties is noted and reasons are suggested for this trend. Section VII continues this theme and examines the consequences of these trends.

The author would like to acknowledge the following individuals for their thoughtful reviews of the entire manuscript or of specific chapters: Richard W. Boyd, James Ceaser, William J. Crotty, John C. Donovan, Edward C. Dreyer, John A. Hamilton, Jr., Ruth S. Jones, William Keech, Richard Murray, and Henry A. Turner. Thanks also go to Neil McFeeley and Alwyn R. Rouyer for their helpful input for the sections on the courts and the national party organizations, respectively. Stan Wakefield of Prentice-Hall deserves much credit and thanks for his encouragement and support of this project. While all of the above individuals share in strengthening the final product, obviously any omissions or weaknesses of the book are the sole responsibility of the author.

Special acknowledgement also goes to Linda Fulton and Linda Phipps for typing various portions of the manuscript. Finally, Mallory Blank deserves much credit not only for her typing of earlier chapters, but also for allowing the author to spend evenings and weekends writing by keeping Jeremy and Mai-Ling otherwise occupied. It is most appropriate, therefore, that this book be dedicated to her.

SECTION I

DEFINING
POLITICAL PARTIES

While each of us has our own impression of what a political party is and how it operates, there is much confusion and disagreement over the definition of "political party." Even among trained political observers, there is no consensus as to what constitutes political party and which characteristics distinguish it from other organizations.

This introductory chapter attempts to provide a comprehensive, yet meaningful, definition of political party. It is argued that a party must be viewed as a complex phenomenon composed of at least three elements: the electoral organization, the governing organization, and psychological affiliation. Only by understanding each of these elements as well as the interaction among them, can a meaningful discussion of American political parties follow. Later sections of the book are organized around each of the three dimensions of parties introduced in this chapter.

In addition to demonstrating the complexity of political parties, this chapter offers a context within which to evaluate the role and functions of political parties in a democracy. To facilitate this, a series of democratic models are discussed as potential frameworks for studying political parties in the United States. Each of these models is scrutinized as to its applicability or inapplicability. The chapter concludes by explaining the importance of studying American political parties despite their less than dominant role in American society.

1

Political Parties:
An Introduction

"Political parties are no good . . . there is no difference between them . . . they offer no choice . . . party leaders can't be trusted . . . they're interested in our votes, not our opinion . . . I vote for political amateurs, not professional politicians." Frequently we have either heard or repeated statements similar to the above. It is easy to criticize parties, whether justifiably or not. At the same time, however, it would be difficult to imagine democratic politics without political parties. Austin Ranney refers to this situation as "ambivalence to parties"and contends that it is not new on the American scene.[1] He sees this ambivalence as resulting in a

> tendency of Americans to deal uneasily with the necessities of partisan political organizations because of their widespread belief that political parties are, at best, unavoidable evils whose propensities for divisiveness, oligarchy, and corruption must be closely watched and sternly controlled.[2]

AMBIVALENCE TO PARTIES IN THE U.S.

Although this ambivalence or even hostility toward parties antedates the U.S. Constitution, political parties today enjoy little approbation from the public.[3] This is reflected in a wide variety of recent public opinion polls. When asked

[1] Austin Ranney, *Curing the Mischiefs of Faction: Party Reform in America* (Berkeley: University of California Press, 1975).

[2] *Ibid.*, p. 22.

[3] See Richard Hofstadter, *The Idea of a Party System* (Berkeley: University of California Press, 1969), for a discussion of the early hostility. For current empirical evidence see Jack Dennis, "Support for the Party System by the Mass Public," *American Political Science Review*, 60 (September, 1966), 600-615.

if parties pretty much kept their promises, 61 percent of a national sample in 1969 responded that they did not, while only 32 percent thought they did.[4] After the 1972 election, in response to a similar question, 59 percent agreed that political parties were interested only in people's votes, not their opinions.[5] A 1974 Gallup survey revealed that only 50 percent of the respondents were satisfied with the present party arrangement in the U.S.[6] A common criticism of the current arrangement, of course, is that the Republican and Democratic parties are so similar that no real alternative is given the electorate. At least one author has linked this perception to increasing cynicism toward politics.[7]

Probably the most telling data reflecting this lack of public confidence in American political parties is found in comparisons of support for various political institutions. At a time when Congress and the President inspire confidence in only approximately one-quarter of the population, political parties come in last. Table 1.1 indicates that not only are parties overwhelmingly chosen as doing the poorest job, but they also are perceived as having the least power. While only 3 percent of those queried selected parties as doing the best job, 42 percent thought they had done the worst over the last couple of years. Sixty percent saw the parties as least powerful of the institutions compared. When asked which institution they trusted to do what is right, less than 1 percent chose political parties in the 1972 survey. From all indications, events since 1972 have further weakened trust and confidence in the political parties. Additional evidence of this mistrust was exhibited in responses of over 26,000 high school juniors and seniors in 1973. Seventy-one percent agreed that "most political campaigns involved espionage in which punishable crimes are committeed by both parties."[8]

The current atmosphere of public opinion toward political parties, then, is not favorable. Although parties have always faced a rather hostile environment, they are presently encountering, and will continue to encounter, a crisis in public support. This cynicism toward political parties, as well as toward government in general, will not subside until major changes are made.

For many readers, this book is the first systematic exposure to political parties. Each of us has impressions of what parties are, what they do, and

[4] G.W. Boynton, *Public Reaction to Civil Disobedience, 1969-70*, (ICPR Study #74).

[5] Center for Political Studies, *1972 American National Election Study* (ICPR Study #7010).

[6] *Gallup Opinion Index*, #107 (May, 1974), p. 19.

[7] Arthur H. Miller, "Political Issues and Trust in Government: 1964-1970," *American Political Science Review*, 68 (September, 1974), 951-1001.

[8] *Who's Who Among American High School Students*, Fourth Annual National Opinion Survey, 1973.

Table 1.1 Comparison of Public Perception of Major U.S. Political Institutions, Fall, 1972

Institution	Done Job[a]		Power[b]		Trust[c]	
	Best	*Worst*	*Most*	*Least*	*Most*	*Least*
Congress	27	7	32	6	28	4
Supreme Court	13	22	25	9	23	15
President	39	10	31	8	34	9
Political Parties	3	42	4	60	1	57
All or none	5	1	1	1	5	2
Don't know	13	18	7	16	9	13
	100%	100%	100%	100%	100%	100%
N	(1072)	(1045)	(1072)	(1053)	(1072)	(1052)

SOURCE: Center for Political Studies, 1972 American National Election Study (ICPR Study #7010).
a) Which of the parts of government on this list do you think has done the best (worst) job in the past couple of years?
b) Which part of government do you think is most (least) powerful?
c) Which part of government do you most (least) often trust to do what is right?

what they should be. For most, the bases of such viewpoints are the accumulation of fragmented and frequently subjective information collected throughout life. Seldom do we objectively analyze the pros and cons of the party system or examine it within a broader social context. It is usually assumed that parties are static, unchanging institutions which are either entirely beneficial or harmful to society.

As a result, the multifaceted criticism of parties at times is contradictory in nature. Parties are criticized by some as weak and ineffective and by others as too strong and exclusive. They have been attacked as corrupt, undemocratic, and unresponsive by political scientists and by much of the public. These criticisms of American political parties are the result not only of actual shortcomings of the parties, but also of a failure to understand fully the role of political parties and the context within which they must operate. There is no clear and meaningful conception of what is meant by the term political party, and therefore, what ought to be expected from it.

This book is an attempt to place American political parties in a more realistic framework. It examines the context of parties in the United States, as well as their characteristics and activities. It emphasizes the impact of political parties on the individual citizen, as well as the role of the individual in the party. While the focus is almost exclusively on the two major parties in the United States and the party system within which they exist, when appropriate, party systems and parties of other countries and minor parties in the U.S. are used for comparative purposes.

In this chapter, several preliminary considerations are discussed. The most fundamental of these relates to the definition of "political party." In other words, what is a political party? A second concern here is the role of political parties in a democracy. It makes little sense to study parties if they are determined to be unimportant to government and society. It is vital to understand the basic attributes, roles, and functions of political parties before attempting to assess their place in American politics.

THE CONCEPT OF POLITICAL PARTY

There is no consensus among political scientists or practitioners as to what constitutes a political party and distinguishes it from other political organizations. In formal terms, each state legally defines a political party in its statutes, leading to a wide divergence in meanings. There is also a multitude of conceptual definitions of political party which differ in detail and emphasis, and at times are contradictory in content.

When analyzing these disparate definitions, several crucial points of emphasis are evident. To some observers, emphasis is directed toward parties as an ideological framework. Parties are defined in terms of a shared ideology or a common issue-orientation of the members. Very seldom is such a definition applied in the United States, however.[9] Others focus on the various functions parties perform or roles they are expected to play.[10] In such definitions the stress is on activities unique to the political party that distinguish it from other organizations. Still other observers emphasize structure or formal organization when defining the party concept.[11] These observers describe political parties as structures with attendant functions and activities.

In defining political parties here, a more elaborate concept is presented. Too often we fail to understand all aspects and oversimplify party politics. To overcome this tendency, parties are perceived as composed of many dimensions. It is not possible precisely and neatly to define such a complex phenomenon in a sentence or two, as some writers have done. Emphasis on selected aspects of political party organization tends to obscure other di-

---

[9] Maurice Duverger, *Political Parties* (New York: John Wiley and Sons, 1954). For a more in-depth discussion of the rationale for political parties, see Giovanni Sartori, *Parties and Party Systems* (London: Cambridge University Press, 1976), especially Chapters 1 and 2.

[10] Austin Ranney and Willmoore Kendall, *Democracy and the American Party System* (New York: Harcourt, Brace and Company, 1956), for instance, emphasize the functions of parties for democracy.

[11] See Samuel J. Eldersveld, *Political Parties: A Behavioral Analysis* (Chicago: Rand McNally and Company, 1964).

mensions of the party, resulting in distortions. Although it is tempting to select several characteristics of political parties and define them on that basis, that approach is here rejected as too simplistic. In order to see the many ramifications of modifying or restructuring the parties, all relevant dimensions should be examined. Only in this way can the criticisms of political parties be fully analyzed and the success or failure of American parties be appraised.

Political parties here are viewed as complex, multidimensional phenomena with components that at times might be in conflict among themselves. In defining political party, at least three dimensions must be included. Parties are simultaneously electoral organizations, governing organizations, and psychological affiliations.[12] Roles are played and functions performed in each dimension. All three dimensions are composed of a series of structures which, although overlapping and interrelated, are analytically separable. This book is concerned with the development, configuration, and consequences of parties in each of these areas. The strengths and weaknesses of parties in the United States are examined on the basis of these three dimensions.

PARTIES AS ELECTORAL ORGANIZATIONS: THE NUCLEAR PARTY

One objective of this book is to moderate the emphasis placed on the formal/ legal party structure. Most observers agree that American political parties are organizations with neither elaborate requirements for membership nor highly formal organizational structures. National party organizations are usually dismissed as loose coalitions of state and local party organizations, with a semblance of a real existence only during the national conventions. It is here argued that parties, as organizations in any real sense, exist primarily as coalitions during campaign periods. What look like conscious, continuous, goal-oriented efforts by a structured organization are, for the most part, illusions. In actuality, party organizations are series of loosely connected nuclear candidate groups which unite only through the symbols of the party. The formal/legal organizations created by state laws play only a minor role in American elections.

Parties are perceived as coalitions of candidate organizations over time.

---

[12] These are similar to the three dimensions of Frank J. Sorauf, *Party Politics in America*, 3rd ed. (Boston: Little, Brown and Company, 1976), although they are not identical. Sorauf's dimensions are the party organization, the party in office, and the party in the electorate. The original emphasis on these three aspects was V.O. Key, Jr., *Politics, Parties and Pressure Groups* 5th ed. (New York: Thomas Y. Crowell Company, 1964), especially Chapters 12 through 25.

The basic unit of party organization is not necessarily the formal local or county party but rather a "collective effort devoted to the capture of a single public office," or a nucleus.[13] This corresponds to a precinct only when the precinct controls the contested office. For a real nucleus to exist, there must be some expectation that organizational activity will lead to a victory in the nuclear office. One reason for the decentralization of parties in the United States is the extraordinary number of independently elected public officials, each of whom might, and most often does, create an independent campaign organization.

When campaigns and elections are examined in later chapters, it must be remembered that the electoral activities of political parties in primary as well as general elections are performed typically by these nuclear parties which revolve around each candidacy for office. Although parties have always functioned in this way, recent trends have extended this pattern of decentralization. Historically, there have never existed elaborate, continuous, and centralized institutions for party cooperation at the national level. Political parties have always been decentralized, nuclear coalitions of local entrepreneurs and part time politicians.[14] The historical continuity of nuclear or candidate-centered parties under one party label or another has created the illusion of a two-party system.

One difficulty in describing the organizational aspect of American parties is their lack of sharply defined structures. They are so interrelated with the political environment that it is difficult to distinguish their organization from either the government or the electorate. While parties in many countries temper their electoral activities with ideological goals, American parties exist primarily to contest offices and win elections. They nominate candidates for a variety of state, local and national offices and loosely gather the multitude of nuclear candidate organizations together under a common symbol. In order to survive as parties, they must continue to elect officials under their labels. Only by remaining competitive can political parties be effective. Nominating candidates without concern for the electorate's opinion does not further a party's cause, despite ideological considerations. As a result, party organization in the United States is loosely structured and electorally based.

[13] Joseph A. Schlesinger, "Political Party Organization," in James G. March, 3d., *Handbook of Organization* (Chicago: Rand McNally and Company, 1965), 764-801, introduced the concept of the nuclear party discussed here.

[14] Schlesinger, "Political Party Organization," p. 786, terms this a multi-nuclear organization or complex party.

PARTIES AS GOVERNING ORGANIZATIONS

The structures characterizing the party as a governing organization are quite different from the nuclear parties and coalitions defining the party's electoral organization dimension. Once elected to office on a party label, the officeholder becomes a viable spokesman for the party even though he is not subject to the discipline or control of the legally prescribed party leaders. It can be argued that survival of a party's officeholders is the most conspicuous sign of party success. The relationship between any officeholder and the leadership of the formal party organization is tenuous, however. Elected officials are independent and at times in open conflict with the formal party leaders. Again, it is crucial to note that American political parties must compete, not only with each other, but with many other sources of influence in the policy-making process. Parties seldom influence legislators or executives to the exclusion of other sources.

That political parties in the United States are notoriously weak in their ability to govern is an understatement. Schattschneider, in his classic work on parties, argues that parties are unable to hold their lines on controversial public issues when the pressure is on. He contends that this condition "constitutes the most important single fact" concerning American political parties.[15] In other words, once the electoral party wins elections and takes control of government, insofar as this is possible under a federal system with separation of power,[16] the party in government has few incentives or sanctions for guaranteeing the discipline of those elected under its label. On most controversial bills, the legislator is free to vote his own conscience or his constituency's wishes. It is a rare substantive bill where party is an overriding factor in deciding the vote of every congressman.[17] This ineffectiveness of the party as a governing organization is the basis for much criticism. It is one area where the expectations of party proponents have far exceeded party success in performance of this role.

[15] E.E. Schattschneider, *Party Government* (New York: Rinehart and Company, Inc., 1942), pp. 131-132.

[16] In a federal system it is difficult to control both the national government and all 50 states. Under the separation of powers it is unlikely that one party will control all branches of government. The interaction of these institutions reduces the likelihood of one party's controlling the entire government. See Chapter 3 for more details.

[17] See Aage R. Clausen, *How Congressmen Decide: A Policy Focus* (New York: St. Martin's Press, 1973). He finds that only for one dimension of voting, government management, is political party the dominant factor on the decisions of most congressmen.

The influence of the parties in government should not be negated completely, however. Structures do exist which attempt to govern in the name of the party in all states but Nebraska. Both houses of Congress are organized along party lines. The success of these structures in achieving control of policy making and governing the nation and states is examined in Chapter 8. At this point, it is only necessary to understand the nature of this party dimension and to recognize its distinctive features.

PARTY AS PSYCHOLOGICAL AFFILIATION

For most Americans, political party means something quite different from a set of electoral or governing structures. Very early in life, most children form basic attachments to the nation as well as to one of the major parties. For approximately two-thirds of the electorate, party is defined in terms of attachment to some rather ambiguous party label. As discussed here, party label attachment constitutes the third dimension of party, that of psychological affiliation. Membership in parties can be defined in various ways; but in any real sense, most of the population is a member of a political party only through identification with it or psychological attachment to it.[18]

Although formal membership in American parties is possible, only a few of the electorate actually join a party as they would an association or club. Dues are not required, and one need not prove allegiance in order to claim membership to either party. Support in elections is not even essential, though the party might serve as a reference point or cue, resulting in generally consistent support. Parties, in psychological terms, screen perception by filtering out certain communications that do not readily fit the individual's view of the world. The party symbol or label aids the citizen in understanding and simplifying a rather complex and confusing political world. Like a chart or compass, party labels give direction to those who identify with them. Party membership for most of the citizenry of the United States, then, is "principally a state of mind—a matter of self-identification."[19]

In addition to providing cues for voters and simplifying politics for the electorate, psychological attachment to a political party is also important in formation of political attitudes. We tend to view actions of "our" party and its representatives in a favorable light and to accept the programs and policies espoused by them as our own. In the United States, it is likely that

[18] The most comprehensive work on party identification is still Angus Campbell, et.al., *The American Voter* (New York: John Wiley and Sons, 1960).
    [19] Randall B. Ripley, *American National Government and Public Policy* (New York: The Free Press, 1974), p. 46.

opinions and attitudes are shaped in part by party affiliation. It is an exception when a person becomes identified with a party because its stands are similar to his own. Parties form attitudes more often than attitudes form parties.[20]

In light of the scope and importance of party identification in the United States, political parties can be defined as a coalition of individuals and groups sharing some long-term psychological attachment to a party name or symbol. Andrew Greeley astutely envisions American political parties as affiliations, very similar to churches, ideologies, or ethnic groups. Parties are something to which Americans belong with a greater or lesser degree of loyalty, much as they belong to a church. Political parties serve as a map that guides us through the "confusions of the bargaining, coalition-forming American political environment."[21]

The dimension of party as an affiliation cannot be overemphasized because the other two dimensions are heavily dependent on the nature of the electorate. The extent of party identification and psychological affiliation with parties will be discussed in Chapters 9 and 10.

INTERDEPENDENCE OF PARTY DIMENSIONS

These three dimensions of political parties are highly interrelated. Together they constitute a party. Not one of them can be analyzed totally in isolation from the others without distorting the situation. The degree of psychological affiliation exhibited by much of the electorate, for instance, has a great impact on parties as electoral organizations. That we have had two fairly stable parties over the years has been attributed to the pervasive party identification of the American electorate. According to the Survey Research Center, party identification limits the parties to two by providing rather stable reservoirs of support for them. It also strengthens the second party by stabilizing party competition and minimizing the possibility of a total landslide at all levels. Party identification reduces the amplitude of electoral shifts from one party to the other.[22] Alterations in patterns of party identification will result in organizational changes as well.

The party as a governing organization, in turn, is reflective of the electoral organization. The weak, decentralized nature of the electoral party organization is translated into a minor governing role. The expanded influence of nonparty candidate organizations results in what some term irresponsible

---

[20] Andrew M. Greeley, *Building Coalitions: American Politics in the 1970's* (New York: Franklin Watts, Inc., New Viewpoints, 1974), p. 172.

[21] *Ibid.,* p. 170.

[22] Campbell, et al., *The American Voter*, p. 287.

parties in government, that is, parties unable to discipline those elected under their label. If the election of party candidates depended solely on the party electoral organization, voting in the legislative bodies would undoubtedly be more party-cohesive. Also the party would be likely to demonstrate a more affirmative policy-making role. Given the nature of the electorate and the current role of party organizations in elections, it would appear that the party in government exists only superficially.

The three dimensions of party are interrelated but not always in harmony. The party in government, that is, the one elected under a party label, many times plays a major role in the party electoral organization for a brief time during campaign periods, but then is quite independent of any party ties until the next election when it again plays a major role. This situation is possible only because parties tend to be nothing more than coalitions of nuclear candidate organizations. A highly centralized party system could not tolerate such discrepancies among its components.

POLITICAL PARTIES AND DEMOCRACY

One question the reader may be asking at this point is: why study political parties at all? Why spend time examining this rather confusing combination of elements which mean so many different things? With the current trend away from parties as electoral and governing organizations and the decreasing dependence on party labels, it is easy to dismiss parties as relics of the past. It is here argued that such conclusions are not completely warranted. By examining the nature and roles of parties in a more realistic manner, it will be apparent that parties still occupy a position, albeit a limited one, in American society and government.

Despite their many shortcomings, political parties are a part of the electoral process we take for granted. A great disservice has been perpetrated by expecting too much from political parties. We do a similar disservice when we expect nothing from them. Some middle ground seems to be more justified and, hopefully, is offered in this book. In order to appreciate the disparate roles and functions of political parties, several democratic models are briefly examined. A good starting point for this exploration is direct democracy, under which no need exists for organizations such as political parties.

DIRECT DEMOCRACY

Under direct or classical democratic theory, the citizens simply come together and jointly make decisions. Representatives or intermediary organizations are unnecessary because all citizens have an equal and direct voice in all decisions. In any nation as large as the United States, this dream of the classical democrats fades rapidly. Not only is it physically impossible for citizens directly to make policy, it is also very difficult to accept certain assumptions on which the classical theory is based. The assumptions of direct democracy include: (1) that all citizens are interested and informed about every issue, (2) that all citizens' convictions are equally intense about each issue, (3) that a majority can in all cases be achieved, and (4) that the majority decision will be in the public interest.

Both research and common knowledge about the electorate indicate that the first two assumptions are not met in the United States. Only a very small portion of the electorate is informed and interested on even the broadest of issues. As issues become more complicated, the knowledge and interest of even the more politically-minded citizens wanes. Also, intensity of opinion on issues is not a constant, as the second assumption requires. Few people have strong or highly emotional opinions on a range of issues and many people fail to have an opinion on most issues concerning policy alternatives.[23]

The third assumption of direct democracy also lacks empirical support. Rare is the issue on which a majority decision can be reached without eliminating alternatives by narrowing the "choice" down to two.[24] The question here is how the selection of legitimate alternatives is made, but theorists offer little in the way of explanations. Even if majority rule could be attained on every issue, there is no guarantee that the resulting decisions would be in the public interest. Strict majority rule discriminates against militant minorities, since it does not account for intensity of opinion. The danger here is that a rather unconcerned majority might dominate minorities who have much more at stake in the outcome of an election.

For these reasons, in addition to the physical impossibility of assembling over 225 million individuals, whether as a whole or in segments, direct policy-making by the public is not workable in the United States. Public opinion is not translated directly into public policy as suggested in the direct democracy model (Figure 1.1), with the possible exception of New England town meetings. It is unlikely, therefore, that anything approximating a direct linkage exists between public opinion and governmental decisions.

[23] See James J. Best, *Public Opinion: Micro and Macro* (Homewood, Ill.: The Dorsey Press, 1973), Chapter 5 and Bernard C. Hennessy, *Public Opinion*, 3rd ed. (North Scituate, Mass.: Duxbury Press, 1975), especially Chapters 2 and 21.

[24] James M. Buchanan and Gordon Tullock, *The Calculus of Consent* (Ann Arbor: University of Michigan Press, 1962), pp. 129-145, for instance, contend that majorities without some type of mechanism for exchanging votes are extremely difficult to achieve.

Public ⟶ Policy Decisions

Figure 1.1 Direct Democracy: Classical Democratic Model

ELECTIONS LINKAGE MODEL

In order to compensate for the inherent limitations of direct democracy, other models of democracy have been introduced which demonstrate the necessity of a linkage or intermediary between public desires and public policy.[25] The need for such linkages is an implicit rejection of the direct democracy model. Two variations of the linkage model are presented in Figure 1.2.[26] In the first variation, elections are the link between the public and the government. The people select representatives through formal, free elections. These representatives then protect the interests of their constituents.

Public —Votes⟶ Representatives ⟶ Policy Decision

Public —Votes⟶ Parties ⟶ Policy Decision

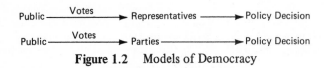

Figure 1.2 Models of Democracy

Proponents of this linkage model view democracy primarily in terms of competition through free elections. Democracy is seen as an institutional arrangement in which individuals have the power to make political decisions through their vote. Seymour Lipset defines democracy simply as a political system that provides constitutional opportunities for changing governing officials.[27] The key element is a free election system that links the citizens to the government.

[25] For a more in-depth discussion of linkage models see Norman R. Luttbeg, ed., *Public Opinion and Public Policy: Models of Political Linkage*, revised edition (Homewood, Ill.: The Dorsey Press, 1974), especially pp. 1-10. The two models in Figure 1.2 are simplified versions of Luttbeg's linkage models on p. 9.

[26] A third linkage model places interest groups at the center. Robert A. Dahl, *Pluralist Democracy in the United States* (Chicago: Rand McNally and Company, 1967), is perhaps the major proponent of this model. In addition to Dahl's works, see David B. Truman, *The Government Process*, 2nd ed. (New York: Alfred A. Knopf, 1971), for a defense of interest-group pluralism. For criticisms of this theory or its application to the U.S., read Theodore J. Lowi, *The End of Liberalism* (New York: W.W. Norton and Company, 1969) and Murray Edelman, *The Symbolic Uses of Politics* (Urbana: University of Illinois Press, 1964).

[27] Seymour Martin Lipset, "Some Social Requisites of Democracy: Economic Development and Political Legitimacy," *American Political Science Review*, 53 (March, 1959), 71.

But just as the direct democracy model was found to be limited by its assumptions, the elections linkage model also fails to reflect reality. The inequality of resources in a free election system, for instance, maximizes the expression of portions of the public and minimizes others. Although almost all adults may vote, few realistically can run for office. They have neither the skills, knowledge, nor resources to enter the electoral process as a full participant.

The elections linkage model also assumes that elections will always offer a reasonable choice on issues. In order for the voters to have a voice in policy decisions through elections, the choice must be available. We will see that U.S. elections are seldom issue-oriented and in most cases fail to offer a clear choice. Although elections are a possible linkage between the public and policy decisions, they are far from complete in themselves.

PARTY GOVERNMENT MODEL

A second linkage model of democracy introduces political parties as the crucial intermediary, although elections are necessary also. According to the proponents of this model, the parties are not limited to an electoral or a minimal governing role. Instead, they constitute the central institution of democracy. Parties have been tied to democracy in many ways. Clinton Rossiter perceives parties and democracy as arising together and existing in a reciprocal relationship. He suggests that democracy cannot exist without political parties, and that if parties are seriously weakened or disappear, democracy will cease to exist.[28]

Under this model, parties also serve to bridge the divisions of power in American politics by aggregating voters into groups with fairly common interests. E.E. Schattschneider sees the party government model as good democratic doctrine, because parties alone among political organizations are designed to aggregate the electorate and mobilize majorities.[29] Without the opportunity to choose between competing political parties, popular sovereignty cannot exist. According to the party model, these competing parties and their leaders define the alternatives of public policy and the people then choose between the parties. Political parties provide both the government and the opposition in this linkage model.

Other observers, although not contending that competition among parties is a precondition of democracy, envision the necessary political freedoms in a democracy as resulting from the formation of strong political

---

[28] Clinton Rossiter, *Parties and Politics in America* (Ithaca, N.Y.: Cornell University Press, 1960), p. 67.

[29] Schattschneider, *Party Government*, pp. 206-207.

parties.[30] These parties, composed of different slates of candidates, will reflect different outlooks and policy alternatives. It would be impossible to prohibit political parties and still permit the liberties necessary for an authentic democracy. Rival parties not only ensure popular control over decision-makers at election time, but also keep open the channels to legitimate influence at all times.[31] To many political theorists, competition between two strong, centralized political parties is vital to democracy. Parties are the major link between the people and their government in this model.

COMPLEX DEMOCRACY:
THE LIMITED ROLE OF PARTIES

None of these simple linkage or direct democracy models is applicable to the U.S. Although each has merit as a theory, all are all too simple to explain American politics. They either overemphasize political parties or ignore them. In order to understand the American political process more fully, we must envision parties as one element in a complex political system. The entire political process, of which parties are a part, itself is in constant interaction with the non-political aspects of society. Also, we must recognize the interplay between the three dimensions of political parties and the complexity of the world. These three simple models fail to explain because they exclude the complications of actual politics.

Certainly, political parties in combination with elections serve as a potential linkage between the public and the government. This book, however, will emphasize the limited realization of this potential in the policy-making process. As stated earlier, there is little evidence that American political parties ever have been adequate linkages. Neither parties nor elections are issue-oriented enough to define public policy. The data and trends discussed in this book afford little hope for an increased role of political parties in the near future. They suggest instead that expectations of party potential must be tempered with the realization that many other political and non-political elements also have major roles in American democracy.

SUMMARY: WHY STUDY POLITICAL PARTIES?

Why study political parties if their role in the policy-making process is severely limited? It was stated in the early pages of this chapter that American parties face a hostile environment, and that, more than any other institution, they

---

[30] For instance: see H.B. Mayo, *An Introduction to Democratic Theory* (New York: Oxford University Press, 1966), pp. 60-70.

[31] Dahl, *Pluralist Democracy*, p. 209.

lack the confidence of the public. One reason for studying parties is to see why they find themselves in this predicament. Why their weakness as a political linkage? Why the negative public attitudes? It is hoped that the answers to such questions are provided in succeeding chapters.

Another reason for studying political parties is that, despite their limitations, they have been one of the most persistent elements of American society. Contrary to frequent predictions of their demise, parties have persisted as one of many political institutions. Although parties fail to monopolize or even dominate the electoral process, neither does any other institution in the U.S. In other words, if we fail to study political parties, what institutions should we study to explain American politics? Or should we simply give up? The answer, or course, is that we must examine the political party system, not as an institution of singular importance, but as one element in a highly complex and at times confusing political system. This text attempts to provide the framework for such an examination of American political parties.

SECTION II

THE UNIQUE SETTING
AND TRAITS
OF THE
AMERICAN PARTY SYSTEM

Most Americans assume that political parties are similar around the world. They expect foreign elections to be like U.S. elections and foreign politics to be conducted along U.S. lines. This section attempts to describe the unique characteristics of U.S. parties and the electoral system. We shall see that U.S. parties have few parallels in organization, goals, membership, and activity. We shall also see that two-party systems are a rarity in a world of multiparty or one-party systems.

The main question is: Why are U.S. parties different? A related question is: How has this unique party system managed to continue relatively unchanged during U.S. history? In order to answer these questions, this chapter examines the historical and cultural context of U.S. parties and elections. Their development, isolated from most outside influences and historical restrictions such as feudalism, has been gradual but continuous. The combination of various institutional constraints, such as federalism and separation of powers, has established the broad context within which political parties operate in the U.S.

Finally, the unique nature of the American electorate has helped to mold the party and electoral system. America's large, heterogeneous population has managed to remain supportive of parties only through limited party identification. Most of the population remains skeptical of political parties and views politics as spectators, not as active participants. Their hostility has had a profound impact on our party system and on our elections. It has resulted in a party system not duplicated anywhere in the world.

2

Characteristics
of American Parties
and the Party System

The purpose of this chapter is to describe the general characteristics of parties and the party system of the United States. American parties are distinctive in many ways. In order to demonstrate the uniqueness of political parties in the U.S., several classification schemes are introduced. The first concentrates on internal characteristics of party organizations and categorizes them by structure, functions, and orientation. A second scheme classifies parties on the basis of their composition by class and religion.

In addition to examining characteristics of American parties, this chapter will also analyze the party system in the U.S. One of the most striking traits of the American party system is the dominance of two parties. It will be demonstrated that the two-party system is a rarity among democracies. Multiparty and one-party systems are much more common. The two-party system of the U.S. will be analyzed in detail at various levels. Finally, the role of third parties in American politics will be discussed and their future chances for success will be evaluated.

CADRE PARTIES:
ORGANIZATION AND MEMBERSHIP

In his classic work on political party organization, Maurice Duverger classifies parties as either mass membership or cadre parties.[1] The mass membership party is by far the most common in western democracies. It is characterized

[1] Maurice Duverger, *Political Parties* (New York: John Wiley and Sons, Inc., 1954). For a summary of comparative studies of political parties see Leon D. Epstein, *Political Parties in Western Democracies* (New York: Praeger Publishers, 1967), and Kay Lawson, *The Comparative Study of Political Parties* (New York: St. Martin's Press, 1976).

by a large formal membership which pays dues and is actively recruited. Its survival depends on its continued ability to maintain these large membership rolls. Like many nonpolitical associations, leadership is well defined and internal lines of control emanate from the top. Leadership is centralized and develops from within, resulting in a permanent bureaucracy of career professionals.

Duverger views mass membership parties as primarily doctrinaire in ideology. Although they desire to win elections, their central goal is further acceptance of some ideology or set of principles. Finally, mass membership parties are oriented toward change. They tend to be politically extreme, and reformist in nature. Mass membership parties, then, are similar to any large membership organization that attempts to further its own interests through political means.

While Duverger classifies most political parties as mass membership, both the Republican and Democratic parties are described as cadre. In the U.S. only a very few of the "third parties" exhibit mass membership party characteristics. In light of this finding, what characteristics do major American parties manifest that distinguish them from most other political parties in the world?

MEMBERSHIP

Cadre parties are characterized by a lack of membership in formal terms. Very few Americans are members of cadre parties on the same basis as they are in other organizations. Cadre party members do not pay party dues, receive a membership card, or attend meetings. What is cadre party membership then? Although defining membership under these circumstances is difficult, there are at least six levels of participation which could be used. The resulting categories have been ordered in a series of concentric circles for illustrative purposes (see Figure 2.1).

At the center is the small group of *leaders* which includes precinct committeemen, county and district leaders, and state party leaders. These are crucial to the success of any party at all levels. Generally the leaders are more ideologically sophisticated than the other members. Immediately surrounding the leaders are the party *workers*. These workers represent past and future leaders, and have influence by virtue of their continuous participation. Many times concurrent with the workers are the official party *members*. These individuals most closely correspond to the members of the European parties, although their proportion in the U.S. electorate is comparatively minute. They formally join a party by applying for membership, subscribing to party principles, paying dues and the like. All students of parties agree that the ac-

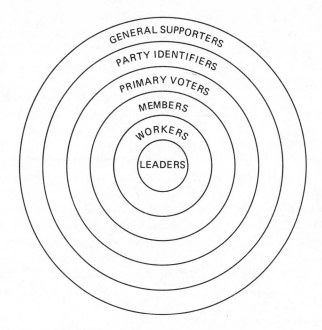

Figure 2-1　　Levels of Party Involvement

tivities and interrelations of leaders, workers, and members should be included as elements of political parties.[2] James Q. Wilson limits party membership only to these three.[3] Disagreement centers on the remaining categories.

A more inclusive definition of membership includes voters who participate in the selection of party nominees by voting in the primary. Since the U.S. is the only nation that uses direct primaries extensively, there is disagreement over inclusion of primary voters. Despite the fact that the vast majority of primary voters are not active party members and fail to participate in any other party activity, they do control ultimately the most crucial of the party functions; they nominate the standardbearers. Samuel Eldersveld, therefore, includes primary voters as party members.[4]

The other party supporters who might be included are those who vote for all, or almost all, of a party's candidates in the general election. Evidence

[2] Austin Ranney, *Curing the Mischiefs of Faction: Party Reform in America* (Berkeley: University of California Press, 1975), p. 152.

[3] James Q. Wilson, *Political Organizations* (New York: Basic Books, Inc., 1974), p. 96.

[4] Samuel J. Eldersveld, *Political Parties: A Behavioral Analysis* (Chicago: Rand McNally and Company, 1964), p. 2.

presented in Chapter 10, however, suggests that such voting is less consistent and less frequent than in the past, and that a greater proportion of the electorate divides its votes between the parties. It would be difficult, indeed, to assign voters to either party on the basis of anything less than unvarying votes for the candidates of that party.

The final category at times included in party membership is psychological attachment—more commonly referred to as party identification. It will be demonstrated in Chapter 9 that party attachment may or may not be associated with actual voting support. Large numbers of party identifiers fail to vote at all or vote for candidates of the opposing party. The Michigan Survey Research Center, however, defines party affiliation solely on the basis of identification.[5]

An all-encompassing definition of party would include all six of the categories described above. It is unlikely that political observers will ever agree on such a simple item as the composition of party membership. American parties are unlike most other parties in which membership is formally defined and there are procedures for admitting and expelling members.[6]

NATURE OF ORGANIZATION

In addition to the limited number of actives and a restricted definition of party membership, the activities of U.S. cadre organizations are minimal. Even the few members who are active tend to participate only during the period before elections. This periodic activity, coupled with unclear lines of authority within the party, results in highly decentralized and diffuse organizations. Seldom is there one leader or set of leaders who are responsible and accountable for party actions.

Perhaps the most distinctive feature of U.S. parties is their emphasis on winning elections. While American parties are not totally devoid of ideological concerns, such interests are secondary. Unlike the mass membership parties of Western Europe, American parties concentrate on electoral, not ideological, concerns. They make very little effort to educate the public on principles and doctrine. Due to the nature of American politics, political parties in the U.S. cannot afford to neglect their electoral function. Their survival depends not on a mass of loyal members, but on their ability to mobilize votes at each election.

[5] Angus Campbell, et.al. *The American Voter* (New York: John Wiley and Sons, 1960).

[6] This book will accept the most inclusive definition of party membership which includes both consistent supporters and psychological affiliation.

Duverger states that cadre parties are characterized by non-professional leadership composed of notables and the socioeconomic elites. While U.S. parties certainly do lack professionally oriented leadership and have few full-time workers or leaders, it does not appear accurate to imply that U.S. party leadership is closed. In fact, it is open to outsiders of all social and economic levels. For those willing to work, leadership positions, at the local level at least, are accessible. The leadership in U.S. parties is more inclusive and open than in mass membership organizations.

MODERATE PARTY ORIENTATION

Due in part to the need to mobilize support to win elections, both major parties are moderate or centrist-oriented. Instead of offering extreme or change-oriented programs, the parties favor the status quo. Very seldom does either party initiate major changes in the social order. Again, because cadre parties depend on support from broad electorates, they must include a wide range of viewpoints. Unless they can appeal to disparate groups of voters, they will fail. In order to have such widespread appeal, American parties must not be identified as too extreme or too reformist.

COMPOSITION OF U.S. PARTIES: HETEROGENEOUS PARTIES

It was mentioned above that American parties must be moderate in orientation because they include many types of supporters. Richard Rose and Derek Urwin found support for this in their study of the social composition of political parties.[7] They classified 76 parties in 17 western countries as either socially homogeneous or heterogeneous. A party was homogeneous if it received most of its support from one region, social group, or class. They found that while class, region, and ethnic identity are all bases of cohesion for many of the parties, religion was the most common single factor. The U.S. was one of only four of the 17 countries that had no religiously cohesive party. Most of the western nations examined had at least one party whose composition was defined by religion. The second, and sometimes reinforcing factor was social class. The U.S. is one of only three countries without a nationwide class-based party. Although the New Deal Coalition of the 1930s was class-oriented, compared to other democracies examined by Rose and Urwin, even during that period class had a limited role.

[7] Richard Rose and Derek Urwin, "Social Cohesion, Political Parties and Strains in Regimes," *Comparative Political Studies*, 2 (April, 1969), 7-44.

Both U.S. parties are among the 19 parties classified as heterogeneous by Rose and Urwin. The Republican and Democratic parties have demonstrated an ability to absorb various social groups which in other countries would form new parties. There is no Catholic party, Protestant party, Working Class party, etc., and voting by specific religious and socioeconomic groups fails to support consistently one major party over the other. Although each party has been more or less successful in attracting support from these disparate sources, the pattern is neither solid nor dependable. Neither party can depend solely on the support of any group in society.

THE AMERICAN TWO-PARTY SYSTEM

Perhaps the most common means of classifying political party systems is a numerical one. The simplistic numerical scheme is to describe systems as either one-party, two-party, or multiparty. In order to increase precision, more categories such as modified one-party and authoritarian can be added. Most party systems, however, are either one-, two-, or multiparty, with the latter being by far the most common in western democracies. This designation by numbers is based on a measure of how many parties are able to compete for office with a "reasonable chance of success."[8] Criteria used to judge what is meant by the phrase "reasonable chance" differ from person to person and result in inconsistency from scale to scale.

Historically, the U.S. party system has been placed in the two-party category with little hesitancy. Most researchers see the U.S. as a model of this rare type of party system. They cite percentages of two-party balance at the national level since the Civil War, both in the presidential and congressional votes. They refer to the generally close national averages for congressional elections as well as the resiliency of the two parties over the last 100 years. Certainly the balance of Republican and Democratic strength since 1872 is impressive. Table 2.1 illustrates this balance. Also, both political parties have demonstrated a remarkable ability to recover from what appeared to be electoral disasters. For instance, the Democrats rebounded from a series of massive defeats at the polls during the 1920s. The Republicans also recouped, though not nearly as strongly, after disastrous defeats in the 1964 election. In 1966 alone they recovered 47 congressional seats. They also won the next two presidential elections, and, without Watergate and related events, might

[8] See Austin Ranney and Willmoore Kendall, *Democracy and the American Party System* (New York: Harcourt, Brace and Company, 1956), pp. 156-58.

Table 2.1   Two-Party Balance, President and Congress, 1872-1978

	Republican	Democrat
President Terms	15	12
Mean Vote for President	48.5	46.6
Senate Control	28	26
House Control	20	34
Mean Vote for House	42.1	52.1

have extended that string of victories. Time after time a party declared dead or dying has demonstrated its persistence.

On the surface it appears that the U.S. has had a consistent two-party system since 1860. Upon closer examination, however, it becomes obvious that this generalization is misleading in several ways. James MacGregor Burns argues, for instance, that we have a four-party system in the U.S.[9] In terms of organization and functions, there are very real subdivisions in each of the major parties. Burns contends that in each party there is a liberally-oriented presidential unit and a more conservative congressional one. Not only is there an absence of organizational coordination among the four parties; they also represent different constituencies. The presidential wings must appeal to broad constituencies while a large percentage of Congressmen come from safe districts. Burns sees presidential parties as urban-oriented and congressional parties as rural and small-town-oriented. Whether these divisions actually represent separate parties or simply internal divisions depends on one's definition of political parties. At the minimum, they illustrate the diffuse and decentralized nature of American parties.

One might also argue that despite a long history of the use of the Republican and Democratic party labels, in actuality we have a 100-party system, since each of the two national parties is nothing more than a coalition of the 50 autonomous state party organizations convening for several days once every four years. To conceive of parties as ongoing, dynamic organizations one must focus on the state parties. Also, many times the variation of the 50 state units within either national party is greater than among the state organizations of the opposing party. Certainly, many of the southern Democratic state parties are more similar in orientation to Republican parties than they are to Massachusetts or New York Democrats. In other states, such as Washington, there is a tendency for the Republican party to be the more

[9] James MacGregor Burns, *The Deadlock of Democracy* (Englewood, Cliffs, N.J.: Prentice-Hall, Inc., 1963).

progressive force, despite the converse at the national level. There is much evidence to support the position that the U.S. manifests a more complex party system than simply two competing national parties. Whether these inconsistencies are best resolved by reducing parties to the state level is questionable. Once this is done, the next step would be to fragment the party units even more and say we have six thousand county parties or 200,000 precinct parties. Despite the organizational deficiencies of the national parties, it still appears most useful to define our party system as composed of two and not multiple parties.

There are several serious problems resulting from the classification of the U.S. as a two-party competitive system, however. The first deals with taking averages over time and the second with the use of national aggregates. Although the figures in Table 2.1 indicate that the success of the parties has been relatively balanced over the last century, they obscure the domination of Democrats or Republicans during portions of that period. Competition among the parties is commonly unequal at any one time, sometimes severely so. Only by averaging election results over extended periods do the parties reflect a competitive two-party setting. The use of such averages, however, can be misleading in studying shorter time periods.

A more important distortion results from the use of national aggregates. American elections for all offices except the presidency are statewide or narrower in orientation. In discussing party competition, it is imperative to examine variation by states or smaller electoral units. There is a reasonable chance that competition that looks evenly balanced for a single election year represents only an artificial competitiveness. Table 2.2 indicates three possible sets of election figures that when averaged provide examples of two-party competition. In each case, the aggregate of these six states is a 50-50 split between the parties. For a complete analysis, however, attention must be directed toward analysis of party competition within the 50 states. What represents an adequate amount of consistency to be labeled two-party

Table 2.2   Party Competition: An Example

Percent Democratic	Case 1	Case 2	Case 3	Case 4
State A	50	60	70	100
B	50	50	50	0
C	50	40	30	100
D	50	60	70	0
E	50	50	50	100
F	50	40	30	0
Average	50	50	50	50

competition? Although there is little doubt that case 4 is not competitive and case 1 is, questions concerning the other two possibilities are significant. How do we define competition?

MEASURING PARTY COMPETITION

One of the problems in examining party competition within the states is the lack of a standard measure of competitiveness. Every researcher has somewhat different criteria for defining this concept.[10] While some authors have looked only at the total percentage of offices won by each party, others include the percentages of the vote given each party. Using the latter criterion, a state where one party loses but consistently receives 45 percent of the vote would be considered more competitive than a state where the party lost consistently with only 10 percent of the vote. Most observers would agree that the first measurement, counting only the number of elections won or lost, obscures the question of whether the party has a "reasonable chance" of success.

Another inconsistency in measurement of party competition relates to the offices included. As we will see later, voting criteria differ as one moves from the highly visible presidential contest to lower-level offices. Therefore, classification of states as to competitiveness is dependent on the nature of the offices included. Scales of competition which include only the national offices of President, Senate, and House yield competition scores different from those which include only state offices such as governor and state legislator. Several attempts to measure party competition are summarized here.

Austin Ranney and Willmoore Kendall developed a simple method for classifying state party systems based on the number of elections won and the percentage of victory for candidates of each party.[11] They computed competitiveness primarily from a national orientation employing the vote for president, U.S. Senate, and governor. Using this base, Ranney and Kendall arrived at three categories: two-party, one-party, and modified one-party. Of the 48 states analyzed, 25 were classified as two-party, 10 as one-party, and 12 as modified one-party.

Richard Dawson and James Robinson constructed a more complex measure of competitiveness based on both houses of the state legislatures and the governor.[12] They identified three dimensions of party competition. The

---

[10] Philip Coulter and Glen Gordon, "Urbanization and Party Competition: Critique and Reflection of Theoretical Research," *Western Political Quarterly*, 21 (June, 1968), contend that problems in measuring competition are the major reasons why the concept has not been examined adequately.

[11] Ranney and Kendall, *Democracy*, pp. 161-64.

[12] Richard Dawson and James Robinson, "Inter-Party Competition, Economic Variables, and Welfare Policies in the Fifty States," *Journal of Politics*, 25 (1963), 265-84.

three dimensions include: (1) the margin of comparative popular support in terms of the percentage of votes held by the majority party, (2) the relative percentage of time each party controlled the offices, and (3) the proportion of time that control of these bodies was divided. The three dimensions were found to be highly correlated, but the authors concluded that a composite index of the first dimension for all three bodies offered the best single measure of party competition. Of the 46 states ranked, 22 exhibited a two-party status, 10 were classified one-party and 14 modified one-party. The highest degree of competition was present in Montana while South Carolina and Mississippi registered the lowest composite score.

One of the most sophisticated indices of party competition is an adaptation of the Dawson-Robinson scale. Austin Ranney constructed a 50-state index based on the percentages of the vote for governor received by each party from 1946 to 1963 and the percentages of the seats in each state house held by each party in every legislative session.[13] He then computed three percentage figures for each state: (1) the average percentage of popular vote won by Democratic gubernatorial candidates; (2) the average percentage of state senate seats held by the Democrats; and (3) the percentage of all terms for governor, senate, and house, in which the Democrats had control. These indicators were then averaged and placed on a continuum ranging from .0000 (total Republican success) to 1.000 (total Democratic success), with .5000 representing a balanced two-party situation (see Table 2.3). Although technically there are five categories, no states fall into the one-party Republican slot. Of the 50 states, 28 are classified two-party, 15 modified one-party, and seven one-party.

The major finding of this summary of three disparate measures of competition is the consistency of the number of states classified as two-party. In each case fewer than 30 states demonstrate moderate to high degrees of competition. Although the specific state rankings vary somewhat, significant proportions of one-party dominated states are common to each.[14]

---

[13] Austin Ranney, "Parties in State Politics," in Herbert Jacob and Kenneth Vines, ed., *Politics in the American States*, 2nd ed. (Boston: Little, Brown and Company, 1971), pp. 82-121. For additional measures see Paul T. David, *Party Strength in the United States, 1872-1970* (Charlottesville: University of Virginia Press, 1972); Joseph A. Schlesinger, "A Two-Dimensional Scheme for Classifying the States According to Degree of Inter-Party Competition," *American Political Science Review*, 49 (December, 1955), 1120-28; and Mark Stern, "Measuring Inter-Party Competition: A Proposal and Test of a Model," *Journal of Politics*, 34 (November, 1972), 889-904.

[14] Richard E. Zody and Norman R. Luttbeg, "An Evaluation of Various Measures of State Party Competition," *Western Political Quarterly*, 21 (December, 1968), 723-24 found a high degree of correlation among the various measures of competition.

Table 2.3 The Fifty States Classified According to Degree of Interparty Competition

One-Party Democratic	Modified One-Party Democratic	Two-Party	Modified One-Party Republican
Louisiana (.9877)	North Carolina (.8332)	Hawaii (.6870)	New Jersey (.5122)	North Dakota (.3305)
Alabama (.9685)	Virginia (.8235)	Rhode Island (.6590)	Pennsylvania (.4800)	Kansas (.3297)
Mississippi (.9407)	Florida (.8052)	Massachusetts (.6430)	Colorado (.4725)	New Hampshire (.3282)
South Carolina (.9292)	Tennessee (.7942)	Alaska (.6383)	Michigan (.4622)	South Dakota (.3142)
Texas (.9132)	Maryland (.7905)	California (.6150)	Utah (.4565)	Vermont (.2822)
Georgia (.9080)	Oklahoma (.7792)	Nebraska (.6065)	Indiana (.4450)	
Arkansas (.8850)	Missouri (.7415)	Washington (.6047)	Illinois (.4235)	
	Kentucky (.7170)	Minnesota (.5910)	Wisconsin (.4102)	
	West Virginia (.7152)	Nevada (.5742)	Idaho (.4077)	
	New Mexico (.7150)	Connecticut (.5732)	Iowa (.3965)	
		Delaware (.5687)	Ohio (.3837)	
		Arizona (.5663)	New York (.3835)	
		Montana (.5480)	Maine (.3820)	
		Oregon (.5387)	Wyoming (.3537)	

SOURCE: Austin Ranney, "Parties in State Politics," in *Politics in the American States*, 2nd ed. Herbert Jacob and Kenneth Vines eds. (Reading, Mass.: Little, Brown and Company, Inc., 1971), p. 87.

CONGRESSIONAL DISTRICT COMPETITION

The state analysis indicates that competition between the parties is less impressive than the two-party classification implies. One substate level central to this analysis is the congressional district. In examining the aggregate figures for Congress over the last 100 years, the parties are split rather evenly. However, such figures tell us nothing about the presence or absence of competition within the particular districts. In actuality, there is little interparty competition within most districts and the trend is toward a further decline.[15] "Indeed the principal attribute that most congressional districts have in common is a history of one-party domination."[16] Keefe concludes that only 15 to 20 percent of recent House elections have been marginal or competitive.[17]

Although there has been a trend towards more equal competition across states and districts in the vote for president, most congressional seats continue to be "safe" for one party. Furthermore, one-party dominance of House seats is not a southern phenomenon as commonly assumed, but is nationwide. In only about 70 to 100 districts out of the 435 is there a chance that the party holding an office will lose. Much of this has been attributed to the phenomenal rate of incumbent success in re-election.[18] The figures in Table 2.4 indicate that generally over 90 percent of incumbents seeking re-election win. In only a very small percentage of the districts in any one year will there be much probability of changing parties. Even in those few districts where no incumbent is running for re-election, it is unusual for the district to change parties. Due to the greater visibility of Senate candidates, incumbency plays a lesser role in that house. In 1976, for instance the turnover in senators was high.

[15] David Mayhew, "Congressional Elections: The Case of the Vanishing Marginals," *Polity*, 6 (Spring, 1974), 295-314. Also see John A. Ferejohn, "On the Decline of Competition in Congressional Elections," *American Political Science Review*, 71 (March, 1977), 166-76; Morris P. Fiorina, "The Case of the Vanishing Marginals: The Bureaucracy Did It," *American Political Science Review*, 71 (March, 1977), 177-81; and Edward R. Tufte, "The Relationship Between Seats and Votes in Two-Party Systems," *American Political Science Review*, 67 (June, 1973), 504-54.

[16] William J. Keefe, *Parties, Politics and Public Policy in America*, 2nd ed. (Hinsdale: The Dryden Press, 1976), p. 37.

[17] Keefe defines marginal as districts won by less than 55 percent of the vote. In 1974, 10 percent were considered marginal Democrat and 12 percent marginal Republican. See *Ibid*, Table 6, p. 38.

[18] Robert S. Erikson, "The Advantage of Incumbency in Congressional Elections," *Polity*, 3 (Spring, 1971), 395-405, concludes that the advantage of incumbency more than doubled between the 1950s and 1966. Also see Warren Lee Kostroski, "Party and Incumbency in Postwar Senate Elections," *American Political Science Review*, 67 (December, 1973), 1213-34.

Table 2.4 Incumbent Success Rate House and Senate, 1958-1970

Year	House			Senate		
	Attempt	Success		Attempt	Success	
1958	394	354	90%	26	17	65%
1960	403	372	92%	28	27	96%
1962	393	368	94%	30	27	90%
1964	397	345	87%	30	28	93%
1966	407	362	89%	31	28	90%
1968	409	396	97%	28	20	71%
1970	392	370	94%	28	21	75%
1972	376	350	93%	27	20	74%
1974	391	343	88%	27	23	85%
1976	381	365	96%	25	16	64%

The closeness of competition between the two major parties at the national level is at least in part the result of averaging or balancing out many one-party states. This analysis could, of course, be carried below the state level but to do so would be impractical. It is likely, however, that state competition figures are nothing more than averages of one-party dominated substate units. In the measures studied here only about half the states and about one-quarter of the Congressional districts are classified as two-party competitive. Although competition between the two major parties at the national level has been evident for over a hundred years, at any point in space and time, some degree of one-party control is common. While the U.S. is considered by most authors to be a two-party system, many political units manifest dominance by one party or the other.

THIRD PARTIES IN AMERICAN POLITICS

Although there might be some question as to whether the U.S. has a two-party system or a modified one-party system, there never has been evidence of a multiparty system. Seldom have more than two parties competed meaningfully at the national level. Despite some exceptions such as the four-party politics of New York State (see Box 2.1), third parties have exhibited little possibility of electoral victory. The election structure as well as the nature of American politics has moderated the potential success of any but the two major parties. Although Chapter 3 will examine the reasons in more detail, a brief summary of third parties in America is included here.

Despite the general lack of success of third parties in the electoral process, many party labels continue to appear on presidential ballots. In any

BOX 2.1 MODIFIED TWO-PARTY SYSTEM
NEW YORK STATE

The European multiparty system is not the only alternative to the two-party system with episodic third-party activity. New York State has a highly competitive party system with two major contenders and third-party contestants that are able to sustain themselves over time. Two of the minor parties currently not only participate in the elective process, but contribute directly to the formulation of policy in the state's government. This is all achieved within a system of direct election of a single chief executive, plurality rule, single-member districts, two major parties, and other common features of American party systems.

The most important of New York's third parties are the Liberals and the Conservatives. The two are similar in the breadth of their appeal and oftentimes in their political behavior, but they have distinctly different origins and goals . . .

The essential attribute of New York's modified two-party system is the options it provides to both individual voters and political parties. For the issue oriented voter the presence of fairly durable third parties affords a greater variety of choices among party platforms and candidates than does a two-party contest. Alternative arenas are available for potential activists who find the major-party organizations either preoccupied with winning office or dominated by an older generation of politicians. Furthermore, the system does not force voters to choose between "throwing their vote away" or voting for one of two major parties. The modified system allows third parties to retain their specialized constituencies while contributing to election outcomes through coalitions with the major parties. Finally, the ability of third parties to survive over time makes them vehicles for new issues and new programs that otherwise would have to await acceptance by a much broader audience before the major parties would address them. Thus, durable third parties, even more than the short-lived parties that emerge in the present national two-party system, hold the potential for stimulating political discussion and compelling politicians in power to stay abreast of current public trends.

Changing the election laws of other states to replicate those of New York would not, of course, automatically generate third parties or placate those groups demanding new forms of political participation. But it would certainly tend to facilitate change.

SOURCE: Daniel A. Mazmanian, *Third Parties in Presidential Elections*, (Washington, D.C.: The Brookings Institution, 1974), pp. 115 and 134-35.

presidential election there will be many party names on the ballot in addition to the Democrats and Republicans. It has been unusual, however, for these minor parties to collect more than a small fraction of the vote. Table 2.5 presents the vote percentages of the most successful third parties in U.S. history. Daniel Mazmanian suggests that all ten of these "significant" parties have emerged in periods of severe political crisis.

Only in times of extraordinary stress do the division of public opinion, the positions taken by the major parties, and the energies of third-party entrepreneurs take on importance.[19]

Table 2.5   Significant Third Parties in Presidential Elections

Year	Party	Vote Percentage
1832	Anti-Mason	8.0
1848	Free Soil	10.1
1856	American	21.4
1860	Breckinridge Democrats	18.2
1860	Constitutional Union	12.6
1892	Populist	8.5
1912	Progressive (Roosevelt)	27.4
1912	Socialist	6.0
1924	Progressive (LaFollette)	16.6
1968	American Independent	13.5

SOURCE: Daniel A. Mazmanian, *Third Parties in Presidential Elections*, (Washington, D.C.: The Brookings Institution, 1974), p. 5.

While there is evidence that third parties achieve their greatest success during crisis periods, this does not ensure success, nor is it sufficient for third party formation. In addition to the crisis, both major parties must fail to offer reasonable alternatives on the major issues. If one or both of the parties face the issue of concern the potential for the third party is reduced. After the Civil War and during the Depression, for instance, the Republican and Democratic parties, respectively, monopolized the crisis issues and effectively denied third parties a significant role despite the severity of the crisis.

[19] Daniel A. Mazmanian, *Third Parties in Presidential Elections* (Washington, D.C.: The Brookings Institution, 1974), p. 27.

Even in crisis periods where third parties have emerged, their electoral efforts have been restricted to attempts to deny the electoral college victory to either major party. Never has a third party come close to winning the popular vote for president, and seldom has one effectively organized at the other levels of government. Some contend that the presence of third parties in a number of cases has prevented the formation of electoral majorities.[20] There is also a question whether the presence of third parties has ever affected the outcome of the election by drawing off votes from the favored party. Although there is no proof that the latter event ever occurred, it is mathematically possible that the outcomes of 1848, 1956, 1960, 1892, and 1968 would have been reversed without the third party vote as reflected in Table 2.5. Regarding 1968, Converse concludes that there is little evidence that "the Wallace instrusion by itself" changed the outcome.[21] Similarly, most observers of the remaining elections offer little or no support for such a supposition.[22]

FORMS OF THIRD PARTIES

It is significant that the most successful third parties at the polls have been splinters of one of the major parties and not autonomous organizations. Both minor parties of 1860 and the Progressive parties of 1912 and 1924 (Table 2.5) were of this type. As such they tended to be highly personalized around a charismatic leader (i.e., Breckinridge, Teddy Roosevelt and Robert LaFollette). In a similar manner, the American Independent Party (AIP) success in 1968 represented a personal achievement for George Wallace and was limited to his attempt to block an electoral college victory by Humphrey or Nixon, thereby gaining leverage. His success was not extended to other AIP candidates, nor has the party been able to retain the momentum in succeeding elections without Wallace. In glancing at the parties in Figure 2.2, it is interesting that none of these personalized third parties have maintained their electoral success beyond one election.

In addition to these personalized or splinter-party movements there has been a type of organization which, although lacking the dramatic vote percentages of the splinters, is more long-term in nature. These parties tend to have foundations in ideological groups of European origin. The various

[20] *Ibid.*, p. 69.

[21] Philip E. Converse, *et al.*, "Continuity and Change in American Politics: Parties and Issues in the 1968 Election," *American Political Science Review*, 63 (December, 1969), 1092.

[22] See Mazmanian, *Third Parties*, pp. 71-74.

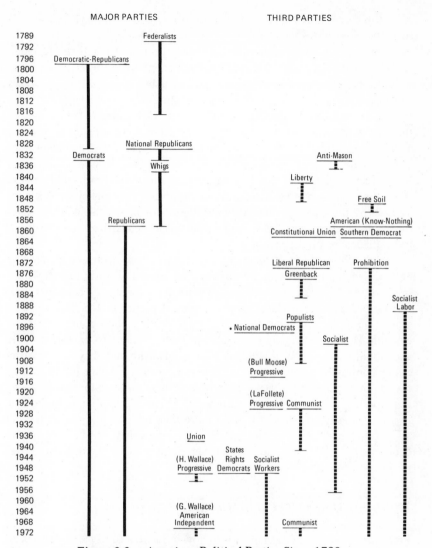

Figure 2.2   American Political Parties Since 1789

SOURCE: *Guide to U.S. Elections* (Washington, D.C.: Congressional Quarterly, Inc., 1975), p. 176.

Socialist parties, the Communist Party, and the Prohibition Party are examples of mass membership organizations that have surfaced in the U.S. Although they have won few elections, they are most persistent in offering presidential candidates. Figure 2.2 illustrates this persistency. In almost every case, the efforts of these parties have been ideologically-oriented, although several have succeeded in securing local offices.[23]

In addition to the electorally-oriented third parties and the ideologically-oriented organizations, there have been at infrequent intervals attempts to form new parties around specific critical issues. The early third parties (the Anti-Mason, Free Soil, and Populist stand out as most successful) were formed as responses to specific conditions. Although strong traces of some of these party orientations still exist in specific states, they have not been viable at the national level for some time. Once the issue is absorbed by one or both of the major parties these issue-oriented organizations have disappeared. Some recent examples of this type of organization are the Peace and Freedom and other minor parties arising out of disillusion over policy on Vietnam pursued by the major parties. Although the minor parties failed to win significant electoral support, they were successful in publicizing their views and protesting current policies.

Like the earlier splinter party movements, these organizations tend to be transient and limited to the presidential contest. Efforts to carry their organization to other levels of government most frequently have met with frustration. Despite the large number of third parties in U.S. history, they seldom have received much attention or significant support at more than one election. Due to this, many have failed in their attempts to dramatize issues and mobilize support for their ideological stands. Although they are unrestricted by continuing commitments and able to take more extreme positions than the major parties, third parties have found voters difficult to convince. The third parties tend either to fade away due to lack of continuing support or to turn inward and become nothing more than interest groups representing a loyal but small corps of members. Seldom, unless they strike a sympathetic chord in the electorate, do they attract support much beyond their mass members.

THIRD PARTIES AND PUBLIC POLICY

Frequently the question is raised as to how influential third parties have been in electoral politics and in determining public policy. On the first point, some contend that although third parties are ineffective in altering results, they broaden the base of electoral politics by appealing to those who are uninvolved in politics and alienated from the major parties.[24] This contention is unsupported by election turnout data, which indicate a general decline in

---

[23] The Socialist Party held several mayoral offices in the 1950s including Milwaukee (Frank P. Zeidler).

[24] Mazmanian, *Third Parties*, p. 77.

turnout as third parties become more evident. Those elections in which third parties are able to garner large vote percentages exhibit low participation rates. This implies that third party voting might serve as one means of protesting the major party candidates while nonvoting might be another manifestation of the same phenomenon.[25] Third parties appear to offer only one of several alternatives for dissatisfied voters.

In terms of public policy, the most frequent credit given third parties is that they present new issues to the public which the major parties are unable or unwilling to pursue. Although few observers suggest that third parties directly effect such changes, many contend that the major parties eventually adopt the innovations and ideas initiated by the more flexible minor parties. Mazmanian, for instance, concludes that "many of their ideas have eventually been incorporated into the programs of major parties and translated into public policies."[26] He offers such examples as the slavery restrictions of the Free Soil party during the 1850s becoming public policy under the Republicans a decade later. More dramatically, he contends that most of the progressive ideas on taxation, regulation of railroads, and social insurance implemented in the New Deal era were initially introduced by earlier Socialist, Populist and Progressive parties. Also, third parties were at the forefront of the battles over suffrage and election reforms.

After all is said and these convincing examples are given, there is still very little evidence that it was the efforts of the third parties that effected these policy changes. Although third parties might have quickened the pace of change, support for even such a limited thesis is mixed. In any case, the minority views represented by these third parties require a broader public acceptance and ultimate adoption by one or both major parties before they can be translated into public policy. How much the efforts of third parties facilitate such a process is open to question. With a few possible exceptions it appears most likely that third parties throughout the history of the U.S. have represented a minimal policy influence. As in the case of electoral success, third parties have had a very minor role in shaping policy.

CONSTRAINTS OF THIRD PARTIES: WHY A MINOR ROLE?

Access to Ballot. Although the major reason for the ineffectiveness of third party attempts is rooted in our culture and in the nature of our electoral process (Chapter 3), there are several obvious biases against third parties that have impeded their development. The first is the attempt by the major

---

[25] See Chapter 10 of this book for more details.

[26] Mazmanian, *Third Parties*, p. 81.

parties to limit competition by making it difficult or nearly impossible for additional parties to get their candidates listed on the ballot. In theory, filing dates, petitions, and other devices are utilized to reduce the number of candidates to a reasonable number. In practice, whether intended or not, they have constrained the development of third party challenges. Walter Dean Burnham contends that most if not all of the fundamental progressive procedural reforms were in "effect devices of political stabilization and control" and not neutral in intent.[27] Although no state forbids third-party candidates, many make it procedurally confusing and time-consuming to be placed on the ballot.

One of George Wallace's major accomplishments of 1968 was to gain access to the ballot in all 50 states. However, despite obtaining almost 3 million signatures, he was still unable to run on a single party label across the nation. In addition, the time and money used to collect these required signatures on petitions distracted from more pressing campaign objectives. Wallace was ultimately aided by the Supreme Court, which ruled that Ohio's law required an unreasonable number of signatures and directed that the AIP be placed on the ballot.[28] The Court's willingness to enter this arena, previously considered a political domain, has moved towards reducing this restraint on third parties. Despite this and succeeding decisions against the states, [29] there continues to be room for violation since the Court failed to issue definitive guidelines. Also, few new political groups have the resources available to take the matter to court across a number of states.

Access to Media.   Another disadvantage to third parties is the difficulty they experience in attracting the attention of the mass media. While the candidates of the two major parties receive unlimited free publicity through regular news programming and special interview shows, third-party candidates are virtually excluded (see Box 2.2). Any exposure they get must be paid for through personal advertisements. In light of the extreme importance of the mass media coverage, and the government restrictions on spending for media, third party candidates face insurmountable odds.

The obstacles facing minor party candidates have been an issue for many years. In the 1934 Communications Act, Section 315 (a), Congress

[27] Walter Dean Burnham, *Critical Elections and the Mainsprings of American Politics* (New York: W.W. Norton and Company, Inc., 1970), p. 74.

[28] *Williams v. Rhodes, Governor of Ohio*, 393 U.S. 23 (1968). For more discussion see Thomas G. Walker, *American Politics and the Constitution* (North Scituate, Mass.: Duxbury Press, 1978), pp. 110-116.

[29] *Moore v. Ogilvie*, 394 U.S. 814 (1969).

BOX 2.2   CONSTRAINTS ON
THIRD PARTIES

Under-publicized and under-financed, the various third-party candidates together received barely 1.5 million votes, less than 2 percent of the national total. Spokesmen for several were critical of scanty media coverage and inequities in the new federal campaign finance law, which they felt contributed to their low vote totals.

McCarthy was a major opponent of the new campaign finance law even before the campaign began and he has vowed to continue to challenge its constitutionality. McCarthy claims that the law threatens to institutionalize the two-party system by supplying public funds for the Democrats and Republicans while placing tight limits on the size of contributions, which are the major source of funds for third parties. "I would have needed $100-million to compete this year," McCarthy said in a panel discussion November 15. "Let me raise money and compete."

McCarthy's bitterness was not limited to fund-raising restrictions. In a press conference November 5, he sharply criticized the lack of media coverage his candidacy received. A major problem for third party contenders, he said, was exclusion from the debates. McCarthy felt the debates cemented the impression in voter's minds that there were only two candidates.

"I think we are in a new era of politics," he said, "in which the great mother goddess is the President of the League of Women Voters. She decides who the candidates are. Then the three minor gods are the heads of the three networks. They confirm what the mother goddess has said. They say, 'We agree. These are the two candidates—these two, and no more.' "

Ed Crane, chairman of the Libertarian Party, shared McCarthy's disappointment. He claimed that the only times his party received national attention were in human interest stories.

Like McCarthy, Crane was also critical of the campaign finance law. The Libertarians were only able to raise about $600,000, a small fraction of the $21.8-million in federal funds provided to the major parties for the general election campaign. Crane noted that most of his party's money had to be pumped into ballot drives, which did not leave any money to mount an effective campaign.

Finances and media attention were also major problems for

the two right-wing offshoots of the 1968 Wallace campaign—Thomas Anderson's American Party and William Shearer's American Independent Party, which ran Maddox. Both parties raised less than $200,000.

SOURCE: *Congressional Quarterly Weekly Report*, Vol. 34, No. 51 (December 18, 1976), 3336.

guaranteed all parties equal access to the media. In 1959, however, the equal-time statute was amended to exclude the most crucial elements of the original Act. Equal candidate time on newscasts, interviews, or documentaries was no longer required, provided the appearance was incidental to the subject matter presented. The equal-time clause was also temporarily suspended during the presidential debates of 1960 and 1976, when minor party candidates were excluded from the debate format. Generally, the rulings on this statute have limited equal-time responses to candidates of the Republican and Democratic parties.[30]

FUTURE THIRD PARTIES

While third party efforts continue to be hampered by unequal access to the media, restrictive ballot procedures, and the electoral process in general, some authors contend that independent and minor party candidates may have greater success in the future.[31] They argue that trends toward more independent voting, a more issue-oriented consciousness, and the ability to use the media for rapid exposure give attractive candidates means of offsetting some of the disadvantages. They cite Wallace's success and his personalized-movement type of organization as examples of what can happen when a candidate is able to draw disillusioned members of the two major parties to an issue orientation through effective, though limited, use of the media. Despite warnings of such possibilities, it seems highly unlikely in the near future that we will approach a multiparty system like most of the European systems. There are too many aspects of American culture and political institutions that promise to perpetuate our unique two-party system.

[30] Mazmanian, *Third Parties,* p. 105.

[31] For instance, see Samuel Lubell, *The Hidden Crisis in American Politics* (New York: W.W. Norton and Company, Inc., 1970), p. 68 and Frederick G. Dutton, *Changing Sources of Power: American Politics in the 1970's* (New York: McGraw-Hill Book Company, 1971), p. 242.

CHARACTERISTICS OF AMERICAN PARTY
SYSTEM: A SUMMARY

It has been demonstrated that the American party system and the parties which operate within it are unique among western democracies. Unlike most other nations in the world, the U.S. has shown little tendency toward a multi-party system. For over a century the Republican and Democratic parties have dominated American politics with little sustained challenge from any third party. While there are some indications that third party movements might have greater potential due to weakening party attachments and growing importance of the media, there is no evidence that we are moving toward multi-party politics.

There is more danger of one-party politics increasing below the national level. Despite a remarkably equal balance of support of the major parties over the last hundred years, there are many one-party dominated congressional districts and states. For a variety of reasons, including the growing power of incumbency, the trend is toward less rather than greater interparty competition. Similarly, despite the competition over the last century, there has existed one-party domination for extended periods of time. Only in the aggregate in space and time do we really have balanced two-party competition. Still it appears most accurate to label our party system as two-party in nature since throughout our history there have tended to be two parties with a reasonable chance of success in winning the presidency.

Just as the American party system is unique, so are the two major parties distinctive. Both parties are heterogeneous in composition, each incorporating many religious, ethnic, and class groups. Neither party can depend fully on consistent support from any one group, and each must, therefore, attempt to gain support from as wide a coalition as possible. As a result, American parties are moderate or centrist in nature, and ideology and issues are minimized in an effort to maintain as much support as possible from these diverse sources.

The Republican and Democratic parties are also distinctive in their organization. Both are considered cadre in nature while a large proportion of parties in western democracies are classified as mass membership. U.S. parties are characterized by a lack of formal membership and by periodic activity. Although membership can be defined in many ways, very few Americans formally join a party as they would other organizations. Those who are active concentrate their efforts during the campaign period. Leadership in U.S. parties tends to be more amorphous and more decentralized than party leadership of other nations.

The most distinctive characteristic of American parties is their emphasis on winning elections. While each party has a somewhat different ideological orientation, the similarities are much more obvious and seldom are elections conducted on ideological grounds. The nature of the electorate, in combination with the decentralized character of the party organizations, minimizes the role of ideology or doctrine in party activities. American parties are electoral organizations, not mass membership associations, and their survival is based on maintenance of electoral support. As such, they are as uniquely American as the two-party system. Chapter 3 will attempt to offer explanations as to why they are unique. Why do U.S. parties and the U.S. party system manifest characteristics uncommon to those found in other democracies?

3

The Context
of American Political Parties

The uniqueness of the American parties and party system was illustrated in Chapter 2. Even among western democracies, U.S. parties stand out as exceptions. Both major parties are of the cadre type: highly decentralized, status-quo-oriented, and win-centered. They depend on supporters, not members, and attempt to appeal to all major social groups to secure electoral support. The presence of two parties is an exclusively American distinction. Whether we have meaningful, two-party competition or a balance of various one-party districts has been questioned, but there is no doubt that a multiparty system is alien to American politics.

This chapter examines some aspects of American society which have shaped political parties and the party system. Everett Ladd sees parties as creatures of American society and contends that changes in the party system can be understood only within the context of social change.

> The American party system took shape in the closing years of the eighteenth century as a principal early response in political institutions to egalitarianism. The type of party system then formed reflected the many features of the socio-political setting which was the U.S. of that time, and the changes and adaptations in the party system speak to the continuing transformation of American society.[1]

Although there is not enough time here to discuss all aspects of American society which may have influenced parties, the most crucial ones are examined. After describing the relevant historical context of party development, the role of the formal governmental institutions in shaping the party system is pre-

---

[1] Everett Carll Ladd, Jr. *American Political Parties: Social Change and Political Response* (New York: W.W. Norton and Company, 1970), p. 27.

sented. Finally, the characteristics of the population and of political culture are discussed in an effort to understand better why our party system is unique.

HISTORICAL CONTEXT

Although the evolution of electoral machinery can be traced back a thousand years in England and a rudimentary form of party organization began to appear after that, "early indications are vague and elusive."[2] The earliest organizations took the form of political groupings within the legislatures. While early parliaments were used mainly to legitimize the Monarch's tax practices, divisions began to occur within the parliaments. Although these legislative groupings appeared for over 700 years, they tended to be far from our present conception of party organizations.[3] It was not until 19th century America that stable party organizations developed (see Box 3.1).

As long as parties were limited to legislative groupings, little change was evident. Although factions were present to varying degrees in the colonies, they tended to be "shifting, kaleidoscopic groups, banding together from time to time, then exploding into unfamiliar patterns."[4] They took on various forms and names, including clique, caucus, junto, and faction, but never party. Frequently, they were nothing more than intricate agreements among legislators across a range of issues.

Parties became important when the vote was extended and elections had to be contested. Despite almost unanimous opposition by early American political leaders to the concept of party, some mechanism was necessary to (1) conduct nominations, (2) organize elections, and (3) manage government. These functions were performed by nonparty means, but all failed ultimately because they lacked the basic coordination that accompanies parties and provides clarity and continuity to the electoral process. Although it is difficult to imagine elections without party labels, that is what took place before the 1790s. Prior to that time, parties that existed in the states were loose and subject to frequent change.

[2] Roy F. Nichols, *The Invention of the American Political Parties* (New York: The MacMillan Company, 1967), p. 7.

[3] For an excellent description of parties in the early period see William Nisbet Chambers, *Political Parties in a New Nation: An American Experience, 1776-1809* (New York: Oxford University Press, 1963).

[4] Alison Gilbert Olson, *Anglo-American Politics, 1766-1775* (Oxford: Clarendon Press, 1973), p. x, disputes this description, however.

BOX 3.1   ORIGIN OF U.S. PARTIES

The system of government called American democracy is Anglo-American in origin and history. It was never completely planned nor projected, and even in the laws and constitutions which have been its charters, it was never fully described. Certain of its chief elements were neither designed nor authorized, while some of its most effective instruments of operation have been unspecified improvisations and adaptations . . .

One of the most elaborate of these inventions has been a unique instrument, the American political party machine. Its design was long in the making, and not until the mid-nineteenth century was it, for all intents and purposes, completed in the form of an organized and institutionalized two-party system, a device which enabled the community to carry on the periodic contests for power which are one of the chief features of the practice of self-government. Interestingly enough, this instrument was conceived and developed without any statutory or constitutional authorization.

SOURCE: Roy F. Nichols, *The Invention of the American Political Parties* (New York: The MacMillan Company, 1967), pp. xi and xii.

Although the need for a means of organizing nominations and elections became evident early in the development of the Republic, the opposition to political "factions"[5] slowed parties' initial development. Even Thomas Jefferson, who had a major part in creating the first truly popular party in the western world and was a central figure in developing responsible constitutional opposition, had no use for political parties. "If I could not go to heaven but with a party, I would not go there at all."[6] Benjamin Franklin warned against factions and "the infinite mutual abuse of parties, tearing to pieces the best of characters."[7] John Adams believed that "a division of the

[5] *Ibid.*, discusses the use of the term faction in describing the early political units.

[6] Richard Hofstadter, *The Idea of a Party System: The Rise of Legitimate Opposition in the United States, 1780-1840* (Berkeley: University of California Press, 1969), p. 123.

[7] *Ibid.*, p. 2.

republic into two great parties ... is to be dreaded as the greatest political evil under our constitution."[8] Despite their condemnations of parties, the critics engaged in partisan action and were driven to develop a party system. Hofstadter's analysis presented in Box 3.2 illustrates the dilemma in which the framers found themselves. They each saw their own party as the means of ending party politics and restoring government by consensus.

BOX 3.2   PARTIES AND THE FOUNDING FATHERS

Of course it is important to realize that the Founding Fathers were more accurately criticizing the rudimentary parties they had seen in action or had read of in their histories than the modern parties they were themselves beginning to build for the future. They stood at a moment of fecund inconsistency, suspended between their acceptance on one side of political differences and opposition criticism, and on the other their rejection of parties as agencies to organize social conflict and political debate. They well understood that conflicts of opinion are inevitable in a state of republican freedom, but they wanted to minimize such conflicts and hoped to achieve a comprehensive unity or harmony. They did not usually see conflict as functional to society, and above all they could not see how organized and institutionalized party conflict could be made useful, or could be anything other than divisive, distracting, and dangerous.

For this reason the history of the United States during the first quarter century of government under the federal Constitution marked a focal episode in the development of the idea of legitimate opposition. In Anglo-American experience the idea of free political criticism had made vital gains in the eighteenth century ... Even in America, where the battle with royal governors had created a strong tradition of oppositional politics, the idea of a mass party as an extension of parliamentary discussion and opposition was not widely accepted. It was held by most men to be particularly unsuited to government under a representative republic, where representative institutions themselves were believed sufficient to serve the public interest ... In America, where party opposition had been much more fully developed, it had been carried on in the face of a firm conviction by each side in the party battle that the other was not

---

[8] *Ibid.*

legitimate, and in a healthy state of affairs would be put out of business. Neither party had thought of the other either as a legitimate opposition or as an alternative government; neither side thought of the two parties as engaged in a sustained competition that would result in rotations of power. Each party hoped to bring about the other's destruction by devouring and absorbing as many of its more amenable followers as could be won over, and by forcing the remaining top leadership into disorganization and impotence.

SOURCE: Richard Hofstadter, *Idea of a Party System,* (Berkeley: University of California Press, 1969), pp. ix and x.

The Constitution makes no mention of political parties. In the debate over the Constitution, however, both the Federalists and Anti-Federalists indicated their fear and disdain of parties or "factions" (one of the few matters on which they agreed so fully). In *The Federalist Papers*, Number 10, one of a set of documents favoring ratification of the Constitution, James Madison warns of factions, but concludes that the best way to counter them is to provide for a large variety of groups, thereby diluting the power of any one. He accepted parties as unavoidable by-products of a free state; to be checked and restricted, but never eliminated. Alexander Hamilton's stand against parties was more extreme and more orthodox. He saw parties as evils that could be avoided or abolished. By the 1790s the best that was said about parties was that they were unavoidable evils. A more common justification for the existence of parties was that through parties ultimately all parties would be eliminated.[9] George Washington considered himself above parties and had a tendency to brand all political opposition as sedition.

In this ominous and hostile environment, parties in the United States were nurtured. The various elements which constituted the Federalist party were brought together by Hamilton, whose views on parties were cited above. He was able to build a rather broad base of support of capitalists and wage earners, and thereby provided the first stable if still quite tenuous links between the public and the government. His organization marked the first party at the national level. It had (1) a structure with leaders and followers, (2) continuing procedures for performing nomination and election tasks, (3) a unique ideological perspective, and (4) representation of a wide range of interests. Although, by current standards, public participation was limited, the Federalist party represented a step in the direction of a stable, ongoing, electoral organization.

[9]*Ibid.,* p. 6.

Partly as a personal reaction to Hamilton and partly as a response to the need for an effective opposition mechanism, the young intellectuals, represented most clearly by Jefferson and Madison, formed a capital faction which led to the creation of the Democrat-Republican party. Despite Jefferson's cautions attitude toward parties, events during the 1790s intensified conflict between the Federalists and the Republicans, strengthened the party divisions in Congress, and led to party voting in the electorate. By 1800 the schism within the Federalist party reached major proportions and Jefferson won the election through a broad appeal to the voters and a clearly defined program.

With the Republicans came some of the organizational features which characterize parties today. In addition to the use of nominating caucuses, local party conventions, and state party committees, came the specter of the professional politician. Patronage was used to strengthen the party and a leadership corps developed. This party was so successful that the dreams of Washington and Hamilton were almost realized, ironically, through the new party that replaced theirs. Between 1800 and 1828, the U.S. had virtually a one-party government, the Republicans. Factionalism, however, destroyed the Republican coalition soon after the Federalists disbanded. Again the need for an opposition won out over the complacency toward party organization. By 1828, Jackson and his Democratic party were in competition with a new opposition, in this case the Whigs.

Richard Hofstadter puts much emphasis on the phase of party development between 1828 and 1840. He contends that the second-generation leaders began to realize the merits of party organization and saw two-party competition as an asset, not a liability, in the public interest.[10] Martin Van Buren is seen as typical of the new breed of politicians, less ideological or fixed in their view of issues and more interested in organization. As these leaders recognized the legitimacy of parties, they accepted patronage, the caucus, and other party mechanisms as necessary and fundamentally good.

The value of opposition itself as a cohesive political force was recognized first by Van Buren and his New York Republican cohorts. They welcomed the idea of a permanent opposition. Hofstadter states that this "marked the single longest stride toward the idea of a party system."[11] The

[10] *Ibid.*, pp. 212-52. Also see Richard P. McCormick, *The Second American Party System: Party Formation in the Jackson Era* (Chapel Hill: University of North Carolina Press, 1966). Ronald P. Formisano, "Deferential-Participant Politics: The Early Republic's Political Culture, 1789-1840," *American Political Science Review*, 68 (June, 1974), 473-87, presents a more analytical approach to the early party period.

[11] Hofstadter, *Idea of a Party System*, p. 226.

lesson of the first quarter of the nineteenth century had been clear: The divisive impact of personal factions was far more dangerous to a democracy than open and principled conflict between two stable and permanent parties. Active party competition was presumed to cure apathy, inform the public, reduce competition, and help insure the social peace. That parties have failed to meet the goals of these second-generation leaders has not been due to their lack of confidence. Parties had come into their own as legitimate political organizations.

Although many changes have accompanied parties and the party system since 1840, most have represented adjustments to changing conditions, not basic alterations in the concept. The Lincoln Republican replacement of the fading Whig party and the following realignments were reflections of shifts in the electorate, not major modifications of the party system. Although significant reforms have occurred over the last 140 years, none have been as profound as the changes that took place in the century preceding it. By 1840, the two-party system had been tested and demonstrated to be necessary. More crucially, it was grounded in the very institutions that defined the government and the society at large.

BOX 3.3   WINNING COALITIONS IN
U.S. HISTORY

I. *Federalist (1789-1801).* The Federalists received most of their support from New England and from coastal areas around the country. Their coalition was composed of the rich, well-born landowners plus the commercial interests.

II. *Jeffersonian Democrat-Republicans (1801-1827).* The major element of this broad-based coalition was the agricultural interests that constituted 80 percent of the population during this period. Although the Republicans were opposed by the manufacturing interests, the intensity of opposition was low. Strongest early support came from small farmers that produced for themselves, not for trade.

III. *Jacksonian Democrats (1828-1859).* Most evident in this coalition was the inland or backwoods population. This rapidly growing category was supplemented by a well-balanced coalition across most of the states especially among laborers and small landowners. The opposition Whig coalition never really challenged the broad Democrat coalition.

IV. *Union Republicans (1860-1895).* The only solid regional winning coalition in our history. Composed of industrial support in the North and agrarian support from the West. Basically North and West versus South during this entire period.

V. *Industrial Republicans (1896-1932).* Despite a major realignment in the mid-1890s, the Republican label stayed with the revamped coalition. During this period urban support for the Republicans eroded with the immigration of large numbers of Catholic ethnics. Rural support in some subregions weakened as the areas were settled by immigrants from the South. The main elements of the industrial Republicans were northern businessmen and middle-class Protestants as well as Middle-Western farmers.

VI. *New Deal Democrats (1932-1968).* The New Deal coalition was an amalgamation of the traditional Southern Democrats and the new urban Democrats of the North. While holding the support of the farmer-labor-South coalition that evolved in the prior period, the New Deal Democrats were able to add the urban-unemployed, the blacks and various ethnic minorities. The question is what will follow this coalition.

FORMAL GOVERNMENTAL CONTEXT
OF PARTIES

In the preceding section, political parties were viewed as having evolved within a unique historical context. The isolation of the U.S. from Europe, the resulting lack of built-in governmental constraints, and the westward expansion all helped to shape a new type of party system unique to the United States.

As noted in Chapter 1, the party system is but one element in the governmental process. Any function it performs is interrelated with other government institutions and the constitutional framework within which they operate. To understand the nature of our party system more fully, an examination of the primary constitutional and governmental restraints on the system is warranted. Not surprisingly, the U.S. exhibits a distinctive combination of political institutions which help to define the characteristics of its political parties.

FEDERALISM

The U.S. is a federal system. In other words, the Constitution delegates specific powers to the central government while reserving other powers for the states. Since the national constitution was written by delegates from the states, instead of the states being created by a central government, the states specifically protected their interests by limiting the powers of the central government. Additionally, areas where agreement could not be reached at the Constitutional Convention were left up to the states to solve.

While a major shift toward centralization of power has occurred over the past 190 years, regulation of most aspects of political parties and elections is still within the domain of the states. Some states provide detailed laws defining parties, specifying their structure and responsibilities, and regulating their contributions and expenditures. Other states outline the nature of the party system, but leave it to the parties themselves to provide more detailed bylaws.[12] In either case, centralization of party authority in a national organization is thwarted by inconsistent and uncoordinated state laws regulating parties and elections.

In addition to decentralizing political parties, federalism encourages parties to put emphasis on winning elections by providing a vast array of elective offices. While there are only 536 elective offices at the national level there are over 520,000 at the state and local level.[13] Due to the number of offices and frequency of elections, the parties must direct most of their energy and resources toward winning. Only by capturing many offices at the national level, as well as in the states, can a party have a chance to influence policy. Ironically, once a party gains control it must spend more time and resources in order to maintain its power. Its task is complicated greatly by the need to control both states and the national government.

The decentralization of power resulting in the federal system in turn leads to internal diversity within each party. In examining Congress later it will be illustrated that state constituency issues at times conflict directly with party stands. In the most crucial cases, the constituency is not betrayed.

Federalism is a major factor in explaining the decentralized nature of American parties. A modification in the federal system would be necessary to produce increased levels of party cohesion and centralization of authority.

[12] Robert J. Huckshorn, *Party Leadership in the States* (Amherst, Mass.: University of Massachusetts Press, 1976), p. 2.

[13] Richard G. Smolka, Committee on Post Office and Civil Service, *Hearings on Voter Registration* (Washington: U.S. Government Printing Office, 1973), p. 192, estimates that there are over 521,000 elected officials in the U.S.

SEPARATION OF POWERS

An even more distinctive American institution which shapes the structure and functions of political parties is the separation of powers. Due in part to their suspicions of centralized government and control by factions, the Constitution's authors went to great lengths to minimize the possibility of dominance by any one branch. In order to accomplish this, they established a series of checks and balances among the executive, legislative, and judicial branches. None would become dominant, since each could limit, constitutionally, actions of the others.

This separation of powers not only succeeded in checking the powers of the various branches, but also diluted the power of the political parties. Since there is no single locus of power in the national government, it is improbable that either party will control all branches at the same time. Contrarily, under a parliamentary system, the party that controls the lower house creates the government. The prime minister and his cabinet have seats in parliament. They hold their executive positions as leaders of the majority party in the legislative branch and serve at the pleasure of the majority. In the U.S., conversely, a party can have comfortable majorities in both houses of Congress, yet have no control or even influence over the executive branch. This might occur because of ideological differences between the presidential and congressional wings of a single party[14] or because of a divided government. The latter is the situation when one party controls one or both houses of Congress and the other holds the presidency. Divided government over the last three decades has been as common (see Table 3.1) as one-party control of both branches. It is not surprising that few presidents have been successful in dealing with a Congress controlled by the opposing party.

In addition to producing potential conflict situations within the national government, separation of powers reinforces federalism by reducing party discipline and cohesion. Since control of the government is not solely dependent on maintaining a majority, members are more free to vote their constituencies without being perceived as traitors. Party label, although important on many votes, is subsumed on others since members are not bound to vote as their leaders demand.

> In a parliamentary country like Britain, the chief executive is part of the legislature . . . Since the executive requires a legislative majority, the failure of Labour (or Conservative) party members of Parliament to support their government brings down their government. It is hardly surprising, then, that members of the

[14] See James McGregor Burns, *Deadlock of Democracy: Four Party Politics in America* (Englewood Cliffs: Prentice-Hall, Inc., 1963), Chapter 2.

Table 3.1   Party Control of President and Congress, 1947-1978

Congress	Years	President	House	Senate	Divided
80th	1947-48	D	R	R	Yes
81st	1949-50	D	D	D	No
82nd	1951-52	D	D	D	No
83rd	1953-54	R	R	R	No
84th	1955-56	R	D	D	Yes
85th	1957-58	R	D	D	Yes
86th	1959-60	R	D	D	Yes
87th	1961-62	D	D	D	No
88th	1963-64	D	D	D	No
89th	1965-66	D	D	D	No
90th	1967-68	D	D	D	No
91st	1969-70	R	D	D	Yes
92nd	1971-72	R	D	D	Yes
93rd	1973-74	R	D	D	Yes
94th	1975-76	R	D	D	Yes
95th	1977-78	D	D	D	No

majority party do not frivolously vote against the programs on which the executive—their party's leaders—stakes the governments' life.[15]

While the joint executive-legislative parliamentary system encourages party cohesion, our separated system provides few incentives for party unity.

ONE-MAN EXECUTIVES
AND SINGLE-MEMBER DISTRICTS

A related American phenomenon that has influenced the development of parties is the single or one-man executive. From the president to the state governors to the mayors of the large cities, the executive is a single person, ultimately responsible for the action of all subordinates. He, not his party, is elected, and he serves the term. The election of executives in the U.S. is an all-or-nothing situation. This works against third parties because the executive office cannot be divided among parties as it can under a parliamentary system. In order to win the Presidency, a broad coalition of diverse groupings must be formed prior to the election. Despite the vote proportions of the losers, there is only one winner with no sharing of power. Third parties have a

[15] Ladd, *American Political Parties*, p. 50.

difficult time convincing the voters that a vote for their candidate is not wasted.

Reinforcing the one-man executive is the use of single-member districts in selecting most other officials. There is no inherent justification for electing only one legislator from each district. France, for instance, makes use of a proportional representation system which includes multimember districts. This system gives minority parties in each district the chance to win a proportion, no matter how small, of the seats in a district. Under the winner-take-all, single-member scheme there is no representation except for the winning party in each district. It is not surprising that we have many districts continually dominated by one party and that third parties have been unsuccessful in gaining representation in the various legislative bodies of the U.S. Single-member districts help explain the durability of our two-party system.

ADMINISTRATIVE INSTITUTIONS

In addition to the core institutions of federalism and separation of powers and the electoral institutions of single-member districts and single executives, there are many other aspects of government which have influenced and shaped the party system. In Chapter 5 the impact of various administrative reforms on party organization will be examined in detail.

Perhaps no one factor has weakened parties more than the inclusion of the direct primary as the major means of nomination. This one administrative change is most crucial in any discussion of party organization. Also important in weakening party organizations have been: (1) the introduction of the civil service system (which eliminated major sources of party patronage) and (2) social welfare reforms (which minimized the social role of urban party machines). Again, it is clear that parties must be examined within the institutional as well as the historical context.

POPULATION CHARACTERISTICS OF THE U.S.

Just as the historical and institutional framework within which American parties operate is unique, so are the characteristics which define the population. Throughout this discussion it will be obvious that the population of the U.S. is not comparable in composition to any other country in the world. The American party system in part reflects this unique composition.

LARGE, DIVERSE POPULATION

Although the United States population of 225 million ranks fourth in the world, it is by far the largest of the western democracies. In addition, its population is more widely dispersed than any of the other democracies except Canada. Its various regions run the gamut of climatic conditions, terrain, and ecological categories. As a result, concerns and desires of those in specific regions naturally differ and must be accommodated in the party system.

Complementing and reinforcing the population size is its complexity. As seen in Chapter 2, both U.S. parties are classified as heterogeneous, representing cross-sections of diverse social, religious, and ethnic groups. Third parties too closely identified with any one of these groups have failed to gain broad support. There is an obvious reason why U.S. parties are mere coalitions of diverse groupings. Simply put, the U.S. population is the most heterogeneous of any nation in the world. Since it is a nation of relatively recent immigrants, virtually all nationalities are represented among its members. Along with the varied backgrounds have come identifications that, although sublimated, are quite lasting. These divisions are expected to result in political divisions unless parties are able to serve as brokers of the various interests.

In addition to the multiplicity of ethnic backgrounds, there are divisions by race. Although 80 percent of Americans are Caucasian, there are significant racial minorities. Blacks represent about 11 percent of the population while Hispanics, Asians, and native American Indians constitute the remainder. The political importance of these minorities, especially the blacks, is heightened since they tend to be concentrated in urban areas of the North and rural areas of the South. Jimmy Carter in 1976 owed much to the high levels of black support he received in certain key northern states.

Unlike many other democracies, such as Britain and Sweden, the U.S. has no established church. As a result there is wide diversity of religious orientation with no sect being a majority. Although the largest single religious grouping is the Protestants, it actually is composed of over 200 different denominations, ranging politically from liberal to highly conservative. Despite the diversity, most teach obedience to authority and seldom are openly critical of the political system. Most Protestant denominations use a similar political system to run their internal affairs.

The Roman Catholic religion is the single largest church organization in the U.S. with approximately 25 percent of the population nominally members. Historically, Catholics have been discriminated against politically and socially, though this discrimination has now diminished. The concentration of Catholics in the urban East and in parts of the Midwest and West has created another challenge to the major parties. How does one openly court the Catholics without alienating Protestant support? Both parties have attempted this with varying degrees of success throughout history.

The final major religious group in the U.S. is numerically by far the smallest. The Jewish religion and culture are largely indistinguishable. Although organizationally there are three major branches of Judaism which constitute in total less than 4 percent of the U.S. population, the concentration of Jews in several large electoral vote states, their traditionally high interest in politics, and their historical affinity to vote as a bloc, have given them greater influence than their numbers would suggest. Neither party can write off the Jewish vote in key states such as New York and Massachusetts.

LACK OF RIGID CLASS SYSTEM

While many divisions exist in the U.S. population which have forced the major parties to accommodate conflicting interests, the lack of a rigid social class system has eased this burden. Unlike the continental and British societies, where social class is predetermined, U.S. citizens have always enjoyed an open class system. While there have been many theories offered to explain this uniqueness, the absence of the feudal system and the presence of the open frontier appear to be most useful in tracing U.S. social development.[16]

> It is hard to overemphasize the importance of American society's being established 'de nouveau', cut off from the social, economic, and political institutions—and the ideological defenses—of ascriptive class societies.[17]

Due to the ambivalent attitude of Americans toward class, parties have been able to pursue their task of accommodating diverse groups without being constrained by social class considerations.[18]

REGIONAL DISTINCTIONS

Regional differences were alluded to before. It is important to note here that the greatest challenge to the Union came as the result of a regional cleavage. Prior to the Civil War, region was a crucial factor in determining party alignments. Although region has recently been diluted as a major political division, it continues to provide a primary line of potential conflict of which both

---

[16] See Louis Hartz, *The Liberal Tradition in America* (New York: Harcourt, Brace and World, Inc., 1955), and Frederick Jackson Turner, *The Frontier in American History* (New York: Holt, 1921).

[17] Ladd, *American Political Parties*, p. 35.

[18] To some extent, however, "objective" class measures such as education, income, and occupational status have replaced traditional class influence. See Chapter 9 of this book.

parties are aware. Regional differences historically have given each party concentrated areas of popular support as well as electoral votes. Much of the uniqueness of the present party system reflects regional distinctions.

Important in all discussions of the heterogeneous nature of the U.S. population is the concept of overlapping membership. Because there are so many divisions, it is unlikely that all members of any group will share all other memberships. This, too, has blurred the major lines of division in American society and facilitated party moderation and the accommodation of diverse interests.

HIGHLY MOBILE POPULATION

In addition to being large and diverse, the population of the United States is highly mobile. Americans move from state to state and region to region at unequaled rates. It is estimated by the Census Bureau that approximately 20 percent of the population changes residence each year and that 40 percent of the adults live in a state other than the one where they were born. Supplementing change of residence is the open and frequent travel of Americans within the nation. The use of the automobile and a vast array of recreation vehicles permit travel to all parts of the continental U.S. by a cross-section of American society.

This mobility has political impact in that it tends to minimize regional and state differences. The continuous movement of people transcends local and regional ties and has reduced parochialism over the last half century. It also means that the most transient elements of the population seldom become active or even interested in local politics. This mobility has facilitated the nationalization of American politics for many people. Significantly, the most mobile of the electorate are the most educated, that is, those who normally are most active and informed about politics. It is possible that many potential party activists among the highly mobile are eliminated on this basis.

ENVIRONMENTAL INFLUENCES
AND THE ECONOMY

Before examining the values and beliefs of this large, diverse population, it must be noted that many other environmental factors have helped shape the unique American political setting. Certainly the economic system of the U.S. and the presence of vast natural resources have enormous political significance. The abundance of natural resources has made it easy to fulfill the material demands of a large population. Problems of distribution under this situation are much less acute than in a state of market scarcity.[19]

The economy of the U.S. is primarily a private enterprise and market economy. The continued expansion of material output has been the result of mass production techniques. While this has led to the highest standard of living in the world, it has also resulted in unbelievable degrees of wastefulness. The high rate of consumption has been dependent on the utilization of resources well in excess of the population. It has been estimated that Americans, who constitute 5 percent of the world's population, use approximately 30 percent of the world's resources. As the resources of the earth become more scarce, it is expected that Americans will have to adjust their standard of living downward and eliminate most of the waste. Meanwhile both parties support a free economy and are identified to varying degrees with continuance of the current economic system. Neither major party can afford to challenge the bases of American economic life.

POLITICAL CULTURE: VALUE AND BELIEFS
OF AMERICANS

In every country there are certain widely held beliefs and values which shape the nature of society and define the limits of government. Although not formalized and largely unwritten, these political beliefs reflect the deepest foundations of public support for the system. With some danger of oversimplification, the term political culture is used here to refer to this complex set of beliefs and values held by the public. This definition corresponds closely to Donald Devine's conception of political culture as a value system which can influence political and social behavior.[20] Any attempt to describe the context of political parties must examine relevant aspects of the American political culture. The political culture not only shapes political life, it also serves to maintain support for a particular type of government and the attendant institutions.

The U.S. political culture has been described as integrated rather than fragmented.[21] An integrated political culture is marked by a stable, broad consensus on basic fundamentals as to how political life should be conducted. It also is characterized by reasonably durable and strong loyalties to the

[19] William C. Mitchell, *The American Policy: A Social and Cultural Interpretation* (New York: The Free Press, 1970), Chapter 2.

[20] Donald J. Devine, *The Political Culture of the United States* (Boston: Little, Brown and Company, 1972), pp. 14-18.

[21] Walter Rosenbaum, *Political Culture* (New York: Praeger Publishers, 1975).

government as well as to the nation. There tend to be low levels of political violence and a dominance of civil procedures for management of conflict. Finally, an integrated political culture contains a high degree of underlying trust among the various social groups. This trust arises out of their shared orientations toward political life. In the U.S. the basic political values and beliefs are characterized by the "liberal tradition."[22]

THE LIBERAL TRADITION

Although there are various interpretations of and dimensions to the liberal tradition, much of its content can be traced to John Locke via the Declaration of Independence. Its basic premise is that government is created by men to further their own ends of life, liberty, and property. The people come first and the government has limitations not present in all political systems. Out of this liberal tradition have come a series of tenets which shape political life in the U.S.

Politics is not a way of life for most Americans, nor a preferred occupation. There is a strong belief that politics should be minimized in society. The antiparty sentiment expressed throughout history is but one manifestation of this belief. At its extremity is the feeling that political power itself is evil, that politics is dirty. Americans tend to be suspicious of power, especially when concentrated in the hands of a few. Due to this suspicion, most of our political documents reflect attempts to control power. Most of the Constitutional Amendments and the progressive reforms were adopted to limit the power of the government or its extensions (that is, parties). Under the liberal tradition, power is a "thing" which must be limited in quantity. The liberal tradition places much emphasis on the concept of rational-legal authority, which defines conditions under which power may be wielded legitimately. The basis of political power is legal and lies in the office and not in the person occupying the office. In order to be legitimate, power must satisfy all criteria of rational-legal standards.

Citizenship is considered a duty in U.S. culture. Even voting is perceived as a duty and is emphasized in the socialization process. Popular rule is assumed, although it, too, has limits. It is expected that the public interest will be served, though it is unclear what the public interest is. In no case is self-interest expected to be a goal of either officials or citizens. Officials are expected to vote their consciences and not blindly follow party leaders. We shall see later that this admiration for independent representatives has had a negative impact on party discipline in Congress.

Some inconsistencies arise in the liberal tradition as expressed by Americans. Most believe strongly in majority rule and minority rights and

[22] See Devine, *The Political Culture of the U.S.*, pp. 47-65.

fail to see that they are logically inconsistent. The same holds true for liberty and equality. Although these are contradictory concepts in absolute terms, Americans have embraced both with fervor. Other values which are strongly upheld in our political tradition are property rights, federalism, political competition and a strong sense of altruism.

A final component of the liberal tradition which has helped shape political behavior in the U.S. is the conception of politics as a game. This has several disparate implications. First, election results tend not to be so important that a loss is tragic. A return match is always possible at some time in the future. It is expected, therefore, that the losers will be gracious and that transfers of power will be peaceful and as smooth as possible. In large measure American politics is free from the tensions and crises apparent in transfers of power in other nations. Politics, after all, is only a game.

Another result of this belief is that spectators outnumber participants. American politics is basically a spectator sport, with most citizens involved only minimally through the vote. At the very most, 5 percent of Americans can be said to be active participants in politics on a continuing basis. Another 50 to 60 percent might run across the field infrequently during elections, while the remainder never even show up to watch. This pattern of course has wide implications for political parties. They cannot depend on continued or consistent participation from their identifiers, their organizations are skeletal in nature, and few people readily follow party politics. It is not surprising that both major parties are cadre in nature. The basis for mass membership simply is not present in the U.S.

The specific provisions of the liberal tradition are viewed as having a major impact on political parties and the conduct of politics in the U.S. The fact that there is a high degree of consensus on these values itself has shaped electoral politics. Ladd contends that the U.S. exhibits a "remarkably homogeneous political culture."[23] Disagreements that exist have been within the liberal tradition. Consequently, parties are not preoccupied with doctrinal matters, since almost everyone adheres to a similar ideological orientation. Although there are differences in degree and style, there is no sharp ideological conflict between the parties.

STATUS QUO AND CONFORMITY: THE MODERATE ELECTORATE

A related cultural trait of Americans is their tendency to conform. This is partially the result of status uncertainty in a system without a class base. Americans are highly sensitive to how other people view them, and conformity is one way of pleasing others. David Riesman refers to this as "other-

[23] Ladd, *American Political Parties*, p. 35.

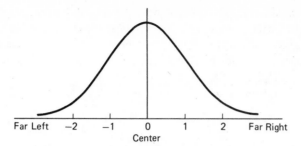

Figure 3.1   Normal Distribution of Voters

directedness," which he contends is a major characteristic of Americans.[24] We tend to rely on what others think, to accept others' standards, and to conform materially as well as emotionally. Out of conformity comes general support for the status quo. Americans tend to be satisfied with things as they are, including the political institutions. There is little impetus for major changes in political parties or other institutions.

One means used to describe the moderate nature of the Ameican electorate is the normal curve model.[25] The normal curve is a distribution in which most of the values are near the middle, with decreasing proportions as one moves to either extreme. Many observers of American politics contend that the electorate is distributed roughly in this manner. In other words, the bulk of the voters are close to some middle ground in ideological terms, while very few voters are found in either the extreme conservative or liberal categories as presented in Figure 3.1. Obviously, under this model a party must gain the support of the votes clustering around the center, especially between +1 and −1.

Since both parties are centrist, and most presidential elections are decided by the extent to which candidates can maintain a moderate image, the criticism that there is little difference among candidates is more understandable. In an electorate distributed around the two extremes, the

[24] David Riesman, *The Lonely Crowd* (New York: Doubleday Anchor Books, 1953). Hartz, *Liberal Tradition in America*, p. 5, contends that universal acceptance of the Lockean Tradition has produced a stifling and oppressive conformity in the U.S.

[25] See Norman H. Nie, Sidney Verba, and John R. Petrocik, *The Changing American Voter* (Cambridge: Harvard University Press, 1976), pp. 307-344 for a more sophisticated examination of this phenomenon.

parties would naturally represent different aspects of the electorate. In the U.S., both parties compete for the strategic middle ground. Under normal circumstances one might expect the Democrat party straddling the center line from the left and the Republican party overlapping from the right (see Figure 3-2). The far extremes in the U.S. tend not to be associated with either major party and are largely alienated from electoral politics.

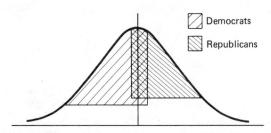

Figure 3.2   Party Support in Normal Distribution

A major problem arises for either party when its candidate is perceived as being too extreme. In 1964, Goldwater lost support of some moderate Republicans, as well as the independents and conservative Democrats so necessary for a Republican victory, because he was seen as too "dangerous," that is, too extreme. In 1972, McGovern found himself in a similar position, though on the other end of the spectrum. During the primaries he became too identified with the more extreme left activists, an image he was unable to

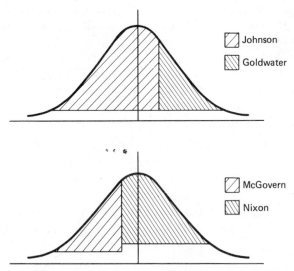

Figure 3.3   Candidate Support in Normal Distribution, 1964 and 1972

overcome during the general election. As a consequence he did very poorly among traditional moderate-conservative Democrats, especially the ethnics and laborers.[26] Figure 3-3 attempts to describe the losses of Goldwater and McGovern through the normal curve model.

LIBERALS AND CONSERVATIVES

Despite the consensus support for basic values in the liberal tradition and the moderate nature of the American electorate, ideological differences do exist. Although Liberals and Conservatives generally agree on the broad goals of public policy and on the principles of democratic government, they disagree, at times sharply, on the means of achieving these ends. They also disagree on the institutions which should have primary responsibility for implementation of these goals. According to William Bluhm, Liberals are those persons who believe in the implementation of comprehensive national welfare legislation to improve the lot of the disadvantaged. Liberals also see the need for extensive national government intervention in the economy and the integration of minority groups into the mainstream of American life. On the other hand,

> Conservatives, like the Classical Liberals a century ago, stress the importance of private initiative and local government responsibility for the achievement of all these goals. And they are very strongly attached to the work ethic.[27]

The Liberal-Conservative division in the United States, then, centers largely on the means of achieving democratic ends, not on the legitimacy of these ends, nor on the basic principles themselves. Despite the suggestion by some observers that we have come to the "end of ideology,"[28] there remain genuine political distinctions between Liberals and Conservatives in American politics. Except for a few persons on either extreme, however, the disagreements which exist occur within the context of American political culture.

[26] For more details see Andrew M. Greeley, *Building Coalitions: American Politics in the 1970's* (New York: Franklin Watts, Inc., New Viewpoints, 1974).

[27] William T. Bluhm, *Ideologies and Attitudes: Modern Political Culture* (Englewood Cliffs, N.J.: Prentice-Hall, Inc., 1974), p. 117. This book is an excellent summary of the literature on ideology and political culture. Also see William E. Connolly, *Political Science and Ideology* (New York: Atherton Press, 1967), especially pp. 21-30, for a comparison of an elitist and pluralist interpretation of American politics.

[28] For instance, see Daniel Bell, *The End of Ideology* (New York: The Free Press, 1962).

CONTEXT OF THE AMERICAN PARTY SYSTEM:
A SUMMARY

After examining major components of the context of political parties and the party system of the U.S., it is easier to understand why they are unique. Political parties evolved in response to demands that were distinctly American. This, despite an ambivalent and at times hostile environment. This remarkably stable party system is also intricately tied to the institutional framework grounded in federalism and the separation of powers. Decentralization of the party system is a natural extension of decentralization of all other aspects of American government. In addition, party dualism has been fostered by a system of one-man executives and single-member districts which works against the organization of third parties.

Reinforcing the historical-institutional context has been a political tradition that emphasizes consensus and minimizes ideological division. In American political culture, politics is perceived as a game where few play and most are spectators. The stakes of this game are lower than in other countries. A loss in any one election, though not a desired event, does not preclude a win in the next. Since federalism offers a multitude of elective offices, losses of one party are rarely complete and the value system is not directly challenged. Separation of powers also minimizes the stakes and facilitates a relatively peaceful and orderly election process. Parties have profited from the non-ideological nature of the American electorate and have adjusted to it.

Interrelated with all these influences is a distinctive population, both in size, and, most importantly, diversity. The heterogeneity of the U.S. electorate is unmatched anywhere in the world. This characteristic has compelled the parties to serve as brokers of many disparate interests. Neither party can become identified with any one segment of society without risking the support of other segments. Under such conditions, it is not surprising that the parties are cadre and oriented towards elections.

4

Suffrage
and Elections
in the United States

In the last two chapters, the unique characteristics of U.S. parties were examined and an attempt was made to explain their evolvement within the context of American history, culture, and institutions. It was concluded that there is a complex of reasons for the development of this unusual political party system, none of which alone is a sufficient explanation. One factor, central to any discussion of American parties, has been intentionally excluded up to this point—the electoral framework. Due to the electoral orientation and win-centered nature of U.S. political parties, it is essential to examine the electoral context in detail. Who can vote, what are the voting regulations, and what variations exist among the states? Each of these questions is crucial in describing the electoral context.

UNIVERSAL ADULT SUFFRAGE

The basic qualifications for voting in the United States are quite simple. One must be at least 18 years of age by election day, a U.S. citizen, and a resident of one of the 50 states. On the face of it, we have achieved universal adult suffrage. Although additional state requirements restrict this universal suffrage somewhat, with few exceptions all adult citizens today are eligible to vote in state as well as national elections. This has not always been the case in the U.S. Actually, it is a relatively recent phenomenon. The history of the American electorate has been one of continual expansion. Before examining the current electoral framework, a brief presentation of this historical expansion of suffrage will be useful.

PROPERTY AND TAXPAYING
QUALIFICATIONS

Although religious barriers to voting were mostly eliminated by the time of the American Revolution, property and taxpaying qualifications for white males were used in some states through the 1850s. Since few people owned property this meant that only a small proportion of the adult population was allowed to vote. The rationale for such restrictions was that since their vote would influence the amount of money to be spent, only those who paid taxes should be able to vote. While some states seriously enforced property requirements, others were quite lax. The western states, for instance, seldom enforced such restrictions. Many property qualification laws were made so complex that it became easier to ignore them. Although taxpaying qualifications (except the poll tax) presumably were eliminated by the Civil War in all states, the issue reemerged again recently in terms of school bond elections. It was argued that only those who pay property taxes should be allowed to vote on how tax funds were spent. By 1860, however, almost all white males could vote in most of the states.

RACIAL RESTRICTIONS ON VOTING

The next major expansion of the electorate came in 1870 with the 15th Amendment to the Constitution. It stated simply and clearly that no state could deny the vote on "account of race, color, or previous condition of servitude." Although the clear language of this amendment should have given the vote to all males, black or white, its goal was not reached until almost one century later. Soon after ratification of the 15th Amendment, efforts were made in the South to disfranchise the blacks. Although the initial moves towards nullification of the Amendment were made soon after the election of 1876, when the last federal troops were removed from the South, full black disfranchisement began with the Mississippi Constitutional Convention of 1890, and was completed by 1903 when all former Confederate states had barred blacks from participating in the Democratic party nominating process. In addition to the "white primary" where only whites could vote in the all-important party contest, many other legal devices were introduced in a concerted effort to eliminate the black vote.[1]

Literacy tests were used by states, both North and South, on the assumption that only those who were literate could make a meaningful electoral choice. In the South this device was overtly used to restrict the black

---

[1] Gerald M. Pomper, *Elections in America: Control and Influence in Democratic Politics* (New York: Dodd, Mead and Company, 1970), pp. 213-20.

vote. These "tests" naturally eliminated a high proportion of the uneducated and illiterate black population. In order to ensure such disfranchisement, however, the tests were applied to the races unequally. Illiterate whites were given questions they could answer easily, while highly educated blacks were given impossible questions at the discretion of the registrar.

Poll taxes also were used in northern as well as southern states. The rationale for poll taxes was that elections cost money and somebody must pay for them. Who better than those who exercise the privilege of voting? Even when applied in good conscience, however, poll taxes discriminate against those who have little money. Although one or two dollars is a small price for a rich man to pay, it might be a day's food for an entire poor family. The sacrifice is unequal. In the South the poll tax effectively barred the poor blacks from voting, while poor whites might be given money to vote.

In addition to the application of literacy tests and poll taxes that also were common in northern states, southern states used other "legal means" to minimize the black vote. These included various property and residency requirements, difficult and easily manipulated registration procedures, "grandfather" clauses, and disfranchisement for minor criminal offenses (applied to blacks only, of course). Any loopholes were closed by fraud, intimidation, or discriminatory administration of the laws.[2]

For those few blacks who successfully overcame the legal barriers, there were more serious extralegal deterrents to voting. Harassment of blacks by the Ku Klux Klan and other white organizations was a well-documented and effective means of keeping potential black voters away from the polls. Although much of this harassment was nonphysical, it occasionally resulted in violence against the would-be voters. A burning cross on the lawn and the harassment of one's family might be followed by a physical attack if the former did not discourage the vote. Lynching was not uncommon in some areas of the deep South.

Despite passage of the 15th Amendment in 1870, it was not until a series of Supreme Court decisions were handed down in the twentieth century that this discriminatory process was reversed. The voiding of the "white primary" by *Smith v. Allright* (1944) demonstrated the Court's willingness to enter the election arena. *Smith v. Allright* was followed by a series of Civil Rights Acts between 1957 and 1970, notably those of 1965 and 1970. In each case, however, resistance to the reforms was strong and the actual impact in some cases was less than the decisions would imply.[3]

[2] *Ibid.,* p. 214.

[3] For instance, see Robert H. Talbert, "Poll Tax Repeal in Texas: A Three-Year Individual Performance Evaluation," *Journal of Politics,* 36 (November, 1974), 1050-56, who finds a "slippage" between promise and fulfillment of elimination of the poll taxes.

The 24th Amendment (1964) invalidated the use of poll taxes in elections for national offices. Attempts to circumvent this amendment for state elections and on technical grounds, however, minimized its impact on some states. As a result, the Supreme Court in *Harper v. Virginia Board of Elections* (1966) voided use of the poll tax in state and local elections as well as national, ruling it denied the "equal protection" guaranteed under the 14th Amendment.

The moves to eliminate literacy tests took a different route. In 1965, 20 states still used literacy tests. The Voting Rights Act of 1965 selectively outlawed literacy tests in those states that administered them to deny or abridge voting rights. The Act was applied only to those states in which less than 50 percent of the eligible voting age population was registered or voted in the 1964 presidential election. This so-called "triggering clause" obviously was aimed directly at the southern states. The Act also provided federal examiners to ensure compliance with the law. Instead of simply extending these same provisions, the Voting Rights Act of 1970 totally voided literacy tests in all states as discriminatory against minorities. Later legislation and court cases have extended this concept by requiring bi- or multilingual ballots in areas that contain specified proportions of non-English speaking minorities.

In 1970, blacks finally were guaranteed the franchise promised a century earlier. The Voting Rights Acts, in combination with key court decisions, resulted in an expansion of the electorate across racial boundaries. Although discrimination still exists in some areas, it is no longer sanctioned by the legal electoral structure.

WOMEN GAIN THE VOTE

Although women's suffrage first gained national attention at the Seneca Falls Conference of 1848, it took many years of struggle to gain the vote nationwide. Although 15 states allowed women to vote prior to 1919, the eastern states, with the bulk of the population, resisted.[4] Finally, in 1920, the 19th Amendment was adopted, forbidding the states to deny the vote on the basis of sex. Like the 15th Amendment 50 years earlier, the 19th Amendment standardized voting qualifications across the states and reduced the broad powers of the states to control suffrage. It represented the single largest expansion, doubling, at least in theory, the potential electorate. Actually, it took two generations for women to vote in proportions similar to men.

[4] Wyoming was first in women suffrage in 1890, but New York waited until 1917.

THE 18 YEAR-OLD VOTE

Throughout our history the age of an adult entitled to vote, in most states, has been 21. Although four states allowed voting at a younger age (Kentucky and Georgia, 18; Alaska, 19, and Hawaii,* 20), most states required that a person be at least 21 on the day of the election. In 1970 the Voting Rights Act included a provision to allow 18 year-olds to vote in state and national elections. The rationale was that 18 year-olds were more mature than in the past. Also, the point was made that while many of those fighting and dying in Vietnam were under 21, they could not vote.

After passage of the Voting Rights Act of 1970, the vote-at-18 clause was challenged in the courts and the requirement that the voting age in state elections be set at 18 was thrown out as unconstitutional. Congress could regulate national but not state suffrage, according to the Court. This decision made registration in many states most confusing, since 18 year-olds could vote in national but not state elections. To resolve this confusion, the 26th Amendment was hastily proposed and ratified in June, 1971. For the first time in U.S. history anyone 18 or over by election day could vote in all states.

IMPLICATIONS OF EXPANDING ELECTORATE FOR POLITICAL PARTIES

The continual expansion of the electorate has not taken place without an impact on political parties. At the very minimum, both parties have had to adjust to the changing constituency in order to remain competitive. The infusion of large numbers of women, blacks, and young voters into the electorate has resulted in appeals from both parties to gain their loyalty. One characteristic of these new potential voters is their lack of attachment to either party. Therefore, they offer a relatively uncommitted and flexible bloc of voters open to appeals from either party. Following each of the major expansions in suffrage, there has been an adjustment period during which the parties have attempted to mobilize support, and the newly enfranchised groups have become the focus of attention. After a short interval these voters have tended to be assimilated in varying degrees into the party system.

NATIONAL FRAMEWORK OF ELECTIONS

In addition to the basic qualifications of voters, other aspects of elections have been nationalized since the framing of the Constitution. The impact of one-man executives and single-member districts on elections was discussed in Chapter 3, along with federalism and separation of powers. Before variations of election laws by state are examined, several other general aspects of the U.S. electoral system must be reviewed. They relate to the way in which people vote and the terms of office and timing of elections. Each has a major impact on the conduct of elections in the U.S., and thus each affects the political parties.

THE AUSTRALIAN BALLOT

Several major changes in the mechanics of conducting elections occurred in the beginning of the 20th century. One of these was the shift to official, secret ballots, commonly referred to as Australian Ballots since they originated with the Ballot Law of 1856 in Australia. Prior to 1890, voting took place on unofficial or party strip ballots prepared and distributed by the parties, not the government. Each party had a separate ballot which listed its candidates for each office. Party hawkers peddled these ballots to voters around the polling stations in a carnival-like atmosphere. The ballots were of different sizes and colors, which made voting obvious with no chance of secrecy. The party strip ballots also made ticket-splitting virtually impossible in some areas and difficult in others. Before selecting a ballot, the voter had to "reduce his several choices to one and then take the party ballot corresponding to that decision."[5]

After the adoption of the Australian Ballot by Massachusetts in 1888, many other states quickly followed suit. By 1896, 90 percent of the states had switched to official ballots. These ballots were prepared and administered by the states, not the parties. They were uniform and listed the candidates of both parties in a standard order. Most importantly, the voting was conducted in secret, not under the eyes of watchful party observers. This more than any other reform was designed to reduce the buying of votes. It was assumed that since the vote ultimately was secret, it was futile for someone to pay another to vote in a particular manner, since there was no way of guaranteeing that, in the secrecy of the voting booth, the voter would comply. This change to the standardized secret ballot, therefore, is seen as a crucial and necessary ballot reform.

Office Bloc Ballot.   Although the states rushed toward the Australian Ballot in principle, there continued to be variations in the ballot. The most common distinction which still exists is between the "office bloc" and "party column" ballot arrangements. The office bloc ballot represents the most nonpartisan format. Candidates of all parties are grouped by office.

---

[5] Jerrold G. Rusk, "The Effect of the Australian Ballot Reform on Split Ticket Voting: 1876-1908," *American Political Science Review*, 64 (December, 1970), 1223.

Although the party names generally are listed after each candidate's name, this form facilitates split-ticket voting since the voter is faced with a series of decisions across the offices listed on the ballot. The decision for each office is a separate, distinct choice.

Party Column Ballot. The "party column" ballot format is basically a consolidation of the old party strip ballots placed side by side on a single piece of paper. This ballot lists party candidates for all offices in a column, as its name suggests. Although official, uniform, and secret, this format differs from the office bloc in making it easier to vote straight ticket. Although the office bloc ballot was more popular in the beginning, after 1890 the party column design predominated and increased in popularity over the years.[6]

In many states party voting is encouraged by provision for a straight ticket vote. This option is incorporated most often into party column ballots by providing one box or lever which represents a vote for all candidates of the party selected. By marking the appropriate box or pulling the lever a voter can complete his entire set of choices. In many ways this is similar to the party strips used prior to 1890, since by a single action all decisions are consolidated into a vote for the party. It is suggested by some that such devices increase straight-party voting.[7] Rusk sees the increase of split-ticket voting between 1876 and 1808 as the result, at least in part, of the change in ballot format, especially the shift to the office bloc type. In fact, he sees ballot format as the dominant factor during this period. Walker concludes, similarly, that the office bloc format leads to more roll-off or voter fatigue than the party column ballot.[8] The many separate decisions required on the office bloc ballots tend to tire the voters, who then do not complete the ballot. Usually this means fewer votes the further one moves down the ballot.

TERMS OF OFFICE AND
AND TIMING OF ELECTIONS

The U.S. election machinery is also unique in that terms of office are for fixed, predetermined periods of time. Constitutionally, the President is elected for a four-year term, congressmen a two-year term, and senators for

[6] *Ibid.*, p. 1221.

[7] Angus Campbell and Warren E. Miller, "The Motivational Basis of Straight and Split Ticket Voting," *American Political Science Review,* 51 (June, 1957), 293-312.

[8] Jack L. Walker, "Ballot Forms and Voter Fatigue: An Analysis of the Office Bloc and Party Column Ballots," *Midwest Journal of Political Science,* 10 (November, 1966), 448-63. For a discussion of the advantages of being listed first on the ballot, see Delbert A. Taebel, "The Effect of Ballot Position on Electoral Success," *American Journal of Political Science,* 19 (August, 1975), 519-26.

six years. Once elected, the winner knows exactly when he or she must face reelection and the loser knows when the rematch is scheduled. For over a hundred years, national elections have been held on the first Tuesday after the first Monday in November of even-numbered years. In 1845 Congress exercised its constitutional power to declare that presidential electors would be selected on that day, when the harvest would be completed. Congressional elections would be conducted concurrently unless otherwise provided by the state constitution. All 50 states now use the November date for national elections and most have adopted it for statewide contests.

Although many Americans assume that elections worldwide are based on the concept of fixed terms in office, in most democratic systems they are not. Under the parliamentary systems of western Europe, the winning party stays in office only as long as it maintains a basic level of public support. An electoral vote of confidence may be called by the government at any time within a specified period, generally five years. Or the opposition may force the government to call the election. Under such a system, crisis situations often lead to national elections well before the stated limit is reached. While the distinctive fixed-term system of the U.S. does function as a stabilizer in times of conflict, it does not ensure that any important issues will call for resolution at the predesignated year and date of the election. Due in part to their fixed terms, U.S. elections are not dependent on issues, although by coincidence or design an issue may peak at election time. Unlike parliamentary elections, fixed terms minimize the impact of issues and shift emphasis to candidate personalities. Also, due to the predictability of terms, office holders are able to plan their reelection strategies much more thoroughly, thereby significantly extending the campaign period.

An attendant characteristic of fixed-term elections in the U.S. is the use of staggered elections. In other words, not all officials face election at the same time. At the national level, for instance, only a third of the senatorships are contested at each congressional election, while there is a presidential race half of the time. In addition, the federal nature of U.S. elections results in off-year and odd-year elections in many states. One result of staggered elections is that one party cannot capture the whole government in any one election. Even in a disastrous year the party's losses are moderated because many offices have not been contested. The losing party in one election has time to build upon the offices it still holds. By the time the remainder of the offices come to term, the conditions may have shifted toward the party which lost in the prior election.

Finally, the features of fixed and staggered terms of office, combined with direct primaries, runoff elections, and the like, have resulted in a multiplication of the number of elections held. The frequency of elections in the

U.S. is surpassed in only a few democracies, notably in Switzerland, where a citizen can vote four or five times a year. In some U.S. states there is a general election each year (odd years for state offices only). Each general election is accompanied by a primary and, if necessary, a runoff. In addition, local elections, bond issue elections, and special district elections are held throughout the year in most states. Such a multiplicity of elections has a numbing effect on the electorate. The sheer number of elections has contributed to low levels of participation, especially in the infrequent local issue elections. It also means that the parties and candidates must continually prepare for upcoming elections.

STATE VARIATION IN ELECTORAL STRUCTURE

Although the history of American elections reflects a growing willingness of the central government to standardize certain aspects of election administration, the "preeminent authority for election management in the United States is still the individual state."[9] Not only are many of the laws governing elections state laws, but it is also the states that administer the federal standards. The regulation of elections at one time was almost completely within the jurisdiction of the states. The 'Time, Places, and Manner' clause (Article 1, Section 4) of the Constitution and the reserve power in the Tenth Amendment ensured this, while tradition reinforced the dominance of the states for many years.

While the Voting Rights Acts of 1965 and 1970 and a series of Supreme Court decisions during the 1960s and early 1970s narrowed state discretion in determining voting qualifications and the Constitution now guarantees a vote for all citizens over 18 who are residents of a state, there remains much variation in election laws from state to state. Despite the simplicity of the stated voting qualifications in the Constitution, the specific requirements and procedures in many states are quite complex. The administration of elections is far from uniform within the 50 states. Rules applied in some states are inappropriate in others. The political parties, it must be remembered, must also operate within 50 different sets of rules. Some of the major distinctions remaining at this writing are discussed here.

[9] Jae-On Kim, John R. Petrocik, and Stephen N. Enokson, "Voter Turnout Among the American States: Systemic and Individual Components," *American Political Science Review*, 69 (March, 1975), 110.

REGISTRATION SYSTEMS

In the United States it generally requires two deliberate acts at different times to vote. Prior to voting on election day, some act of registration is necessary. Detailed registration systems were introduced nationwide between 1890 and 1910. They were justified on the grounds of minimizing electoral fraud by insuring that only those legally eligible to vote did, although the real reasons in some cases were to limit participation by certain groups. While registration in its simplest form is merely a listing of qualified voters used on election day to determine who is eligible and to limit each person to one vote, the actual mechanics of registration can be quite complex and discouraging.

Timing. Prior to passage of the Voting Rights Act of 1970, which prohibited any state from closing registration more than 30 days before the election [upheld in *Oregon vs. Mitchell* (1971)], some states closed registration 90 days before the election date. In their study of registration in 104 major U.S. cities, Kelly, Ayres, and Bowen argued that "registration requirements are a more effective deterrent to voting than anything that normally operates to deter citizens from voting once they have registered, at least in presidential elections."[10] One of the most striking findings of their analysis was the strong correlation between the closing date for registration and the percentages of citizens that registered. The longer period of registration not only increased the convenience and, therefore, lowered the cost of voting, but also allowed the campaign process to stimulate voters to register. An index of "convenience of the times and place of registration" was also found to be closely related to variation in rates of registration.[11]

Place of Registration. While the 1970 Voting Rights Act voided the states' authority to close registration more than 30 days before the election, many other inequities have remained. Most states require in-person registration. In other words, one must personally appear at some location and fill out the necessary forms. But the registration center may be far from the voter's home and the hours the registration center is open may force some employees to take time off from work to register. A 1971 study commissioned by the League of Women Voters demonstrated that "the current system of registration and voting functions inefficiently for citizens throughout the United States."[12] They found state registration laws to be ambiguous and

---

[10] Stanley Kelly, Jr., Richard E. Ayres, and William G. Bowen, "Registration and Voting: Putting First Things First," *American Political Science Review*, 61 (June, 1967), 362.

[11] *Ibid.*, p. 363.

[12] William J. Crotty, *Political Reform and the American Experiment* (New York: Thomas Y. Crowell Company, 1977), p. 59.

local administration in most states to be obstructive to voting. The President's Commission recommended easily accessible registration places in each precinct as close to election day as possible.[13]

Type of Registration System. There are two basic types of registration practiced in the United States. Periodic registration, as the name implies, requires that a person register at frequent intervals, generally before each election. Permanent registration, conversely, allows one to register and vote without having to register again if his voting record is consistent. Most, but not all, permanent registration states require reregistration if a person fails to vote over a specified period of time, generally 4 years. As might be expected, permanent registration is easier for the voter and facilitates voting.

A controversy over periodic vs. permanent registration has centered on the possibility of fradulent registration. Some argue that periodic registration provides "clean" lists, while permanent registration allows fraud. This argument is not supported by experience, according to Key, and neither system is foolproof.[14] From the standpoint of convenience to the voters and increased voting turnout, there is strong justification for permanent registration. Also, if the lists are constantly updated and purged of those no longer eligible, there should be little chance of fraud. Most states now use some form of permanent registration, either on a statewide basis or in designated, generally urban, areas.

RESIDENCY REQUIREMENTS

Each year more than 20 million adults in the United States move to new residences. In the past, many lost their voting rights because of state residency requirements. Most states not only had minimum residency requirements which affected those moving from state to state, but also had county and district residency requirements which disfranchised many people who moved only short distances within a state or even within a city. State residency requirements prior to 1972 ranged from six months to two years. According to Fredman:

> These requirements are a relic of the old days when it was necessary to establish local contact and rely on challenges at the polling places to detect fraud. The result is that thousands are disenfranchised in a nation whose very traditions encourage mobility.[15]

[13] The President's Commission on Registration and Voting Participation proposed a series of electoral changes in their 1963 report.

[14] V.O. Key, Jr., *Politics, Parties and Pressure Groups*, 5th ed. (New York: Thomas Y. Crowell Company, 1964), p. 627.

[15] L.E. Fredman, *The Australian Ballot: The Story of an American Reform* (Lansing: Michigan State University Press, 1968), p. 129.

The 1970 Voting Rights Act voided all state residency requirements for presidential elections, arguing that these requirements did not relate to any compelling state interest in the conduct of elections. In 1972, the Supreme Court in *Dunn v. Blumstein* extended this ban on excessively long residency requirements to other elections. The Court declared that lengthy residency requirements for voting in state and local elections were unconstitutional and suggested that a 30-day period should be sufficient to guarantee completion of the necessary paperwork. Within one year, residency qualifications in most states complied with the Supreme Court's guideline.

> By 1972, 31 states and the District of Columbia had no residency criteria (subject, however to various qualifications), 16 applied the Supreme Court suggestion of a 30-day grace period, and one state (Kansas) required only 20 days. Only 2 of the 50 exceeded the Court's rule-of-thumb and these (60 days in Florida, 45 in Michigan) are modest by previous standards.[16]

ABSENTEE VOTING PROVISIONS

Access to the polls is of two kinds, direct and indirect. Direct voting means that a person goes to his home precinct and votes according to the provisions of law. Indirect voting is provided under absentee voting laws, which vary considerably among the states. Some states offer absentee voting for anyone who is not present on election day, while others limit the right of voting in absentia to specific categories of people. The categories of absentee voters unable to register or vote at their designated polling place commonly include registered voters who are temporarily away from home or ill, military personnel, college students, and Americans living abroad.

According to Crotty, the absentee registration and voting requirements of the states are extraordinarily complex.[17] While the Voting Rights Act of 1970 simplified these requirements, the paperwork required by some states effectively disfranchises many citizens living abroad. The President's Commission urged that the entire process of absentee voting be made less complicated and more flexible to allow for last-minute changes. The Commission recommended that absentee voting by mail should be allowed for all qualified voters who are absent on primary or general election day, as well as for those who are physically unable to reach the polling place.

[16] Crotty, *Political Reform*, p. 86.
[17] *Ibid.*, p. 95.

DISQUALIFICATIONS

There are many disqualifications written into various state constitutions and statutes. Some, like those in the Idaho Constitution that prohibit voting by prostitutes, persons who frequent houses of ill fame or lewdly cohabit, or those who are of Chinese or Mongolian descent, are not enforced. However, 44 states currently prohibit voting by those deemed mentally incompetent. Forty-seven of the states disqualify institutionalized persons, prison inmates, and former convicts as voters. In some states a felony conviction disfranchises a person for life unless a pardon is granted.

Aliens are now denied the vote in all 50 states. Arkansas in 1926 was the last state to require U.S. citizenship as a precondition for voting. Most states, ironically, still deny the vote to citizens living on federal reservations, including military bases, national parks, and veterans' hospitals. The rationale is that these federal employees are not state residents, are exempt from state taxes, generally have their own schools and services, and represent distinct legal entities. In most states, military personnel living on bases must vote by absentee ballot in the state of their residence. Not surprisingly, many people in this category do not vote in any state elections.

POLLING PLACES AND TIMES

Another area of states' discretion in election administration is the establishment of the times and places of voting. Although the actual administration is commonly the responsibility of local officials (that is, county clerks, election commissioners, precinct officials), recently there has been a trend toward increased state responsibility in this area.[18] The designated polling places are usually located in public buildings such as schools, courthouses, and fire stations, or in other available locations. The local election administrators are accountable in most cases to the Secretary of State and must follow certain prescribed practices. In those places where voting machines or punchcards are used, the Secretary of State's Office usually has to certify the process. There is no national involvement in the selection of polling places or in the method of voting used.

The number of hours polling places are required to remain open varies from fifteen hours in New York to five hours in parts of New Hampshire. In most cases, the polls are open either twelve or thirteen hours, opening between 6 and 8 a.m. and closing between 7 and 9 p.m. It seems logical that the longer

[18] *The Book of the States: 1976-77,* 21 (Lexington, Mass.: Council of State Governments, 1976), p. 207.

the polls are open, the more convenient it is for a voter and the more likely he will be to vote. In many European countries the polls are open all weekend. Not surprisingly, these countries exhibit much higher turnout figures than the U.S. In those areas where the polls are only open during working hours, an additional strain is placed on the voter. It seems reasonable for polling places to remain open at least until 9:00 p.m. The need for an early closing time in order to hand-count ballots is past. There is little reason to close the polls early, especially in urban areas. Although there have been many proposals to extend the hours of voting uniformly across the states, there is much opposition from the states, which see this as a local matter.

ELECTORAL LAW VARIATION AND VOTING TURNOUT

It has been suggested throughout this section that the variation in election laws from state to state results in different rates of voting turnout. One prominent theory of voting assumes that the decision to vote is governed by a cost/return model. If returns or benefits outweigh the costs, a person votes, but if the costs are too high, the person abstains.[19] These can be monetary costs, costs of inconvenience, or costs of information.[20] Although monetary costs are present even in the absence of poll taxes, a more common cost is that of inconvenience. Certain registration procedures, like periodic registration, can be highly complicated and burdensome. In states without precinct registration, travel to the place of registration becomes difficult for some people. Voting itself can be inconvenient if the polls are open only a limited number of hours. Since most citizens are not highly political in nature and they give priority to daily personal needs, this inconvenience may prove to be too dear a cost.[21]

Closely related to the cost of inconvenience is the cost of obtaining information on how and where to register and vote. It may be assumed that the cost of obtaining this information is in direct proportion to the complications of the registration and absentee-vote provisions. And, the higher the cost, the lower the turnout rates.

Another form of nonvoting related to election laws, however, has even more of an impact on democratic theory. Involuntary nonvoting occurs when persons who desire to vote are excluded because of restrictive legal or administrative election procedures. Until 1972, residency requirements, which

[19] Anthony Downs, *An Economic Theory of Democracy* (New York: Harper and Row, 1957).

[20] Kelly, "Registration and Voting".

[21] See Bernard H. Berelson, Paul F. Lazarsfeld, and William N. McPhee, *Voting* (Chicago: University of Chicago Press, 1954), pp. 322-323.

varied greatly from state to state, were very effective in disfranchising many would-be voters. Strict absentee-voting qualifications and lack of absentee-registration procedures can also obstruct voting under certain circumstances.

Whether they result in voluntary or involuntary nonvoting, state election laws are an important determinant of voting turnout. Although some features, like the date of general elections, are standard across the nation, overall variations in state election laws are widespread.

According to the President's Commission, "restrictive legal and administrative procedures for registration and voting are a major reason for low participation." The Commission criticized many election laws for being "unreasonable, unfair, and outmoded," and for disfranchising millions of would-be voters in the highly mobile American society.[22] Andrews suggests that the actual turnout rates in the United States are misleading, and that over 80 percent of those legally and physically able do vote. He contends that the law excludes a much larger portion of the citizens from voting than is usually assumed. He estimates that in 1960 approximately 22 million persons of voting age were either legally excluded or were unable to vote for other legitimate reasons.[23]

Those who have included electoral structure variations in their studies have generally found these variations to have an impact on voting. Kim and associates conclude that legal factors must be included in any attempt to study variation in turnout among the 50 states.[24] In a follow-up comment, Douglas Rose suggests that "states can still affect turnout by discouraging voting by particular social groups" through registration and other electoral system factors.[25] Registration is found to be a crucial variable which produces most of the turnout differences among states. Blank demonstrates that a combination of political variables, including a scale of electoral structure, explains turnout variation much more fully than social or economic conditions.[26] Those states in which registration and absentee voting are easy,

---

[22] The President's Commission on Registration and Voting Participation was especially concerned about this type of nonvoting. *Report of the President's Commission on Registration and Voting Participation* (Washington, D.C.: U.S. Government Printing Office, 1963).

[23] William G. Andrews, "American Voting Participation," *Western Political Quarterly*, 19 (December, 1966), 639-52.

[24] Kim, "Voter Turnout Among the American States," 123.

[25] Douglas D. Rose, "The American States' Impact on Voter Turnout," *American Political Science Review*, 69 (March, 1975), 124-31.

[26] Robert H. Blank, "Socioeconomic Determinism of Voting Turnout: A Challenge," *Journal of Politics*, 36 (August, 1974), 731-52. Steven J. Rosenstone and Raymond E. Wolfinger, "The Effect of Registration Laws on Voter Turnout," *American Political Science Review*, 72 (March, 1978), 22-45, present a detailed discussion of the impact of registration laws.

residency requirements are minimal, and the polls are open longer, have higher turnout rates. Obviously, the laws of these states facilitate voting, while other states make voting more difficult.

> There is not a great deal anyone can do to force a higher turnout or to command a more enlightened vote. It is possible, however, to reduce the formal barriers that have developed over the years that hinder and, in some cases, entirely prohibit more inclusive electoral participation.[27]

SUGGESTED REGISTRATION REFORMS

Suggestions for revising voter registration with the intention of increasing voter turnout have included some form of universal registration by mail and election day registration. Universal registration would include an automatic means of registering all eligible voters, most likely administered by the Social Security Administration.

> A separate voter-registration card would be issued to qualified electors to be presented at the polling place. Registration would be permanent. A postal ballot for the presidential race could be issued at any polling place in the country to electors absent from their residences. States would, of course, be invited to use the federal rolls as their own.[28]

Less inclusive postcard registration systems might be administered by the states, or registration could be discontinued, especially in the rural states. Box 4.1 suggests some of the strengths and weaknesses of a mail system, while Table 4.1 demonstrates public opposition to eliminating registration. Election day registration would require each person to present some identification at the polling place before he or she could vote. It has been estimated that had election day registration been used in 1972, voting would have risen by over 9 percent or 12 million voters.[29]

The step beyond universal registration and abolition of registration is

[27] Crotty, *Political Reform*, p. 52.

[28] Kevin P. Phillips and Paul H. Blackman, *Electoral Reform and Voter Participation* (Washington: American Enterprise Institute for Public Policy Research, 1975), p. 68.

[29] Rosenstone and Wolfinger, "Effect of Registration Laws on Voter Turnout," 33-34. They estimate a net gain of .5 percentage points for the Democrats and a slight increase in voting of the less educated and affluent.

Table 4.1   Opposition to Universal Registration*

	Favor	Oppose	No Opinion
National	40%	55	5
Republicans	30%	67	3
Democrats	43%	53	4
Independents	44%	49	7
East	48%	46	6
Midwest	40%	56	4
South	35%	60	5
West	38%	58	4
College background	39%	58	3
High School	40%	56	4
Grade school	45%	46	9
Under 30 years old	49%	46	5
30-49 years old	35%	60	5
50 and older	38%	57	5
City size:			
One million and over	49%	43	8
500,000-999,999	37%	57	6
50,000-499,999	42%	55	3
2,500-49,999	44%	52	4
Under 2,500, rural	34%	61	5

*In order to vote in elections, each person must now be registered. It has been proposed that registration NOT be required in elections for national office if a person can produce proper identification, such as a driver's license, on election day. Would you favor or oppose this plan?

SOURCE: The Gallup Poll, March 25-28, 1977. Copyright 1977, Field Enterprises, Inc. National adult sample of 1,550.

to make voting compulsory as it is in other western democracies, most notably Australia. It has been proposed that either a fine be imposed on non-voters or a tax incentive given to those who vote.[30] Although this proposal would most effectively and directly increase turnout, it is not popular in the U.S. It has been suggested that compulsory voting would have a direct impact on the political parties.

[30] U.S. Congress, House, Committee on Post Office and Civil Service, *The Concept of National Voter Registration*, p. 16; *Election News*, vol. 2, no. 9 (February, 1973), p. 2.

BOX 4.1   MAIL REGISTRATION

Mail registration provides an added convenience to persons who wish to register and vote. By itself, it does not necessarily increase voter registration. The standard pattern in most states—high registration in presidential election years, low registration in non-presidential election years—confirms the fact that voter interest in the offices and candidates on the ballot, and in the issues, is a far more important factor than the method of voter registration in determining how many names are on the registry. No appreciable increase in voter turnout was related to mail registration. Persons who registered by mail during 1974 voted in approximately the same percentages as other registered voters.

The relationship between mail registration and party identification is inconclusive. Evidence does suggest that persons who register by mail are less likely to affiliate with either party, and that the increase in "declines" in Maryland in 1974 reduced Republican more than Democratic registration.

The cost of registering by mail seems to be about $1.00 per registered voter. This figure covers the postage-paid registration form, printing and processing, voter-registration lists, and polling place rosters. Variations from a low of fifty cents to a high of $2.00 were reported . . .

There is a potential for vote fraud under the mail-registration system. The safeguards written into the law are stronger than those actually implemented in practice . . . Mail registration combined with absentee voting might be exploited in a type of vote fraud which would be very difficult to detect.

Maryland and New Jersey officials in general support the concept of voter registration by mail. Few, however, favor federal legislation on mail registration. Most were very critical of the proposed mass distribution of federal mail registration forms to every household . . . Other officials expressed concern that national legislation would supersede state legislation and might contain even fewer security checks.

Mail registration, if adopted by the states, poses no problem of dual voter-registration systems. If congressional legislation is passed, states will have to determine whether to abolish registration entirely for federal elections, maintain dual systems of voter registration, or adopt the federal system for state elections. As this study shows, many methods of mail registration are possible. Although each can increase voter convenience, though not necessarily total registration, each could conceivably increase the incidence of fraud.

> SOURCE: Richard G. Smolka, *Registering Voters By Mail* (Washington, D.C.: American Enterprise Institute for Public Policy Research, 1975), pp. 82-83.

Under present circumstances, compulsory voting in the United States would tend to increase the ideological content of party politics. Both minority-group liberals and George Wallace sympathizers are heavily represented in the ranks of present nonvoters. A massive infusion of youth and minority voters would definitely shake up the existing partisan pattern, probably pushing the Democratic party well to the left and moving conservatives into another framework.[31]

It appears most likely that some form of postcard registration or automatic registration will preclude the more extreme option of making voting mandatory.

DIRECT ELECTORAL DEMOCRACY

Out of the same progressive reforms that resulted in the secret ballot and the registration system came a series of mechanisms introduced to provide direct democracy through votes on issues. These attempts to check the power of political institutions, especially the legislatures, placed power in the hands of the electorate. It was assumed that such devices would give a large segment of the voters the opportunity to enact policies when the legislature refused to respond. Also, such reforms were expected to result in more egalitarian policy-making with less manipulation by interest groups. Despite controversy over whether these goals have been met or not, the *initiative, referendum*, and *recall* have become intricate parts of the political systems of at least 20 states.

INITIATIVE

Although the specific provisions differ by state, the initiative is a mechanism through which a specified number or percent of eligible voters (generally 5-10 percent) petition to have a legislative proposal or amendment placed on the

---

[31] Phillips, *Electoral Reform*, p. 69. This book presents election reform from a conservative viewpoint.

ballot for acceptance or rejection by the electorate. The most common types of initiatives can be placed into four categories:

1. a constitutional initiative, which allows citizens to alter or amend a state's basic document;

2. a direct initiative, which lets citizens enact or amend statutes;

3. an indirect initiative, which stipulates that the initiative must be resubmitted, after approval of the voters, to the legislature for final approval; and

4. an advisory initiative, which is a sort of nonbinding statement of public opinion which supposedly helps to guide a legislature's decision-making.[32]

The most significant initiatives are the first two on the list.

Most of the states using initiatives are in the West. Out of the 21 states that had provisions for initiatives in 1975, only four were east of the Mississippi River. California makes the most use of this device, followed by Washington, Colorado, Oregon, and North Dakota. Between 1970 and 1974 alone, 12 initiatives appeared on the California ballot. In these states and several others, the initiative has become a permanent institution and a commonplace feature of the political process. Interestingly, states with more disciplined, cohesive legislative parties have less use for the initiative than weak party states.[33]

Recently there has been much criticism of the initiative as a policy-making device. It has been suggested that it has negative consequences for the American political system. It is said that the frequent use of the initiative indicates legislative failure as well as voter dissatisfaction and frustration. Furthermore, it has been argued that the high-use states are more restricted and therefore, less innovative than those states without the initiative. Legislators in initiative states are constrained by the fear of an electorate challenge. Finally, it is said that the initiative itself has become a vehicle for special interests instead of a weapon for citizens.

Price dismisses these allegations and questions the "prevailing negative assessment of initiatives" by academics as well as politicians.[34] He contends

---

[32] Charles M. Price, "The Initiative: A Comparative State Analysis and Reassessment of a Western Phenomenon," *Western Political Quarterly*, 28 (June, 1975), 246.

[33] *Ibid.*, pp. 252-54. For a look at use of the initiative in one state, see Carl E. Lutrin, "The Public and Ecology: The Role of Initiatives in California's Environmental Politics," *Western Political Quarterly*, 28 (June, 1975), 352-71.

[34] *Ibid.*, p. 261.

that the initiative does provide the public with a means of last resort by which to bypass the traditional political channels. Bone agrees that some of Washington state's most exciting battles are centered around initiatives of various types.[35]

REFERENDUM

The referendum is a direct legislation device through which decisions of legislatures are kept from becoming policy until approved by the electorate. Three types of referenda are available in various combinations in 39 states.[36] Twenty-four states allow the people to petition for a referendum, usually with intention of repealing existing legislation. Nineteen states have provisions for the legislature to voluntarily submit laws to the electorate for approval, while the constitutions of 21 states require that certain questions, such as debt authorization, be submitted to the people.

In each case, the legislative actions are subject to a popular vote, which, in effect, can veto acts of the legislature. In some cases the threat of a referendum has made legislators reluctant to pass bills which might result in mobilization of a referendum effort. In the state of Washington for instance, bills passed by the legislature can be challenged if 4 percent of those voting for governor institute a petition for referendum. If the petition drive is successful, the legislature is required to place the bill on the ballot. As might be expected, these issues are often among the most crucial and controversial. Although less used than the initiative, the referendum has become an important instrument of popular control in some states.

RECALL

Recall laws usually stipulate that when a specified percentage of voters so petition, a special election will be held to determine whether a particular official will remain in an office or immediately vacate it. The rationale for the inclusion of recall provisions is to make office holders directly responsible to the electorate. At present twelve states have recall for state offices. Another 25 or so provide some form of recall procedures for municipal office holders. Although used infrequently, recall votes tend to be emotional and divisive when they are held.

[35] Hugh A. Bone and Robert C. Benedict, "Perspectives on Direct Legislation: Washington State's Experience, 1914-1973," *Western Political Quarterly*, 28 (June, 1975), 349.

[36] Seven additional states have a referendum process available only to local units of government.

VOTING TURNOUT ON DIRECT LEGISLATION

Voting for initiatives and referenda (sometimes jointly termed propositions) averages between 10 and 30 percent less than the corresponding vote for the governor, although it frequently approximates the turnout for lesser state offices. This is not impressive evidence for direct legislation theory. Bone finds, however, that participation rates for all types of ballot propositions have increased consistently since 1930.[37] Turnout on moral issues tends to be highest, while questions of governmental structure register the least voter participation. Turnout for initiatives is higher than for referenda, while constitutional amendments arouse the least interest.

Although some have contended that voters are predisposed to cast a negative vote on all propositions, John Mueller finds little evidence to support this thesis.[38] While some voters might be alienated, bloc negative voting is minor. Although Mueller concludes that the parties can be important influences on propositions, they take positions on very few ballot measures.[39] Voting and interest appear to be closely tied to the saliency of the issues.

According to Bone, the direct legislation procedures have initiated or sanctioned far more changes than is commonly realized. Also, they have helped educate the citizens about a number of public problems. One need only look at California propositions of the last five years to see the scope of the subjects.[40] Initiatives and referenda provide additional channels for political expression and are intricate parts of electoral machinery in many of the states.

IMPLICATIONS OF NONPARTISAN ELECTIONS

Another progressive reform of electoral structure is the introduction of nonpartisan elections, especially in city elections. This reform was an attempt to neutralize the power of political parties in the urban areas by taking "politics" out of the elections, thereby making them somehow less corrupt and vulnerable to political control. By 1959, over 60 percent of all American cities with over five thousand population had adopted nonpartisan elections,

[37] Bone, "Perspectives on Direct Legislation," p. 340.

[38] John E. Mueller, "Voting on the Propositions: Ballot Patterns and Historical Trends in California," *American Political Science Review*, 63 (December, 1969), 1210.

[39] *Ibid.*, p. 1206.

[40] For instance, nuclear power plants, capital punishment, legalizing marijuana.

with the trend continuing in that direction.[41] Despite the intentions of the reformers, several implications of the nonpartisan election structure have been unfavorable.

Although nonpartisan contests have succeeded in reducing party control, they have also resulted in a corresponding decrease in voting turnout, which averages about 30 percent. In a 1962 survey of cities over 25,000, partisan election cities averaged 50 percent turnout while those using nonpartisan elections averaged only 30 percent.[42] Several reasons for this gap are obvious. In nonpartisan elections two major stimuli for voting are absent: party identification and local party activity in getting out the vote. It has been demonstrated that nonparty informational sources are insufficient substitutes.[43]

In addition, Hamilton contends that the goal of expelling "politics" from the election process results in "issueless elections" and "name lotteries." This pattern is intensified by other components of the reform model of city government, such as the at-large election of councilmen, that produce a long ballot and a heavy informational burden on the electorate.[44] Finally, the goal of nonpartisan elections itself can be questioned. As local party organizations are weakened, the reward system which has motivated citizens to be active in politics disintegrates and leads not only to lower turnout figures, but also to lessened interest and activity in local politics. Nonpartisan elections have weakened party organization in cities without providing a substitute set of incentives.[45]

INSTITUTIONAL FRAMEWORK OF
ELECTIONS: A DEBATE

The crucial importance of the institutional framework of elections to parties and voting behavior is best exemplified by an ongoing debate in political science. Although many scholars have noted their positions, the major com-

[41] Eugene C. Lee, The *Politics of Non-partisanship: A Study of California City Elections* (Berkeley: University of California Press, 1960), p. 25.

[42] Howard D. Hamilton, "The Municipal Vote: Voting and Nonvoting in City Elections," *American Political Science Review*, 65 (December, 1971), 1139.

[43] M. Margaret Conway, "Voter Information Sources in a Non-Partisan Local Election," *Western Political Quarterly*, 21 (March, 1968), 69-71. Also see Phillip Cutright, "Activities of Precinct Committeemen in Partisan and Non-Partisan Elections," *Western Political Quarterly*, 17 (March, 1964), 93-108.

[44] Hamilton, "The Municipal Voter," pp. 1139-40.

[45] See Chapter 5 in this book for a detailed account of the importance of various types of incentives for political activity.

batants are Burnham, Converse, and Rusk. This debate demonstrates the complexity of the institutional framework and its interrelationship with political party activities.

The debate started in 1965 with an article by Walter Dean Burnham in which he traced a decline in partisanship and participation in elections since 1896. He offered as evidence:

1. the decline in voting turnout
2. the increase in ticket splitting
3. the large decrease in voting during nonpresidential years (drop-off)
4. the tendency to vote only for the highest offices on the ballot
5. the increase in partisan vote swings from election to election.[46]

This deterioration in the electorate was caused by the solid Republican dominance after 1896 and a resulting lack of competition. In addition, Burnham contends that the capitalist leaders of the industrial revolution stole the electoral system from the voters, which alienated the voters and demoralized them. While the 19th century electorate was informed and active, the 20th century electorate is marked by lower participation rates as well as by decreased levels of partisanship. To Burnham this represents not only a deterioration of a once enlightened electorate, but also the beginning of the decomposition of the party system.[47]

In a series of articles, Philip Converse[48] and Jerrold Rusk[49] have countered Burnham by citing institutional changes in the electoral system which account for much of the discrepencies between the two periods. They contend that major alterations in the mechanisms of conducting elections were also occurring around 1896. They argue that Burnham's trends are the result of election reforms, and do not indicate a "decline of party."

> ... institutional properties of the electoral system, considered either as an entity or as a network of component parts, have played

[46] Walter Dean Burnham, "The Changing Shape of the American Political Universe," *American Political Science Review*, 59 (March, 1965), 9-10.

[47] Burnham best presents this thesis in *Critical Elections and the Mainsprings of American Politics* (New York: W.W. Norton and Company, Inc., 1970).

[48] Philip E. Converse, "Change in the American Electorate," in *The Human Meaning of Social Change*, ed. Angus Campbell and Philip E. Converse (New York: Russell Sage Foundation, 1972), pp. 263-337.

[49] Jerrold G. Rusk, "Comment: The American Electoral Universe: Speculation and Evidence," *American Political Science Review*, 68 (September, 1974), 1028-49.

and continue to play a crucial role in influencing and shaping voting behavior—in essentially defining the conditions and boundaries of decision-making at the polls.[50]

Specifically, the introduction of the Australian Ballot and personal registration systems are offered as institutional elements affecting the electorate during this time period.

Converse argues that registration systems, which generally were introduced between 1890 and 1910, might have caused the drop in turnout by: (1) significantly reducing fraud (especially repeat voting and voting the graveyard); and (2) eliminating from voting those who have failed to register but would otherwise vote.[51] Rusk contends that weak registration systems had to exist for corruption to flourish.[52] In other words, the high turnout prior to 1896 might have been due to corruption which was possible only in the absence of a registration system. Adoption of personal registration lowered the turnout rates by reducing fraud. Complementing the introduction of registration systems was the widespread adoption of the secret, official ballot early in this period. In combination with strict registration requirements, the secret ballot all but eliminated vote fraud. In the process, ticket splitting increased, since those eliminated by the reforms were those who tended to vote straight ticket. According to Rusk, those most frequently disfranchised were: (1) corrupt voters who were paid by party hacks to vote straight ticket; and (2) marginally involved voters who voted only in response to "militaristic drilling" by the party.[53] According to Rusk, the changing voting trends in the North between 1890 and 1920 are largely explained by the ballot and registration changes. In the South, inclusion of the poll tax and literacy tests significantly reduced turnout during this same period.

An additional institutional alteration which Rusk and Converse contend had an impact on the electorate was the enfranchisement of women in 1920. Rusk estimates that this single action decreased turnout by 10 percent immediately after 1920.[54] This is because women were unaccustomed to voting and largely heeded the long-standing prohibition against it. Those who did vote frequently engaged in ticket splitting since they, initially, at least, lacked strong party loyalty. What appears to be a simple alteration in voting behavior is based on a complex set of institutional changes.

In response to these criticisms of Rusk and Converse, Burnham acknowledges the impact of these structural changes, although he disputes the mag-

---

[50] *Ibid.*, p. 1237.

[51] Converse, "Change in The American Electorate," pp. 282-85.

[52] Rusk, "The American Electoral Universe," p. 1033.

[53] *Ibid.*, p. 1042.

[54] Rusk, "The American Electoral Universe," p. 1044.

nitude of their influence. While Converse and Rusk see the reforms as basically positive, that is, eliminating the "most questionable elements of the earlier electorate,"[55] Burnham contends that they represent attempts by the capitalist elite to weaken opposition and take control of government.[56] Despite this, he, too, recognizes the vast impact of the "most cumbersome sets of procedural requirements in the western world," which

> ... creates a major 'double hurdle' for prospective voters which does not exist in Western Europe: the requirements associated with residence and registration, usually entailing periodic registration at frequent intervals, and the fact that elections are held on a normal working day in this employee society rather than on Sundays or holidays.[57]

Although this debate is expected to continue, perhaps with new arguments and participants, the role of institutional electoral structures will continue to be central to any discussions of political parties. Parties do not exist in a vacuum. Instead, they operate within a complicated institutional framework. As elections are central to political parties, the electoral context determines the conduct of elections. This debate indicates that voting patterns, too, are dependent on the institutional framework. Whether one agrees with Burnham that the electorate has deteriorated, or with Rusk and Converse that institutional changes have strengthened the electorate, the role of the structure of elections is undisputed.

PARTIES WITHIN THE ELECTORAL
CONTEXT: A SUMMARY

This chapter has examined the electoral system within which parties must operate. This cannot be overemphasized, because U.S. parties are basically election-oriented. Anything that affects voting and elections ultimately influences political parties. Three elements examined in this chapter appear to be most crucial to political parties. First, the expansion of the electorate over the last two centuries has meant that the parties have had to be flexible to adapt to the changing nature of their potential supporters. Both parties have

[55] *Ibid.*, p. 1049.

[56] Walter Dean Burnham, "Theory and Voting Research: Some Reflections on Converse's 'Change in the American Electorate,'" *American Political Science Review*, 68 (September, 1974), 1022.

[57] Burnham, "The Changing Shape," p. 13.

been largely successful in absorbing the changes at each new expansionary stage, although their adaptability has been inconsistent.

This discussion has implied that the political parties themselves have seldom been in the forefront of moves to expand the electorate. They have supported moves to expand where they are likely to benefit, but as a whole have not initiated action. Rather, they have responded to changes after they were made. In some cases, that is, southern Democrats and the 15th Amendment, party response has been to obscure and delay the expansion as long as possible. Once the electorate has been modified, that is, blacks voting in the South, the parties have enjoyed a reasonable amount of success in drawing the new voters to their ranks. In many cases, however, this apparent success might be the result of the lack of alternatives available to the newly franchised voters. These new voters most often have a simple three-way choice: vote Republican, vote Democrat, or don't vote at all.

A second aspect of the electoral system noted in this chapter relates to the federal nature of the U.S. Laws regulating most aspects of elections are state laws. The actual administration of elections is conducted through the secretaries of the 50 states. Despite a nationalization of many aspects of election laws through constitutional amendments, voting rights acts, and Supreme Court decisions, the states still vary significantly in registration residency requirements, poll procedures, and the like. There is much evidence that the structure of elections does influence turnout rates. Those states where voting is made easier exhibit significantly higher turnout rates. This variation in voting regulations must be noted in any discussion of the electorate, since the nature of voting regulations does vary from state to state. Disqualifications and voluntary nonvoting due to complicated laws eliminate large segments of the population in some states.

A final aspect of elections discussed here relates to variation in turnout rates not by state, but by type of election. It was demonstrated that voting turnout in nonpartisan elections and in various forms of direct-issue voting is much lower than in the general elections. While nonpartisan elections are the result of progressive movements designed to gain more democratic elections and public input, they have failed to attain minimal standards of participation as compared to partisan contests. There is tentative evidence here to suggest that the presence of a partisan dimension increases turnout in elections. We shall now turn to an examination of this partisan element in our unique electoral system.

SECTION III

PARTIES
AS ELECTORAL
ORGANIZATIONS:
DECENTRALIZED
PARTY SYSTEM

In this section, party organization in the U.S. is examined. As noted in Chapter 2, one unique feature of American parties is their organization. It was argued that the decentralized nature of political parties has resulted in part from the role played by states and localities in our federal system and the division of power between the various branches. The dispersion of political power in the government has led to similar distributions within the political parties. While most political parties have hierarchical organization with control at the national party level, U.S. party organization is fragile and decentralized. Power and activity are most common at the lowest organizational levels, while the national party leaders struggle for recognition. This will be apparent throughout this discussion of parties as electoral organizations.

The national organization is inhibited by each state's control over many party electoral functions. The states define a political party and designate various substate organization levels. In terms of activity, the smallest unit or precinct is generally strongest, though the county organization retains most of the decision-making authority. The county and precinct organizations, plus intermediary party organizations in some states, form the backbone of the U.S. party system. The state organization is generally composed of past or present members of these smaller party units. In many cases, the state committees have little influence over the county committees and the precinct committeemen. The state committees also are most commonly well defined by state law.

As power is decentralized within the states, it is also decentralized nationally. The national organization is a creation of the national convention which, in turn, is composed of delegates from the states. The state delegates, in turn, are representative of the counties, and so forth. In addition to the decentralized organizational structure, the emergence of candidate organiza-

tions independent of the parties has tended to reduce further the power of the U.S. parties, especially at the national and state levels. The destiny of U.S. parties as electoral organizations appears to be uncertain if they are measured against a centralized party system. The next two chapters will examine first the state and local organization, and then the national organization of U.S. parties.

5

Decentralized
Party System:
State and Local
Organization

One of the major characteristics of the American political party system pointed out in Chapter 2 was the highly fragmented and decentralized nature of party organization. It was suggested in Chapter 3 that this resulted from a combination of historical, cultural and institutional forces operating on the party system. In this chapter, the bottom levels of political party organization in the U.S. are discussed. It is expected that effective power and control reside in these local organizations instead of at the national level. In addition to tracing through the various formal/legal levels of party organization, we shall examine the activities, membership, and effectiveness of party units.

FORMAL/LEGAL PARTY STRUCTURE

Although political parties developed outside of the formal governmental institutions, they largely are governed by state laws. Most states outline the formal structure of parties and define the power of party officials. Some states provide detailed regulation of state and local party organization, while others offer limited guidance and allow the parties to regulate themselves through self-imposed bylaws.

> The laws covering primaries, caucuses, elections and political parties of the Commonwealth of Massachusetts are published in a bound volume, 7 1/2 by 10 inches, and containing 534 pages. South Carolina, on the other hand, repealed all laws regulating the parties in 1944 to give the Democrats the best possible chance of evading regulation by the federal courts after the U.S. Supreme Court outlawed the "white primary."[1]

[1] Robert J. Huckshorn, *Party Leadership in the States* (Amherst: University of Massachusetts Press, 1976), p. 12.

In most states, some combination of state laws and internal party regulations define the activities, membership, and procedures of party organizations. State and local organizations are assumed to be public, or at least semi-public, institutions. Unlike the national organization, they are not totally the product of their own making.

The formal/legal structure of parties results in a fragmentation of functions and powers among a wide variety of units. One question here is how meaningful these legal divisions are in terms of effective control of the party machinery. Where does the actual power lie, what defines actual membership in the party units, and what activities are parties expected to perform in the U.S.? While the decentralized nature of the formal party system makes it impossible to describe accurately, some generalizations are useful.

In his analysis of European political parties, Robert Michels contends that parties are like other large-scale organizations in concentrating effective power among a few at the top.[2] In effect, the leadership becomes a ruling elite which makes decisions and controls the organization. Michels terms this tendency toward elite control the Iron Law of Oligarchy. In the hierarchy of parties a gulf develops between the rank-and-file and the leadership. The dominance of the leadership is assured, however, because it controls the flow of information and monopolizes the skills and talents necessary to run the organization. The rank-and-file are characterized by low interest and skill and an inability to control the organization. Furthermore, Michels argues that party leaders are not representative of the members, and that policies reflect the desire of the elites, not the mass membership. Even if a successful challenge to the leadership is made, a new elite will form with characteristics very similar to the old one.

If Michels' strict hierarchical model were applied to U.S. parties, one would expect highly centralized control at the national level. Power would flow from the higher-level party organizations to the lower. Those at the lower levels, such as the precinct and counties, would be directly responsible to the leader at the next higher level, and so forth. Lower level leaders would be selected by the centralized leadership and the elite would control the lines of communication. Most decision-making activity would be concentrated at the top. A strict hierarchy of the major U.S. party units could be illustrated as in Figure 5.1.

Samuel Eldersveld contends that party organization in the U.S. fails to reflect a pyramidal hierarchy with power concentrated at the top, as suggested by Michels' oligarchical model.[3] In examining the party organization of

[2] Robert Michels, *Political Parties* (New York: The Free Press, 1949).

[3] Samuel J. Eldersveld, *Political Parties: A Behavioral Analysis* (Chicago: Rand McNally and Company, 1964).

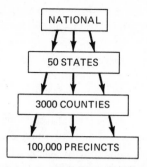

Figure 5.1   Levels of Party Organization

one county, Eldersveld offers an alternative model of hierarchy. Power under this model is dispersed throughout the various party "strata."

> ... although authority to speak for the organization may remain in the hands of the top elite nucleus, there is great autonomy in operations at the lower 'strata' or echelons of the hierarchy and control from the top is minimal... [4]

Unlike Michels' model, this model does not present party control as monolithic, but rather as a highly proliferated and tenuous coalition of local leaders. Party organizations are open and clientele-oriented, not closed and elite-oriented groups. Leadership is recruited from all socioeconomic levels and access to the structure is broad, resulting in a heterogeneous elite, socially as well as ideologically.

Communication in the "stratarchy" moves from the bottom up and is "highly voluntaristic", with little coercion from the top.[5] Most county leaders are unable even to maintain direct contact with their precinct leaders, and they are aware of this deficiency and frustrated by it.[6] Decision making takes the form of bargaining among subgroups rather than the issuance of directives from above. The formal leadership has few rewards and virtually no sanctions available. The resulting leadership process is very disorganized since consideration must be given to many opinions in order to maximize mobilization of support. The precinct leaders run their operations virtually alone, with limited contact and involvement of the county leaders.

Although it appears that the stratarchical model is generally most descriptive of U.S. party organizations, the wide variation of state laws and

[4] *Ibid.*, p. 99.
[5] *Ibid.*, p. 377.
[6] *Ibid.*, p. 407.

local conditions indicates the need for a more complex model. One approach is to classify parties on the basis of specified characteristics and then place them on a continuum from most to least organized. David Olson has categorized county party organizations into four types on the basis of activities, cohesiveness, structure, and role orientation.[7]

Olson's four types of party organization are:

1. The *organizational party* has an autonomous structure of communication and concerted activity which dominates candidate recruitment, nomination, and campaigning. It typically involves itself in campaigns for all levels of office. Little important electoral activity occurs outside the control of the organizational party.

2. The *factionally organized party* consists of two or more factions, each similar to the organizational party. Each faction tends to dominate all stages of the electoral cycle for its candidates and campaigns for all levels of office.

3. The *party of partial activity* participates in nominations and elections, but fails to monopolize any function. Individual candidates are largely responsible for running their own campaigns, but they do find the party organization helpful in their efforts. The extent of activity of this party type varies by office.

4. The *candidate-centered party* is a minimal party in which the formal/legal structure is limited or nonexistent. If factions exist, they are unstable and not very effective. Candidates rarely align themselves with other candidates and each candidate manages his or her own campaign. Most support is given by persons or groups lacking in party orientation and concerned primarily with advancing their own purposes.[8]

STATE AND SUBSTATE PARTY ORGANIZATION

Few Americans are even superficially informed about state political parties. This is not surprising, given the emphasis placed on national politics and national institutions. The news media seldom cover state party activities in

[7] David M. Olson, "Toward a Typology of County Party Organizations," *Southwestern Social Science Quarterly,* 48 (March, 1968), 558-72.

[8] *Ibid.,* p. 570. For a somewhat different typology see David M. Olson, "District Party Organization and Legislative Performance in Congress," *Journal of Politics,* 36 (May, 1974), 482-86.

any detail, and the parties themselves often fail to publicize their activities. There is a tendency for party workers to constitute small, self-contained groups unknown to the public. It is a rare person that can name the state party chairman of either party in his or her state. For most of us, state parties are an enigma. Although membership entails nothing more than an expression of identification, few citizens become active or knowledgeable of the internal workings of the political parties at the state level. This is unfortunate, because the state parties are quite accessible to concerned citizens.[9]

STATE CENTRAL COMMITTEE

One factor contributing to the lack of knowledge about state parties is the lack of uniformity from state to state. In actuality, it is difficult to generalize about any aspects of party organization at the state level, since state laws often specify names as well as membership selection, size, and functions. Most commonly, the state organization is referred to as the State Central Committee. The size of these committees ranges from less than 100 to over 800 in California. In most cases, an executive committee is selected to make most of the decisions which are then ratified by the full central committee. A state chairman generally is appointed by the party's gubernatorial candidate, and his position may be either a paid full-time position or, more commonly, a part-time avocation. Some state parties have an executive director to handle day to day decisions and routine party work. The executive director is ultimately accountable to the state central committee.

One major aspect of variation by state revolves around two related elements: the lower unit from which state committee members are chosen and the means by which they are actually selected. In many states the state committeemen are chosen from the county committees, while in others they are chosen from the state legislative district, congressional district, state convention, or a combination of these units. The actual methods of choosing members include: (1) selection in party primary, (2) election by a lower committee, (3) selection at a state party convention, and (4) automatic or ex-officio selection based on position in lower committees (for example, the chairman of each county central committee.)

The activities and roles of the state central committees also reflect the impact of state law, as well as party custom and formal bylaws of each

[9] The most comprehensive coverage of state political parties is Malcolm E. Jewell and David M. Olson, *American State Political Parties and Elections* (Homewood, Ill.: The Dorsey Press, 1978).

party. Some state central committees, especially in the East, are active, powerful political units. They draft party platforms, distribute and raise campaign funds and, in a few states, organize slates of statewide candidates. In other states, the central committees are little more than a name, with few attendant responsibilities and powers. The majority of state central committees falls somewhere between inactivity and a signficant middle-level party unit.

EXPANDING ROLE OF STATE PARTIES

As demonstrated in Chapter 3, the Founding Fathers placed little trust in political parties and consciously failed to provide a structure through which they could evolve. Partly because of this distrust and partly because of federalism, state parties grew as distinct and autonomous entities. The national organizations followed the development of state parties, and they continue to be coalitions of the 50 state parties.

> Seldom did they become organized as pyramidal hierarchies with lower levels responsible to the higher. Seldom was authority concentrated in a single individual or statewide office. Seldom did the membership maintain a sustained interest in party affairs. Finally, there was seldom any attempt to enforce even rudimentary party responsibility.[10]

Throughout history, however, state parties have failed to take advantage of this constitutional vacuum, and much criticism has been levelled at their apparent weakness.

Huckshorn argues, however, that presently state parties demonstrate more vitality than ever before. Although the changes have not been uniform or universal across the states, widespread progress is apparent. The growth of modern campaign techniques, including public opinion surveys and data processing, has been accompanied by demands for organizational continuity and long-range planning. In response, a new breed of state party leaders has established permanent state headquarters with paid state chairmen and/or state executive directors to provide continuity.[11] The establishment of national associations of state chairmen is another evidence of the new vitality of state party organizations.

[10] Huckshorn, *Party Leadership in the States,* p. 3
[11] *Ibid.,* p. 5.

Party leaders in some areas have managed to reverse the antiparty trends of past decades by assuming greater leadership roles and by seeking to refocus public attention and loyalty toward the party as opposed to individual candidates.[12]

There are several convincing reasons why state parties are presently in a favorable position to claim a larger leadership role in the national parties. First, since state and local units are so much more numerous than the national ones, greater experimentation and easier control over party affairs are possible. State and local units tend to be more homogeneous and therefore facilitate actions which would be divisive at the national level. Second, state parties are small enough to adopt new campaign and administration techniques without being absorbed by the momentum of the new politics. There is much need for coordination and cooperation in exploiting new techniques such as surveys, advertising, data processing and electoral analysis. Rather than precluding state parties, as some contend, these new demands offer parties in the states an indispensable role as clearing-houses for state and local candidate organizations.[13]

Another advantage of state parties is the predominance of elected and appointed officials at the state and substate level. Only a handful of the over 500,000 elected officials in the U.S. are national. Despite a decrease in patronage at both the national and state levels, it is obvious that the opportunities for rewarding party work remain much broader in the state and county parties. Conway and Feigert found that workers motivated by material rewards are more likely to be active than those ideologically rewarded.[14] Most activity remains at the local and state levels where the rewards are most abundant and the politics most personal.

Since the states offer a large number and wide diversity of elected offices, the minority party generally is assured control of some offices. The states provide more opportunity for the party out of power to serve a useful function. Even a small proportion of the offices is enough to build an organizational base. The federal system offers the most protection for minority parties at the state or substate level. Continuance of the national party depends on strong and active organization at these local levels. The evidence presented by Huckshorn indicates that many state parties are exhibiting a

---

[12] *Ibid.*, p. 263.

[13] *Ibid.*, p. 266.

[14] M. Margarat Conway and Frank B. Feigert, "Incentives and Task Performance Among Party Precinct Workers," *Western Political Quarterly*, 27 (December, 1974), 693-709.

resurgence of effort to maintain their traditional position in the multilevel political parties of the U.S.

SUBSTATE PARTY UNITS

Although national politics is the most salient and the states control the legal structure, most activity rests at the substate level. It is here that volunteers are recruited to distribute campaign literature, canvass the voters, raise small contributions, and transport voters to the polls. It is at this grass-roots level that the parties come into direct contact with the voters and ultimately mobilize them or fail to do so. It is here that parties succeed or fail. Despite the variation by state, two features are common to party organizations across the nation. First, parties are organized in a series of committees from the precinct level to the national committee. Second, party organization generally parallels the arrangement of electoral districts in the states.

Table 5.1   Substate Party Committees*

Level	Number of States
Precinct	50
County	45
Legislative district	27
Congressional district	20
City	20
Ward	13
Town or Township	13
Judicial districts	3
Regional districts	2

*The unpublished survey by Herbert Duncombe and Robert Blank was conducted in 1975, and responses were received from the Secretary of State and/or party officials in all fifty states. If either party in a state listed the use of a particular type of local party committee, the state was shown as having that type of committee.

Although the precinct is the smallest level of party organization in all states, the intermediary levels vary by state. Table 5.1 indicates that county party committees are the most prevalent units across the 50 states. Other units include the state legislative district, congressional districts, and various smaller units. City committees and the ward committees within cities are found most commonly in the East, as are town committees. Party organization at these levels will be summarized here, beginning with the precinct.

Precinct Committee. The precinct is the smallest unit of political organization. In metropolitan areas it might contain between 1,000 and 2,000 voters, while in sparsely populated areas the number might be as low as a dozen. The boundaries of the precincts are most commonly determined by a county governing board, which is also responsible for altering the boundaries when the population changes. There generally is an attempt to keep the size of precincts as balanced as possible.

Precinct committeemen or committeewomen are chosen either by voters in a primary election or by party members attending a precinct caucus. The number of committeemen in each precinct varies by state. One study found twelve states in which there was one precinct committeeman or woman, and at least thirteen states where each precinct had one committeeman and one committeewoman.[15] The remaining states were found to have more than two precinct committee officials. Oregon precincts, for instance, have one male and one female precinct member for each 500 votes cast in the district. North Carolina precincts each have a precinct chairman, three vice-chairmen, and a secretary-treasurer.

How crucial is precinct activity during the campaign? Although there are conflicting conclusions regarding the effectiveness of precinct work, it is generally agreed that strong precinct organization during campaigns is an essential element of success. One of the difficulties in assessing the role of precinct activity is the problem of isolating it from other factors such as the social and economic characteristics of the precinct residents.[16] Katz and Eldersveld, for instance, found that while strength of party organization was related to voting, demographic characteristics were a better predictor of the vote.[17] Eldersveld also pointed out the limited nature of party contact in Detroit, where over 60 percent of the electorate was never exposed to party contact. Only 17 percent had been contacted more than once.[18]

Despite these cited limitations, it is estimated that precinct activity can increase a candidate's vote in a precinct by 5 to 10 percent over what might have been expected in its absence.[19] There is substantial evidence that per-

[15] See Herbert Sydney Duncombe, *Modern County Government* (Washington, D.C.: National Association of Counties, 1977), pp. 70-71.

[16] William J. Crotty, "Party Effort and its Impact on the Vote," *American Political Science Review,* 65 (June, 1971), 439-50.

[17] Daniel Katz and Samuel J. Eldersveld, "The Impact of Local Party Activity upon the Electorate," *Public Opinion Quarterly,* 25 (Spring, 1961), 1-24.

[18] Eldersveld, *Political Parties.*

[19] Phillips Cutright, "Measuring the Impact of Local Party Activity on the General Election Vote," *Public Opinion Quarterly,* 27 (Fall, 1963), 372-86.

sonal contact is the most successful form of persuasion, even in this era of mass media.[20] The efforts of local organizations appear to be more crucial in primary than general elections.[21] Also, Wolfinger confirms the fact that precinct work has considerable impact on voting, especially in low-stimulus elections.[22] In summing up the importance of precinct activity, Bartholomew contends:

> The importance of the precinct committeeman to the orthodox politician can hardly be overemphasized. It is in the precinct that elections are frequently won or lost... This is the grassroots area where the party has its basic strength with the committeeman in direct contact with the voters... The specifics of a precinct committeeman's work will vary with the precinct but the basic point remains that here is where the professional politician presumably maintains his real power and security.[23]

The work of precinct officials is concentrated during the election campiagn. An effective precinct committeeman will contact the voters, organize party workers, distribute campaign literature, organize rallies and meetings, and arrange transportation to the polls on election day. During the interim between elections, precinct committeemen supposedly attempt to contact new voters moving into the area, intercede with government officials on behalf of constituents, and attend party meetings. Frequently they will have joint duties as members of district or county committees. In many areas of the country it is very difficult to maintain adequate precinct leadership, however, and in many precincts there is no effective precinct organization for one or both parties. There are few real rewards for precinct activities, and precinct officials lack the visibility of a higher level position. In spite of this situation, however, precinct party officials are probably the most important participants in parties, since they are the only party personnel in contact with the voters on a continuing basis.

County Central Committee. Although precinct committeemen are the base of U.S. political parties, the single most powerful committee in most

[20] John C. Blydenburgh, "A Controlled Experiment to Measure the Effects of Personal Contact Campaigning," *Midwest Journal of Political Science,* 15 (May, 1971), 365-81.

[21] Phillips Cutright and Peter H. Rossi, "Party Organization in Primary Elections," *American Journal of Sociology,* 64 (November, 1958), 269.

[22] Raymond E. Wolfinger, "The Influence of Precinct Work on Voting Behavior," *Public Opinion Quarterly,* 27 (Fall, 1963), 387-98.

[23] Paul Bartholomew, *Profile of a Precinct Committeeman* (Dobbs Ferry, N.Y.: Oceana Publications, Inc., 1968), p. 7.

states is the county central committee. Table 5.1 indicates that 45 states have county committees, the exceptions being Alaska, Connecticut, Massachusetts, North Dakota and Rhode Island. Despite wide variations among states in party organization, the county central committees are surprisingly similar. Generally, they are composed of a county chairman, vice-chairman, secretary, and treasurer. These officials, in most cases, are elected by the entire county committee membership. The central committee membership varies but usually includes all precinct committeepersons. The county chairman is a key figure in many counties.[24] In point of fact, the county officials may actually recruit candidates for the precinct positions in order to solidify their political base.[25]

The county is central to the party organization for several reasons. First, the counties are political divisions with many elected and appointed officials. Often they are the major remaining source of patronage available to the parties. Control of the county can be lucrative politically. Second, the county seat, especially in rural areas, is a central gathering place and economic center as well as the housing for the county court. Third, the laws of most states recognize the importance of the county central committee and give it a special place among party committees. It not only performs various campaign activities, but also secures signatures for candidates' petitions, selects members to state conventions and the state central committees in some states, and approves patronage appointments.

One indication of the importance of county party organizations is the high ranking given them by state political officials. The results of these rankings in Table 5.2 demonstrate that county central committees and county party chairmen are considered crucial in most states except New England, where city and town committees are more important.

Other Substate Committees. Several other substate party committees are worth mentioning. Twenty-seven states have party committees that correspond to state legislative districts. Generally, they are composed of all precinct officials in the district. In many cases, these committees overlap with the county committee, although the powers and functions of the district committee are much more constrained. An additional 20 states have party committees corresponding to congressional districts. In some states these organizations function as the congressman's personal organization, set off from the rest of the party.

---

[24] It was Richard Daley's position as Cook County Chairman, not his position as Mayor, that gave him most of his patronage power.

[25] See Alice DeGanton Schrank, *Political Parties: Promise and Performance* (Bay City, Michigan: Rich-Errington, 1975).

Table 5.2 Rating of the Importance of Local Party
Offices and Organizations

	All States	States Outside of New England	New England States
Precinct committeemen	1.61	1.74	.50
County party committees	2.19	2.39	.50
County party chairmen	2.24	2.42	.75
Legislative district committees	.97	.94	1.25
Legislative district chairmen	1.00	.97	1.25
City party committees	.69	.45	2.50
City party chairmen	.77	.53	2.75
Town or township committees	.47	.26	2.25
Town or township chairmen	.55	.29	2.75

SOURCE: Herbert Sydney Duncombe, *Modern County Government* (Washington: National Association of Counties, 1977), p. 75. Data from Herbert Duncombe and Robert H. Blank, unpublished survey, 1975. This question was answered by secretaries of state and state party leaders in thirty-eight states. All scores in this table are averages for the states in each category. A score of "3" represents "very important;" 2, "important;" 1, "somewhat important;" and 0, "not important."

Although it is very difficult to generalize, most states have some combination of party committees between the precinct and county levels. Many eastern states, for instance, provide city, town, and ward organizations. Generalizations for the rest of the nation are even more hazardous, though city and ward organizations are common to many of the urban states. Town and township committees are rare west of the Mississippi. As a rule, all of these subcounty committees are centered around campaign activities.

STATE AND LOCAL PARTY ACTIVITIES

Although there have been many classifications of party activities, one of the most useful is that of Paul Allen Beck, in which he distinguishes four types (dimensions) of party activity.[26] These include: (1) organizational, (2)

[26] Paul Allen Beck, "Environment and Party: The Impact of Political and Demographic County Characteristics on Party Behavior," *American Political Science Review,* 68 (September, 1974), 1229-44. For other typologies, see William J. Crotty, "The Party Organization and Its Activities," in *Approaches to the Study of Party Organization,* ed. by William J. Crotty (Boston: Allyn and Bacon, 1968), pp. 247-306 and Eldersveld, *Political Parties,* pp. 333-409.

service, (3) mobilization, and (4) persuasion. The last two are campaign-oriented, while the first two relate mostly to inter-campaign activity.

Organizational. Organizational activities are those that are directly related with maintenance of the party organization at each level.

> The political party is an organization and may be expected like all organizations, to engage in activities designed to maintain its organizational vitality.[27]

Such activities include selecting leaders, hiring a staff, holding regular meetings to conduct party business, and keeping records. None of these organizational activities is unique to parties. Interest groups, churches, and high school clubs use basically the same rules and procedures as parties.

What distinguishes parties from other types of organizations, however, is their explicit goal of winning elections and attempting to control government. The three activities remaining to be discussed are all aimed at the goal of winning. Each reflects a different approach to strengthening support for the continued existence of parties as organizations. Fulfillment of this goal, however, is based on the assumption that organizational activities proceed smoothly.

Service. Service activities are future-oriented activities designed to build allegiances among the constituency which can be translated into votes at election time. Although party machines are identified most closely with service activities, party organizations of all kinds attempt to build support through such activities. The most common types of services include: (1) patronage jobs, (2) legal assistance and help in dealing with the bureaucracy, (3) priority in material services, and (4) direct aid (for example, cash in hard times). The main effort of the party machine is to provide continuous material benefits and a wide range of services directly to local constituents through the local party leaders.

Mobilization. Although service activities may build support, they are indirect and may not always be the most efficient means of winning elections. Also, the performance of service activities alone is rarely sufficient to insure support on election day.

> In order to collect the debts which have been accumulated by continuous servicing of constitutents, machine leaders place heavy

[27]Paul Allen Beck, "Environment and Party: The Impact of Political and Demographic County Characteristics on Party Behavior," *American Political Science Review,* p. 1231.

emphasis on voter mobilization activities. Performance of these activities is particularly important among the poor because they often lack the motivational force which propels the more affluent or educated votes to the polls.[28]

Since most party organizations lack the means of providing adequate services, mobilization activities are much more typical.

Mobilization is an attempt to draw out latent support. It is most common during campaigns, especially during the last several weeks. It includes canvassing of voters, registration drives, and transportation to the polls on election day. Local party workers are crucial to mobilizing attempts. Although mobilization is a more common party activity than servicing constituents, many party organizations do a poor job of "getting out the vote."

Persuasion.   The final activity of parties, according to Beck, also is concentrated during the campaign period and directly concerned with winning elections. Persuasion is an attempt to convince voters to support the party and its candidates. Here the parties must compete with candidate organizations and various ad hoc issue-oriented groups. Generally, parties are less successful in persuasion than in mobilization. Beck argues that parties have turned away from service activities toward more direct vote-getting methods to adjust to the changing needs of the electorate (see Table 5.3).[29] As levels of education have increased, parties have reduced emphasis on mobilization and attempted to compete with the candidate organizations in campaign persuasion activities. Ultimately, however, success in both mobilization and persuasion depends upon strong organization.

PARTY ACTIVISTS

Parties tend to be relatively open organizations with few, if any, formal prerequisites for active participation. Despite this accessibility, estimates are that at the most, 2 percent of the electorate is active in party affairs. This small percentage raises two related questions. The first is why the vast majority of the electorate fails to participate, and the second, which is examined here, is why this small minority is active. What distinguishes party activists from the rest of the electorate and what motivates them to partici-

[28] *Ibid.*, p. 1230.

[29] Also see, Gerald H. Kramer, "The Effects of Precinct-Level Canvassing on Voter Behavior," *Public Opinion Quarterly,* 34 (Winter, 1970), 560-72.

Table 5.3   Activities Mentioned By The Party Officials

Orientation of Activity	Description of Job	Most Important
Campaign-Related	(58.3%)	(67.8%)
Contacting Voters	26.5%	43.5%
Raising Money	12.5	6.9
Getting people to register	10.6	6.9
Campaigning	3.4	6.1
Public relations	3.4	1.7
Contacting new voters	1.9	1.7
Party-Organized	(27.6%)	(19.9%)
Participating in party meetings and business	11.7%	10.4%
Recruiting and organizing workers	9.8	5.2
County party organizational work	6.1	4.3
Ideological	(8.3%)	(9.6%)
Increasing political information	7.2%	9.6%
Policy formulation	1.1	0.0
Nomination	(5.7%)	(3.5%)
Getting candidates for local office	3.4%	2.6%
General activities	2.3	0.9

SOURCE: Lewis Bowman and G.R. Boynton, "Activities and Role Definitions of Grass Roots Party Officials," *Journal of Politics,* 28 (February, 1966), p. 126.

pate in political party affairs? An examination of the characteristics of party actives and a discussion of the incentives offered by the parties might illuminate this situation.

CHARACTERISTICS OF PARTY ACTIVES

Although not all party leaders are of higher social and economic status (SES), as a group they tend to be more educated, have higher incomes, and to be in professional higher-status occupations. They are also more informed and politically aware. Lawyers are the most overrepresented group among party actives. While they constitute less than 1 percent of the labor force, their proportion among party leaders is generally between 15 and 30 percent

(Table 5.4). In most states Republican actives are of higher SES than Democrats, although Samuel Patterson found this trend to be reversed in Oklahoma.[30] In addition, party leaders tend to be long-term residents of the counties in which they hold office. Especially in rural counties, they tend to be active in other organizations, perhaps because of their social and economic characteristics.

Surprisingly, party leaders seldom run for elective office. They recruit, and in some cases, select, candidates but they themselves stay outside the competition for office. One reason may be that entrance into the election arena might compromise their party position. Another reason cited by Avery Lieserson is that party leaders recognize "that competent party work alone does not constitute a qualification for a place on a winning ticket."[31] A leader who runs for office and loses might have difficulty in maintaining his party position. To be sure, there are some people who see party activity as a route to elective office. The leaders, however, tend to be separated from this process.

There is mixed evidence on the ideological composition of party actives. McClosky found major divisions among the leaders not evident in the followers:

> Whereas the leaders of the two parties diverge strongly, their follow-ers differ only moderately in their attitudes toward issues. The hypothesis that party beliefs unite adherents and bring them into the party ranks may hold more for their active members . . . not for its rank-and-file supporters.[32]

A recent study by Nie and associates has concurred that party activists are not representative rank-and-file members in regard to issue orientation.[33]

---

[30] Samuel C. Patterson, "Characteristics of Party Leaders," *Western Political Quarterly*, 16 (June, 1963), 333-52. Also see Richard J. Heuwinkel and Charles W. Wiggins, "Party Competition and Party Leadership Attri-butes," *American Journal of Political Science*, 17 (February, 1973), 159-69.

[31] Avery Lieserson, *Parties and Politics: An Institutional and Behavioral Approach*, (New York: Alfred A. Knopf, 1958), p. 201.

[32] Herbert McClosky, Paul J. Hoffman, and Rosemary O'Hara, "Issue Conflict and Consensus Among Party Leaders and Followers," *American Political Science Review*, 54 (June 1960), 426. Also see David Nexon "Asym-metry in the Political System: Occasional Activists in the Democratic and Republican Parties," *American Political Science Review*, 65 (September, 1971), 716-30.

[33] Norman H. Nie, Sidney Verba, and John R. Petrocik, *The Changing American Voter*, (Cambridge: Harvard University Press, 1976), pp. 200-05.

Table 5.4 Variations in Occupational Background of County Party Chairmen: Seven States

Occupational	Ohio Dem	Ohio Rep	Oklahoma Dem	Oklahoma Rep	Kansas Dem	Kansas Rep	Wisconsin Dem	Wisconsin Rep	New York Dem	New York Rep	Maryland* Dem	Maryland* Rep	Tennessee* Dem	Tennessee* Rep
Professional	3	4	15	18	8	10	6	12	14	13	42	36	13	5
Lawyer	18	19	24	12	14	28	19	30	–	–	–	–	–	–
Business	26	27	22	20	19	33	17	45	29	34	8	11	3	3
Sales-Clerical	10	8	10	13	15	6	8	5	13	15	13	14	10	38
Farmer	6	20	19	25	29	15	16	3	–	–	0	2	8	16
Laborer	11	6	2	5	1	4	23	0	32	28	10	6	62	16
Housewife	10	5	2	0	7	1	5	0	–	–	20	17	2	5
Retired	–	–	3	3	6	0	3	3	–	–	3	9	2	5
Public Office	–	–	2	0	1	1	2	0	3	5	–	–	–	–
Other	15	11	1	2	0	0	0	0	–	–	3	1	0	3
No Response	–	–	0	2	0	3	1	2	8	6	0	4	0	8
	99	100	100	100	100	101	100	100	99	101	99	100	100	99

*Note: Maryland data only Montgomery County, Tennessee data only Knox County, Precinct Chairman.

SOURCES: (1) Ohio Figures: Thomas A. Flinn and Frederick M. Wirt, "Local Party Leaders: Groups of Like Minded Men," *Midwest Journal of Political Science*, 9 (February, 1965), 77-98; (2) Oklahoma, Kansas, Wisconsin: Samuel C. Patterson, "Characteristics of Party Leaders," *Western Political Quarterly*, 16 (June, 1963), 332-52; (3) New York: Robert S. Hirshfield, Bert E. Swanson and Blanche D. Blank, "A Profile of Political Activists in Manhattan," *Western Political Quarterly*, 15 (September, 1962), 489-506; (4) Maryland and Tennessee: M. Margaret Conway and Frank B. Feigert, "Motivation, Incentive Systems, and the Political Party Organization," *APSR* 62 (1968), 1159-73.

The study indicates that activists in the 1970s more frequently were in the extreme ideological positions. Although Republican supporters tend to cluster on the right of the issue scale, Republican leaders outflank them further to the right. The Democratic supporters, unlike the Republicans, are divided between conservatives and liberals. The Democratic activists, however, have become more unifed in the liberal direction than they were in the 1950s.[34]

Conversely, Eldersveld demonstrates that leadership exhibits very weak ideology at the local level. He finds that 30 percent of the Democratic leaders are conservatives and 33 percent of the Republicans are liberals. He concludes that party leaders consciously tone down their ideology in order to gain the support of the large numbers of citizens whose ideology might be at odds with their ideological orientation.[35] Herbert McClosky also suggests that leaders must moderate their own views to build support among the less ideological followers.[36] Other authors find a general consensus among local party members and leaders sharing a "consistent point of view."[37]

Another element is introduced by Edmond Costantini, who finds that the top political leaders are more moderate than the middle-level actives. He suggests that the McClosky findings obscure this crucial cleavage between attitudes in the party. One of the functions of the top party leaders, according to Costantini, is to serve as "ideological intermediaries between the radicalism of lower-level party actives, and the centrist electorate."[38] Leaders must try to restrain the extremists among the party ranks and hold together various divergent and conflicting elements within the party.

In summary, party leaders tend to be more articulate, informed, and concerned about politics. Although types vary, they tend to overrepresent the higher SES groupings of education, income and occupation. Party actives are usually respectable, solid middle-class citizens, not the party hacks of the cigar-smoked backrooms in political stories. The evidence, though unclear,

[34] *Ibid.*, p. 204.

[35] Eldersveld, *Political Parties*, p. 540.

[36] McClosky, "Issue Conflict and Consensus," p. 426.

[37] See Thomas A. Flinn and Frederick M. Wirt, "Local Party Leaders: Groups of Like-Minded Men," *Midwest Journal of Political Science,* 9 (February, 1965), 77-98. Robert S. Hirshfield, Bert E. Swanson, and Blanche D. Blank, "A Profile of Political Activities in Manhattan," *Western Political Quarterly,* 15 (September, 1972), 489-506, concludes that ideological orientation is an important factor in determining party affiliation of Manhattan activists.

[38] Edward Costantini, "Intraparty Attitude Conflict: Democratic Party Leadership in California," *Western Political Quarterly,* 25 (December, 1963), 972.

indicates that party actives are more ideologically oriented than the public at large. The magnitude of this difference varies in time and place, however.

Some authors have suggested that it is external stimuli, more than SES or ideology, that make some people party leaders and keep others inactive.[39] Almost three-fourths of the local party officials thought the triggering mechanism of their involvement had been a situation where they were urged to seek or fill a local party position. Bowman and Boynton contend that those active in parties are not unlike many others in the community with similar socioeconomic backgrounds. Only a few are pushed over the threshold through the recruitment process, however. The more open the recruitment system, the larger the proportion of potential activists who are brought in.

INCENTIVES FOR PARTY INVOLVEMENT

Party actives are found to be higher SES, established members of the community, and only slightly more ideological than the general public. This still fails to explain why some people with these characteristics are motivated while the vast majority are not. Clark and Wilson have suggested that three types of incentives are available to organizations as inducements.[40] They hypothesize that the motivation to be active in political parties is supplied by some combination of the three.

Material Incentives. The first term that comes to mind when material incentives are noted is political patronage. Patronage is the provision of government jobs in return for party service and continued party support. Many times those individuals given jobs by the party leaders are expected to "kick back" a certain percentage to the party coffers. Patronage is most often identified with machine politics and is crucial to machine organizations. Although Civil Service reforms have eliminated many patronage positions, there is evidence that more exist than many assume (see Box 5.1).

Patronage is still an incentive for party work at the municipal and county levels, although paid patronage positions have declined. Even in patronage positions, parties have a less than efficient means of motivation, since the party seldom receives full support from patronage appointees except voluntarily. The restriction on higher level patronage jobs in the

[39] Lewis Bowman and G. R. Boynton, "Activities and Role Definitions of Grass Roots Party Officials," *Journal of Politics,* 28 (February, 1966), 121-43.

[40] Peter B. Clark and James Q. Wilson, "Incentive Systems: A Theory of Organization," *Administrative Science Quarterly,* 6 (September, 1961), 134-37.

BOX 5.1   PATRONAGE IS ALIVE AND WELL

A *New York Times* survey of city and state government in
New York concluded that patronage has vastly expanded in the
last several decades because of the tremendous growth of government, spiraling government spending, and the expansion of
government's discretionary powers to regulate, control, and supervise private industry. The same story reported that the annual
payroll in city jobs exempt from civil-service regulations, which
had been $10 million in the Wagner administration soared to
$32.8 million under Mayor Lindsay in poverty-program jobs alone.
During the first three years of Mayor Lindsay's regime the number of "provisional" employees increased from 1,500 to 12,800.
Under Mayor Wagner the City of New York also had 50,000
"noncompetitive" jobs; 24,000 more "noncompetitive" positions
were added after Lindsay took office. In the last year of the
Wagner administration the city let $8 million in consulting con-
tracts without competitive bidding. By 1969, the city's annual
expenditure for outside consultants had risen to $75 million, with
many indications that Lindsay was using these contracts as a form
of patronage. In addition to the jobs and contracts at his disposal,
the Mayor of New York also can wield tremendous patronage
power through his control of the municipal agencies that grant
zoning variances.

The patronage resources of the New York mayor's office are
not much greater than those of the Manhattan Surrogates' Court,
which does about $1 billion worth of estate work each year,
appointing attorneys to administer estates. These appointments,
which are often both undemanding and lucrative, generally are
made on the basis of political considerations. Other courts in New
York City name referees, trustees, guardians, and receivers in a
variety of situations. These appointments also are both rewarding
and politically determined. Trustees, in turn, decide where to bank
the funds for which they are responsible, and their power in this
respect constitutes another form of patronage if decisions are made
politically—as they seem to be.

Cities other than New Haven and New York have political
systems in which patronage plays a crucial part. Mayor Richard
Daley of Chicago is also chairman of the Cook County Democratic
Committee. These two positions together give him control of

132

about 35,000 patronage jobs. It is reported that Daley personally scrutinizes each job application. Since there are 3,412 voting precincts in Chicago, the Democratic organization can deploy an average of ten workers to each precinct just on the basis of job patronage.

... Over 8,000 state employees in Indiana owe their jobs to patronage and are assessed two percent of their salaries for the coffers of the ruling party's state committee.

SOURCE: Raymond E. Wolfinger, "Why Political Machines Have Not Withered Away and Other Revisionist Thoughts," *Journal of Politics,* 34 (May, 1972), 372-74.

national and state governments has resulted in a new emphasis on appointments to honorary governors' or presidential commissions. It is not unusual to see large party contributors rewarded with such appointments, though it is doubtful that the promise of such a position in itself would be incentive enough to elicit the contribution. Though job patronage is not uncommon, it appears unlikely that it is an important enough motivation to explain more than a small portion of party activity.

Another, less direct, incentive for being active in a party organization is the hope of a political career. Prior to the advent of direct primaries, when parties controlled the nominating process, party work was an effective and perhaps sole avenue to elective office. Parties controlled appointive offices as well as the nominations for elective offices. Once in office, elected officials kept party ties, since renomination could be refused by party leaders.

Under the direct primary system, reinforced by the emphasis on candidate organizations, the party's role in the nomination process has dwindled to one of relative weakness. Party connections and a lifetime of party work no longer guarantee a nomination. Many of the attractive and successful media-oriented candidates (see Chapter 13) bypass the party organization and appeal directly to the primary voters. Although some might be active in parties as a means to a career in politics, this alone cannot be considered an important material incentive.

Related to the incentive for a political career is social or economic mobility. Patronage may no longer be widespread, but some people are active in political parties because the contacts made and the publicity resulting from party work further their job or business. Lawyers, insurance men, and real estate brokers become active in party work because it offers them the chance of interaction with community influentials. The publicity resulting from party activity for these individuals is a valuable form of self-advertisement.

A final category of material incentives which potentially motivate certain persons to be active in party organizations might be grouped under a general heading of "preferments." There are billions of dollars of contracts offered by state and local governments each year. All governments buy millions of dollars in insurance and other services which are quite lucrative to those obtaining the contracts. It is very helpful to know ahead of time where a highway is going to be constructed, or to be able to have land rezoned for profit. Although many of these transactions are regulated—through the bidding required on government contracts, for example—favors are a part of political life. It is likely that contracts within political parties are helpful in getting privileged information and special attention not afforded those without such party contacts.

Other types of preferment include the distribution of liquor licenses, franchises to handle automobile licenses, safety inspection centers, etc.

> ... the Indiana method of issuing automobile and drivers licenses and automobile titles is unique. These matters are handled by a franchise system, rather like service stations or Kentucky Fried Chicken outlets. Local "license branches" are "awarded to the county chairman of the Governor's party, or the persons they designate." The branch pays the state party committee four cents for each license sold; otherwise, it retains all fees up to $10,000. Above that figure, half the take must be returned to the state Bureau of Motor Vehicles.[41]

Many times such preferments are controlled by the local politicians and party leaders. At a more personal level, fixing of traffic tickets and leniency in enforcing the law may be incentives for party work. Also, the frequency and quality of government services might be tied to party support. Not surprisingly, those sections of major cities that have the highest levels of support for the incumbent party also tend to have the most frequent garbage collection, the best police protection, and the clearest streets in the winter. Such incentives for party work, though much less direct than patronage, influence a larger proportion of party activists.

Solidary Incentives.   Solidary incentives refer to social and psychological satisfactions achieved through group membership. Such satisfactions are nonmaterial and relate instead to feelings of prestige, status, and social

---

[41] Raymond E. Wolfinger, "Why Political Machines Have Not Withered Away and Other Revisionist Thoughts," *Journal of Politics*, 34 (May, 1972), 374.

acceptance. Psychologists suggest that all individuals have a need for acceptance by a group. We all desire social approval and the feeling that we are being recognized for our achievements. According to James Q. Wilson, party activity is one easily accessible means of satisfying such a need. Due to the openness of party organizations:

> ... it is likely that the majority of persons who are active members of local party organizations seek neither material benefits nor the achievement of large ends, but merely find politics—or at least coming together to work at politics—intrinsically enjoyable.[42]

This was demonstrated by Detroit precinct leaders, among whom 75 percent of the Democrats and 55 percent of the Republican mentioned social contacts, fun, and the pleasure of being accepted by the group as the chief attractions of party work.[43] Table 5.5 contains comparative figures for New York county leaders.

Once accepted by a group, one's identification with the group intensifies if the association is psychologically satisfying. In addition, the social status and prestige acquired through party activity may serve to keep the member active. Bowman found that although parties can attract activists through purposive incentives, the continuance of activism depends on "the eventual positive orientation of the activist toward the party as a group and toward his position in the party."[44] Personal satisfaction, then, may not only explain why people become active, but also why they remain active despite the meager material benefits. Although more difficult to measure than material benefits such as patronage, contracts and favors, solidary benefits might be crucial to continued party activity. Especially in a period when material benefits are modest, these personal nonmaterial incentives help explain why some people are party actives.

Purposive Incentives.   Purposive incentives refer to ideological motivation for group activity. Although this is minimized in a system where political parties are win-centered, pragmatic organizations, some people join a party to express their ideology. In fact, a party at the local level might be more committed to certain ideological concerns than it is at the state and national

---

[42] James Q. Wilson, *Political Organizations* (New York: Basic Books, 1974), p. 110.

[43] Eldersveld, *Political Parties*, p. 278.

[44] Lewis Bowman, Dennis Ippolito, and William Donaldson, "Incentives for the Maintenance of Grassroots Political Activism," *Midwest Journal of Political Science*, 13 (February, 1969), p. 139.

Table 5.5 Reasons of New York County Committeemen for Interest in Politics

Reasons	Democrat Number	Democrat Percent	Republican Number	Republican Percent	Liberal Number	Liberal Percent
Desire to change community	67	29	25	10	23	43
Friends	27	12	14	11	3	6
Personality	21	9	11	9	7	13
Enjoy dealing with people	21	9	14	11	6	11
Family or relatives in politics	15	6	26	16	2	4
Make job and business contacts	10	4	6	5	2	4
Desire for prestige	7	3	0	0	1	2
Acquaintances on job	3	1	3	2	1	2
Influence of teacher	3	1	1	1	2	4
Other	22	10	15	12	4	6
No answer	38	16	14	11	2	4

SOURCE: Robert S. Hirshfield, Bert E. Swanson, and Blanche D. Blank, "A Profile of Political Activists in Manhattan," *Western Political Quarterly* 15 (September, 1962), 500.

Table 5.6   The Importance of Solidary, Purposive, and
Material Incentives by Area and Party

	Categories of Incentives (Grand Mean Score)*		
	Purposive	*Solidary*	*Material*
North Carolina Republicans	1.17	2.14	3.15
North Carolina Democrats	1.10	1.96	2.85
Massachusetts Republicans	1.21	2.15	3.39
Massachusetts Democrats	1.43	1.87	3.08
Total	1.18	2.01	3.12

*The possible ratings are: (1) "very important"; (2) "somewhat important"; (3) "not very important"; and (4) "not important at all." Thus, the higher the grant mean, the lower the incentive category in importance.

SOURCE: Reprinted from "Incentives for the Maintenance of Grassroots Political Activism," *Midwest Journal of Political Science,* 13 (1969), p. 133, by Lewis Bowman, Dennis Ippolito, and William Donaldson by permission of the Wayne State University Press.

levels. Table 5.6 illustrates that purposive incentives are viewed as most important by leaders in at least two states.

An additional dimension of purposive incentives refers to the well-being of the organization itself. Certain political actives, especially those from families with a tradition of party activity, see the continuance of the party as an end in itself. Their strong identification with the party blurs distinctions between their own purposive benefits and those of the party. Although many who say they are most concerned with the party itself perhaps misread their more selfish motivation, some may actually participate "for the good of the party."

IMPLICATIONS OF PARTY INCENTIVES

Several studies of party incentives have demonstrated their potential effects on the party organization. Margaret Conway and Frank Feigert found that task performance and perception of one's role in the party organization was related to the incentive sought in being active. They concluded that the most effective organization is one which is capable of providing a range of incentives. Only by providing a variety of incentives would a party maximize its effectiveness in performing both campaign and non-campaign tasks.[45]

[45] Conway and Feigert, "Incentives and Task Performance," p. 709.

Joseph Schlesinger contends that the type of incentive used affects the capacity of the party organization to make decisions and adapt to changing conditions.[46] He suggests that dependence on material incentives produces the greatest flexibility in defining goals and choosing strategy. Conversely, an organization utilizing largely social incentives is less flexible, since every decision will to some extent affect the motives of each of the participants. Finally, purposive incentives introduce rigidity in organizational goals. Emphasis on ideologies or issues tends to create conflict over what the goals should be, and is potentially divisive.

Although material benefits are still an incentive for party activity for some, solidary and purposive incentives have increased. Meeting social and psychological needs and fulfilling ideological or issue-oriented objectives appear to be necessary incentives for most local parties. The shift away from material incentives has brought an increased commitment to the value of participation. Whether this commitment stems from concern over issues or an increasing need for social approval is not clear. In any case, the parties cannot rely on any single type of incentive as they did in the days of patronage and social service. In order to obtain and maintain active members, they must emphasize the solidary and purposive goals.

CHALLENGES TO FORMAL
PARTY ORGANIZATION

While there is evidence that material incentives are available to a limited extent, most emphasis has shifted toward solidary and purposive benefits. This shift means that the parties must compete much more vigorously with many nonparty organizations which supply similar incentives. Solidary incentives are available from a host of nonparty clubs and voluntary associations at a lesser cost to the prospective member. As long as parties controlled patronage and other material rewards, they had the advantage. With the movement toward solidary and purposive incentive systems, however, this monopoly has been lost. Parties now find themselves struggling to maintain support primarily through ideological or purposive channels. Even here, however, they face a challenge from a variety of other organizations such as candidate organizations, political clubs, and ad hoc issue-oriented groups which are also vying for the 2 to 3 percent of the electorate that is active in politics.

[46] Joseph A. Schlesinger, "Political Party Organization," in *Handbook of Organizations*, ed. James G. March (Chicago: Rand McNally, 1965), p. 770.

In addition to the formal/legal party committees, there are many semi-official groups designed to serve party members. Although lacking legal recognition in the state statutes, at times they speak for segments of the party. Some of these operate under the sponsorship of the party, while others emerge from party inaction. The very existence of these alternative groups indicates the parties' difficulty in satisfying all purposive and solidary demands. These groups may be formed by party members who desire a certain ideological or policy orientation, who are dissatisfied with the regular party organization, or who have personal ambitions that are frustrated by the formal party committees.

PARTY CREATED GROUPS

Both major parties have created a series of auxiliaries at all levels. Women's organizations have been sponsored by parties to raise money, to sponsor educational and social events, and to seek the active support of women. Although women's auxiliaries appeared to peak in number and enthusiasm in the 1950s and 1960s, many local and state groups remain active. In general, these women's groups take stands corresponding to that of the parent body.

A more visible and less compliant auxiliary is the youth group. Young Republican and Democratic clubs are organized from the national level to the precinct level. These youth groups tend to be oriented toward purposive incentives, especially ideological ones. At times they have taken stands at odds with the parent organization, thereby causing it embarassment. Since the senior organizations began absorbing youth into the regular organizations in the late 1960s, the Young Republican and Democrats have had difficulty in retaining their membership. They also have faced challenges from nonparty ideological groups in which there are no constraints imposed by formal party leaders.

NONPARTY ALTERNATIVES

In some urban areas, ward or district clubs have been formed to provide a club-style membership for political activists interested in an issue orientation not found in the formal party committees. The most famous of these clubs are found in New York City. Many times the clubs serve the personal ambitions of an assembly or ward leader. They tend to be dominated by educated, middle-class activists generally committed to liberal policy and ideological orientations. They serve as an alternative purposive organization. Past patterns, however, indicate that these clubs need an urban environment to be successful.

Similar to the clubs, though more numerous, are the ideological groups, most commonly a liberal or conservative response to the regular party organization. They are generally dissatisfied with the party committee's preoccupation with winning elections, and emphasize ideological concerns and issues instead. The Democrats of Texas Club, for instance, holds its own state convention and supports various liberal programs and candidates. In Wisconsin, voluntary organizations, originally created to represent ideological stands of both parties, have actually replaced the regular party committees. In 1974, the Wisconsin legislature abolished the statutory committees and vested all legal powers in the voluntary organizations.

The most researched of all alternative organizations are the California clubs.[47] In 1934, the California Republican Assembly was founded by party members who were unhappy with the conservative leadership of the party. In 1964, the conservative United Republicans of California gained control of the original club. On the Democratic side, the California Democratic Council was formed in 1953 to strengthen the party and provide liberal alternatives. These clubs provide continual educational programs and social functions and serve as viable alternatives to the regular party organization. California clubs, like those in New York and Wisconsin, overrepresent the middle-class business and professional people. In addition to offering program alternatives, these clubs participate in preprimary endorsement of party candidates. By supporting slates of candidates in the primaries, they occasionally succeed in controlling the nominating processes of their parties.

CANDIDATE ORGANIZATION

In Chapter 1 it was argued that what looks like conscious, continuous, goal-oriented efforts by a structured organization are illusions. Parties are primarily coalitions of nuclear candidate groups. The formal/legal organizations created by state laws play only minor roles. Mostly they serve as a means of pooling individuals and groups under an electoral label. Nothing in the present chapter rejects this conception. In examining the statutory organizations for structure, membership, leadership, and activities, it is obvious that party units, with very few exceptions, are loose coalitions of actives with diverse incentives and objectives.

The statutory parties, although never consistently strong, today are weaker than in the past. Although part of their weakness can be blamed on electoral reforms, especially direct primaries, and on administrative reforms

[47] See Robert L. Morlan and Leroy C. Hardy, *Politics in California* (Belmont: Dickenson, 1968), pp. 26-32 for a good summary.

such as the civil service system, the development of candidate-centered campaigns and the shift toward purposive incentives have had a devastating impact on party organization. Virtually all candidates for elective office, from the national to the local levels, establish their own campaign organizations.[48] These autonomous groups compete with the party organization for the support of the small proportion of political activities in the electorate. Since the parties have lost their advantages of patronage and ability to control the nomination process, the incentives for working within the formal party structure are not strong. The mistaken emphasis on media-oriented campaigns has reduced the use of volunteer precinct workers. It is the independent candidate organizations which mobilize and persuade voters in practice as parties do in theory, although the independents seldom participate in service activities and do not have to sustain a permanent organization.

Nuclear organizations are formed and abolished as candidates come and go. The activity of such groups is cyclical, peaking during the campaign and then lapsing into inactivity until the next election. While some of the nuclear group leaders might also be formal organizational leaders, it is more likely that they will not be active in the party. It is possible that the candidate-organization leaders might be in conflict with the party regulars. In other words, while the functioning parties can be seen as a loose coalition of regular party leaders, political clubs, and ad hoc issue-oriented or candidate-oriented groups, as well as various types of ideological groupings, these elements might be at odds with each other. When viewed from this perspective, it is not surprising that party organization at the state and local levels appears weak and vacillating. Although parties as electoral organizations vary in structure as well as function from state to state and locale to locale, they tend to be minimally effective, shifting alliances of activists. If the statutory party organizations ever dominated the electoral process, they no longer do so. This will be illustrated more fully in Chapter 11, by examining the nomination process.

STATE AND LOCAL PARTY ORGANIZATION: A SUMMARY

Fundamentally, the U.S. party system is most meaningfully examined at the local level. It is at the precinct and county levels, not the state or national, where individual citizen participation occurs. Leadership comes from the bottom up in what Eldersveld terms a "stratarchical" organization. Precinct committeemen most often select county leaders, county leaders choose

[48] See Chapter 13 for more details.

state leaders, etc. The state party organization is most accurately seen as a loose coalition of local leaders, to whom it is responsible. Both during campaigns and between them, most activity is centered at the local level. Although there is evidence of attempts to revitalize the state parties and centralize many party activities, they continue to hold little autonomous power. Although they function within the framework established by the individual states, the local organizations are at the core of our party system.

Even the local units, however, are nothing but loose coalitions of the formal/legal organization components, allied auxiliary and nonparty political groups, and candidate-centered organizations. Various nuclei interact and, for a period of time, they constitute the party. The composition of the parties, therefore, shifts over time and is in no way fixed. Joseph Schlesinger suggests that one reason for this looseness is that nuclear organizations go through "recurring phases" that require cooperation with other nuclear organizations in varying degrees.[49] The weakness of the state and local electoral organizations poses a related question. What conditions surround the national party organization? If state and local parties are supposed to be the strongest party units and they are found to be lacking, where does that place the national parties? Chapter 6 looks specifically at national party organization in the U.S.

[49] Schlesinger, "Political Party Organization," p. 786.

6

National
Party
Organization

The last chapter illustrated the decentralized nature of state and local parties. The overall impression is one of lack of clear purpose, weak leadership, amorphous membership, and minimal activities. The formal/legal parties realistically give way to the ad hoc coalition of candidate organizations or nuclei. It might be expected that, although disorganization is a common feature of state and local political units, the national parties, with their party headquarters, professional staffs, multimillion dollar budgets, and national party chairmen, would maintain control, or at least act as coordinators of state and local parties. Perhaps power does reside in the point of the pyramid after all?

Nothing could be further from the reality of the situation. The decentralization of American parties is reflected most clearly in the weak national committees. Despite the vestiges of hierarchical organization (national committee, executive committee, chairman, professional staff), the national party exists in name and shape only, devoid of substance. It has been suggested that the national committees are nothing but shadow committees. They have been referred to as "anachronisms, deadwood, and gigantic frauds" by leaders of both parties.[1] Cotter and Hennessy describe the activities of the national committees as "politics without power."[2] This should not be surprising, since the national level of party organization, more than any other level, is a product of the federal, decentralized nature of the American political system. The vast number of elective offices are state and local, not national. State and local recruitment, nominations, and campaigns are not

[1] John S. Saloma III and Frederick H. Sontag, *Parties: The Real Opportunity for Effective Citizen Politics* (New York: Random House, 1972), p. 92.

[2] Cornelius P. Cotter and Bernard C. Hennessy, *Politics Without Power* (New York: Atherton Press, 1964).

145

easily elevated to the national level. The variation of state statutes of defining parties and regulating elections guarantees a diversity that has frustrated many efforts at strengthening the national party. Although the absence of statutory or constitutional proscriptions concerning the national organization allows it to develop without legal limits, this situation also has meant that it lacks any legal power base. More than any other level of party organization, the national parties mirror the environment within which they have evolved. They have no legal disciplinary powers or sanctions and no power to control or even influence the nominations of the vast majority of candidates in the U.S. Most surprising, perhaps, is their lack of control over the selection of congressional offices. In effect, they are concerned with and have influence over only one office in the nation—the presidency. Even here their involvement is minimal and their power negligible.

Despite the limited power of the national party organizations and the accuracy of the criticisms leveled at them, there have recently been manifestations of increased activity and initiative in those bodies. The national organizations of the 1970s, though weak and disabled, are attempting to shape their future more than at any previous time. Although they find it difficult to bargain from their respective power vacuums, there is evidence of attempts to reformulate and solidify their positions. In a perhaps futile attempt, they are trying to exert greater influence over the selection of presidential nominees and to extend this influence to other offices. In this attempt, the national organization faces formidable cross pressures from both the states and from Congress.

If the national party exists at all, it exists in the national convention held every four years. For those three or four days, a coalition made up of various state organizations, presidential candidate supporters, and a vast array of ad hoc groups, constitutes the party. It was early understood, however, that the national convention had serious drawbacks as a party organization. Even the most primitive organization requires continuity over time. Figure 6.1 illustrates the failure of conventions to meet this need. It is impossible to consider the convention as anything other than what it is—a grouping of various interests for a very short period of time.

In order to provide continuity between conventions, national committees were established. Selected at one convention, they would serve until the next. In addition to other tasks, to be discussed later, they would plan the

Figure 6.1   Convention as Party

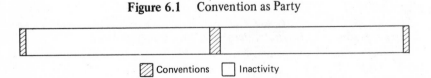

◪ Conventions   ☐ Inactivity

Figure 6.2   National Committe as Party

subsequent convention. Since these committees were composed of unpaid members from across the U.S., they could meet (especially prior to the jet age) at most once or twice a year. This meant that even this interim decision-making group was unable to exert a continuous influence over party matters (see Figure 6.2). While the committees lent the national conventions permanence in theory, they failed to provide continuous direction and administration of party responsibilities.

In response to the need for an ongoing administrative unit to carry out day to day party business and oversee planning for subsequent conventions, party headquarters evolved. Professional staff members were hired to serve as the permanent nucleus of the national organization. Chosen to head this party bureaucracy was the national chairman, for some, the symbol of the national party. Thus the party headquarters, the budget, and the air of a national organization developed. This chapter will examine in more detail the structural elements of the national party organizations. While they are much less effective than they at first appear, they are all we have to work with.

THE NATIONAL COMMITTEE

Theoretically, the national committees are designed to frame national party policy and programs, carry out the mandates of the national convention, manage the presidential campaign, and elect a national chairman. In practice they do little but ratify or legitimize the actions of the chairman and staff. Committee members are not able to exercise any significant control over the national headquarters, since they generally are unfamiliar with its details and meet only several times a year. Actually, the national committees never have exhibited identifiable and definable being, and in some ways are "non-things."[3] Although they have existed in fundamentally the same form for over a century, the national party committees remain enigmas.

As stated earlier, the national committee arose out of a need for a continuing body to serve as a link from one convention to the next. As such, it

[3] *Ibid.*, p. 11.

147

was consciously restricted in the scope of its authority. The Democratic committee was first established in 1848 by this motion of the National Convention:

> Ordered, that a committee of one from each state, to be named by the respective delegations, be appointed to promote the Democratic cause, with power to fill vacancies and to be designated "the Democratic National Committee."[4]

Prior to this, interstate presidential campaign committees and committees of correspondence had served as informal links among state party leaders. With this 1848 Democratic action, the National Committee was formalized. The federal nature of the DNC was reflected clearly in the equal representation it granted the states and the states' control over the selection of members. In 1856 the Republicans followed suit by establishing a similar national committee, composed of one member from each state. It, too, had the major function of deciding where the next convention would be held, but little additional authority. Both committees were to serve from adjournment of one convention to adjournment of the succeeding convention, at which time they would be dissolved and new committees created.

COMPOSITION OF NATIONAL COMMITTEES

The national committees of both parties until 1920 were composed of one man from each state. With ratification of the 19th Amendment, equal representation of the states, as well as of the sexes, was preserved by simply adding one woman from each state. In 1952, in an attempt to reward party support, the Republicans awarded states and territories an extra member, a state chairman, if one of three conditions was met. The conditions were that: (1) the state had voted for the Republican presidential candidate in the previous election, (2) the state had a Republican governor, or (3) the majority of the state's congressional delegation was Republican. This resulted in a maximum membership of 162 members. Since these provisions for state chairman inclusion are so broad, there has been little evidence of rewarding party support and the RNC has had about 140-160 members. Equality of the states was largely maintained despite the expansion in size.

The most sweeping change in national committee composition was made at the 1972 Democratic convention. In the midst of a movement for representation of various components of the party, the federation aspect of the DNC was discarded and additional weight was given to the distribution

[4]*Ibid.*, p. 14

of party support and population. States were no longer given equal representation, despite great variation in size of population and extent of party support. The reconstituted national committee in 1972 took the following form:

1. Chairperson and next ranking officer of the opposite sex from each state, D.C., and Puerto Rico (104).
2. Additional members apportioned on the same basis as delegates to the national convention (200).
3. Chairman of Democratic Governors Conference and two additional governors (3).
4. Democratic leader and one additional person from each house of Congress (4).
5. Chairman of Democratic Mayors Conference and two additional mayors (3).
6. President and two additional members of the Young Democrats (3).
7. Additional members, not to exceed 25, to be added to provide balanced representation of minorities (0-25).

The total membership of the DNC ranges from 317 to 342. Although this size provides more opportunities for participation, it has resulted in an even less manageable decision-making body. Its size and composition preclude any actual deliberation and control over party affairs.

Selection of Members. Both parties allow the state organizations to select national committee members, though each is attempting to increase supervision of the process. In all but a few cases, the states have attempted to retain as much control over their selection processes as possible. Therefore, only a handful of parties use the primaries for selection. The most common means of selection is at the state party convention. Approximately 20 of the Democratic state parties and half of the Republican parties elect their national committeemen and committeewomen at the state convention. Other means in order of use include selection by: (1) the state party delegation to the national convention and (2) the state central committee.

Characteristics of Members. No matter how they are selected, the national committee members tend to be of higher socioeconomic status than the average citizen. Cotter and Hennessy found that over 60 percent of the members between 1948-1963 had a college degree.[5] Over 40 percent of

[5] *Ibid.*, pp. 47-48.

the committeemen appear to be lawyers, while committeewomen reflect a balance between housewives and career women. Other professional and executive occupations also are overrepresented. Committee members tend to be middle-aged (40-60), with less than 10 percent under 35 years of age. Democrat members are fairly representative of the major religions, while Republicans heavily overrepresent Protestants.

Most significant of all characteristics of committee members is that almost 90 percent held party or elected office before their selection. This implies that many were chosen because they were already important in their state parties. Their power bases were established prior to selection. The age of many also indicates that in some cases, selection was a reward for faithful party service. Many appear to have made the right political connections, especially friendships with governors.[6]

A final characteristic of national committee members is that they have the time, as well as the money, needed for the job. Since most committee members not only must pay their own expenses in attending meetings and conventions, but also are expected to contribute to campaign funds and attend party functions, most members are well-off financially. This monetary factor is probably less important now than in the past, since money is available to minority members and partial or full funding is sometimes provided by state central committees. Time, perhaps, is more crucial. National committee members must be able to take time off from their regular jobs, without remuneration, to attend committee functions. It is not surprising under these circumstances that committee members tend to be the more well established and professionally oriented of state party members.

LIMITED ROLE OF NATIONAL COMMITTEES

According to the Democratic party charter, the DNC shall meet at least once a year at the call of the national chairman, the executive committee, or the request of at least one-quarter of its members.[7] Similarly, the Republican party rules stipulate that the full RNC shall meet at least twice a year.[8] Each committee is given responsibility, among other things, for issuing the call for the next convention, formulating and disseminating statements of party policy, conducting the campaign of the party's presidential candidate, and electing or appointing the various officers of the committee. Quite an imposing list of duties for a group that meets so infrequently.

[6] *Ibid.*, p. 54.

[7] *Charter of the Democratic Party of the United States* (December 7, 1974), Art. 3, Sec. 5.

[8] *Rules*, Adopted by the 1976 Republican National Convention (August 17, 1976), Rule 28.

Despite the institutionalized character of the national committees and their many formal roles, neither the RNC or DNC exerts control over the national party. According to Hugh Bone, "The committee members themselves are hardly able to exercise any significant control over the chairman or the general headquarters staff."[9] National committee members have no actual role in planning party strategy, formulating party issue positions, or overseeing internal party affairs. Little information is transmitted from party headquarters staff to national committee members at their infrequent meetings. Although members are expected to attend national committee meetings at their own expense or that of their state party, little of substance is accomplished. Much time at these meetings is spent listening to introductory remarks by party and congressional leaders, sitting through lengthy introductions of new members, and attending receptions.

Committee members are seldom given detailed information concerning what is going on within the party headquarters. No financial statements or budgets are made available to the members, nor are these matters open for discussion. One often-cited example of the secrecy surrounding party finance is the successful concealment of a $4.1 million debt of the DNC from 1964 to 1966 from the DNC members as well as most Democratic party leaders. Campaign funds and services also are distributed without committee knowledge or approval. Contrary to the formal responsibilities of the national committees, as stated in party documents and by tradition, there is little if any leadership accountability to the committee members. The committee members' role appears to be limited to some involvement in planning the convention through membership on various subcommittees.[10] Surprisingly, there has never been a major attempt by either national committee to force the issue and gain control. The nature of the members and their infrequent contact with each other reinforce their passive acceptance of decisions made by the staff.

One reason always cited for minimal committee influence is that they meet so infrequently and for such short intervals that it is impossible for them to be informed on all the issues. Although this rationale is justified to a point, the party headquarters have made few attempts to inform the members more fully. Neither party, for instance, distributes informative materials about internal party matters to members. The official publications of both parties tend to be composed of party propaganda, generally giving the impression of

[9] Hugh A. Bone, *Party Committees and National Politics* (Seattle: University of Washington Press, 1958), p. 8.

[10] Charles O. Jones, *The Republican Party in American Politics* (New York: The MacMillan Company, 1965), p. 28, discusses the distribution of convention patronage such as Pages, Sergeant at Arms, and so forth, to each state's representative on the Committee on arrangements.

a hardworking, effective, and centralized party bureaucracy. Newsletters tend to be written to glamorize headquarters activities and rally support for the national chairman. *First Monday,* the official publication of the RNC, is a professionally done and colorful monthly, but it contains virtually no material on the conduct of business of the RNC.

EXECUTIVE COMMITTEES

To overcome the limitations of the full membership, both national committees have created executive committees that are selected at the first organizational meeting after each convention. Members of the executive committees serve at the pleasure of the full committee and in theory carry out the executive as well as administrative functions of the national committee between meetings. The Republican executive committee numbers 15 and the Democratic normally 11. Supposedly, the small size of these executive groups enables the national chairman to have more frequent meetings with them and consult on a more continuous basis than is possible with the full committees. Both parties specify that the executive committees must meet at least four times annually.[11] Despite these provisions, it appears that these bodies have little actual decision-making power and are seldom consulted by the party chairmen.

NATIONAL PARTY EXECUTIVES

The national party chairman well illustrates the ambivalent nature of American parties. While the potential responsibilities of the national chairman are broad, they are intentionally ill-defined. The chairman must respond to many elements in the party and attempt to reconcile differences among presidential, state, and congressional influences. In addition, the chairman must satisfy campaign contributors, leaders of auxiliary party organizations, and leaders of potential support groups.

The rules of both national parties provide for a national chairman.[12] Only recently have chairmanships been made full-time, paid positions. They are elected at the first meeting after the convention. Republican chairmen

[11] See *Democratic Charter,* Article 4 and Republican *Rules,* Rule 26 for more details on the composition of the executive committees.

[12] The DNC uses the term "chairperson" while the RNC retains "chairman." National chairman is used exclusively here solely for readability purposes.

serve a two-year term of office and Democrats serves until the next convention. Though the fact is not stated in any party documents, party chairmen serve at the pleasure of the president or presidential candidate. Formally, they can be removed by the national committee at any time, though in practice the national committee seldom takes that step. The Democrats require a majority vote for removal, while the Republicans require a two-thirds majority.

ROLES OF PARTY CHAIRMEN

The ideal chairman, according to Cotter and Hennessey, must among other things be (1) an image-maker, (2) a hell-raiser, (3) a fund-raiser, (4) a campaign manager, and (5) an administrator of the national headquarters.[13] He should be able to coordinate the public relations efforts of the disparate groups that use the party label, while at the same time avoiding issues. "His hope is to make the audience identify or empathize with his cause by appealing to symbols with emotional content."[14] His public relations role for the general public must be carefully balanced with a continuous, open, and "unremittingly partisan" stance among the party faithful. The chairman must be able to generate enthusiasm and sharpen the issues among party loyalists. In addition, the chairman is expected to give direction and general supervision to the staff of the national headquarters, help coordinate fund-raising efforts, and less frequently, serve as campaign manager.

In reality the chairman has few resources available for achieving these goals. Time especially is limited for the part-time chairman. Authority is also a limited quantity for most national chairmen. It appears that recent chairmen have devoted more effort to public relations and building internal party unity and less to fund raising and campaign management. Fund raising has become increasingly specialized and monopolized by the the presidential campaign organizations. Similarly, the chairmen's role in the presidential campaign has become minimal at best.

> The generalization seems to be that, when a new chairman is chosen after the convention, without having been part of the nominee's pre-convention team, he is not likely to be given any campaign leadership role.[15]

[13] Cotter and Hennessy, *Politics Without Power*, pp. 67-106.

[14] *Ibid.*, p. 69.

[15] *Ibid.*, p. 74.

Since candidate organizations develop well before the convention, without the involvement of the national party leaders, the national chairman usually has a minimal role and frequently is chosen with that condition in mind. The actual role of the chairman in the campaign, of course, depends solely on his relation with the presidential nominee.

SELECTION AND CHARACTERISTICS

Who are these chairmen and how are they selected? The data on recent chairmen in Table 6.1 indicate that there is no one road to the chairmanship. There is a fairly equal balance among congressmen, state party leaders, and others. Although some chairmen have been wealthy, more commonly they are of modest income in law or business. They might be the choice of the presidential candidate, the dominant party faction, or in some cases a compromise choice. It is not known how many potential chairmen are "unavailable" (see Box 6.1), but the job is demanding and generally offers few rewards.

The selection process varies most according to whether or not the party holds the presidency. A recent example will serve to illustrate this distinction. In 1977, the Democrats selected a chairman to replace Robert Strauss, who was stepping down after an unusually long tenure of over four years. Although Kenneth Curtis was not well known by most members of the DNC, he was elected by acclamation. Why was he unopposed? The answer is simply that he was President Carter's choice. He had been an early supporter of Carter and it was made known that the President desired his service. As always, the President received his choice.

On the other hand, the Republicans had lost the presidency after a bitterly fought primary contest between Ford and Reagan. After the loss the seated chairperson resigned, as usual, leaving the position open. Unlike the winning Democrats, the Republicans contested their chair. On the third ballot a compromise candidate, William Brock, was selected by a 90 to 46 vote. He immediately was able to take the initiative in party matters and became an outspoken critic of the Democratic administration. Meanwhile Curtis, chosen without opposition, faded into the background, as is expected when the party controls the White House.

Although the context within which the national chairman must function largely defines his role, his tenure tends to be extremely abbreviated. Perhaps because there are so many people and groups to be pleased, the average tenure is less than two and a half years. This is not sufficient time to become proficient in a job of this scope. It is not surprising, therefore, that most chairmen are less than successful in gaining an independent base of

Table 6.1 National Party Chairmen, 1950-1979

Name	Tenure	Prior Position
Republicans		
Guy G. Gabrielson	1949-52	State Speaker of House
Arthur Summerfield	1952-53	Eisenhower Campaign Manager
C. Wesley Roberts	1953	State Party Chairman
Leonard W. Hall	1953-57	U.S. Representative
H. Meade Alcorn, Jr.	1957-59	State Party Leader
Thurston B. Morton	1959-61	U.S. Senator
William E. Miller	1961-64	U.S. Representative
Dean Burch	1964-65	Goldwater Campaign Organizer
Ray Bliss	1965-69	State Party Chairman
Roger C. Morton	1969-71	U.S. Representative
Robert J. Dole	1971-73	U.S. Senator
George Bush	1973-74	U.S. Ambassador to U.N.
Mary Louise Smith	1974-77	Co-Chairman RNC
William Brock	1977-	Defeated Senator

Mean tenure: 2.0 years

Name	Tenure	Prior Position
Democrats		
William M. Boyle	1949-51	DNC Executive Vice-Chairman
Frank E. McKinney	1951-52	State Party Leader
Stephen A. Mitchell	1952-54	Stevenson Supporter
Paul M. Butler	1955-60	National Committeeman
Henry M. Jackson	1960-61	U.S. Senator
John M. Bailey	1961-68	State Party Chairman
Lawrence F. O'Brien	1968-69	U.S. Postmaster General
Fred R. Harris	1969-70	U.S. Senator
Lawrence F. O'Brien	1970-72	Former DNC Chairman
Jean Westwood	1972	McGovern Campaign Organizer
Robert Strauss	1972-77	DNC Treasurer
Kenneth M. Curtis	1977-78	Former Governor
John White	1978	Deputy Agriculture Secretary

Mean tenure: 2.2 years

power. They remain totally dependent on the wishes of presidential nominees, as well as those of various factions within the party. Their ability to initiate and carry out new programs also suffers from the uncertainty of their position. Although party chairmen are generally the most dominant and visible persons in the national party organization, they do in fact practice "politics without power."

BOX 6.1   DRAFTING A PARTY CHAIRMAN

As 1970 began, I was busy with O'Brien Associates and with work on this book. Then, early in February, Senator Fred Harris resigned as chairman of the Democratic National Committee and I found myself under intense pressures to replace him.

The unsalaried post of national chairman was not, to be sure, much of a plum at that point. Our party was divided and deeply in debt. I had been surprised when Fred Harris sought the post a year earlier. He apparently hoped the chairmanship would work to his political advantage by giving him national visibility, but instead his increasing association with the liberal wing of the Democratic Party was giving him political problems back in Oklahoma.

A number of reporters called me on the day Harris announced his resignation and I told them all that I was not the least interested in the job. Hubert Humphrey called me a few days later and said that as the party's titular leader he felt a responsibility to recommend a new chairman to the National Committee, whose members were to meet within thirty days to elect a replacement for Harris. Humphrey asked me to refrain from flatly ruling out the possibility until we had time to talk in person.

I agreed to do so, but I made it clear to him that I was not a candidate. However, in the days ahead, pressures continued to build. Humphrey called to report that Bob Strauss, a Dallas lawyer and Texas national committeeman, had agreed to become the party's treasurer if I became chairman. I commented that any man who would become the treasurer of a party that was over nine million dollars in debt was obviously a good Democrat.

Humphrey and I met in Washington and he told me he had been in touch with party leaders around the country and there was a consensus that I was the man for the job. I replied that I doubted if any real consensus existed, since, for example, I'd heard that George Meany, head of the AFL-CIO, was cool toward my return.

"Let's just see about that," Hubert responded and immediately called Meany, who told him he could be comfortable with me as chairman. . . .

But I decided I could not do it and, after advising Humphrey, I made a public statement that I was not a candidate.

I assumed the matter was closed. However, after the executive committee of the National Committee began its deliberations, I received a call from the chairman, Colonel Jake Arvey, a close friend of mine and the long-time Democratic leader in Chicago, who

156

announced that the executive committee had unanimously drafted me. "We don't want any response from you now," he said. "Just think about it." While I thought about it, there was a call from Humphrey and I filled him in on what was taking place. He was highly amused and pleased. "We've got you on the spot now," he said.

I began to be swayed by the mounting pressures. Finally, I said I would accept the draft of the executive committee if it was backed up by similar approval of the full National Committee. Eventually Arvey and other party leaders persuaded the active announced contenders not to enter the race so that my selection would be unanimous. Given that on-the-record support from the National Committee, I accepted the chairmanship.

Some reporters wrote that I had engineered a brilliant political coup to obtain this unanimous draft. That wasn't true. I did not seek the job and I accepted only when old friends in the party persuaded me.

SOURCE: Excerpt from *No Final Victories,* copyright © 1974 by Lawrence F. O'Brien. Used by permission of Doubleday and Company, Inc., pp. 271-73.

NATIONAL PARTY HEADQUARTERS

The bylaws of each party designate other officers of the national committee, in addition to the national chairman. Both parties require co- or vice-chairmen and have sex qualifications for filling them. The co-chairman of the RNC is elected simultaneously with the chairman and must be of the opposite sex. Also, the Republicans select one man and one woman vice-chairman from each of four regions. The Democrats have one male and one female vice-chairman. The parties also provide for the election of a party treasurer and a secretary. Terms of office are two years for the Republicans and four years for the Democrats.

Both national chairmen have rather broad appointive powers, though most must be ratified by the committee. The RNC chairman, for instance, appoints a general counsel, a finance chairman, and a series of committees composed of national committee members. The Site, Call, Arrangements, Rules, and Contest committees all must be organized at least two years prior to each convention. Each RNC member is on one of these committees. In response to problems arising out of Watergate, the Republicans in 1976 established the Select Committee on Presidential Campaign Affairs. Composed of the chairman and treasurer, along with five additional RNC

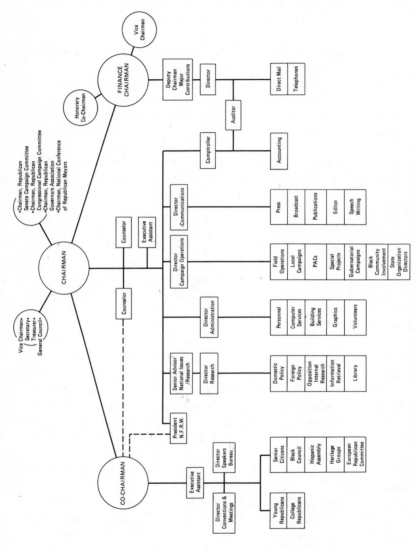

Figure 6.3 Organizational Chart: Republican National Committee

158

members, this committee is responsible for preserving and protecting the integrity of the presidential election process, especially in regard to campaign expenditures. Each Republican candidate for the president must agree in writing to this rule prior to nomination.

At the center of the national party organization is the headquarters staff. A staff of professionals is hired under the supervision of the national chairman to run the day to day activities of each party. While the number varies greatly, usually there are between 75 and 150 paid employees at the headquarters of each party. During presidential campaign years, this number tends to triple. The composition of the staff ranges from high-paid professionals to clerical workers and interns. An executive director is hired by the chairman to coordinate activities and supervise the staff.

The organizational chart in Figure 6.3 illustrates the multitude of elements that constitute the national headquarters. Each division is semi-autonomous and is responsible for specific activities. Both parties have research divisions which conduct polls, analyze voting data, and provide research services to state parties. Other divisions focus on specific constituencies such as women, ethnic minorities, or senior citizens, or handle technical matters such as public relations, patronage, and publications. The director of each division is appointed by the national chairman, as are the chairman's personal advisors on legal, political, and financial matters.

In addition to the various elements of the national party headquarters are many satellite organizations which cluster around the national committee. These include the Young Democrat and Republican clubs, the Federations of Women, the Governors' Associations of the respective parties, and a multitude of regional organizations composed of state party leaders. Ideological satellite groups such as the Ripon Society (liberal Republican) and the Americans for Democratic Action (Democrats) exist outside the national committee and frequently are vocal critics of party organization leadership. In some cases these groups have been created because the national committee has not been responsive to their desires. For instance, the Young Americans for Freedom (YAF) was established in the early 1960s as a conservative rival to the Young Republicans Federaton. These satellite organizations continue to operate on the fringes of the formal national party structure, adding yet another dimension of fragmentation to the national parties.

PARTY POLICY COUNCILS

Both national parties have made attempts to create bodies to provide policy statements. Interestingly, these have been relatively recent phenomena. Prior to 1920, neither party established policy-making bodies. The efforts of the RNC between 1920 and 1944 resulted in the creation of three advisory committees, all directed toward the platform, however. In 1962, under the initiative of Eisenhower, who expressed more interest in the party after he left office, the National Republican Citizens Committee was formed to provide policy alternatives to the Democratic Administration.[16] This initial attempt at party policy making failed when Goldwater won the 1964 nomination. Significantly, no sitting members of the RNC or congressmen were included on the Citizens Committee.

After the disastrous results of the 1964 election were tallied, the RNC, under the Chairmanship of Ray Bliss, created another policy committee. The Republican Coordinating Committee (RCC) was formed to promote party unity and provide a broadly based representative leadership group which would speak for the party on major issues. Between 1965 and 1968 this committee established working task forces that published almost 75 position papers and statements on a wide range of issues.[17] Many of these recommendations were included in the 1968 Republican platform. After the Nixon victory, however, the RCC faded and was dismantled by the Nixon organization. It was not until 1977, after losing the presidency, that the Republicans again established a policy council. At the recommendation of Gerald Ford, a new coordinating committee was created.

The first attempt of the Democrats to provide a party forum for policy making was the Democratic Advisory Countil (DAC), created after Adlai Stevenson's defeat in 1956. Its functions were to enhance the image of the party by focusing on issues and to provide clear opposition to the policies of Eisenhower. Although the DAC met only two to three times a year, it created ten working committees that published over 60 policy statements between 1957 and 1959. While the DAC was a more successful fundraiser than the DNC, it failed, largely because most congressional leaders refused to recognize it, and because its liberal orientation was opposed by southern conservatives. The final blow to the DAC was Kennedy's victory. His organization absorbed many elements of the council and it died of uselessness.[18] There is no place for an alternative party voice to that of the president. Party Chairman Bailey's eulogy for the DAC stated that while it had served a function when the party did not control the presidency, after winning the office, "policy should be made at the White House and by the leadership of Congress."[19]

[16] Cotter and Hennessy, *Politics Without Power*, pp. 204-210.

[17] See *Choice for America: Republican Answers to the Challenge of Now* (Washington, D.C.: RNC, July, 1968), for a 500 page summary of the separate reports.

[18] Cotter and Hennessy, *Politics Without Power*, p. 222.

[19] John D. Morris, "Democrats End Advisory Council," *New York Times,* March 12, 1961, sec. 1, p. 1.

In 1969, the Democratic Policy Council (DPC) was established by the national committee to make statements on national issues. Its chairman, Hubert Humphrey, stated that the major assignment of the DPC was "to build a winning agenda of Democratic issues for the 1970s."[20] To this end, 66 nationally prominent leaders were asked to serve on the council. From the start, it faced opposition from congressional leaders, who saw it as competition, and from the defeated forces of McCarthy and Kennedy, who were suspicious of its moderate policy orientation. Although Humphrey offered many pronouncements in his position as chairman and some policy work was accomplished, the divisions within the Democratic party in the early 1970s minimized the role of the DPC.

One unmistakable pattern in all these attempts at creating policy councils is their demise immediately upon winning the presidency. The DAC died when Kennedy won in 1960. The RCC likewise was dismantled when Nixon won in 1968, while the DPC had little role after Carter's victory. The irony of this situation is that at the very time the party has an opportunity to affect policy making, the mechanisms established to do just that are eliminated. Policy councils are less than successful in achieving their modest goals when they are the out party. However, the national committees retain no independent policy-making body when they hold the presidency. This reflects not only the dominance of the president in party affairs, but also the general tendency of all presidents to minimize competition from the national committee and therefore keep it as weak as possible.

The general failure of policy councils and committees at the national party level also illustrates the difficulties of policy making in a heterogeneous, election-oriented organization. Opposition within the party along ideological lines consistently weakens the role of these policy-making bodies. Similarly, the failure to obtain even minimal congressional backing has reduced the impact of these attempts at making policy. Party policy councils, though at times producing impressive arrays of reports on numerous substantive issues, have been of minor significance in American politics.

PROBLEMS OF NATIONAL
PARTY ORGANIZATION

Why are the national parties so weak? Obviously it is easy to say they are weak because power is decentralized and the national organization is nothing more than a loose coalition of many political interests. This, however, begs the

[20] *America in the 1970's* (Washington, D.C.: DNC, February, 1970), preface.

question: What specific problems minimizing their ability to move toward centralization do the national electoral organizations face?

COMPETITION FOR INFLUENCE

It was stated above that presidents traditionally have desired weak national chairmen and have tended to discourage and inhibit efforts to strengthen the organization at the expense of their prerogatives. Both presidents and the congressional leadership prefer weak national committees which will offer no challenge to their leadership (see Box 6.2). The Senate and House committees serve as competition for national committees, both for policy influence and for monetary support.

In addition, the state and local party leaders favor a limited national organization. Naturally these leaders wish to maximize their autonomy and reject efforts to centralize authority in the national committee. Although they fear presidential domination of the national party and have little sympathy for the congressional party committees, the state and local party leaders also have attempted to limit any potential aggrandizement of the national organization. While they desire a national headquarters that can provide organizational services, campaign assistance, and some patronage, they oppose efforts to increase authority at the top. It is ironic that the very forces that are crucial to building strong national organizations are those that jealously guard their own powers and frustrate attempts to strengthen the national party.

PASSIVE NATIONAL COMMITTEE

Another problem of the national party organization is a twofold one. The current procedures for selecting national committee members result in a nonactivist orientation of that body. In fact, these members primarily view their role as a ratifying and legitimizing one. There is little evidence of national committee challenges to the national party chairman and staff. In large part, committee members passively follow the directions of the headquarters leaders. This is not surprising, since Committee members are remarkably unprepared and ignorant of internal party affairs. Although they may be important, active leaders in their home states, their infrequent meetings and lack of communication result in little activity. Compounding this is the fact that national committee members are often chosen from the older and wealthier party members who have the time and money to serve. Often the membership is an honor, and few people who feel themselves so honored attempt to exert influence over party headquarters.

BOX 6.2   WHITE HOUSE DOMINANCE

Carter's intention to expand the responsibility of the national committee is not unprecedented in recent American history, although its implementation at the urging of an incumbent President would be. Traditionally the President staffs the national committee with his own people, as Carter has done, and then removes responsibility from it. Usually the emasculation of the committee is not the result of executive policy, but the natural outcome of the struggle between the committee and the White House for national party leadership.

Harry C. McPherson, a White House aide under President Johnson, described the presidential attitude toward the party during the last Democratic administration: "The party as far as I can tell is a quadrennial happening," he told a January meeting of the National Democratic Forum. "The party was not important at all under Kennedy or Johnson. They were activist Presidents who did not use the party much. Once in office, the President wants to be the President of all the people. He does not want to be the respresentative of one political party. The [role of the] Democratic Party in the next four years will be determined almost entirely by Carter."

White House dominance of its national committee, however, has not been restricted to Democratic administrations. President Nixon had three national chairmen during his five years in office. Kansas Sen. Robert Dole, who chaired the committee during the 1972 campaign, reflected once on the impotence of his chairmanship. Not only did the Republican National Committee have nothing to do with Watergate, he said, but it had nothing to do with Nixon's nomination, campaign, election or inauguration.

SOURCE: *Congressional Quarterly Guide to American Politics,* Fall, 1977 (Washington, D.C.: Congressional Quarterly, Inc., 1977), p. 83.

While the selection process favors a less active and more submissive national committee, there is no evidence that the national chairmen desire a more activist-oriented constituency. They appear to be satisfied with a national committee that gives them the most leeway—one that does not rock the boat. National chairmen and their staffs play the same game of competition that the national office holders and state-local party leaders play. By attempting to maximize their own autonomy, the national chairmen and their cohorts perpetuate a weak national committee. Again, the national party suffers from a lack of enthusiasm and initiative.

LACK OF NATIONAL MEMBERSHIP BASE

Throughout this work the uniqueness of U.S. cadre party membership has been stressed. Americans are not actually "members" of a party organization in large numbers. Those who are active, however, are active in state, and especially local, parties, not in a national party. The limited party membership, excluding party identifiers, is basically a local membership. The national organization is isolated from the workers and party loyalists who provide a continuing base of support at the local and state levels, where the rewards of office are found in abundance. The federal nature of the electoral system and the emphasis of U.S. parties on winning elections almost preclude national party activity. What would these "national activists" be active over? The presidency is the only office at this level. It has been demonstrated, however, that the presidential campaign is, in practice, controlled not by the national party, but by a nucleus independent of the party—the candidate's own personal organization. Therefore, incentives for party work at the national level are nonexistent.

Due in part to the lack of a membership base, the national committee has no sanctions against state and local organizations or congressional or Senate candidates who bolt the party. With what could they be threatened? Reduced campaign support is no sanction, since there is very little of it to begin with. The national organization depends on the state and local parties, not vice versa. The national committee cannot influence, to any extent, nominations in the states. They have little influence over the selection of state and local party officials, since this selection is largely controlled by state laws. The lack of a national membership, therefore, leads to the impotence which characterizes both national committees.

FINANCES

The lack of a continuing membership base results in another critical problem for the national committees, that of finance. Although both parties recently have implemented mass mailings to build a continuing grassroots financial base, these mailings have not been highly successful. In the mid-1970s, the Democrats, under the direction of Robert Strauss, attempted to take party finance directly to the television audience. In a series of telethons, the Democrats were able to raise millions of dollars, with about one third going to the national organization.

> In September 1973, the Democratic National Committee conducted a highly successful fund-raising telethon on NBC that raised $5.5 million from 575,000 contributors. The net proceeds were divided evenly between the DNC and the states where the money was raised.[21]

Although the telethons, especially the initial ones, were successful in raising immediate sums of cash and in public relations, they were less successful in building a long-term, broad-based financial base.[22]

The Republicans have had more success with conventional mass-mailing solicitations under the leadership of able chairmen of the National Finance Committee. During the early 1970s, however, they faced a disastrous decline in contributions, first, because of competition from Richard Nixon's re-election committee, and second, as a reaction to the Watergate scandal. The decreasing base of Republican identifiers implies more difficulty ahead for Republican party finances.

The Democrats' predicament is perhaps more the result of many years of inattention than lack of a grassroots base. In the early 1960s, Paul Butler, the national chairman, attempted to establish a solid financial base through a Dollars for Democrats appeal. This was to provide a national membership at annual dues of $10.00. President Kennedy chose instead to create an elite one-thousand-dollar club. Although this route apparently was more lucrative, in light of Kennedy's popularity, it was inimical to long-term, broad-based financing.[23] Butler's attempts at creating a well-financed professional national organizational staff were dismissed by Kennedy as well as Johnson. Perhaps telethons are the closest the Democrats can come to a broad-based appeal, but more is needed for an active national party.

[21] John G. Stewart, *One Last Change: The Democratic Party, 1974-76* (New York: Praeger Publishers, 1974), p. 179.

[22] Herbert E. Alexander, *Financing Politics: Money, Elections and Political Reform* (Washington: Congressional Quarterly Press, 1976), pp. 94-96.

[23] Membership in the $1000 Club peaked at about 4000 in 1964 and then entered a sharp decline until its demise in 1968. This decline indicates how speculative such funding is and to what extent it is personalized in the presidency. The Democrats also depend heavily on million dollar fund-raising dinners. For more details see "The Personal Touch," *National Journal* Vol. 9, No. 29 (July 16, 1977), p. 1126.

Another source of income for the national organizations in the past were quotas levied on the state organizations by the national chairmen. Since the chairmen hold no sanctions through which to ensure compliance, these have been very unsatisfactory means of raising money. They also introduce an unstable and unpredictable situation. Not having any idea what revenue might be expected makes for a poor budgeting system. In addition, the continuous solicitation of quotas from the states further strains the relationships between the national and state organizations. If the parties are to be successful in increasing their power, they must establish their autonomous and broad base of continuing monetary support.

NATIONAL PARTY REFORM EFFORTS

DEMOCRATS

Both national parties have gone through extended periods of reform since the late 1960s. The Democratic party reform has been most visible and comprehensive. In 1964, the Special Equal Rights Committee was established by the Democratic convention. This committee set a precedent by shifting authority toward the national party, which could enforce its "six basic elements" among all state parties. The penalty for noncompliance was to be the refusal to seat the state delegation at the 1968 convention. The state parties were informed that they must obey the rules or face the consequences. Although the actual impact of these rule changes was minor, the stage was set for more substantial reform.

Out of the disastrous 1968 Chicago convention came a little-noticed mandate for the creation of two reform bodies. The Commission on Party Structure and Delegate Selection (McGovern-Fraser) was authorized to modify the delegate selection process, while the Commission on Rules (O'Hara) had responsibility for modernizing and improving convention procedures. While the O'Hara Commission quietly updated convention procedures, most of which were adopted at the 1972 convention, the McGovern-Fraser Commission became the center of controversy between reformers and regulars and led to perhaps the most significant modifications of a national party since its inception. A series of 17 hearings across the country accentuated the debate by publicizing abuses of party procedures in the states.[24] The result was a set of 18 guidelines or rules of fair play. These

---

[24] See William J. Crotty, *Political Reform and the American Experiment* (New York: Thomas Y. Crowell, 1977), especially pp. 243-47 and Chapter 12.

guidelines were supposed to guarantee open access and fair representation of all elements of the party.

The means of implementing these guidelines was as drastic an innovation as their content. In 1970, two notices were sent along with the guidelines to the state parties. The first measured current state regulations against the guidelines and indicated where and how the state must change its procedures to comply with the standards. The second notice stated that the changes were mandatory. Any state in violation would have to demonstrate conclusively that it made "all feasible efforts" to comply with the changes. By 1971, it was estimated that 40 state parties were in full compliance with the guidelines, while the remainder were in substantial compliance.[25] For the first time

> . . . a national party had promulgated and each state had adapted to federal criteria determining how a party should behave to insure due process procedural guarantees and standards of fair representation . . . it could mark a turning point for a rather loose association of state parties whose organization and decision making had changed little during the history of its confederation.[26]

These changes were not without conflict, however. Most controversial among the reform provisions were the first two guidelines which required the state parties to take affirmative steps to include minority groups, youth (18-30), and women in proportions reasonably close to their presence in the state. This quota system was frequently and viciously attacked. Although there was a great deal of animosity from state party leaders, they lacked coordination and their effectiveness was minimal.

The real debate over the guidelines occurred at the 1972 convention, where 82 challenges to the delegations of 31 states were filed. The situation deteriorated after that. A New Delegate Selection Commission was created to reevaluate (that is, to weaken) the reforms of delegate selection. This (Mikulski) commission eliminated the quotas and replaced them by "affirmative action programs." Among other provisions of this compromise between regulars and reformers were the following: (1) the state parties were allowed to appoint up to 25 percent of the state's delegates; (2) national committee members and various elected officials were given convention privileges (without vote) solely on the basis of their positions; and (3) a Compliance Review Commission was created to monitor the states' efforts.

Another reform action coming out of the 1972 convention was author-

[25] Commission on Party Structure and Delegate Selection, *The Party Reformed* (Washington, D.C.: DNC, July 7, 1972).

[26] Crotty, *Political Reform*, p. 245.

ization of a Charter Commission. Also approved was a highly controversial midterm convention to be held in 1974. In December, 1974, following an emotionally filled Charter Commission meeting culminating in a walkout of the liberals (led by the blacks), the "mini-convention" was held in Kansas City. Under the strong direction of the national chairman, Robert Strauss, and through his efforts to unify the regulars and reformers, a progressive party constitution was adopted, the first document of this scope for either party. According to Crotty, this:

> signaled the beginning of a concerted drive to revivify the party. The intent was to make the party relevant to the demands of a technologically advanced society and an increasingly more sophisticated electorate.[27]

The revision of delegate selection was continued under the Commission on the role and Future of Presidential Primaries created in 1976.

REPUBLICANS

Although Republican reform efforts were less visible and more moderate, they largely coincided with the Democrat efforts to modernize the party. Due to the stronger organization and homogeneity of the Republican party, the major issues focused on the streamlining of convention procedures and better dissemination of RNC policy positions. Throughout the reform efforts, the federal nature of the national party was emphasized. Unlike the Democrats, the Republicans made no moves to centralize authority over the delegate selection process.

> . . . any reform actions that impinged upon what were considered state processes, even if adopted by the national convention, were accepted only as suggestions. The differences between the two parties in approaching this issue were fundamentally and diametrically opposed.[28]

While attempts were made to strengthen the Republican national staff and services, ultimate authority remained in the states.

The 1968 Republican convention authorized creation of the Delegates and Organization (DO) Committee, composed of RNC personnel. Although the DO Committee was less successful than the McGovern-Fraser Commission

[27] *Ibid.*, p. 255.
[28] *Ibid.*, p. 256.

in increasing minority representation, Rule 32 prohibited discriminatory practices and urged state committees to take positive action to achieve broad participation in the delegate selection process by women, young people, minority and ethnic groups, and senior citizens. Rule 29 established a committee to work with the state parties in implementing the reforms. Again, it was stressed that these rules were not binding on the states and in no way constituted quotas, which had been the most controversial aspect of the Democratic reforms.

NEW INITIATIVES

Although the specific provisions of the Democratic and Republican reforms vary, the general direction in each case is toward modernization of party structure and opening up of the party process. While the Democrats have chosen to force state compliance from the national level, the Republicans continue to emphasize the federal nature of the party by offering suggested guidelines to the states, and assuming some degree of voluntary compliance. While these reforms have been debated and finally actualized, significant changes have also been apparent within the national committees relating to the means of achieving their objectives. Both party headquarters are taking new initiatives to increase their visibility and usefulness to the states as well as to Congress.

There is much evidence of increasing efforts by the Republican headquarters to intervene in primaries in favor of candidates it feels can win in November. For instance:

> The Republican National Committee acted in May to help a black bank official win nomination for a state legislative seat in a largely black district in California. More important, Senate G.O.P. campaign chairman Bob Packwood of Oregon is asking local politicians in states with a Senate election in 1978 to compile priority lists of strong candidates for the national party to recruit.[29]

Any attempts of the RNC to intervene in state politics in the past would have been rejected out of hand. In order to stimulate local organizations, the RNC created a Communications and Registration Program in the mid-1970s. It was designed to give local party organizations technical assistance such as polling and voting analyses which they could not afford on their own. Increasingly, the Republican headquarters is attempting to sell itself as a service organiza-

---

[29] *Congressional Quarterly Guide to American Politics, Fall, 1977.* (Washington, D.C.: Congressional Quarterly Press, 1977), p. 73.

tion for candidates. It is expected that new efforts will be made by the RNC to take an even more active role in recruitment, as well as in campaign management, to reverse the current trend away from the party.

The Democratic National Headquarters, although lagging behind the Republicans, has also greatly expanded the services offered to candidates. In addition, the DNC has attempted to generate party activity at the local levels by conducting grassroots hearings on national issues such as government reorganization, energy, and human rights.[30]   Increased effort and resources are directed at identifying congressional districts where funding should be concentrated. Both the DNC and the RNC are attempting to revitalize their image for party leaders and candidates as well as for the public.

NATIONAL PARTY ORGANIZATION:
A SUMMARY

Despite the efforts to energize the party organizations, the national committees suffer from several inherent weaknesses that make them vulnerable and lessen their chances of success. Most obvious is the almost complete dominance by the presidential office. In effect, the national committee is the captive of the president when they hold the presidency, and without direction when they do not. This domination of one office is compounded by competition from congressional leaders, who display their own ambitions to control the party. Together, presidential and congressional forces are able to minimize the influence of the national chairman.

The other major weakness of the national committees emphasized in the last two chapters is the federal nature of the party system. The key description of U.S. parties is decentralized. In the national party, this is reflected in the dependence of any national efforts on the state and local parties. As stated earlier, the national party is nothing but a coalition of state parties, in spite of all the bureaucratic trappings discussed here. This fact, combined with the innate weakness of the national committees and the strength of independent candidate organizations, suggests that renewal of the national parties is difficult, at best, and perhaps, futile.

Any attempts to vitalize and strengthen the national parties are bound to fail unless parties can organize from the bottom up. Strong local and state organization is a prerequisite for strong national parties. Another precondition is the resolution of the rivalries between the various elements of the

---

[30] "The Democrats Under Carter," *National Journal*, Vol. 9, No. 21 (June 21, 1977), p. 797.

party and a truly unified effort at party renewal. The probability of such a sustained effort is not good. While it is certain that both national organizations will continue to improve communications with the states and will provide increasingly useful services to candidates, the nature of party politics in the U.S. will minimize the impact of these efforts.

SECTION IV

PARTIES
AS GOVERNING
ORGANIZATIONS:
THE FAILURE OF PARTIES
TO GOVERN

In addition to serving as electoral organizations, political parties traditionally are expected to organize the government and provide the loyal opposition. The adherents of the responsible party model suggest means by which U.S. parties might achieve these goals. However, at the present time, U.S. political parties have failed to act as governing organizations. Although there is some influence of political parties in each branch, their overall impact is minimal.

The chapters in this section will examine the failure of U.S. parties to govern. Chapter 7 analyzes the relationship of presidents to other elements of the party. It also examines the limited influence of political parties over the day to day activities of the government bureaucracy. It is argued that the independence of these agencies and bureaus, even from the president, has isolated them almost totally from party control. The courts, surprisingly, offer one branch where political parties offer some control in the recruitment process, especially at the county and state levels.

Chapter 8 emphasizes the limited nature of party control of Congress. It stresses the division between the national committee and the respective leadership in Congress. Although Congress is organized along party lines and the party label is still the best single indicator of congressional voting, the inability of the leadership to control its members is obvious when Congress is compared to parliamentary systems of government. The dispersion of power among various alternatives to party leadership, such as committee chairmen, reinforces the decentralized and fragmentized nature of parties in Congress. Despite the contention of some political observers that U.S. parties must be made "responsible," there is little evidence that such a pattern is evolving.

7

Parties
and the President,
Bureaucracy,
and Courts

The most obvious place to examine party in government is the presidency. Presidential politics is the summit of party politics, and the presidency is the single most important prize. Most of the efforts of the national party are directed at and limited to the contest for president. A party that holds the presidency is dominated in many ways by the president. He alone speaks for the party, determines party programs and policies, and selects national party officers.

Despite the president's dominance of the party, it is unlikely that party politics will be uppermost in his activities. Also, the national party is weak and in continuous competition with state parties and congressional party committees and leaders, and the president has little influence at those levels. Actual presidential leadership of the party depends on his personality and perspective toward party politics and his role as leader. While some presidents, such as FDR, have expended much effort for the party, most recent presidents have failed actively to lead their party, instead depending solely on their inherent symbolic leadership. Even those presidents who have attempted to lead a united party have been frustrated by the dispersion of government power among the various branches.

PARTISAN ROLES OF PRESIDENT

The president's role as a party leader has evolved slowly over the last two centuries. According to James Burns, presidential aggrandizement has been most marked in the sphere of party politics.

> There was a time when conventions refused to renominate incumbent Presidents, when the national chairman was independent of

179

presidential control, when the national party apparatus was dominated by competing leaders or factions. Things are very different
now.[1]

Throughout this period, due to several strong presidential leaders, there has
been increased recognition of the president as party leader. Certainly, the
activities of Jackson, Lincoln, Wilson, and both Roosevelts illustrate that
presidents draw much of their power from their positions as party leaders.

> By playing the grand politician with unashamed zest, the first of
> these men gave his epic administration a unique sense of cohesion,
> the second rallied doubting Republican leaders and their followings
> to the cause of the Union, and the other three achieved genuine
> triumphs as catalysts of congressional action.[2]

Even Eisenhower, who perceived himself above partisan politics, admitted
that a president must devote one or two hours of every working day to being
Chief Republican or Chief Democrat.

The role a president plays as party leader is derived from a multitude of
capacities he is expected to perform to some degree. As such, it is heavily
dependent on the individual president's perception of the office and its
attendant responsibilities. Success or failure as party leader varies with the
abilities and orientations of the president. The "character" of the president
in large part defines his orientation toward the many roles he is expected
to perform.[3] Not surprisingly, the party leadership role of presidents has
ranged from substantial control over party affairs to performance of a weak
symbolic role. Despite the actual role exhibited, potential party leadership
is reflected in several overlapping capacities at the base of the presidency.

SPOKESMAN OF NATIONAL CONSTITUENCY

Of the over 500,000 elected offices in the United States, only one, that of
president, represents a national constituency. The president is the only party
nominee for whom the entire nation votes. House and Senate members are

---

[1] James MacGregor Burns, *Presidential Government: The Crucible of
Leadership* (Boston: Houghton Mifflin, 1965), p. 315.

[2] Clinton Rossiter, "The Presidency as the Focus of Leadership," in *The
Power of the Presidency,* ed. Robert S. Hirschfield (Chicago: Atherton Press,
Inc., 1968), p. 231.

[3] See James David Barber, *The Presidential Character* (Englewood Cliffs,
N.J.: Prentice-Hall, Inc., 1972).

representatives of localities and as such tend to be more parochial in their interests, reflect only sections of voters, and speak for at most only a portion of the party. There is no national party choice except the president. No one else represents the people as a whole and exercises a national choice. In the words of Woodrow Wilson:

> He can dominate his party by being a spokesman for the real senti-
> ment and purpose of the country, by giving direction to opinion, by
> giving the country at once the information and the statements of
> policy which will enable it to form its judgements alike of parties
> and of men.[4]

In a strict sense, then, the president *is* the national party. Most of the party effort at the national level is directed at nomination and election of the president. While party leadership is the last thing the Constitution intended, the national constituency of the presidency has given the occupant of that office a monopoly over the national party base of support. Since no other officeholder represents nearly as broad a constituency, there is no effective alternative to the president as spokesman of the party. Even in cases of presidents who exhibited little interest in the party, effective competition for party leadership is unlikely. No one else is able to speak for the party, because no one else has demonstrated a national base of support.

SYMBOLIC PARTY LEADER

In addition to reflecting the broadest base of support, the president is by far the most visible representative of the party. The inherent ability of a president to make news ensures a central role in party politics. Since the president is the most striking manifestation of the party, his programs become identified as party programs, his successes become party successes, and his failures become party failures. As hard as the Republican party candidates attempted to separate themselves from the fate of Richard Nixon in 1974, their attempt was futile. Whatever else Nixon meant to the party, he was identified by the public as the Republican in the White House. While this symbolic leadership need not be transformed into moral or organizational leadership, it does tie the party irreversibly to the man. As a symbol of the party, the president has another point of power which he may or may not exploit in his role as party organization leader.

[4] Woodrow Wilson, "The President's Role in American Government," in *Power of the Presidency,* ed. Hirschfield, p. 92.

ORGANIZATIONAL PARTY LEADER

While the ability to speak for the national party and the president's symbolic leadership come with the office, whether he takes an active organizational leadership role or not is uncertain. While the presidency provides the opportunity for party control, the president must take the initiative. Although Clinton Rossiter is certainly overstating the president's powers when he states that he is the nation's number one political boss,[5] the president does have several potential areas of influence. The party leadership of the president related to (1) leadership of his congressional party and (2) leadership of the national committee.

There is little doubt that a willing president can control the national committee. The convention and the platform frequently are dominated by the presidential candidate. When an incumbent is running for reelection, there is little doubt that the platform is a close reflection of the president's program. The closely orchestrated party conventions for reelection of Johnson and Nixon left no doubt as to who was in charge. The national chairman has become a political lieutenant of the president and serves at his will. James Burns contends that the national party chairman frequently has less power than many political aides in the White House.[6] Although many recent presidents have been less than active leaders of their party, none has been willing to allow leadership to go to another. While Eisenhower became increasingly disenchanted with his party to the point of questioning its right to live, and Johnson and Nixon appeared most interested in using the party to build their own personal support, all accepted at least nominal leadership of the national party organization.

The party influence of the president does not generally extend to the state parties, however, nor to congressional committees. His dominance is limited to the national committee organization. Although an active president might campaign for party candidates at the state and local levels, it is unwise to intervene directly in party nominations or become embroiled in state party disputes. Presidents Roosevelt and Kennedy, among others, learned the boundaries of presidential influence the hard way. Both FDR and Kennedy felt the backlash of party leaders when they intervened in state party politics.

The second dimension of presidential party organization leadership relates to attempts to lead the congressional parties. Since all presidents must work with Congress, it becomes imperative that they be able to work with party leadership in that body. In those cases where the Congress is controlled by the opposite party, the president might be forced to minimize partisan-

[5] Rossiter, "Focus of Leadership," p. 231.
[6] Burns, *Presidential Government,* p. 316.

ship, but in no case can he ignore his own party. Since Thomas Jefferson first achieved leadership of the congressional party caucus in order to provide party cohesion for his program on the floor of Congress, presidents have been aware of their potential congressional leadership.[7]

Although John Kennedy was less than successful in his leadership over congressional Democrats and his program suffered accordingly, he argued that party leadership, in the most political sense, was a precondition of legislative success.

> But no President, it seems to me, can escape politics. He has not only been chosen by the nation—he has been chosen by his party . . . if he blurs the issues and differences between the parties— if he neglects the party machinery and avoids his party's leadership— then he has not only weakened the political party as an instrument of the democratic process—he has dealt a blow to the democratic process itself.[8]

In this, Kennedy reflects the thinking of Woodrow Wilson, who suggests that the president cannot "escape being the leader of his party except by incapacity and lack of personal face," since he is at the same time a choice of the party and the nation.[9]

ELECTORAL LEADER

A final leadership capacity of the president relating to parties is his potential for aiding other party candidates on the ballot. There is some evidence that presidential success does influence the success of other party candidates. This phenomenon is termed the *coattail effect,* implying that a popular president might carry other candidates into office in the wake of his victory. This might happen when: (1) party faithful turn out not only to support the presidential candidate but also to vote for lower-level candidates, or (2) a popular incumbent president campaigns particularly for key individual candidates who then win. In light of increased ticket splitting (see Chapter 10) and the increased issue-awareness of many voters, it is likely that electoral leadership by the president might decrease in the future. In the current mood of presidential

---

[7] Edward S. Corwin, "The Aggrandizement of Presidential Power," in *Power of the Presidency,* ed. Hirschfield, p. 216.

[8] John F. Kennedy, Speech to the National Press Club, January 14, 1960.

[9] Wilson, "The President's Role," p. 92.

elections, it is just as likely that lower-level candidates will lead the presidential candidate, except in the cases of extreme landslides. While the success or failure of a presidential candidate is certain to affect other party candidates under extreme conditions, the role of the president as an electoral leader is of questionable utility to most candidates.[10]

LIMITATIONS TO PARTISAN LEADERSHIP

As the highest elected official in the country, the president is certain to have much influence over the party organization and the party electorate. His stature and prestige hold not only symbolic rewards for the party, but also a reservoir, though limited, of patronage and other perquisites. His leadership of public opinion and his dominance of the mass media do provide him with a substantial base of potential party leadership. Despite this potential, however, there are significant limits to presidential leadership. Since the president has a broader responsibility to the nation as a whole, any perception of a president as being too partisan will result in public resentment and criticism. The president must balance his need to mobilize party support with the need to maintain broader public support. In this era of public opinion polls and widespread media exposure, presidents have become even more aware of limits on partisan activity. It must be remembered that hostility toward partisan politics runs deep in the United States. The opposing party would like nothing more than to exploit this, if given the chance.

The decentralized nature of the parties also minimizes presidential leadership. As noted earlier, the party influence of presidents does not extend to state and local party organizations. While the president dominates the national committee, the limitations of the national parties are well documented. The congressional party committees remain autonomous, largely independent of presidential and national party control. The president falls far short of leading a centralized and cohesive party, because the actual power lies in state and local party organizations.

Reinforcing the lack of centralization in party structure is the great potential for divided party control in the United States. Even if presidential

[10] For more detailed analysis, see Milton C. Cummings, *Congressmen and the Electorate* (New York: The Free Press, 1966); Malcolm Moos, *Politics, Presidents and Coattails* (Baltimore: Johns Hopkins Press, 1952); Charles Press, "Presidential Coattails and Party Cohesion," *Midwest Journal of Political Science,* 7 (November, 1963), 320-35; and Warren E. Miller, "Presidential Coattails: A Study in Political Myth and Methodology," *Public Opinion Quarterly,* 19 (Winter, 1955), 353-68.

leadership can be transformed successfully to congressional leadership, there recently has been about a 50 percent chance that Congress would be controlled by the opposition. This situation obviously minimizes the party leadership role of the president, since he must achieve some degree of bipartisanship in order to get legislation passed. Woodrow Wilson's excessive partisanship, for instance, led to a rejection of the League of Nations in the Senate and hastened his downfall.[11] While he demonstrated earlier in his career that a president can be a strong partisan leader in a weak party system, in the end this approach proved too rigid.[12]

In addition to the cultural and institutional factors limiting the party role of a president are several specific provisions. The Twenty-Second Amendment, which limits the president to two full terms, tends to reduce substantially a president's ability to lead during the last two years in office. The Civil Service reforms have removed most patronage positions and thereby limited the president's resources. The lack of control by the president over the vast bureaucracy also limits the president's ability to provide active party leadership.[13]

Finally, the president's personality and perception of the office might restrict his partisan role. The practice of surrounding oneself with personal advisors and the continuing expansion of the White House staff tend to isolate a president from party leaders.[14] The creation of personal campaign committees, such as the Committee to Re-Elect the President in 1972, further reduces the need for some presidents to lead a weak national party organization. Also, the preoccupation with other, more central presidential activities makes it very difficult for presidents to contribute one or two hours a day to party endeavors. In many cases, therefore, this is delegated to an advisor or, perhaps more commonly, ignored. Robert Hirshfield contends that the result is that presidential party leadership is "at best uncertain and at worst non-existent."[15]

---

[11] Robert J. Sickels, *Presidential Transactions* (Englewood Cliffs, N.J.: Prentice-Hall, Inc., 1974), p. 18.

[12] *Ibid.*, p. 21.

[13] For a good discussion of the limitations on the president's powers of appointment see James W. Davis, Jr. *The National Executive Branch* (New York: The Free Press, 1970). Also see Richard F. Fenno, Jr., *The President's Cabinet* (New York: Random House, Vintage Books, 1959) for a discussion of factors influencing cabinet appointments.

[14] See Stephen Hess, *Organizing the Presidency* (Washington, D.C.: The Brookings Institution, 1976), pp. 16-17. Also, John H. Kessel, *The Domestic Presidency* (North Scituate, Mass.: Duxbury Press, 1975).

[15] Robert S. Hirschfield, *Power of the Presidency*, p. 3.

PRESIDENTS AND PARTIES: A SUMMARY

While the limitations of presidential party leadership might be overstated, the weak leadership exhibited by most recent presidents, despite the impressive potential of the office, emphasizes the weakness of parties in government. While the symbolic emphasis of the parties is centered in the chief executive, actual leadership is fragmented and ineffective. Infrequently in the last three decades has a president been able to unify and strengthen a party. The nature of the party system and the institutional and cultural context of the presidency, as well as of the parties, negates centralized control, even by the highest elected official in the land. Nowhere is this more clear than in the relations with the federal bureaucracy.

PARTIES AND THE BUREAUCRACY

When parties are well disciplined and operate within a political system that ensures simultaneous control of the executive and legislative branches, one would expect them to exercise a major role in the formulation of policy. Under such circumstances, the bureaucracy might closely reflect the goals of the political administration and be responsive to party politics. Obviously, the U.S. system does not fit this description. While parties in the United States do help shape public policy through their control of certain executive and legislative positions and the inherent subordination of nonelected to elected officials, party impact is weak, oblique, and hopelessly fragmented. Due to their weakness, the parties have effectively contributed to the relatively autonomous powers of the bureaucracy, especially at the national level.[16]

While little comprehensive analysis of parties in the bureaucracy is available, probably because they play such a limited role, several areas of research are helpful in estimating the impact of political parties on the bureaucracy. These areas include: (1) studies of the civil service system and the corresponding demise of widespread patronage, (2) establishment of career executives and their relationships with political executives, and (3) the impact of parties on bureaucratic effectiveness and responsiveness. While it is extremely difficult to isolate the influence of political parties, since they are so intertwined with other factors, a brief examination of the available data might be instructive. As more and more functions of government have been subsumed in the bureaucracy, it is most imperative that any discussion of party in government include this topic.

[16] James A. Medeiros and David E. Schmitt, *Public Bureaucracy: Values and Perspectives* (North Scituate, Mass.: Duxbury Press, 1977), p. 47.

THE CIVIL SERVICE SYSTEM

The tie between parties and the bureaucracy, except for several periods in history, has been ambiguous, partially because neither the parties nor the bureaucracy is specified in the Constitution. Both institutions have evolved without specific constitutional authorization: without a clear definition of their powers and responsibilities. Until the Jackson "spoils" system made the tie between parties and bureaucracy explicit by subjugating the bureaucracy to party politics, little notice was paid to the role of parties in public administration. Out of response to a long series of obvious corruption and malfeasance, the Pendleton Act of 1883 reduced partisan influence by provision of a bipartisan Civil Service Commission, accompanied by competitive exams. By making employment dependent on merit rather than on patronage, partisan influence over administration was to be curtailed and administrative performance improved. Both appointments and removals were removed from politics and party leaders were prohibited from requiring campaign contributions from government employees.[17] This latter aspect was strengthened and extended in the Hatch Acts of 1939 and 1940, which were passed out of fear that President Roosevelt would use public employees to build his own machine.[18] By subsequent congressional and presidential action, the merit system came to cover approximately 90 percent of all federal employees by 1970.[19]

While patronage subsequently has been reduced in most states, county and rural governments remain strongholds of the patronage system.

> By and large, administrative agencies in the states and localities are much more intimately involved in the political process than are similar units at the national level . . . Moreover, in some of the more backward jurisdictions, patronage is still rife, and agencies serve mainly as auxiliaries for the party organizations.[20]

In many states, parties remain a potent force of control over the administration process. Pennsylvania, for instance, has about 50,000 positions available

[17] Although we saw in Chapter 5 that this is still common practice in some states and localities.

[18] Lewis C. Mainzer, *Political Bureaucracy* (Glenview, Ill.: Scott, Foresman and Company, 1973), p. 103.

[19] This is compared to 10 percent in 1884. See Robert C. Fried, *Performance in American Bureaucracy* (Boston: Little, Brown and Company, 1976), p. 315.

[20] Francis E. Rourke, *Bureaucracy, Politics, and Public Policy,* 2nd ed. (Boston: Little, Brown, and Company, 1976), p. 75.

to the party in power, since only about 20 percent of the state employees are on a merit system. Conversely, patronage in California and Wisconsin is seen as negligible.[21] Even in some competitive party states, "gentlemen's agreements" on dividing up the spoils are commonplace.[22] While the 1940 Hatch Act required state and local employees whose employment is financed by federal funds to come under a merit system, a major proportion of state and local employees do not fall under that provision. The quality and rigor of state and local civil service systems also varies significantly.

ANTIPARTY GOALS
OF ADMINISTRATIVE REFORMS

Before examining the role of political parties within this context, it is interesting to note why the civil service reforms were instituted. The thrust of these reforms again reflects the hostility toward and fear of political parties in American politics. The goal of these reforms corresponds closely to the goal of most progressive reforms, such as direct primaries, nonpartisan elections, and use of propositions: to weaken party influence. The civil service system was designed to take "administration out of politics." This consciously reflects the contempt for party politics and its central tool of patronage. Furthermore, it indicates a very low estimate of politicians' motivations in appointing political executives.

> Professionalism contains a strong antipolitics component, rejecting the right of laymen, including politicians, to interfere in the decisions that are to be reserved to professional experts.[23]

There is strong preference for "nonpolitical" experts and an assumption that parties are the enemies of bureaucratic integrity, impartiality, and fairness. Within the context of American resentment of party politics, it is not surprising that partisanship is perceived as the antithesis of bureaucratic efficiency and effectiveness. Limited evidence relating to nonpartisan city governments suggests that such a perspective is overstated.[24]

---

[21] Mainzer, *Political Bureaucracy*, p. 98.

[22] Fried, *Performance in American Bureaucracy*, p. 321.

[23] *Ibid.*, p. 324.

[24] For instance, Robert L. Lineberry and Edmund P. Fowler, "Reformism and Public Policies in American Cities," *American Political Science Review*, 61 (September, 1967), 701-16, find that "reformed" cities may be less responsive to lower-class interests than cities with strong political parties.

LIMITATIONS ON PARTY INFLUENCE

The influence of political parties over the federal bureaucracy is limited by many institutional and administrative constraints. The civil service system has removed a large proportion of administrative positions from the political spectrum and has produced a professional bureaucracy that continues largely unaltered as political administrators in Washington rotate from one party to the other. These career executives are isolated from overt political influence through legislation designed to eliminate those very pressures. Even the several thousand political appointments at the highest levels of administration within the political domain are inhibited from extreme partisan use of office. Not only must these appointees act in the interest of some wider public, but they also often become captives of the professional bureaucrats.

Many cabinet members and other upper-level appointees have noted their inability to accomplish major innovations because of lack of cooperation from the professionals and the unyielding inertia of the vast bureaucracy. The internal bureaucracy definitely works against partisan efforts to induce change. Also, many of the top executive positions are filled by civil servants because administrations have difficulty recruiting good political executives and keeping them. "The posts are unattractive to many already successful persons who fear political sniping and serious financial losses of salary, pension, or promotion in business."[25] As the media becomes more investigative and the Senate more critical and skeptical of presidential appointees, the pressures on prospective candidates will increase.

Party influence over the bureaucracy is also discouraged by the separation of powers, federalism, and other institutions which dilute power. The president cannot make appointments without compromising with party leaders in Congress. Influence is further reduced by the need for stability and professional competence. Many administrative appointments are restricted by the need for individuals with particular expertise.

> Bureaucratic responsiveness might be encouraged through appointing politically active party loyalists to top administrative jobs, but our national parties are amorphous at best, anemic at worst. The largest single source of political executives (appointments to top level positions which are not under civil service) during the Roosevelt, Truman, Eisenhower, and Kennedy administrations . . . was men who had careers in public service, mostly in appointive positions.[26]

[25] Mainzer, *Political Bureaucracy,* p. 105.

[26] Mainzer, *Political Bureaucracy,* p. 111. Hugh Helco, *A Government of Strangers: Executive Politics in Washington* (Washington, D.C.: The Brookings Institution, 1977), contends that appointees are often ill-prepared to deal with the bureaucracy and that bureaucrats have legitimate grounds to be cautious in dealing with these novices.

It is not unusual for professional bureaucrats to appeal to fellow professionals for support against political interference. As the administrative structure has become more compartmentalized and specialized, overall party and presidential control has been reduced substantially. The patterns of organization, modes of operation, agency conventions and traditions, and the vested interests in keeping agency behavior as it is all minimize partisan influences on the bureaucracy.

Perhaps the most important constraint on partisan influence is the party's limited capacity to act as a united coalition. The extreme diversity in interests and outlooks among members of either party minimizes the possibility of offering unified programs or policies. James Burns details the friction between the presidential and congressional parties which results in the lack of party initiative.[27] The lack of party cohension in Congress results in a fragmented approach to policy making. Neither party is able to present the bureaucracy with any program in which the party is united. In this inability, the party in the bureaucracy simply reflects the weakness of parties in all aspects of government. Due to the nature of the bureaucracy, its emphasis on career executives, and the legal restraints on partisan activities, the role of parties in this branch is most ambivalent.

PARTIES IN THE BUREAUCRACY: A SUMMARY

Despite the strong constraints on partisan influence over the bureaucracy, the parties are not without input. According to Fried, "political parties are important agents in keeping bureaucracies responsive..."[28] Parties serve as a contact point, no matter how limited, between the public and the bureaucracy. Alteration of parties in power is accompanied by changes in administrative policies. Pledges made during campaigns usually reflect a genuine attempt to shift priorities. While these attempts are commonly less than successful in altering the bureaucracy itself, shifts in policy are discernable after each change in administration.

One of the major mechanisms available to parties in power is the budgetary process. Richard Fenno has demonstrated substantial variation in support of particular agencies by party.[29] Republican-controlled Congresses favored

---

[27] James MacGregor Burns, *Deadlock of Democracy* (Englewood Cliffs, N.J.: Prentice-Hall, Inc., 1963).

[28] Fried, *Performance in American Bureaucracy*, p. 323.

[29] Richard F. Fenno, *The Power of the Purse* (Boston: Little, Brown and Company, 1966), p. 370.

"old-line," well-established agencies such as FBI and the Bureau of Narcotics, and were most hostile to the Bureau of Labor Standards and the Bureau of the Census. Democratic Congresses, correspondingly, appropriated significantly more funding to Labor Department bureaus and the less-established agencies. Although they are constrained by the "essentiality and noncontroversiality of the functions performed, how easily budgetary cuts can be made, the grass roots support behind programs, and the reputation of administrators for effective performance,"[30] parties can shape the bureaucracy through the budgetary process on an incremental basis.

Finally, party opposition to a program or agency can result in media attacks, congressional investigations, and budgetary cuts. Administrators unsympathetic to the program or agency they are to administer, if appointed, can alter priorities and possibly wind up demoralizing the career executives. While parties seldom exercise positive influence over the bureaucracy, they, too, can frustrate the bureaucratic process.

PARTIES AND THE JUDICIARY

Despite a common notion to the contrary, the judiciary cannot be studied in isolation from partisan politics. According to Glendon Schubert, there are two major reasons for the "strong and persistent desire" of political parties to influence the judicial system:

1) the national judiciary has always been an important source of patronage, and this consideration has become increasingly important as the proportion of patronage positions in the executive system has diminished; and

2) the federal courts have always (and correctly) been perceived by party leaders as a major instrument for control over the substantive content of public policy.[31]

Supreme Court positions always have been among the most important sources of patronage available to an administration. Add to this the several hundred federal judges generally available for appointment during an eight-year term, and the numerous attendant positions, and one has an imposing amount of judicial patronage. "The staffing of nonjudicial positions in judicial systems typically involves direct brokerage with political parties. Civil

[30] Fried, *Performance in American Bureaucracy*, p. 329.

[31] Glendon A. Schubert, *Judicial Decision-Making* (Glenview, Ill.: Scott, Foresman and Company, 1965), p. 11.

service reform has had little effect upon judicial patronage."[32] The state judicial systems generally offer at least as much in the way of patronage.

PARTIES AND FEDERAL JUDICIAL SELECTION

One of the major points at which the partisan impact on the judicial system is felt is in the selection of judges. At the national level, political party affiliation is considered the most important background factor for appointment to the courts. As far back as statistics are available, judicial appointments have gone overwhelmingly (generally well over 90 percent) to members of the president's party. The figures in Table 7.1 demonstrate this conclusively. Only in rare instances have presidents crossed party lines in appointing Supreme Court Justices.[33] In most of these cases, this action has reflected "a presidential judgement that ideological congruity between the President and his appointee was a more important consideration than party affiliation."[34]

Table 7.1   Federal Court Appointments by Party

President	Democrats	Republicans	Percent of President's Party
FDR	203	8	96.2
Truman	129	13	90.8
Eisenhower	11	176	94.1
Kennedy	113	11	91.1
Johnson	170	11	93.9
Nixon	12	166	93.2

SOURCE: Charles H. Sheldon, *The American Judicial Process* (New York: Harper and Row, Publishers, Inc., 1974), p. 121.

Not only are judicial appointments generally reserved for individuals who are nominally members of the president's party, but they also are usually given to those who have been active in party politics. In Chapter 5 it was demonstrated that lawyers are vastly overrepresented in local and state

[32] *Ibid.*, p. 8.

[33] Joel B. Grossman, *Lawyers and Judges* (New York: John Wiley and Sons, 1965), p. 24 suggests that outparty judges are nominated from time to time in order to observe the custom of having representation from both parties in the courts.

[34] Schubert, *Judicial Decision-Making*, p. 12.

politics. Later it will be seen that lawyers occupy a central place in the recruitment process and that they tend to monopolize crucial routes to office. It is not surprising, then, that many federal judicial appointments go to individuals who have been active in party politics most of their careers. According to Schmidhauser, with only one exception, every member of the Supreme Court has held some political post before appointment to the highest court.[35] At the extreme, judicial posts have been used as overt rewards for campaign contributions.[36]

The selection process in the federal courts ensures a major partisan role. Instead of a selection system based on merit and apprenticeship in a judicial career service, as is common in many western democracies, selection of judges in the United States is based, at least partially, on past partisan activity. Actually, appointment to the lower-level federal courts involves much interaction between the president, party organization leaders, and congressional party members. While the president nominates "his" choice for Senate approval, the norm of "senatorial courtesy" allows any senator of the president's party from the district in which the appointment is being made to veto it. Hearings are conducted by the Senate Judiciary Committee and background reports are compiled by the FBI, the American Bar Association, and other interested groups. While only a majority vote is necessary for Senate confirmation, key members of the president's party on Capital Hill retain an effective veto. All nominees must be cleared with appropriate legislative members prior to announcement of the nomination, in order to reduce possible embarrassment. This again demonstrates the sensitive nature of the nomination process and the many political clearances necessary. Box 7.1 illustrates this process. While Supreme Court nominees go through a similar process, they are more commonly a personal choice of the president.[37]

While the degree of partisan involvement necessary as a precondition for such an appointment varies, party activism at some level is important. According to Schmidhauser, this involvement frequently is intense and many times involves campaign management functions involving ties to the president who later appoints them as justices.[38] There are limits to judicial partisanship, however. The prestige of the courts and the image of nonpartisanship must be protected. Too much partisan interference can backfire on

---

[35] John R. Schmidhauser, *The Supreme Court: Its Politics, Personalities and Procedures* (New York: Holt, Rinehart and Winston, 1960), p. 40.

[36] Fried, *Performance in American Bureaucracy*, p. 320.

[37] See Sheldon Goldman and Thomas P. Jahnige, *The Federal Courts as a Political System*, 2nd ed. (New York: Harper and Row, Publishers, 1976), p. 62.

[38] Schmidhauser, *The Supreme Court*, p. 49.

the elected official, as well as the appointees. Still, the data on partisan affiliation and political activity of prospective judges are highly illustrative of the partisan dimension of the federal judicial system.

BOX 7.1   PARTISAN CONSIDERATIONS IN FEDERAL APPOINTMENT PROCESS

In early January, 1956, Chief Judge Major of the U.S. Court of Appeals for the Seventh Circuit notified President Eisenhower of his intention to retire by the end of the following March. Judge Major came from Illinois. However, there was another Illinois judge on the Court of Appeals. According to the informal tradition of state representation on the appeals courts, it was now Indiana's turn for the appointment. Problems soon arose because the two Republican Senators from Indiana (Capehart and Jenner) could not agree on which candidate to back. Moreover, Indiana Republican Congressman Charles Halleck, high in the Republican House hierarchy, had his own candidate. The senators, however, agreed on one point. They would not clear Halleck's candidate, Federal District Judge Parkinson, because they believed that Halleck had received more than his fair share of patronage. Senator Capehart, running for re-election in 1956, wanted the appointment to go to John Hastings who also happened to be Chairman of the Citizens Committee for Capehart. Senator Jenner wanted the appointment to go to Lloyd Hartzler.

Robert Grant, a former congressman, cognizant of Halleck's influence with the Eisenhower Administration and anticipating the selection of Judge Parkinson for the appeals post, went to Washington to line up support for the vacancy on the district bench that would occur with Parkinson's elevation. Eight Indiana Republican Congressmen promised Grant their support. Thus, within a short time after Judge Major announced his intention to retire, the three most important Republican leaders in Indiana actively supported three different men for the soon-to-be-vacant seat on the appeals court. In addition, eight congressmen backed a candidate for an anticipated vacancy on the district bench.

Stalemate resulted. Republican Senator Dirksen of Illinois was waiting in the wings with his candidate if the Indiana Republicans were unable to "clear" a candidate. Justice Department officials negotiated with the principals, but an impasse existed for over a year. Then apparently accommodation was reached. John Hastings received the appointment to the appeals court. The next appeals court vacancy went to Judge Parkinson. Grant eventually received the district court appointment he so actively sought.

SOURCE: Sheldon Goldman and Thomas P. Jahnige, *The Federal Courts as a Political System*, 2nd ed. (New York: Harper and Row, Publishers, Inc., 1976), pp. 58-59.

PARTIES AND STATE JUDICIAL SELECTION

Whereas all federal judges are appointed, the most common means of selecting judges in the state is to elect them. Approximately two thirds of the states use elections, while the remainder provide for gubernatorial appointment, legislative selection, or the Missouri Plan (see Box 7.2). Those systems of executive appointment are similar to the federal court system of selection. The state judicial systems based on elections are, of course, potentially even more political. About half of these states use partisan elections, under which a judicial candidate must seek party sponsorship and run on a party label. Even in states with nonpartisan elections, however, partisan politics is frequently apparent, although it may operate behind a facade of "citizens' committees."

Canon minimizes the importance of formal distinctions among judicial selection systems across the states.[40] He demonstrates that over 45 percent of state supreme court justices leave the court before completion of their terms. While these judges nominally are chosen by elections in most states, the effective power of choice is exercised by the governor who appoints an interim candidate to finish out the term. In many cases, the appointment is made consciously to give the appointee an advantage in the upcoming election. Seldom is an appointed incumbent challenged, and rarely is one defeated, effectively negating the electoral choice. Ironically, the governor's domination is strongest in states with nonpartisan elections, since incumbency plays an even greater role where party labels are absent.[41] At both the state and

[39] Schubert, *Judicial Decision-Making*, p. 7.

[40] Bradley C. Canon, "Characteristics and Career Patterns of State Supreme Court Justices," *State Government*, 45 (Winter, 1972), 37.

[41] Schubert, *Judicial Decision-Making*, p. 27.

BOX 7.2   THE MISSOURI PLAN

The Missouri Plan for the selection of judges was designed to remove judges from the struggles of party and pressure politics as well as gubernatorial patronage. Judges are nominated by a special commission of lawyers, judges, and lay people. The governor appoints from those names submitted by the commission and, after serving on the bench for a short time, the incumbent must go before the people in an election. However, the plan has merely made partisan and group pressures less obvious. For example, business executives have attempted to influence judicial nominations by writing to the nominating commission in behalf of particular candidates. Also, business groups attempt to influence the governor when he makes his selection from the list of nominees sent him by the commission. Watson and Downing have concluded that ". . . the business community, year in and year out, has continued to have an important voice in the overall selection process" in the State of Missouri. Divisions in the Missouri state and municipal bar associations are reflected in campaigns for election of lawyers and lay members to the nominating commissions. The governor often appoints lay members to the commission who are predominantly of his party. It seems clear that political parties as groups have been active in gaining indirect access to the courts through the selection process of the Missouri Plan despite its design to the contrary.

SOURCE: Charles H. Sheldon, *The American Judicial Process* (New York: Harper and Row Publishers, Inc., 1974), p. 123.

federal levels, the judicial selection process is well within the political thicket.[42]

[42] For an excellent example of the role of partisan politics in Senate action on Supreme Court nominations, see John L. Schmidhauser and Larry L. Berg, *The Supreme Court and Congress* (New York: The Free Press, 1972), pp. 103-133, where the controversies surrounding Abe Fortas in 1968-69 are discussed.

PARTISAN INFLUENCE ON DECISIONS

All of the emphasis on the role of political parties in the selection of judges is of little importance unless party affiliation has an impact on judicial decisions. If one assumes that judges are at least, in part, products of their experiences, it seems reasonable that key background factors do have an influence. But does partisanship make a difference in terms of voting decisions by judges? While the evidence is limited due to the fragmentary studies available, as well as the interrelationship of party affiliation with other background variables, there is support for such a thesis.

In a study of state and federal supreme court justices, Stuart Nagel concluded that Democratic judges sitting on the same bench as comparative Republican judges tend to favor the underprivileged.[43] These underprivileged include, among others: (1) the defense in criminal cases, (2) the consumer, (3) the tenant in tenant-landlord cases, (4) the employee in employee injury cases, and (5) the claimant in unemployment compensation cases. Conversely, Republicans are more likely to favor business, landlords, and management. Similarly, Goldman found that while most background variables are not directly related to voting behavior of appeals court justices, party affiliation "proved to have a moderately strong association with voting behavior on issues involving economic liberalism and, to a lesser extent, political liberalism."[44] On the other hand, Thomas Walker found little association between party affiliation and civil liberties decisions among federal district judges.[45]

While many studies of state courts have demonstrated the existence of voting blocs, the presence of partisan blocs has varied. Several researchers have reported that the Michigan Supreme Court is composed of two blocs which correspond to party affiliations of the judges.[46] Studies of Wisconsin and New York Supreme Courts, however, uncovered no partisan differences. As usual, when examining the role of party, the conclusions differ from state to state.

[43] Stuart S. Nagel, "Political Party Affiliation and Judges' Decisions," *American Political Science Review*, 55 (December, 1961), 844.

[44] Goldman and Jahnige, *The Federal Courts*, p. 175.

[45] Thomas G. Walker, "A Note Concerning Partisan Influence on Trial-Judge Decision Making," *Law and Society Review*, 6 (1972), 645-49.

[46] Glendon A. Schubert, "The Study of Judicial Decision-Making as an Aspect of Political Behavior," *American Political Science Review*, 52 (December, 1958), 1014, and Malcolm M. Feeley, "Another Look at the 'Party Variable' in Judicial Decision-Making: An Analysis of the Michigan Supreme Court," *Polity*, 5 (Fall, 1971), 91.

Although there is substantial support for partisan influence on voting in federal courts and in some state courts, one must not overemphasize this influence. While party differences are certainly present, they surface only occasionally and are by no means consistent. Nagel concludes that there is little evidence to suggest that judges consciously vote for or against a party line.

> It is more likely that in some cases judges rely on their personal standards of value in reaching a decision, and these same personal standards also frequently account for their party affiliation. That is to say that party affiliation and decisional propensity for the liberal conservative position correlate with each other because they are frequently effects of the same cause.[47]

Despite these reservations about the direct impact of parties on voting, the partisan nature of the selection process has effective influence over decisions. Whether party is the cause of the judges' personal standards or the result, appointment of a Democrat or a Republican does, apparently, make a difference in many cases.

Goldman envisions the political recruitment process as encouraging party responsibility and thereby providing a "potential link between court output and the current political climate."[48] Without the political input, the courts might become isolated from the mainstream of the public. One result of this responsiveness to partisan considerations is the diversity of outlooks represented on the federal bench. Due to the politicized context of judicial selection and the many points of clearance necessary, parties attempt to provide a balance of the various groups they depend upon for electoral support. The result might be a more open system than some alternatives which, on the surface, might be inviting. Despite the efforts to minimize partisan influence, especially at the state level, it appears likely that parties will continue to play a major role in judicial recruitment.

> Regardless of judicial tenure and modes of selection, there probably will always be a residue of party-correlated judicial subjectivity so long as political parties are at least partly value-oriented and so long as court cases involve value-oriented controversies.[49]

Thus, parties exercise some influence over the distribution of patronage within the judicial system, and, to a lesser extent, over judicial decisions.

[47] Nagel, "Political Party Affiliation," p. 847.

[48] Goldman and Jahnige, *The Federal Courts*, p. 75.

[49] Nagel, "Political Party Affiliation," p. 850.

PRESIDENT, BUREAUCRACY, AND COURTS:
A SUMMARY

The most striking characteristic of parties in the presidency, the bureaucracy, and the courts is the lack of coordination and cooperation. Although the president, as chief executive, nominally has authority over the bureaucracy and is responsible for appointing federal judges, the independence of the various branches is substantial. Even within the bureaucracy, power is dispersed among hundreds of agencies and bureaus. The heavy dependence of recent presidents on their hand-picked White House advisors further minimizes contact with cabinet members and agency heads. The creation of independent regulatory agencies and the civil service system also has weakened the president's ability to rule over a party government.

The party in government, as applied to these branches, lacks any semblance of discipline. Although the president supposedly speaks for the party, he must work within many constraints. Most importantly, the president has a short tenure by law in comparison with the career executives in the bureaucracy and the federal judges. While administrations come and go, the bureaucracy rambles on. The frustration of presidents in failing to make a lasting impression on the government is often obvious. In some cases, the president may encounter more resistance from the executive branch than from outside, as tension between the permanent government and the temporary administration mounts.[50] Even in the appointment process, a president must share power with interest groups, state and congressional delegations, and the like. There is no evidence here of the presence of a systematic party government, even at the national level. While the influence of political parties is felt throughout these disparate branches, party influence tends to be haphazard and unpredictable. The party lacks a clearly defined structure or organizational form, and exhibits no separate party identity.

[50] Davis, *National Executive Branch,* p. 125.

8

Parties
and Congress

In the last chapter, it was found that political parties play a minimal role in the executive and judicial branches of government in the United States. One of the major limitations of parties in these institutions is their lack of a complete and coordinated structure. Where the presence of party is apparent, it tends to be diffuse and fragmented. In no situation is the national party organization in evidence, except indirectly, through the person of the president. This chapter examines parties in the legislature. This subject is treated separately because of the unique organizational structure present in this branch of government. While most emphasis is placed on Congress, state legislative parties, where appropriate, are also discussed.

PARTY ORGANIZATION IN CONGRESS

Unlike the executive and judicial parties, congressional parties have an obvious organizational form with an intricate structure of leadership positions, caucuses, and policy committees. Congress and all state legislatures except Nebraska are organized along party lines. Committee membership is party-based, party leaders have specified functions, and procedural decisions are generally party matters. While there have been periods throughout history when Congress has been dominated by strong leadership, in recent years this has been the exception, rather than the rule. Many congressional reform efforts have diluted leadership sanctions and weakened the formal party leadership positions substantially.

Implied throughout this discussion of the formal party organization in Congress is a most important characteristic of congressional parties. Quite simply, there are actually four party structures in our bicameral legislature: House Democrats, House Republicans, Senate Democrats, and Senate Republicans. While there is some coordination and communication between leaders of each nominal party in the two houses, it is limited, and no party structure transcends house boundaries. This reinforces the fragmented and decentralized nature of parties in government. The president must deal with two sets of congressional leaders. Although it gives the illusion of a power structure, Congress, like the other branches, has no single locus of power. This section will examine in detail the formal party organization in Congress. It will be apparent that in each area, the formal legislative leadership is heavily dependent upon the personal skills of the individuals occupying various positions. And, since formal sanctions are insufficient, these leaders must rely on persuasion and bargaining.

SPEAKER OF THE HOUSE

The speaker is the only congressional leader who extends beyond party lines to the whole chamber. He is, however, always selected in the majority party caucus, since the vote on the House floor merely ratifies the choice of the majority party. Also, this is the only congressional office specified in the Constitution. Speakers gradually accumulated power until early in the twentieth century, when they became all-powerful with unlimited recognitition and control of debate on the floor and the power to appoint committee members and chairmen. In 1910-11, Speaker Cannon was stripped of some of the speaker's key powers and his power was dispersed among substantive committee chairmen, the Rules Committee, seniority leaders, and regional spokesmen. Speakers in many state legislatures still retain substantial powers (see Box 8.1).

Although his direct influence on legislation is now limited, the speaker largely does control the parliamentary machinery. While the speaker shares power with others, if he desires, he still has extensive input into legislative strategy, the development of legislative programs, and initial committee assignments.[1] The speaker also forms a crucial liaison with the president when he is of the majority party. While his dual roles of presidential spokesman and congressional leader at times clash, "The contemporary expectation seems to be that party leaders will support and will even actively work for

[1] The actual appointments to committees are made by autonomous committees on committees. However, the speaker still retains influence over the Ways and Means Committee which serves as the committee on committees for House Democrats. For a good summary, see Nicholas Masters, "Committee Assignments in the House of Representatives," *American Political Science Review*, 55 (June, 1961), 345-57.

BOX 8.1   THE SPEAKER IN THE
STATE LEGISLATURE

In the typical state government the Speaker's powers are very great, second only to those of the governor. Although state legislatures often have emulated congressional organization and style, there has been no counterpart in the states to the 1910 revolution in the U.S. House of Representatives. Ties between the Speaker and the committee system wrenched in the national House during the revolt against Cannonism, are firm in the states—thus helping to centralize decision-making. For example, in all but a handful of states the Speaker continues to be responsible for committee appointments naming the members of standing committees as well as members of special select and conference committees. His influence in the committee structure is reinforced through his power to name committee chairmen in a great many states. . .

The Speaker is frequently a member of the committee on rules—which often plays a critical role near the end of the session in screening proposals—and he may be an *ex officio* member of all committees. Ordinarily, the Speaker does not take an active part in committee deliberations, though his presence may be felt. When he does appear at committee meetings, it may be a good sign that the administration is usually interested in a bill up for consideration.

The Speaker is the principal leader and grand strategist of the majority party in the lower house. Both the majority and minority party caucuses nominate candidates for the office (as well as for other positions), but ordinarily this is only a perfunctory gesture by the minority, since it will not have the votes to elect its candidate. Following the floor vote, the majority's candidate is declared the Speaker, the minority moves to make it unanimous, and the minority's candidate for Speaker becomes his party's floor leader— such is the public record of Speaker selection in the typical legislature. . .

As in Congress, the Speaker in state legislatures engages only rarely in floor debate. On those few occasions when he does take the floor, it is usually to defend an administrative action or to support a major administration bill. His floor appearance is not a casual decision. By not "going to the well too often" he can command greater attention for his views and preserve to some degree the

205

"principle" that the Speaker serves the pleasure of the whole House and is not merely the leader of the majority party.

In summary, the Speaker's influence in the states is compounded of numerous elements. In the first place, he is the guardian of party fortunes and policies. Second, he is charged with many official duties, nearly all of which hold implications for the party interest. Thus, typically, he appoints the members of standing, special, and conference committees; he chairs the rules committee; he refers bills to committee; he presides over house sessions, decides points of order, recognizes members, and puts questions to a vote; he has it within his power to assist a member with a "pet" bill or to sandbag it; he can ease the way for new members or ignore them; he can advance the legislative careers of members or throw up roadblocks before them. All these prerogatives contribute to a network of influence. And, finally, if the Speaker has the strong support of the governor, if he meets with him regularly and is privy to administration plans and secrets, new measures of power and influence come his way. Of all the legislative posts, the one most sought after is the speakership.

SOURCE: William J. Keefe and Morris S. Ogul, *The American Legislative Process: Congress and the States,* 4th ed. 1977, pp. 280-82. Adapted by permission of Prentice-Hall, Inc., Englewood Cliffs, New Jersey.

Presidential programs."[2] The speaker must also balance two functions, which at times may be incompatible. Constitutionally, he is charged with maintenance of the House. He must work to minimize disruptive conflicts and ensure that House business runs smoothly. At the same time, as leader of the congressional party in the House, he must avoid serious conflicts with other party leaders, mobilize support for presidential programs, and maximize party unity. Successful fulfillment of these two funtions depends heavily on the personality and skills of the individual speaker.

Contemporary speakers, therefore, are more than party leaders. While their powers are restricted, they retain a substantial amount of influence, certainly more than any other office, either in the House or the Senate. Among the speaker's other discretionary powers are:

[2] Barbara Hinckley, *Stability and Change in Congress* (New York: Harper and Row, Publishers, 1971), p. 110.

1. recognition of speakers on floor and resulting control over course and timing of debate;
2. assignment of bills to committees in doubtful cases;
3. ruling on appropriateness of parliamentary procedures;
4. appointment of House members to conference committees;
5. final responsibility for scheduling legislation;
6. limited influence over selection of committee members.

Most importantly, the speaker is at the center of the communication network. He knows what members desire, how they intend to vote, and what their mood is.

> In a large and decentralized organization, where information is a highly prized political resource, such a position carries considerable power of its own.[3]

There is no counterpart of the speaker in the Senate, no chamberwide office with any substantial powers. The vice-president officially presides but is seldom present and is considered an outsider. The senior senator of the majority party, the president pro-tempore, is primarily an honorary position. Normally, the chair is occupied by a freshman senator, since unlike the chair in the more procedurally oriented House, the chair in the Senate carries no inherent power.

PARTY FLOOR LEADERS

The chief spokesmen of the parties in the legislatures are the majority and minority floor leaders. They are selected by the caucus of the respective party and are specifically responsible for developing and scheduling the party's legislative program and for steering it through their house. Although they have few formal powers, floor leaders are located at the center of action and do have some fragmentary powers. Lyndon Johnson was able to forge many scattered powers into a strong leadership position through a highly intensive, pragmatic, and personalized leadership style.[4] According to Thomas

---

[3] *Ibid.,* p. 113.

[4] For more information on Lyndon Johnson's leadership style, see Ralph K. Huitt, "Democratic Party Leadership in the Senate," *American Political Science Review,* 55 (June, 1961), 333-44, and Rowland Evans and Robert Novak, *Lyndon B. Johnson: The Exercise of Power* (New York: New American Library, 1966).

Murphey, the House majority leader serves as the speaker's bridge to his party, while in the Senate, the majority leader has most of the speaker's powers and is the single most powerful senator.[5] Party leaders tend to be moderate members with long service in Congress. They cannot be identified with an extreme bloc without hurting their effectiveness to some extent.

The minority leader in the House is the candidate of the minority party nominated for speaker. Generally, the minority leader consults closely with the speaker concerning the agenda, procedures, and so forth. The speaker cannot forget that some day the positions might be reversed if the opposition party takes control.[6] The minority leaders in both houses have a difficult time retaining the support of their members in the face of their minority status. For instance, after large Republican losses in a preceding election, Republicans have replaced the minority leader in hard-fought battles. In a 1959 revolt Charles Halleck replaced Joseph Martin. Five years later, after massive losses in 1964, Gerald Ford replaced Halleck as minority leader.[7] Minority leaders are charged with the welfare of their party and attempt to mobilize support for party strategies. If their party holds the presidency, the minority leaders are chief spokesmen for the president on the floor.

PARTY WHIPS

Since about 1900, party whips have been selected by floor leaders or the party caucus to gather intelligence for the leadership.[8] Over the years, especially in the House, this has resulted in an elaborate network of whips, who are in constant touch with members. While leadership dependence on whips varies with the perception of the floor leader, whips can provide crucial information to the leaders. In addition to polling members about their voting intentions and relaying these data to the floor leaders, whips ensure maximum attendance of supporters for key votes. They apply pressure on supporters to

---

[5] Thomas P. Murphey, *The New Politics Congress* (Lexington, Mass.: D.C. Heath and Company, 1974), p. 115.

[6] Hinckley, *Stability and Change*, p. 115.

[7] For a summary of types of leadership change, see Robert L. Peabody, "Party Leadership Change in the House of Representatives," *American Political Science Reveiw*, (September, 1967), 675-93. For a more detailed examination, see Garrison Nelson, "Partisan Patterns of House Leadership Change, 1789-1977," *American Political Science Review*, 71 (September, 1977), 918-39.

[8] See Randall B. Ripley, "The Party Whip Organizations in the United States House of Representatives," *American Political Science Review*, 58 (September, 1964), 561-76, and Walter J. Oleszek, "Party Whips in the United States Senate," *Journal of Politics*, 33 (November, 1971), 955-79.

be present for the vote, and on nonsupporters to abstain from voting. A strong and effective party whip system can make a substantial impact on party success on crucial votes. In many cases, the party whip succeeds the floor leader in office and therefore the whip's position is sought after by those with higher ambitions.

PARTY CAUCUS OR CONFERENCE

In theory, the caucus is the party mechanism for: (1) selection of party leaders, and (2) consideration of party policy, procedures, and legislative programs. In a strong party system, the caucus includes all party members, who meet frequently and jointly arrive at binding policy decisions. In other words, in a strong caucus system party members are ethically bound to vote along strict party lines when the issue gets to the floor. In the past, the caucus was very strong in Congress, especially while Woodrow Wilson was president. Loyalty to the party was expected and binding caucuses were frequent. About one quarter of the state legislatures have strong party caucuses, some of which meet weekly or even daily.[9]

Not surprisingly, congressional caucuses, or "conferences" as they are termed by all but the House Democrats, now meet infrequently and have no binding force. Caucuses in Congress are usually limited to selection of party leaders at the beginning of each session. Caucuses have some influence over procedural matters, but almost no policy influence. There are no sanctions available against members who vote independently of the caucus decision. Efforts of freshmen House Democrats in 1975-1976 to strengthen the caucus had limited success.[10] The weakness of the "principal governing body"[11] to extend its influence beyond leadership selection is one of the most obvious manifestations of the weakness of congressional parties.

POLICY COMMITTEES

In 1946, the Joint Committee on Legislative Reorganization recommended creation of policy committees "to formulate overall legislative policy of the two parties."[12] Although each party in each house has created policy com-

---

[9] Belle Zeller, ed. *American State Legislatures* (New York: Thomas Y. Crowell Company, 1954), pp. 194-97. Also see Malcolm E. Jewell, *The State Legislature*, 2nd ed. (New York: Random House, 1969), pp. 48-51.

[10] See *Congressional Quarterly Weekly Report*, (November 16, 1974), 3118-20, for a discussion of the objectives of these "reformers."

[11] Murphey, *New Politics Congress*, p. 116.

[12] Report of the Joint Committee on the Organization of Congress, 79th Congress, 2nd Session Senate Report #1011 (March 4, 1946), p. 12.

mittees,[13] they have never become policy-making bodies, nor have they ever been able to present an overall congressional party program. There is little consideration of alternatives, no leadership in establishing a legislative program, and there are no binding decisions. Although policy committees do serve as forums for discussion and communication, they seldom face the most divisive and critical issues.

Randall Ripley suggests that party leaders should work for "modest expansion" of the policy committees in order to achieve an expanded substantive policy-making role for themselves.[14] He sees the policy committee as a crucial mechanism for development of more centralized party leadership. As of this time, however, these committees have not realized even a modest policy-making role. Furthermore, opposition from those upon whom strong policy committees would intrude is substantial. The power of seniority would naturally be reduced if traditional arrangements of authority were modified. Those congressmen who value their individual centers of power view policy committees as envisioned by Ripley as a threat.[15] The prognosis for more effective policy committees does not appear to be good at this time.

EXTRA-PARTY GROUPS

The presence of groups outside the formal party organizations reaffirms the weakness of parties in Congress. One of the best organized and effective of these extra-party groups is the House Democratic Study Group (DSG), which was established in 1959.[16] This loosely knit liberal bloc is an attempt to counterbalance the conservative southern bloc of the party. The DSG has elected officers, a whip system, a professional staff member, and a fund-raising unit. It conducts research on policy questions of interest to members

[13] These committees range in size from 10 in the Senate Democratic Policy Committee to 27 in the House Republican Policy Committee. Both Democratic committees are dominated by party leaders, while the Republican committees are more open, with rotating membership.

[14] Randall B. Ripley, "Party Leaders, Policy Committees, and Policy Analysis in the United States Senate," in *Policymaking Role of Leadership in the Senate,* Commission on the Operation of the Senate, 94th Congress, 2nd Session (Washington, D.C.: U.S. Government Printing Office, 1976), p. 5.

[15] William J. Keefe and Morris S. Ogul, *The American Legislative Process,* 3rd ed. (Englewood Cliffs, N.J.: Prentice-Hall, Inc., 1973), p. 285.

[16] For a full discussion of the DSG, see Arthur G. Stevens, Arthur H. Miller, and Thomas E. Mann, "Mobilization of Liberal Strength in the House, 1955-1970: The Democratic Study Group," *American Political Science Review,* 68 (June, 1974), 667-81.

and provides recommendations on some legislation.[17] The membership of the DSG is approximately 150, or about half of the Democratic congressmen. A corresponding extra-party group on the Republican side is the Wednesday Group. While it is the most liberal and the largest of the informal Republican groups in the House, it has a low profile and is primarily concerned with communication among its members.

PARTY ORGANIZATION IN CONGRESS: A SUMMARY

On the surface, parties in Congress appear well constructed. Formal leadership positions are highly visible, and party conferences and committees are in evidence. When one penetrates the surface, however, it is clear that the formal powers of the leadership are not enough to ensure control over party members. Power is seldom concentrated in any person or group, and fragmentation within the party ranks is obvious. The next section of this chapter attempts to discuss the actual distribution of power in Congress.

DISTRIBUTION OF POWER IN CONGRESS

Randall Ripley contends that three basic patterns of power distribution have been present in the Senate during the last century: centralization, decentralization, and individualism. Table 8.1 demonstrates the major characteristics and consequences of each type. While there has been much fluctuation of the basic patterns during this century,[18] the movement since the early New Deal has been from centralized party leadership to independently powerful committees to an individualized power structure, where each senator is able to be a "leader" or expert in at least one area of specialization.

> When individualism prevails in the Senate, the titular party leaders are not necessarily the real leaders. A large number of members can

[17] Murphey, *New Politics Congress,* p. 129, states that the strength of the DSG research arm resulted in the formation of a Democratic Research Group by the conservative bloc in the early 1970s.

[18] Randall B. Ripley, *Power in the Senate* (New York: St. Martin's Press, 1969), p. 15, suggests the following chronology: 1869-1885 Individualism; 1885-1905 Centralization; 1905-1911 Decentralization; 1911-1917 Centralization; 1917-1933 Individualism; 1933-1937 Centralization; 1937-1955 Decentralization; 1955-1961 Decentralization/Individualism; 1961- Individualism.

Table 8.1 Power in the Senate: Three Models

Competitors for Power	Centralization	Pattern of Power Distribution	
		Decentralization	Individualism
Central party leadership	Powerful and aggressive	Moderately powerful and aggressive	Relatively powerless; unaggressive
Standing committee chairmen	Loyal to the party leaders; moderately powerful	Not necessarily allied with party leadership; independently powerful	Often independent of party leaders; moderately powerful
The individual seantor	Party-oriented; relatively powerless	Committee-oriented; relatively powerless	Subcommittee—or self-oriented; relatively powerful
Consequences			
Nature of the legislative process	Unifed	Partially unified; partially segmented	Segmented
Power acquired by staff members	Low, confined to a few	Moderate; relatively confined	High; relatively widespread
The prospects of organized institutional change (reform)	Most likely	Moderately likely	Least likely

SOURCE: Randall Ripley, *Power in the Senate* (New York: St. Martin's Press, Inc., 1969), p. 14.

be legitimately referred to as "leaders." The formal central party leaders must consult with a large number of members before they feel free to state positions for the party. These leaders are far less aggressive than leaders in centralized or decentralized Senates, and they play only a limited role in trying to promote a united party on important substantive questions.[19]

COMMITTEES AND SUBCOMMITTEES

The expansion of subcommittees, since the 1946 Legislative Reorganization Act reduced the number of full committees, has been phenomenal. There are now over 250 subcommittees in Congress. Since each subcommittee has a chairman with some degree of power over substantive bills, power is significantly dispersed. In the Senate in 1968 there were 103 subcommittee chairmen. Each senator of the majority party is almost assured one chairmanship, while the minority party members are the ranking members on several subcommittees. While the work of many of these subcommittees is minor and limited, they do give each member a base of power and further the individualistic distribution of power in the Senate. While power in the House is more centralized than in the Senate, the tendency to create more subcommittees has reinforced dispersal in both houses.

The daily competition between the formal party leaders and the committee and subcommittee chairmen reflects a basic legislative fact of life: that a strong committee system is the antithesis of centralized party leadership. As soon as power is dispersed to committees, tension arises between the party leaders and individuals in their committee and subcommittee roles. Therefore, party leaders "have generally sought to control the committees; the committees have generally sought autonomy."[20] Over the last six decades, with few exceptions, committees have held the advantage and maintained substantial influence over policy matters.

Committees screen out a very large proportion of bills by not reporting them out. For instance, in the 93rd Congress (1973-74), of the 21,095 bills and resolutions introduced in the House, only 1,333, or 6 percent, were sent from the committees to the floor. Although most major bills are reported, it is the committee, not the full House or Senate, which normally writes the legislation. Amendments on the floor are commonly limited in scope and number, even on major pieces of legislation. In many cases in the House, the Rules Committee can minimize debate and eliminate the use of amendments on the floor. While the floor leaders retain some scheduling prerogatives and

[19] *Ibid.*, p. 11.
[20] *Ibid.*, p. 22.

serve as spokesmen for bills on the floor, many options have already been closed by the committees, especially if the bill has nearly unanimous bipartisan support in committee. In such cases, there is little chance of rejection on the floor.[21]

SENIORITY SYSTEM

The system by which committee chairmen are selected also influences the distribution of power in a legislature. Under a seniority system, with the chair going automatically to the member of the majority party with the longest continuous service on the committee, party leaders have little power. Although the seniority system in Congress has been made more flexible in the last decade (especially by House Democrats), Congress still operates primarily on a straight seniority basis. This reinforces the decentralized character of leadership in Congress by multiplying centers of power down to the level of committee chairmen, who are relatively free from party leader sanctions.

> Lacking the strong centripetal force of powerful leaders or disciplined parties, the House has become even more fractionalized and unmanageable. First the committees and now the subcommittees have become the nexus of activity . . . many of these self-contained work groups have taken on the trappings of feudal domains whose leaders have adopted a policy of mutual noninterference in the affairs of their peers.[22]

The threat of removal by party leaders is not effective unless the committee members themselves desire a chairman out. Leadership is hesitant to enter the sacred arena of committees.

According to Barbara Hinckley, the seniority system also "protects the diverse interests of the members and strengthens Congress's independence of

---

[21] For more discussion on parties and committees see, Richard R. Fenno, Jr. *Congressmen in Committees* (Boston: Little, Brown and Company, 1973); John F. Manley, *The Politics of Finance: The House Committee on Ways and Means* (Boston: Little, Brown and Company, 1970); Richard F. Fenno, *The Power of the Purse: Appropriations Politics in Congress* (Boston: Little Brown and Company, 1966); William L. Morrow, *Congressional Committees* (New York: Charles Scribner's Sons, 1969); George Goodwin, Jr., *The Little Legislatures: Committees of Congress* (Amherst: University of Massachusetts Press, 1970).

[22] Roger H. Davidson and Walter J. Oleszek, *Congress Against Itself* (Bloomington, Ind.: Indiana University Press, 1977), p. x. This pattern of reliance on committees was best illustrated on March 31, 1976, when the Senate created a select committee to study the committee system.

the Presidency,"[23] thus further fragmenting of power. While some critics of the seniority system would have committees more accountable to party leadership, the seniority system does help Congress "to defend itself against outside control by preventing lines of influence from forming between Congress and the White House."[24] The same factor that disperses power in Congress, therefore, also insulates Congress from presidential control. The seniority system is but one additional institution facilitating decentralization in governmental power.

CONGRESSIONAL STAFFS

Due to the heavy workload of congressmen, especially senators, there has been a further fragmentation of power. The proliferation of congressional staffers (see Table 8.2) and their increasing involvement in the details of

Table 8.2   Growth of Personal Staffs of Congressmen,
1960-1974

	1960	1967	1974
Total staff	2,344	3,276	5,109
Percentage of total staff assigned to district offices	14%	26%	34%
Percentage of congressmen whose district offices open only when congressman is home or after adjournment	29%	11%	2%
Percentage of congressmen listing multiple district offices	4%	18%	47%

SOURCE: Morris P. Fiorina, *Congress: Keystone of the Washington Establishment* (New Haven: Yale University Press, 1977), p. 58.

legislation have given many key staff members substantial power in specific areas. Much of the legwork is conducted by the committee staffs. While these individuals maintain a low visibility in public, they have much influence, especially as legislation becomes more technically involved. To a greater

[23] Barbara Hinckley, *The Seniority System in Congress* (Bloomington, Ind.: Indiana University Press, 1971), p. 112. For a good summary of the seniority system, see George Goodwin, Jr., "The Seniority System in Congress," *American Political Science Review,* 53 (June, 1959), 412-36.

[24] *Ibid.*

extent than ever before many legislative decisions in actuality are made by these appointed professional staffers.[25]

CONGRESSMEN'S PERCEPTIONS OF PARTY

The data in Table 8.3 demonstrate the importance of party as perceived by a large sample of Congressmen. Only 10 percent question the legitimacy of parties and agree that the people would be better served if Congressmen were elected without party labels. Eighty-four percent tend to disagree or disagree. Pro-party support decreases, however, when more rigorous qualifications are established. For instance, 52 percent doubt that a member should support the party even when it costs some constituency support. Similarly, 51 percent are against the parties' taking "clearcut, opposing stands" on key issues. The dissenting 51 percent would much rather have the freedom available under the present circumstances. According to Roger Davidson:

> The picture that emerges from these responses is one of overwhelming support for the norm of party activity but considerable disagreement over the degree of loyalty that party membership should imply.[26]

These data lend support for David Mayhew's thesis that parties in Congress serve the members and not vice versa. Since members are not party or program-oriented, but election-oriented, most of their time and effort is directed at getting reelected. They are largely unwilling to risk defeat by following the party line, and the leadership certainly realizes this.

> The fact is that the enactment of party programs is electorally not very important to members. . . What is important to each Congressman, and vitally so, is that he be free to take positions that serve his advantage.[27]

[25] For a good general summary of congressional staffs see, Malcolm E. Jewell and Samuel C. Patterson, *The Legislative Process in the United States,* 2nd ed. (New York: Random House, 1973), pp. 249-277. For more in-depth analysis see James T. Heaphey and Alan P. Balutis, ed., *Legislative Staffing: A Comparative Perspective* (Beverly Hills: Sage Publications, 1975) and Harrison W. Fox, Jr. and Susan Webb Hammond, *Congressional Staffs: The Invisible Force in American Lawmaking* (New York: The Free Press, 1977).

[26] Roger H. Davidson, *The Role of the Congressman* (New York: Pegasus, 1969), p. 149.

[27] David R. Mayhew, *Congress: The Electoral Connection* (New Haven: Yale University Press, 1974), p. 99.

Table 8.3 Attitudes of Congressmen toward Political Parties

	Agree	Tend to Agree	Undecided	Tend to Disagree	Disagree	No Answer
"The best interests of the people would be better served if Congressmen were elected without party labels."	7%	3%	3%	14%	70%	2%
"Under our form of government, every individual should take an interest in government directly, not through a political party."	17%	12%	5%	20%	46%	1%
"If a bill is important for his party's record, a member should vote with his party even if it costs him some support in his district."	9%	26%	7%	15%	37%	6%
"The two parties should take clearcut, opposing stands on more of the important and controversial issues."	17%	28%	3%	16%	35%	1%

SOURCE: Roger H. Davidson, *The Role of the Congressman* (New York: Pegasus, 1969) p. 145.

It is not surprising therefore that the party is perceived by some as a "loose alliance of individual Congressmen."[28] Morris Fiorina agrees that incumbent Congressmen "have managed to structure Washington influence relationships so as to make their reelections ever more certain."[29] With an increasing number of Congressmen wishing to retain office for long periods, party discipline is difficult at best. As reflected in the above data, individual congressmen strongly desire the flexibility to follow the wishes of their constituencies when party-constituency conflicts arise. They favor the use of party labels, but exhibit little interest in party cohesion. The parties as they now exist appear to fulfill the needs of Congressmen quite well.

PARTIES AND VOTING IN CONGRESS

Some have argued that American parties are Tweedledum-Tweedledee[30] or that there "isn't a dime's worth of difference." Others contend that real differences do exist, although they might not apply to all issues or include all members of the party. From what has been seen in all other areas of party politics, it would seem suspicious if there were not substantial internal party divisions. While the debate continues, legislative roll call votes do offer a means of examining divisions within parties as well as differences between the parties. Standards of party cohesion can be established and then applied to the actual voting data. Unfortunately, the use of a wide variety of methods of analysis, time periods, and issues for study has resulted in less than consistent findings regarding the influence of party on congressional voting behavior—if, indeed, such results are possible.

DEFINING A "PARTY" VOTE

When very strict criteria of party voting are applied to voting in the U.S. Congress, the results are not encouraging to those who favor cohesive parties. In a classic study by Julius Turner, a "party vote" was defined as one where

[28] Robert A. Dahl, *Congress and Foreign Policy* (New York: Harcourt, Brace and World, Inc. 1950), p. 51.

[29] Morris P. Fiorina, *Congress: Keystone of the Washington Establishment* (New Haven: Yale University Press, 1977), p. 14.

[30] The Tweedledum—Tweedledee analogy is taken from the identical twins in Lewis Carroll's *Through the Looking Glass* between whom there was no difference in action and thought. Originally applied to American parties by Lord Bryce in 1888, it has served as a description of two parties which are identical in program and policy concerns.

Table 8.4 Proportion of Party Votes in
U.S. House of Representatives,
1921-1967

Year	Percent Party Votes
1921	28.6
1928	7.1
1930-31	31.0
1933	22.5
1937	11.8
1944	10.7
1945	17.5
1946	10.5
1947	15.1
1948	16.4
1950	6.4
1953	7.0
1959	8.0
1963	7.6
1964	6.2
1965	2.8
1966	1.6
1967	3.3

SOURCE: Julius Turner, *Party and Constituency: Pressures on Congress* (Baltimore: Johns Hopkins Press, 1951), p. 24. Data for years since 1950 appear in the revised edition of this volume (Baltimore: Johns Hopkins Press, 1970), prepared by Edward V. Schneier, Jr. (p. 17).

at least 90 percent of one party opposed 90 percent of the other.[31] In comparing the U.S. House to the British House of Commons, using this criterion, Turner found that party voting in the House is substantially lower. The data in Table 8.4 further demonstrate that party voting in the House has declined markedly over the last five decades, with an average of less than 5 percent in the 1960s. The corresponding figure for the House of Commons is generally over 90 percent.

However, if one relaxes this standard to 50 percent versus 50 percent, the picture changes. Under such conditions, approximately 40 percent of the

[31] Julius Turner, *Party and Constituency: Pressures on Congress* (Baltimore: Johns Hopkins Press, 1951). A revised edition was published by Edward V. Schneier, Jr. in 1970. Also see another classic work, David Truman, *The Congressional Party: A Case Study* (New York: John Wiley and Sons, 1959).

roll call votes during the 1960s and 1970s were party votes (Table 8.5). While this still does not illustrate highly cohesive and competitive parties, most of the nonparty votes are bipartisan majorities in which at least 50 percent of both parties agree. Again, the conclusion as to whether party has an important influence on voting depends solely on the subjective standard used. It becomes imperative, therefore, to look at party influence on specific sets of issues and gauge its relative importance to each issue-related dimension of voting.

Table 8.5   Party Cohesion, Simple Majority vs. Majority
1960-1976

Year	Senate	House	Congress
1960	37%	53%	42%
1961	62	50	58
1962	41	46	43
1963	47	49	48
1964	36	55	41
1965	42	52	46
1966	50	41	46
1967	35	36	35
1968	32	35	33
1969	36	31	34
1970	35	27	32
1971	42	38	40
1972	36	27	33
1973	40	42	41
1974	44	29	37
1975	48	48	48
1976	37	36	37
1977	42	42	42

SOURCE: *Congressional Quarterly Almanac* (Washington: Congressional Quarterly, Inc., 1977).

PARTY COHESION IN CONGRESS

Lewis Froman contends that party cohesion as it exists is the result of similar constituency demands on members of each party.[32] In other words, party

---

[32] Lewis A. Froman, Jr. *Congressmen and Their Constituencies* (Chicago: Rand McNally, 1963). Also see David R. Mayhew, *Party Loyalty Among Congressmen* (Cambridge: Harvard University Press, 1966) and Warren E. Miller and Donald E. Stokes, "Constituency Influence in Congress," *American Political Science Review*, 57 (March, 1963), 45-56. Richard

cohesion reflects demographic characteristics of party member districts. This may explain why most deviation from party occurs when constitutency and party interests are at odds. Helmut Norpoth, however, concludes instead that party cohesion is "rooted in policy attitudes shared by members belonging to the same party."[33] Shared policy goals, not similar constituencies, are most crucial for party cohesion, according to Norpoth. Work by John Kingdon supports this contention. Kingdon demonstrates firmly rooted differences in Republican and Democratic issue appeals along a liberal-conservative dimension.

> Not a single Democrat in this study perceived his supporting coalition as including business and professional groups but not labor, and not a single Republican listed a coalition which included organized labor but not business and professional people.[34]

Party members vote together because of their similar attitudes on policy matters, not because of sanctions imposed by the leaders, or simply because of similar constituency demands.

DIMENSIONS OF VOTING

In order to examine the impact of party on actual voting in a meaningful manner, roll call votes can be categorized into issue groupings or "voting dimensions." This method is much superior to depending on a single (generally liberal-conservative) dimension covering a number of issues, because the multidimensional approach allows one to distinguish between issue areas in which party is important and those in which it might not influence individual congressmen. This analysis of voting in Congress is based on the work of Aage Clausen, in which he describes five dimensions of votes: government management, agricultural assistance, social welfare, civil liberties, and international

---

F. Fenno, Jr., "U.S. House Members in Their Constituencies: An Exploration," *American Political Science Review,* 71 (September, 1977), 883-917, discusses the "home style" of congressmen and James H. Kuklinski, "Representativeness and Elections: A Policy Analysis," *American Political Science Review,* 72 (March, 1978), 165-77, examines constituency influence on California state legislators.

[33] Helmut Norpoth, "Explaining Party Cohesion in Congress: The Case of Shared Policy Attitudes," *American Political Science Review,* 70 (December, 1976), 1157.

[34] John W. Kingdon, *Candidates for Office: Beliefs and Strategies* (New York: Random House, 1968), p. 144.

involvement.[35] Together, these five dimensions accounted for approximately 75 percent of the roll call votes in each of the Congresses studied.[36]

As expected, the role of party in congressional voting and the extent of cohesion within each party varies significantly with the issue at hand. The most conflict between the parties occurs, respectively, in the areas of government management, agricultural assistance, and social welfare. Conversely, there is virtually no difference between Democrats and Republicans on civil liberties and international involvement. Significantly, as conflict between the parties increases, there is more cohesion within each party.

The data in Figure 8.1 illustrate the substantial difference in the extent to which party affiliation explains voting in each of the five issue dimensions. Party alone accounts for an average of 83 percent of the variation in voting on government management roll calls. Undoubtedly, it is the management of the economy which most clearly separates Democrats and Republicans.[37] Agricultural assistance also clearly distinguishes between the parties. Party membership is more important than constituency, region, and state combined. Also, while party is the single most important factor in social welfare voting, it only accounts for an average of 31 percent of the votes. In all three of these dimensions, however, party is consistently a strong predictor of congressional voting. Party members are likely to vote together on each of these dimensions, especially on economic matters.

The situation is much different on the remaining dimensions. Party explains only about 4 percent of the vote on civil liberties and none on international involvement. Figure 8.1 demonstrates that civil liberties are a regional dimension, and to a lesser extent are explained by the urban-rural nature of a member's constituency. To a large extent, this reflects the North-South split in the Democratic party, which nullifies any semblance of party cohesion. Since international relations are traditionally the most bipartisan of all issues, it is not surprising that party plays no direct and independent role on this dimension.

These data suggest that one cannot examine party influence without designating the issues under consideration.

[35] Aage R. Clausen, *How Congressmen Decide: A Policy Focus* (New York: St. Martin's Press, 1973). In a later work, Aage R. Clausen and Carl E. Van Horn, "The Congressional Response to a Decade of Change: 1963-1972," *Journal of Politics,* 39 (August, 1977), 624-66, Clausen added two additional policy dimensions: (1) size of agricultural subsidies and (2) national security recommitment.

[36] *Ibid.,* p. 12.

[37] This dimension also includes votes on the role of government in the economy, private versus public development of natural resources, and balancing the budget.

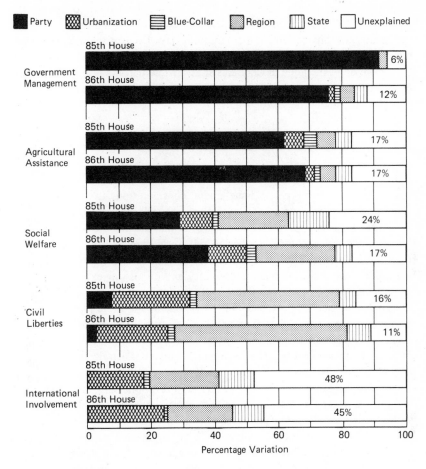

Figure 8.1 Percentage of Variation in Policy Positions
Explained by Party, Constituency (urbanization,
blue-collar percent of work force), Region and State

SOURCE: Aage R. Clausen, *How Congressmen Decide: A Policy Focus* (New York: St. Martin's Press, 1973), p. 168.

The clear absence of partisan influence on civil liberties and international involvement stands in sharp contrast to the clear presence of party influence on the other three dimensions. . .[38]

They also demonstrate that party is but one possible influence on voting. Characteristics of constituency, which might interfere with party influence,

[38] Clausen, *How Congressmen Decide,* p. 143.

are numerous. Also, the perceptions of each congressman are to some extent a result of his or her background. Any decision in a legislature, therefore, is the result of many factors, party and nonparty. Even in the area of government management, about 10 percent of the variation on voting is unexplained by the variables included in Clausen's study. While party is not overwhelmingly important on all issues and under all circumstances, it does continue to play a major role.

INFLUENCE OF PARTY LEADERSHIP IN CONGRESS

In addition to the type of issue under consideration, Lewis Froman and Randall Ripley, in a study of House Democratic leadership, offer six conditions that facilitate party leaders' success in maintaining party cohesion on a vote.[39] First, the greater the cohesion and commitment of the leadership, the more difficult it will be for a member to vote against the party. By designating a particular bill as crucial to the party and by making extensive attempts to persuade party members of that fact, the leaders have a greater chance of attaining member support. Second, party leaders are more likely to achieve unity on procedural rather than substantive issues. The procedural vote for speaker, for instance, is a strictly party vote, while key substantive votes introduce outside influences that minimize member acquiescence to leadership recommendations.

Third, if the issue is less visible to the public and, generally, more complex, a party line vote is easier to achieve. Since the complexity and low visibility of the issue tends to reduce outside influences on the members, they are less likely to be cross-pressured into voting against party leaders. Conversely, the more visible a vote is to a congressman's constituency and the more controversial it is, the greater difficulty the leaders will face.

A fourth and related condition of leadership success is the visibility of action. Since recorded roll call votes on the floor are the most visible type of activity, the greatest proportion of defections from the leadership occur at that level. Voice votes and other unrecorded votes, as well as secret votes in the committees, facilitate leader success. This explains why some congressmen vote differently depending on the type of vote used.

The last two conditions directly relate to outside pressures on congressmen. Obviously, those with constituency attitudes strongly opposed to the

---

[39] Lewis A. Froman, Jr. and Randall B. Ripley, "Conditions for Party Leadership: The Case of House Democrats," *American Political Science Review,* 59 (March, 1965), 52-63.

party leadership will hesitate to follow the party and endanger reelection.[40] It is far more common in these instances to vote with one's constituency, and the leadership recognizes this, since they, too, would act similarly under like circumstances. The most common rationale for voting against the party is strong constituency opposition. The most obvious of the divisions in either party is between the northern and southern Democrats. Table 8.6 summarizes the scope of this division from 1969-1977. Finally, state delegations at times serve as important reference points for members of the party from that state. These informal socializing agencies occasionally provide the member with a rationalization for not voting with the party. At times, state delegations use the threat of such action to gain accommodations from the party leadership. Constituency pressure also is reflected in voting by state delegations, of course.

Table 8.6   North-South Democratic Splits*

	Total Votes	North-South Democratic Splits	Percent of Splits
1969	422	155	36%
1970	684	233	34
1971	743	279	38
1972	861	330	38
1973	1135	318	28
1974	1081	326	30
1975	1214	409	34
1976	1349	378	28
1977	1341	375	28

*At least 50 percent of the southern Democrats against at least 50 percent of the northern democrats.

SOURCE: *Congressional Quarterly Almanac* (Washington, D.C.: Congressional Quarterly, Inc., 1977), p. 39B.

PARTIES IN CONGRESS: A SUMMARY

The impact of party on voting in Congress is a function of many factors including type of legislation, personal background of the member, nonparty demands on member, and importance of the vote to the party leadership.

[40] Regional issues, such as civil rights in the South and water rights and gun control in the Rocky Mountain States, have restricted otherwise liberal Democrats from following party leaders on those issues.

While party affiliation certainly does not determine a congressman's vote on any particular bill, party continues to be the single most important factor in congressional voting.

> Nonetheless, when all the exceptions are listed, totaled, and explained, there are still important differences between the parties. Over the years a majority of the Democratic party has been determined to chart a liberal course for the federal government on labor and social legislation, while a majority of the Republican party has been equally insistent in posing a conservative alternative.[41]

Despite the competition from many nonparty sources and the limitations on partisan voting in Congress, party remains a major influence on the members. Virtually all congressmen manifest loyalty to one party or the other. While every congressman represents a unique constituency, each also has been elected as a partisan. Party remains a primary cue for legislative behavior. In their study on cue-giving in the House, Donald Matthews and James Stimson suggest that members of each congressional party feel a responsibility to strengthen their party, and recognize a common stake in the image it projects.

> Members refer repeatedly to the legitimate role of the Party leader as a cue-giver; he is elected to look after the interests of the party, and when he performs that function he has a legitimate right to make recommendations.[42]

The party leaders account for 16 percent of all mentions of cue-giving and clearly play a major role in shaping the perceptions of members on certain votes. Forty-six percent of the members interviewed by Matthews and Stimson indicated that if they knew nothing else about a bill, they would like to know the position of their party leaders. "Most members feel duty bound to ascertain the views of their party leaders and go along in the absence of contrary inclinations."[43] Similarly, Randall Ripley found that 74 percent of the Democrats and 72 percent of the Republicans in the House indicated that party position was the first consideration in determining their own position.[44] Other studies agree that the desire to find like-minded informants

---

[41] Keefe and Ogul, *The American Legislative Process*, p. 306.

[42] Donald R. Matthews and James A. Stimson, *Yeas and Nays: Normal Decision-Making in the U.S. House of Representatives* (New York: John Wiley and Sons, 1975), p. 96.

[43] *Ibid.*, p. 95.

[44] Randall B. Ripley, *Party Leaders in the House of Representatives* (Washington, D.C.: The Brookings Institution, 1967), p. 141.

generally leads a congressman to a party colleague.[45] Even though individual congressmen deviate from their party's attitude and at times from the party's roll call position, "the significance of this individual relationship pales by comparison with the match between party attitude and party voting."[46] Most legislators have been socialized into party loyalty and they tend to feel most comfortable when they are able to vote with the party, although many times this is not possible.[47] The job of the party leadership is to tap this reservoir of support and consolidate members' loyalties.[48]

Party membership not only offers members a means of personal identity and loyalty, but also provides specific perquisites they could not easily do without. One cannot dismiss the reflection of the party division in the very physical structure of Congress. The aisles divide the parties; office space and parking spaces are delegated by the party leaders; cloakrooms and social activities are based on party membership. Even the softball teams are organized by party! Most importantly, committee assignments are partisan. There is no formal provision for independents or third party candidates in the committee system. Although the party leaders' influence over selection of committee chairmen is limited due to the seniority system, initial assignment to a committee is a party decision. Furthermore, the ratio of members on committee generally reflects the party proportion in the full house. Therefore, the electoral fortunes of the parties are reflected directly in the composition of the committees as well as in the persons of the chairmen, who must be members of the majority party. Finally, political information flows largely through formal and informal communications channels and social relations, that in large part, are formed along party lines. While congressional parties are less cohesive than their counterparts in some state legislatures (Box 8.2), and they lack centralized leadership as well as programmatic orientation, the presence of the two parties is much in evidence on Capitol Hill.

RESPONSIBLE PARTY GOVERNMENT

The lack of highly disciplined, program-oriented parties in Congress has caused some observers to call for a revamping of the American party system. There have been many proposals for such reform, one of the most compre-

---

[45] John W. Kingdon, *Congressmen's Voting Decisions* (New York: Harper and Row, Publishers, 1973), pp. 72-74.

[46] Norpoth, "Explaining Party Cohesion," 1171.

[47] *Ibid.*, p. 1158-59.

[48] Hinckley, *Stability and Change in Congress*, pp. 108-109.

BOX 8.2 PARTY VOTING IN THE STATE LEGISLATURES

Party politics in the legislatures vary in form and intensity from state to state. The dimensions of party conflict and of party differences are not easily compared or contrasted. The reasons for this are several and varied. To begin with, there are wide differences in party competition among the states. There are southern states where Republican politicians come in contact with the legislature only by visiting the state capital and northern states where Democratic legislators have a status only a notch above that of interloper—so dominant are the major parties in their localities.

A second obstacle to generalization about state legislative parties is that they function in disparate environs and under variable conventions. In no two states is rural-urban cleavage of the same intensity and scope, a factor which plainly has a bearing on party behavior. In addition, the way in which legislators are chosen, their tenure and turnover, the power customarily accorded party leaders and the criteria which govern their selection, the existence and utilization of party agencies like the caucus, and the persistence of cohesive elements within each party vary from state to state. Finally, just as party structures differ throughout the country, the legal-constitutional systems within which party processes are carried on differ from state to state. . .

Despite the obstacles to systematic comparison of the role of political parties in fifty state capitals, the general contour of party behavior can be sketched.

1. The model of a responsible two-party system—disciplined and unified parties presenting genuine policy alternatives— is met more nearly in certain northern state legislatures than in Congress. . .

2. As in Congress, party battles in the legislatures are episodic. A great deal of legislative business is transacted with a minimum of controversy. General consensus at the roll-call stage is common, and in many legislatures well over one-half of the roll-call votes are unanimous. . .

3. Party unity fluctuates from issue to issue: party lines are firm on some kinds of questions, rarely visible on others, and, despite the appeals of party leaders, usually collapse on still other kinds.

4. It seems safe to say that in most states parties stay in business by being flexible as to policies. They veer and tack as electoral winds dictate.

5. There is apparently no counterpart in the state legislatures to the conservative coalition of Republicans and southern Democrats which sometimes dominates Congress. Party lines are crossed in the states, to be sure, but the biparty combinations appear to lack the spirit and continuity of the congressional prototype.

6. In northern states distinguished by rigorous party competition in the legislatures, party lines are highly visible on liberal-conservative issues. The Democratic party ordinarily originates and lends considerable support to legislation favorable to the interests of labor, minorities, and low-income groups. . . The Republican party generally is concerned with fostering the interests of the business community, and this objective is likely to take the form of resisting legislation backed by organized labor or of blocking new regulation of business. . .

7. Party conflict often is generated on issues of narrow partisan interest. In one sense, the party organizations perform essentially as interest groups, seeking to strengthen their hand in state politics and to thwart actions which would place them at a disadvantage.

SOURCE: William J. Keefe and Morris S. Ogul, *The American Legislative Process: Congress and the States,* 4th ed., ©1977, pp. 300-304. Adapted by permission of Prentice-Hall, Inc., Englewood Cliffs, New Jersey.

hensive and controversial being that of the responsible party model. When presented in 1950 by the American Political Science Association's Committee on Political Parties, the proposal created a series of debates which have lasted to the present time.[49] Perhaps no other report in political science has ever engendered more controversy and criticism. The proponents of responsible

[49] *Toward a More Responsible Two-Party System,* Supplement to *American Political Science Review,* 44 (1950). See Austin Ranney, *The Doctrine of Responsible Party Government* (Urbana, Ill.: University of Illinois Press, 1962), for a comprehensive examination of the assumption and possible consequences of this theory.

party government, led by E.E. Schattschneider, argued that democracy in America requires two highly centralized competitive parties. Only by making parties responsible to their members as well as to the national electorate could democracy be furthered.

The 1950 committee report presented a model in which the parties had centralized control and were responsive to party members. The committee took the position that a responsible party system is the only institutional mechanism that is able to provide the nation with effective and democratic government. Of all the rival forms of political organization, presidential parties are the principal rallying points for the public interest of the nation. Centralized party government is perceived not only as the most practical means of organizing democracy, but also as a mobilizer of majorities and a protector of liberty. Party government is envisioned as synonymous with democracy by its major supporters.[50]

RESPONSIBLE PARTY FUNCTIONS AND GOALS

Under the responsible party model, three "indispensable" functions would be performed. First, parties would select the particular issues upon which the elections were to be contested. This would enable the public to express itself effectively on the selected issues through their vote. Although selection might, in effect, deprive the people of a chance to express their will on other issues, party government would enable the electorate to choose a general program from two alternatives. The assumption of the responsible party model is that all major issues would fall into one of two hierarchical orderings, each represented by one of the parties. Second, the proponents of the responsible party model argue that it would energize and activate public opinion. The people themselves are not able to assume responsibility for expressions of their own will; some sort of extragovernmental agency is needed to activate public opinion. Under this model, parties provide such an agency. In addition to providing alternative program choices, the parties serve an educational and motivational function. Finally, the advocates of this model contend that party government would establish popular control over government by making those in power collectively responsible to the people. This would be achieved by increasing party discipline and cohesion among the members of legislative bodies. Under this model, an organized and unified group of public officials would be responsible to the entire electorate rather than each official being responsible to his or her particular constituency.

In order to effectuate these three functions and facilitate party respon-

[50] This is evident in all the works of E. E. Schattschneider, especially *Party Government* (New York: Rinehart and Co., Inc., 1942).

sibility, a series of specific reforms have been proposed. They relate to: 1) national party organization, 2) party platforms, 3) congressional party organization, 4) nominations and elections, and 5) intraparty democracy. The responsible party model would be expected to:

1. provide an explicit statement of party programs, priorities, and principles at least once every two years;
2. ensure nomination of candidates loyal to this party platform;
3. conduct issue-oriented campaigns by stressing programmatic differences between the parties and making this choice to the voter straightforward;
4. guarantee widespread and meaningful intraparty participation through democratic party processes and responsible leadership;
5. bind office holders elected under the party label to the party program and to the party policies and priorities.

Under the responsible party model, therefore, parties act as intermediary institutions between the public and the decision makers. Each of the two parties has a conception of what the public desires and each offers a program designed to satisfy the majority of the electorate. During the campaign each party tries to convince the majority of voters in each constituency that its program will best fill the constituents' desires. At the election, the voter, although casting his vote for a specific candidate, supports this candidate primarily because of party label and only secondarily because of individual qualities. Under the responsible party model, the party that wins the majority of the offices takes over the entire power of government. It also has full responsibility for the government's actions and is accountable for the programs it puts into effect.

CRITICISMS OF THE RESPONSIBLE PARTY MODEL

The comprehensive 1950 report drew criticism from two general sources those who found it undesirable and those who saw it as unworkable in the American political system. Some argue that responsible party government weakens federalism by strengthening the national party at the expense of the states. They also contend that this model would lead to a more ideologically intense and ultimately divisive type of politics, and also to the loss of the consensus that now transcends party boundaries. The pluralist flavor of our system would be destroyed, because the party would dominate political respresentation and control of the decision-making process. This new type of party politics would also foster a multiparty system, it is argued. Interest groups and other nonparty organizations are necessary inputs in a pluralist society. Their role would be eliminated, or at least minimized, under this model. Responsible party government is further criticized as undesirable because it would destroy the deliberative and independent nature of our elected officials. Legislators would be forced to vote the party line, and would cease to be free, or dependent only on their constituency. There is reason to believe that this development would be unpopular in the United States. Only 23 percent of the population desire their representative to follow the party line against personal feelings. A majority reject the concept of increased party cohesion or party discipline over candidates.[51]

The possible party model has also been widely criticized as not being realistic within the framework of American politics and society. The critics contend that the American electorate is neither involved nor interested enough in politics to view it in programmatic terms. Voters simply do not view candidates in terms of party programs.[52] The electorate in the United States is not split along ideological lines, nor is there a consistent cleavage on issues. Rather, the electorate is characterized by general consensus around a moderate position. To institute responsible party government would require a sweeping resocialization of the electorate.

Responsible party government also is considered impractical because of the diffuse, decentralized nature of the parties. This model does require a strict organizational hierarchy which is not available in the present political parties. The electoral and governing organizations of political parties would have to be linked. It is argued that the institutions of American government would not facilitate the needed changes. Federalism, separation of powers, and the electoral machinery (especially the direct primary) all tend to decentralize political parties. Any attempts to change the party system would require massive changes in institutions, which are generally supported by the electorate in their present form.

RESPONSIBLE PARTIES AND CONGRESS

The responsible party model relates directly to Congress in several ways. The APSA report contends that party unity in Congress is impaired by the neglect of congressional nominations and elections by party leaders. Without control over the use of party labels, parties will continue to encounter great diffi-

---

[51] Jack Dennis, "Support for the Party System by the Mass Public," *American Political Science Review*, 60 (September, 1966), 606.

[52] Donald E. Stokes and Warren E. Miller, "Party Government and the Saliency of Congress," in Angus Campbell, et al., ed., *Elections and the Political Order* (New York: John Wiley and Sons, Inc., 1966), pp. 194-211.

culty in unifying the membership on policy matters. The committee argued that party organizations in Congress are weak, not because their structure is deficient, but because their powers are not used. It recommended a single leadership committee for each party and each House, with regular meetings between House and Senate leadership committees. These committees would be elected by party caucus and subjected to a vote of confidence every two years. They would be responsible for presenting policy proposals to the membership, controlling the legislative schedule, and managing party affairs.

Under the responsible party model, caucuses would be strengthened and would meet frequently. Caucus decisions on party principles and program would be binding, and sanctions would be imposed upon members who disregarded party decisions. The seniority system would be kept intact, but leaders would be expected to maintain close watch over selection of committee members and chairmen. Members hostile to the goals of the party, under this revised seniority system, would not be assured of a position solely on the basis of seniority.

While it is possible that efforts by congressional leaders to unify and discipline party members might be successful, it is unlikely. Any reforms which attempted to tighten control over legislators' voting would weaken the representational role of congressmen.

> When such changes reach the point where many members of Congress feel that following the national party in their voting threatens reelection from their districts, then the idea of party voting to reflect national electoral mandates becomes unsatisfactory.[53]

As the evidence in this chapter indicates, congressional leaders are not likely to try to extend pressures for party voting to such a point because they, too, represent a constituency in addition to holding a party label. Also, we shall see in later chapters that trends in congressional nominations and campaigns are away from, not toward, a party orientation.

> The decentralized nature of the American party system is nowhere more apparent than in nominations for Congress, in which the national party plays virtually no role.[54]

It seems improbable that leaders, even if so motivated, would be capable of maintaining any significant degree of influence over congressional nomina-

---

[53] David J. Vogler, *The Politics of Congress* (Boston: Allyn and Bacon, Inc., 1974), p. 83.

[54] John F. Bibby and Roger H. Davidson, *On Capital Hill: Studies in the Legislative Process,* 2nd ed. (Hinsdale, Ill.: The Dryden Press, Inc., 1972), p. 14.

tions and elections. Until they are, however, a strict party model, even in the congressional branch, seems unrealistic.

Internal reforms in congressional parties, although more realistic, appear limited. The strong committee system in the House and the individualistic orientation of most senators are major obstacles to effective, centralized party leadership. While policy committees and party conferences conceivably might gain additional influence over members, they will do so only at the expense of the individual members' prerogatives. Few congressmen can be expected to surrender their power bases, which facilitate reelection, without a fight. The leaders understand this. Also, since both houses jealously guard their spheres of responsibility, it is unlikely that the respective party organizations in each will submit to an organization that transcends the houses. Power within Congress is not only fragmented in each house; it is also divided between the House and Senate. Each has traditions and "folkways" which work against a centralized congressional party.

Obviously, when moving to a conception of responsible party government encompassing all branches, fragmentation is substantially increased. Even if, by some extraordinary circumstances, party government succeeds in Congress, there is no assurance that the presidency will be controlled by the majority party. Randall Ripley describes the difficulties presented by a "truncated" majority, in which the presidency is controlled by a party different from that of at least one house.[55] He concludes that to have a productive majority, the president and the majority of both houses must be from the same party. While this in itself will not ensure legislative success, it is necessary for it. Interestingly, American voters prefer divided government. In a 1976 Harris survey, 40 percent favored divided control, and only 38 percent control of both branches by one party.[56] Furthermore, 54 percent felt that it is better to have split control of government, so that opposing power centers can keep watch on one another and keep the federal government honest. With such public sentiment, it is unlikely that American parties in government will become more responsible.

PARTIES IN GOVERNMENT: A SUMMARY

Although the climate for responsible parties may be somewhat more favorable than it was 20 years ago,[57] the potential for fulfillment of this model remains quite minimal. The evidence presented in these two chapters on the

---

[55] See Randall B. Ripley, *Majority Party Leadership in Congress* (Boston: Little, Brown and Company, 1969).

[56] The Harris Survey in *Current Opinion,* 4 (November, 1976), 1.

[57] For a more detailed examination of this debate, see Gerald M. Pomper, "Toward a More Responsible Two-Party System? What, Again?" *Journal*

party in government has demonstrated clearly that parties fail to govern effectively. In many ways, American institutions have succeeded admirably in achieving the framers' desire to minimize centralized control by any one political element. Given the framework of the decentralized governmental system operating in the United States, the lack of highly disciplined and centralized parties is not surprising. The parties simply reflect the government as a whole. The national party organization plays only a minimal role in the executive and judicial branches, and is barely evident in Congress. Moreover, this fragmented "party in government" must compete with many other political influences. While parties do play a role in government, in no way do they monopolize power as they would under a responsible party government.

of Politics, 33 (November, 1971), 916-40; comments by J. Roland Pennock in the same issue; and Pomper's response, *Journal of Politics,* 34 (August, 1972), 952-57. Also see Evron M. Kirkpatrick, "Toward a More Responsible Two-Party System: Political Science, Policy Science, or Pseudo-Science?" *American Political Science Review,* 65 (September, 1971), 965-90.

SECTION V

PARTIES
AS A PSYCHOLOGICAL
AFFILIATION

The third dimension of political parties examined in this book is parties as psychological affiliations. It was stated in Chapter 1 that, for most of the electorate, parties are most meaningful not as a membership organization or a governing device, but as an attachment or identification. Parties, in psychological terms, serve as a screen which filters out messages that do not fit the preconceived view of the world. They serve as reference points or cues for political behavior, although they do not fully determine it. It was demonstrated in Chapter 2 that party membership is frequently defined by this concept of psychological affiliation. Parties can be defined as coalitions of individuals and groups which share a long-term psychological attachment to a party label or symbol.

Chapter 9 examines more closely the context of party as affiliation in the U.S., and looks at patterns of party support across various subgroups in the population. It also describes various forms of political awareness and political behavior and suggests possible explanations. Building on these concepts of political behavior and party attachment, Chapter 10 offers two models of voting in the U.S. The one theory centers on party identification, while the second emphasizes the decline of party loyalty and the increase of independent voting. Through examination of recent behavioral trends, suggestions are offered as to the possible future of the psychological dimension of the political party and its implications for party organization and government.

239

9

Party Affiliation and American Political Behavior

This chapter introduces the concept of party identification within the context of American political behavior. Party affiliation is seen as but one element in the complex set of orientations that constitute political reality for Americans. It is suggested, however, that for many people psychological party affiliation is at the center of their political predispositions, and that it must not be underestimated as a major political influence.

In order to place party affiliation in the proper context, the political socialization process is outlined. This process is the means through which one develops politically, and, as such, it is a crucial area of study. Party identification is then defined, and its role in American politics is examined. The composition of each coalition of party as an affiliation is analyzed in terms of the social groups which make up the coalition. The actual vote support for each party is also discussed briefly.

After the role and nature of party affiliation have been examined, political participation in the U.S. is analyzed. The types of political activity and the degree of public involvement are summarized, with focus on voting turnout and campaign activity. Issue voting and the role of ideology in American elections are described, and the implications of American political behavior on party attachment are noted.

POLITICAL SOCIALIZATION

The political behavior of any society is heavily dependent upon the values and beliefs which constitute political culture. There is evidence that the behavior of citizens is a result of some combination of early political learning and influences in later life. The process through which citizens acquire their political values and beliefs is termed *political socialization*. In addition to individual learning, political socialization serves to transfer political culture from one generation to the next. All societies attempt to perpetuate and strengthen certain values and beliefs through the socialization process.[1] Although this process may lead to change or to the creation of new loyalties, in the U.S. it generally maintains culture across generations.

The individual learning component of socialization is central to this discussion of political culture. During our lives, each of us learns certain political orientations that define our view of politics.[2] We develop a national loyalty, support for the political system, and in many cases an attachment to a political party. We accept varying perceptions of behavior and establish a role-orientation toward politics. Although political behavior is not fully determined by early training, there is evidence that behavior is linked to early socialization.[3]

It has been suggested that while socialization is a continuous process throughout life, three stages are evident. The influences at each stage represent different combinations of socializing agents. The *basic foundation* stage takes place in early childhood and results in the formation of general political attachments and loyalties. It appears likely that the strongest influences during this critical formation stage are those which exercise authority over the child, especially the family and the schools. The second stage shifts emphasis from development of emotional attachments to acquiring *specific knowledge* about political institutions and feelings toward them. The shift in emphasis is marked by the growing importance of agents who stand equal to the person, such as peer groups. The final stage, which arrives in late adolescence, is one of *reactions to specific policies, personalities and events.* Although peer groups are still important during adulthood, political experiences themselves become influential at this time.

Although the conditions and agents change, political socialization continues to shape our perceptions of politics and, to some extent, our political behavior. While new orientations are acquired in response to particular

---

[1] For a good discussion of the role of political socialization see, David Easton and Jack Dennis, "A Political Theory of Political Socialization," in *Socialization to Politics,* ed. Jack Dennis (New York: John Wiley and Sons, Inc., 1973), pp. 32-53.

[2] See Dean Jaros, *Socialization to Politics* (New York: Praeger Publishers, 1973); Kenneth P. Langton, *Political Socialization* (New York: Oxford University Press, 1969); and Richard E. Dawson, Kenneth Prewitt, and Karen S. Dawson, *Political Socialization,* 2nd ed. (Boston: Little, Brown and Company, 1977), for short analyses of the political socialization process.

[3] A major work on the socialization of children is David Easton and Jack Dennis, *Children in the Political System: Origins of Political Legitimacy* (New York: McGraw-Hill Book Company, 1969).

situations, they generally are built upon the basic foundation set during childhood. It is significant that knowledge about politics follows formation of loyalties and basic emotional attachments. This strongly suggests that our views of the world and, specifically, our perceptions of political reality, are molded by a framework constructed early in life. Although alterations are likely to occur during adulthood, they are limited by our basic orientations.

The study of political socialization is complicated and based on various areas of research in political sociology and political psychology. No effort is made here even to summarize this vast body of research.[4] Instead, discussion centers on the major agents of socialization and their impact on voting behavior and on orientation toward political parties. It is assumed that while socialization in the U.S. appears to be an informal, decentralized, and largely unconscious process, it actually has a major influence on the political behavior of the American electorate. In spite of the tendency of the government not to impose specific political orientations, unlike some regimes, certain behavioral patterns evolve that are intricately tied to political socialization.

THE FAMILY

Although its importance has been minimized in recent research, the family at one time was considered the most crucial agent in determining the direction of political learning. It still is recognized by most as a major variable in the socialization process. Fred Greenstein, for instance, argues that the child's opinions about politics are a clear reflection of the parent's views.[5] Others suggest that while the family has little impact on specific opinions, it is the major agency in formation of basic political attachments such as party identification.[6]

It would be surprising if the family did not have a major influence on the political orientations of children. Although politics generally occupies a minor position within the context of family life, the parents have access to

---

[4] Jack Dennis, *Socialization to Politics: A Reader* (New York: John Wiley and Sons, Inc., 1973), is one of the best sources to outline the scope of this research. There are literally hundreds of books and articles relating to various aspects of socialization research.

[5] Fred I. Greenstein, *Children and Politics* (New Haven: Yale University Press, 1965).

[6] Robert D. Hess and Judith V. Torney, *The Development of Political Attitudes in Children* (Garden City, N.Y.: Doubleday and Company, Inc., Anchor Books, 1967).

the child during the most critical formative years. Despite the weakening of family ties and earlier competition from school, friends, television, and teachers, the parents enjoy the most emotionally intense relationship with the child during at least its first five or six years. There is significant evidence that the family plays a major role in the development (or lack) of a sense of trust in the child. Spitz reports that the mother is especially important, and that substitute mothers are largely unsuccessful in developing warmth and satisfying the babies' need for affection.[7] A lack of affection, even during the first six months of life, presents a threatening world. Assuming this is carried over to adulthood, it may result in alienation and isolation of those who continue to feel threatened by the outside world.

In addition to developing the capability to survive in an expanding environment, the family situation transmits basic political roles and values to the child. The child very early learns acceptable as well as unacceptable behavior, through imitation of the parents as well as through direct learning. Rewards and/or punishments suffice to define what is acceptable. Sex roles also have been traced to early childhood and the family environment.[8] Importantly, early childhood socialization generally results in positive, uncritical support for authority. Negative orientations come later, as the individual experiences or views the actual political process, but the positive orientations remain at the core. This pattern tends to moderate attitudes toward politics and minimize rapid shifts in behavior.

While there is evidence that the family situation is important in establishing a feeling of trust and acceptance, there is little evidence that it has a lasting influence on political opinions after the children leave the home. The direction of opinion on specific issues is more related to group influence and direct political experience than to family training. Similarly, behavior orientations are only weakly influenced by the family situation. While those reared in a family with low degrees of political interest tend to have little involvement and interest in politics, those from high interest families tend to be only slightly more involved. When allowance is made for social and economic factors, the familial influence on political participation is minimal.

THE SCHOOLS

While recent research suggests that the role of the family in political socialization is limited to the formation of a nonthreatening environment and basic loyalties, more emphasis has been placed on the role of the schools. Children spend many of their waking hours in a classroom during their first twenty

---

[7] Rene Spitz, *The First Year of Life* (New York: International Universities Press, 1965).

[8] Hess and Torney, *Development of Political Attitudes*, pp. 199-222.

years of life. It would be surprising if the schools were not a major influence over political orientations and behavior. A large number of recent socialization studies have concluded that the schools are a more important agent than the family, especially in transferring political knowledge and developing specific attitudes and opinions.[9] Also, the schools are important in providing a framework for development of informal group relationships.

It has been suggested that schools socialize through various channels. Certainly the curriculum plays a major role in perpetuating values and beliefs fundamental to the political system. Students learn selected American history, literature, and politics. In the early grades, especially, learning is largely supportive of the nation and the regime. There is an attempt to accentuate the positive. In high school, the orientation might become less positive and more critical as emphasis is placed on political and social problems. Whatever the direction of learning, however, much political knowledge is derived from the curricula in the schools. It has been demonstrated that the average American reaches the peak of his political knowledge as a senior in high school. After the individual leaves the formal education system, his knowledge about political institutions decreases.[10]

The schools socialize, through both the curricula and the rituals of classroom life. Young children placed in the school environment learn to tolerate others, learn rules of social life, and experience an expanding environment. They are taught to respect the wishes both of other pupils and the school authorities. The child's mere attendance on a continuing basis at a school with certain ground rules molds his perception of the world. Classroom rituals,[11] including the pledge of allegiance, the presence of flags and other symbols, and the celebration of particular national holidays and events, all serve to reinforce the national loyalties and political orientations of the home.

Teachers have considerable influence over young children and might be expected to serve as a substitute authority figure for the parents, especially if one of the parents is not in the home. It is reasonable to expect that teachers might, in some cases, serve as important motivating forces for future political involvements.

In addition to teachers, classroom rituals, and the curriculum, schools provide socialization through extracurricular activities such as clubs and organizations, athletics, and student politics. These activities serve as one means of becoming integrated into the social structure of the school. By pro-

[9] *Ibid.*

[10] See M. Kent Jennings and Richard G. Niemi, "Continuity and Change in Political Orientations: A Longitudinal Study of Two Generations," in *Political Opinion and Behavior,* 3rd ed., by Edward C. Dreyer and Walter A. Rosenbaum (North Scituate, Mass.: Duxbury Press, 1976), pp. 98-127.

[11] Perhaps performed much less frequently than in the past.

viding status or prestige, they facilitate group acceptance and positive attitudes toward the school environment. In addition, clubs and organizations give the student an opportunity to develop skills useful in politics. It is not known how many political leaders got their start in school politics, but the number is probably significant, since the rules of school and real-world politics are similar. Finally, extracurricular activities reinforce the values learned through the curriculum and the classroom life. These activities appear to be particularly important as a training ground for potential leaders.

In the United States, a large proportion of students go to college. Higher education offers a unique environment for political development and serves as a framework for a broadening exposure to competing political orientations. For many, it marks the first time when parental influence is indirect and distant, and facilitates personal development of the individual apart from the family environment. College also offers a primary means of upward social mobility and trains the future leadership corps. Most political leaders and a large proportion of political activists have college experience. A major route to political office is through law school.

Although there is little evidence that education per se has much influence on direction of opinion, its link to political behavior is well-documented.[12] Those with more education participate more in all forms of political activity. Education teaches the skills necessary to participate and provides positive orientations toward politics and one's place in the political system. Those with higher levels of education exhibit a stronger sense of citizenship and awareness of duty to vote. Not surprisingly, they are also more familiar with political issues. Education teaches a person how to obtain information and creates interest in the social and political world. Those with more education tend to have more opinions. They are much less likely to say they "don't know." Although some of this difference might be because those with more education simply do not want to admit they do not know, education levels are consistenly related to higher levels of familiarity with political issues.

PEER GROUPS

According to David Riesman, peer groups are replacing families as primary authority figures.[13] Peer groups here refer to the informal groups of individuals with whom one associates. They include classmates, fellow workers,

---

[12] For a somewhat dated but excellent discussion of this, see V.O. Key, Jr., *Public Opinion and American Democracy* (New York: Alfred A. Knopf, 1961), pp. 323-341. For an update see Bernard C. Hennessy, *Public Opinion*, 3rd ed. (North Scituate, Mass.: Duxbury Press, 1975), pp. 199-204.

[13] David Riesman, *The Lonely Crowd* (New Haven: Yale University Press, 1950).

and social friends—those closest to us on a day to day basis. Throughout our adult lives, we are influenced by those around us. We desire acceptance and adapt our opinions and behavior to what is acceptable to the group. Riesman terms the tendency to conform to others, to adopt their standards and norms as our own, "other directedness." Few individuals are totally free of group constraints in their political behavior.

Although peer groups become important as soon as children associate with friends outside the family, they take on special importance during adolescence and throughout adulthood. While they tend to reinforce parental values and beliefs formed during childhood, peer groups provide another set of norms. They offer a competing source of cues or reference points for individual behavior and serve as informal channels of communication. There appears to be a significant increase in cross-pressures between parental values and group values during the high school years, as contact with peer group members becomes more frequent and political awareness intensifies. In adulthood, with the absence of parental or school influence, peer groups become the major agent of continuing socialization. The basic orientations formed in the family and school environment might shape reactions to specific political situations later in life, but the major determinant of political opinions and behavior is the most immediate social environment, and this is largely defined by relationships through peer groups.

THE MASS MEDIA AND
POLITICAL SOCIALIZATION

Certainly the mass media, especially television, have a major role in political socialization. Although it is doubtful that TV alone determines political behavior and opinions on issues, it is a highly controllable agent which plays a major role in all aspects of society. Surveys demonstrate that upwards of 60 percent of the public depend primarily on television for political information.[14] Television is consistently perceived as the most trustworthy of all mass media. Despite the highly sophisticated techniques of editing visual presentations and the minute amount of political reality actually covered on TV, people tend to believe what they see on the screen more readily than what they read in print.

As an agent in political socialization, however, the mass media appear to be restricted in several ways. First, there is evidence that only a limited proportion of the public pays much attention to the political coverage in the mass media. Second, even for the small proportion that is attentive directly to the media, early predispositions and political orientations serve to screen

[14] Herbert B. Asher, *Presidential Elections and American Politics* (Homewood, Ill.: The Dorsey Press, 1976), pp. 222-243.

out political stimuli which are discordant. This psychological defense of the basic values and perspectives is termed "selective perception." The image on the television does not directly strike a neural surface of the brain. Instead, a complex network of psychological processes must occur before the message leads to opinions and behavior. In these processes, stimuli are distorted, obscured, exaggerated, or screened out by one's basic value and belief structure. There is no guarantee that a person will be influenced or even be aware of messages that pass through the mass media.

POLITICAL SOCIALIZATION: SUMMARY

Each person carries a package of political orientations which guides his behavior and serves as a framework for his attitudes and opinions. Political actions are influenced, though not determined, by early learning, past experience, and present political stimuli. At the core of the socialization process are basic predispositions that have been found to be most resistant to change. One of the strongest of these orientations, which guides political behavior and shapes attitudes and opinions for large numbers of Americans, is party identification. Party affiliation is a basic orientation which is quite resistant to pressures for change. It is also the third dimension of political parties and a central concept in the study of American political behavior.

PARTY IDENTIFICATION: A CONCEPT

In discussing any concept such as party affiliation, one must first measure it. The psychological dimension of political party is commonly defined as party identification. Although party identification can be measured in many ways, two particular approaches dominate. The simplest method is used by George Gallup and other professional pollsters who ask respondents whether they are (1) Republicans, (2) Democrats, or (3) Independents.

Another method is used by academic researchers. Since they tend to be interested in more precise measurement of concepts, they attempt to include intensity of attachment as well as direction. The Survey Research Center (SRC) of the University of Michigan, which pioneered the study of voting research, measures party identification through a two-part question.[15] The initial question is:

1. Generally speaking, do you think of yourself as a Republican, a Democrat, an Independent, or what?

[15] Angus Campbell, *et al., The American Voter* (New York: John Wiley and Sons, Inc., 1964), pp. 67-68.

Those who classify themselves as a Democrat or Republican are then asked:

    a. Would you call yourself a strong (Democrat, Republican) or a not very strong (Democrat, Republican)?

Those who initially term themselves as Independents are asked:

    b. Do you think of yourself as closer to the Republican or Democratic Party?

From this two-pronged question, seven categories of party identification are derived. Those asked question "a" are classified as strong or weak Republicans or Democrats, depending on their response. Those who say that they think of themselves as closer to one of the parties in question "b" are classified as Independent Democrats or Independent Republicans. Those who answer "b" as "neither" are considered Independents. This seven-fold measurement often is condensed into five categories by combining all three independent designations into Independents.

DEVELOPMENT OF PARTY ATTACHMENT

A central question in the study of party identification (ID) is how it develops in an individual. What makes one person consider himself a strong Democrat while another labels herself a weak Republican? Much research effort has gone into the study of the development and transmission of party identification. The general conclusion of these socialization studies is that party ID is acquired early in life. For instance, Greenstein found that by the fourth grade over 60 percent of the students cited a partisan preference.[16] While this attachment is devoid of substantive content, early attachment serves as a cue for acquisition of information, and shapes perceived political reality. As noted earlier, next to national identity, party attachment appears to become one of the central predispositions early in life.

It is generally agreed that the family is the dominant agent in the transmission of party identification from one generation to the next. Children unconsciously learn party orientation through identification with their parents. Although there are mixed findings, the evidence indicates that mothers might be more important than fathers in this process.[17] While the family is seen as less important in transferring attitudes and political behavior patterns to children, impressive data suggest the influence of families in trans-

[16] Greenstein, *Children and Politics*, p. 71.
[17] Asher, *Presidential Elections*, p. 61.

mitting party affiliation is strong.[18] For instance, despite their findings that the socializing role of the family for most political values and attitudes is restricted, Hess and Torney acknowledge the importance of the family in transferring party ID:

> With respect to general values about partisanship and this specific choice of a party, it has already been established that this area of attitude is influenced strongly by family membership—one of the few political topics, although an important one, on which families seem to exert considerable influence.[19]

Table 9.1 reflects the agreement between parents and children in party identi-fication. While parents' party ID does not determine the child's (that is, not all the children of Democrats are Democrats) the relationship is significant. Although 60 percent of the children of Democratic parents are Democrats, only 7 percent are Republicans. Likewise, 51 percent of children reared in a Republican home are Republican, while only 13 percent are Democrats.

Table 9.1   Student Party Identification by Parent
Party Identification

Student Party Identification	Parental Party Identification		
	Democrat	*Independent*	*Republican*
Democrat	66	29	13
Independent	27	53	36
Republican	7	17	51
Total	100	100	100
Number of cases	914	442	495

SOURCE: *The Political Character of Adolescence: The Influence of Families and Schools* by M. Kent Jennings and Richard G. Niemi (copyright ©1974 by Princeton University Press): Table 2.2 p. 41. Printed by permission of Princeton University Press.

While the data above indicate that the family environment is important to party identification, there are numerous exceptions. Over one quarter of the children of Democrats and one third of the Republicans classify them-

---

[18] M. Kent Jennings and Richard G. Niemi, *The Political Character of Adolescence: The Influence of Families and Schools* (Princeton, N.J.: Prince-ton University Press, 1974), p. 41.

[19] Hess and Torney, *Development of Political Attitudes*, p. 132.

selves as Independents. Also, there are some defections to the opposite party. A central question, then, is: how stable is party identification? Are there substantial defections in adulthood in addition to those evident above? Assuming that party affiliation is the most basic psychological attachment formed in many people, it seems that it should be quite resistant to modification.

STABILITY OF PARTY AFFILIATION

Although the evidence is less than overwhelming, it implies substantial stability in individual party attachment. Consistently since 1952, over 80 percent of those who identify themselves as Democrats and 70 percent of those who call themselves Republicans have reported lifelong affiliation with their party. [20] Although personal forces such as marriage, age, and social mobility might alter the party identification for some, and social forces such as the Civil War and the Great Depression have caused wholesale defections in the past, party attachment is transmitted effectively through the family and tends to be relatively stable for a large proportion of the population.

> Party identification is remarkably constant. A sense of party affiliation is one of the most stable of social or economic group memberships in this complex, everchanging society. It is more stable than occupation or residence. Along with religion, it is an identification that, however strong, persists throughout the entire adult life of most persons. [21]

Furthermore, research has demonstrated that the longer a person has identified with a party, the more intense and stable his party loyalty becomes. [22] The greatest instability is exhibited among the young, that is, among those who have only had the partisan habit briefly, or in whom it has not fully developed.

While recent data demonstrate that there has been a marked decrease in the transfer of party attachment through the family, and that children of politically oriented families do not always remain in the party of their parents, they are far less likely than others to join the opposing party. The family environment is, by far, the single most crucial factor in explaining

---

[20] Asher, *Presidential Elections,* p. 66.

[21] Warren E. Miller and Teresa E. Levitin, *Leadership and Change: The New Politics and the American Electorate* (Cambridge, Mass.: Winthrop Publishers, Inc., 1976), p. 35.

[22] Philip E. Converse, "Of Time and Partisan Stability," *Comparative Political Studies* 2 (July, 1969), pp. 139-171.

party identification. In fact, as demographic factors have become less significant, "family inheritance has become the main support of party loyalty."[23] While an increasing proportion of young voters identify with neither party, those who see themselves as Republicans or Democrats tend to maintain the party of their parents. Partisanship still appears to be "a long-term, habitual commitment of individuals."[24] But Chapter 10 will demonstrate that party identification has weakened considerably, even among those who maintain their attachment.

GROUPS AND PARTY IDENTIFICATION

It was suggested in Chapter 2 that American parties are among a handful in the western democracies without a class base. Neither party can depend fully on support from any social grouping, or presume long-term loyalty from any element of society. In examining party as a psychological affiliation, however, it is important to discover where each party gets its major support. What groups are central to each coalition, and which contribute most to the electoral success of each party organization? Although the coalitions are dynamic and constantly in a state of flux, it is worthwhile to examine levels of party attachment by social grouping.

Although U.S. parties are described as socially heterogeneous, the party electorates exhibit varying degrees of support along class, regional, race-ethnic, religious, and sexual lines of division. While no group consistently aligns itself as a whole with either party, some contribute more extensively to one party than the other. Each party has certain social groupings on which it must depend for extraordinary majorities to balance minority support from other groups. It is significant that, of all the groupings, only one gives either party more than 60 percent of its support on a consistent basis. It will be seen that the blacks are solidly Democratic in loyalty, although this does not guarantee that party their votes.

CLASS DISTINCTIONS

Of all social factors, the most emphasized in traditional party literature is social class. "While the total electorate is generally unpolarized along class lines, these divisions are not completely absent, and the potential for

[23] Gerald M. Pomper, *Voters' Choice: Varieties of American Electoral Behavior* (New York: Dodd, Mead and Company, 1975), p. 29.

[24] Norman H. Nie, Sidney Verba and John R. Petrocik, *The Changing American Voter* (Cambridge, Mass.: Harvard University Press, 1976), p. 73.

class politics does exist in certain groups."[25] Class most simply is measured by self-classification into specified categories such as upper, middle, working, or lower class. Subjective class, as this is termed, is very ambiguous in the U.S. People do not readily identify themselves as members of a particular class, and their awareness of inherent class distinctions is low. The proportion of the population placing itself in each class depends on how the question is worded and what responses are provided. Figure 9.1 shows that while almost 90 percent categorize themselves as middle class on the three-choice option, when working class is included as an option, over 50 percent place themselves in that category, with most of the remainder in middle class and less than 3 percent on either extreme. When working class is eliminated and upper middle and lower middle are inserted, 60 percent identify as middle. In light of this confusion, the proportions identifying with each party are less than impressive. While the working class identify 46 percent Democrat and 20 percent Republican, the corresponding figures for the middle class are 35 and 30 percent, respectively. Most of these differences, however, can be traced to more direct demographic differences.

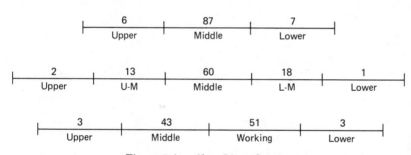

Figure 9.1   Class Identification

A more common measure of class in the U.S. is termed "objective," in that the person does not make a judgment. Rather, a person is placed in a category on the basis of education, income, and/or occupation. The combination of these three indicators is often called socioeconomic status (SES). Although the difference in levels of support for the parties by SES is not as distinct in the U.S. as in other countries, and both parties get substantial support from all classes, there are unique patterns of party affiliation by objective class measures. The data in Table 9.2 illustrate the nature of this variation.

For each of the objective measures of class there is a relationship between higher class and affiliation with the Republican party. As one moves from lowest income and education to highest, the Democratic percentage

[25] Pomper, *Voters' Choice,* p. 50.

Table 9.2 Party Affiliation by Income, Occupation, and Education, 1976

	Democrat	Republican	Independent
Income			
Under $3000	60	18	22
$3000 - 4999	56	20	24
$5000 - 6999	53	22	25
$7000 - 9999	50	20	30
$10,000 - 14,999	47	21	32
$15,000 - 19,999	45	25	30
$20,000 and over	40	31	29
Education			
Grade School	59	22	19
High School	49	22	29
College	39	27	34
Occupation			
Manual	53	17	30
Clerical & Sales	38	27	35
Farmer	44	33	23
Professional and Business	40	29	31

SOURCE: *Gallup Opinion Index,* #137 (December, 1976), p. 50.

decreases, while the Republican percentage increases. More important, however, is that in no category does the Republican party come close to having a plurality. In every case the Democrats hold at least a 4 to 3 majority over the Republicans. Significantly, it is the Independent category which most benefits from the decreased Democratic support at the college level. Over one third of those with a college education are Independent, versus 19 percent of those with grade school education. In occupation, the Democrats have their greatest numerical superiority among manual laborers, while the proportions in the remaining occupational categories are about equal. Despite the pattern of greatest loyalty to the Democratic party among the low SES categories, there is no active cleavage among the parties by class.[26] Certainly, the working class types constitute the most consistent electorate for the Democrats,

[26] Robert H. Salisbury and Gordon Black, "Class and Party in Partisan and Non-partisan Elections: The Case of Des Moines," *American Political Science Review,* 57 (September, 1963), 584-92, conclude that party ID is "relatively independent of class." For more information and a cross-national comparison see Robert R. Alford, *Party and Society: The Anglo-American Democracies* (Chicago: Rand McNally and Company, 1963).

but class alone does not determine party. Class factors, no matter how they are measured, provide a very limited explanation of partisanship at the present time.

REGIONAL DISTINCTIONS

One of the most overemphasized and oversimplified explanations of political distinctions in the U.S. has been regionalism or sectionalism. This explanation centers primarily on the unique party structure and politics of the southern states after the Civil War. The one-party South understandably spawned large majorities of Democratic identifiers. Although some authors also note unique patterns of support in the northeastern and midwestern states, sectionalism largely has been defined in North-South terms.

The data presented in Table 9.3 demonstrate the nature of this division. The patterns of party affiliation for all three non-southern regions are quite similar. In each case, the proportion is less than the two to one Democrat-Republican margin at the national level. The South certainly is conspicuous, with a margin of approximately six Democrats for each Republican. The pro-

Table 9.3   Party Affiliation by Region, 1976

	Democrat	Republican	Independent
East	47	26	27
Midwest	41	26	33
West	46	28	26
South	62	11	27
National	48	23	29

SOURCE: *Gallup Opinion Index*, #137 (December, 1976), p. 50.

portion of Independents, meanwhile, is similar across the four regions. While the South continues to be the most distinctive center of Democratic affiliation, based on long tradition, it is also the region with the highest defection rate in actual voting. Despite the high margin in favor of the Democrats in party ID, the South generally has supported Republican presidential candidates.[27] Also, the South and the other regions have tended to become more similar in party ID patterns over the past 20 years.

[27] For a detailed look at change in the South see Jack Bass and Walter DeVries, *The Transformation of Southern Politics* (New York: New American Library, Inc., 1977).

RELIGIOUS AND ETHNIC DIVISIONS

There are three major religious bodies in the United States, and innumerable ethnic identifications. Although the influence of these groupings on the vote is often exaggerated, party loyalties do vary by religious and ethnic background, even when socioeconomic factors are discounted. Importantly, these two aspects overlap one another, since the strongest ethnic identifications are among Catholics. Figure 9.2 illustrates the disparate patterns of party identification among Protestants, Catholics, and Jews. It is again important to note that no cleavage along religious lines exists in party identification, despite the variation. For all three religions the Democrats represent a plurality, although the proportion of Democrats among Jews and Catholics is approximately 10 percent higher than among the Protestants. Also, the Jews tend to be most disposed toward classifying themselves as Independent, and least likely to be affiliated with the Republican party.

Certainly there is some variation within the 200-plus denominations combined under the Protestant label, although most approximate the pattern in Figure 9.2. The most visible and significant division of Protestants is a regional one. While over 50 percent of the southern Protestants are Demo-

Figure 9.2   Party Affiliation by Religion, 1976

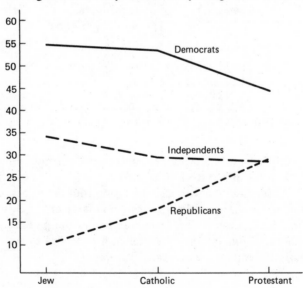

SOURCE: *Gallup Opinion Index,* #137 (December, 1976), p. 50.

258

crats, the corresponding figure for their northern brethren is 34 percent. There is also variation among Catholics along ethnic lines. Irish and Polish Catholics tend to be somewhat more Democratic than German and Italian Catholics, for instance.[28] The Catholics' allegiance to the Democratic party is more a response to historical circumstances and economic status than to any pro-Catholic Democratic party stand. It was the Democratic party that welcomed the Catholic immigrants earlier in this century, and it was the New Deal policies directed at the urban ethnic ghettos that temporarily cemented that foundation and gave the Catholics a central role in the Democratic coalition.[29] Despite a decline in Democratic voting during recent elections and the decrease of about 10 percent in Democratic affiliation since 1960, the Catholics, along with the Jews, continue to identify in large numbers with the Democratic party.[30]

SEX AND PARTY AFFILIATION

Despite assumptions to the contrary, women and men display very similar political attitudes and behavior. The voting turnout of women now is only· slightly lower than that of men, while male-female choices of particular candidates demonstrate few significant differences. According to Gerald Pomper, there are few issues, even those directly related to sex distinctions such as support for a woman presidential candidate, in which the differences between men and women are either large or consistent.[31] The exceptions are issues related to war, human rights, and the use of force. In these three areas, women hold more pacifist views. Because of this, George McGovern received stronger support from women than from men.

The difference between men and women in party loyalty is negligible, with women tending to be slightly more Democrat-oriented. The figures in Table 9.4 indicate the minimal scope of this sex distinction without regard for age. Significantly, however, in the under-30 age group, women tend to be more Democratic than men by a 39 to 24 percent margin. The men in that age group tend to be correspondingly more Independent.

[28] Nie, *The Changing American Voter*, p. 230.

[29] Asher, *Presidential Elections*, p. 72.

[30] For an explanation see Andrew M. Greeley, *Building Coalitions: American Politics in the 1970s* (New York: Franklin Watts, Inc., New Viewpoints, 1972). Also see Mark R. Levy and Michael S. Kramer, *The Ethnic Factor: How America's Minorities Decide Elections* (New York: Simon and Schuster, 1973), especially chapters 4-7.

[31] Pomper, *Voters' Choice*, p. 68.

Table 9.4   Party Identification by Sex, 1972

	Male	Female
Strong Democrat	15.5	14.7
Weak Democrat	22.0	29.1
Independent	39.4	31.9
Weak Republican	13.2	13.4
Strong Republican	9.9	10.9

SOURCE: Gerald M. Pomper, *Voters' Choice: Varieties of American Electoral Behavior* (New York: Dodd, Mead and Company, 1975), p. 77.

RACIAL DIVISIONS

"There is one American social division, however, that is sharp and persistent: the racial strife between blacks and whites."[32] The data in Figure 9.3 display a substantial difference between the races in party identification. Among whites, Democrats have less than a two to one advantage (44 to 26 percent),

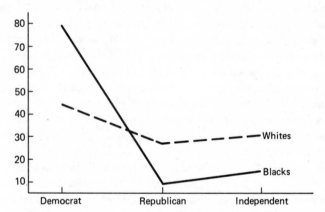

Figure 9.3   Party Affiliation by Race, 1976
SOURCE: *Gallup Opinion Index,* #137 (December, 1976), p. 50.

while among blacks the ratio is eleven to one (78 to 7 percent). Since their conversion to the Democratic party began in response to New Deal policies in the mid-1930s, the blacks have been consistently the most solid identifiers with either party. Their highest attachment was in 1968, when 88 percent identified themselves as Democrats. Due to their Democratic loyalty, the

[32] *Ibid.,* p. 117.

260

blacks are also the least likely group to consider themselves Independents. Nie estimates that while about one fifth of Democrat support comes from blacks, only a very small proportion of Republican support can be traced similarly.[33] The blacks are a central element of the Democratic coalition.

AGE AND PARTY AFFILIATION

Two general propositions have been offered relating to age and party affiliation. The first, and least disputed, is that the older one gets, the stronger identification with a party becomes. Figure 9.4 illustrates the increase in both Democrat and Republican identification in the older age groups. This might be due to the strengthening of attachment over time, but it also could be

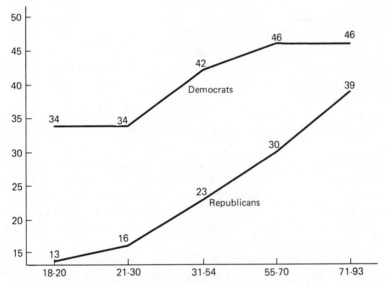

Figure 9.4 Party Affiliation and Age, 1972

SOURCE: Center for Political Studies, 1972 American National Election Study (ICPR Study #7010).

explained as a result of changing circumstances. In other words, those in the upper age categories might tend to be identifiers simply because they were socialized at a time when party lines were more clearly drawn. There is no guarantee that the youth of the 1970s will become more strongly attached to either party as they mature.

[33] Nie, *The Changing American Voter*, p. 242.

The second proposition is more tenuous than the first. It states that aging leads to Republican attachment. Again, the data at first glance would support this proposition, since there is a slightly larger gain in Republican percentage than Democratic. However, the difference is not significant and most studies have found little evidence to support such a trend. While one study found substantial conversions toward Republicanism with age,[34] others have rejected this notion.[35] In general, the young are less partisan, more cynical of politics, and more aware of candidate positions. Although they are no more informed or active than older groups,[36] the youth do represent a "politically meaningful social category"[37] in terms of strength and direction of party affiliation. They are, of course, crucial to the party electorates of the future because they are the future parties.

PARTY IDENTIFICATION
AND SOCIAL GROUPINGS: A SUMMARY

This brief discussion of party identification demonstrates that the party as an affiliation is not simply a reflection of social characteristics.

> Rather than the parties being divided along social lines, they are coming to resemble one another demographically.[38]

One's party is not fixed by one's social status. Although there are some distinctions as to class, whether subjective or objective, with Republicans getting more support from the middle class than the working class, there is no apparent class cleavage. More crucially, the economically mobile voters have tended to carry their Democratic loyalty with them into the middle class, thereby diluting class influence even more.

Similarly, differences in party affiliation along religious and sex lines fail to be significant. Region has also been minimized as a determinant of

[34] John Crittenden, "Aging and Party Affiliation," *Public Opinion Quarterly,* 26 (Winter, 1962), 648-57.

[35] Neal E. Cutler, "Generation, Maturation and Party Affiliation: A Cohort Analysis," *Public Opinion Quarterly,* 33 (Winter, 1969), 583-88; Norval D. Glenn and Ted Hefner, "Further Evidence on Aging and Party Identification," *Public Opinion Quarterly,* 36 (Spring, 1972), 31-47, and Neal E. Cutler, "Demographic, Socio-Psychological, and Political Factors in the Politics of Aging," *American Political Science Review,* 71 (September, 1977), 1011-1025.

[36] Pomper, *Voters' Choice,* p. 114.

[37] Miller and Levitin, *Leadership and Change,* p. 27.

[38] Pomper, *Voters' Choice,* p. 27.

party attachment, although the South still retains its Democratic ties. The one major social cleavage apparent in this brief analysis is along racial lines. Blacks overwhelmingly identify as Democrats. Even here, however, the distinction is not as clear as suggested, since a plurality of whites also identify as Democrats. The difference again is one of degree, not direction. While the data here support the notion of two socially heterogeneous parties, they also indicate that each party must direct its appeals to those groups which most consistently support it. The parties are coalitions of identifiers across various social divisions and, as such, must remain as flexible as possible.

PARTY VOTING SUPPORT

A more direct measure of party support is the vote cast for each party. Although trends in voting are discussed in the next chapter, a summary of the differentiation of the party vote by social group is offered here. Table 9.5 presents data on the Democratic percentage of each major social grouping for recent presidential elections. Although the actual percentages vary from year to year, the overall patterns of vote support in the individual categories are similar to the distribution of party identification.

Those in the higher categories of education and occupation vote significantly less Democratic than those in the lower categories. The greatest Democratic support comes from manual laborers and those with only a grade school education. As with party attachment, however, substantial proportions in every group still support the other party. As expected, Catholics vote more Democratic than Protestants, while non-whites constitute by far the most solid bloc of party support, casting over 80 percent of their vote for Democratic presidential candidates.

The only meaningful deviation from the distribution of party affiliation discussed earlier relates to regional distinctions. The South, which registers a six to one advantage for the Democrats in party identification, fails to support Democratic presidential candidates with anything near that proportion. Over the last three elections, only in 1976, when a southerner was the Democratic candidate, did the South support a Democrat. Even then, Jimmy Carter received less than 54 percent of the vote.

The final distribution of voting support examined here is the vote of party identifiers. As expected, the figures in Table 9.5 demonstrate that party identifiers generally vote for the party of their affiliation. An average of approximately 80 percent of the Democratic affiliates vote for Democratic candidates, while less than 9 percent of the Republicans do. The most obvious defections occurred in 1964, when 20 percent of the Republicans voted for Lyndon Johnson, and in 1972, when almost one third of the

Table 9.5 Vote by Groups in Presidential Elections
1956-1976, Percent Democratic

	1956	1960	1964	1968	1972	1976	Mean 1956-1976
Race							
White	41	49	59	38	32	46	44.2
Non-White	61	68	94	85	87	85	80.0
Education							
Grade School	50	55	66	52	49	58	55.0
High School	42	52	62	42	34	54	47.7
College	31	39	52	37	37	42	39.7
Occupation							
Manual	50	60	71	50	43	58	55.3
White Collar	37	48	57	41	36	50	44.8
Prof. & Business	32	42	54	34	31	42	39.2
Age							
Under 30	43	54	64	47	48	53	51.5
30-49	45	54	63	44	33	48	47.8
50 and over	39	46	59	41	36	52	45.0

Table 9.5 (Cont.)

	1956	1960	1964	1968	1972	1976	Mean 1956-1976
Religion							
Protestants	37	38	55	35	30	46	40.2
Catholics	51	78	76	59	48	57	61.5
Party ID							
Republican	4	5	20	9	5	9	8.7
Democrat	85	84	87	74	67	82	79.8
Independent	30	43	56	31	31	38	38.2
Region							
East	40	53	68	50	42	51	50.6
Midwest	41	48	61	44	40	48	47.0
South	49	51	52	31	29	54	44.3
West	43	49	60	44	41	46	47.2
Total	42.2	50.1	61.3	43.0	38.0	50.0	47.5

SOURCE: *Gallup Opinion Index*, #137, December, 1976, pp. 16-17.

265

Democrats defected and voted for Richard Nixon. Reasons for these defections will be discussed in Chapter 10. One other conclusion here is that those classifying themselves as Independents tend to vote Republican by almost a two to one margin. The only exception, again, is 1964.

While there is a great danger in generalizing from the vote for president to that for other offices, it is evident that the patterns of voting are quite similar to patterns of party identification. The only major exception is the South, which supports Republican presidential candidates frequently despite an overwhelming Democratic advantage in party ID. When voting for offices other than the presidency is considered, this discrepancy is minimized. Voting patterns of the various groupings reinforce the concept of parties as loose coalitions that must gain support from a wide range of social categories.

POLITICAL PARTICIPATION IN AMERICA

Although this book focuses on voting, one must be aware that political participation is a more inclusive concept. In an early work on participation, Lester Milbrath presented a hierarchy of political activity ranging from simple exposure to political stimuli to holding public office.[39] A person at any given level of activity in the hierarchy tends to perform acts at the lower levels also. These activities are classified as gladiatorial, transitional, and spectator. Milbrath estimates that about one third of American adults are apathetic or passive, while 60 percent play largely spectator roles such as voting and paying attention to the campaign. At most, 5-7 percent could be considered gladiators, although Milbrath suggests that 1 or 2 percent is a more reasonable estimate.[40]

While Milbrath's hierarchy broadened the concept of political participation, it still was limited to campaign-related activities and voting. Sidney Verba and Norman Nie expand upon this analysis and conclude that there are four "modes of political participation."[41] In addition to (1) *voting* and (2) *campaign activities,* there are (3) *citizen-initiated contacts* with public officials and (4) *cooperative participation* through groups or organizations. Furthermore, each of these modes entails a variety of activities. While Milbrath concludes that political activities are cumulative, Verba and Nie

[39] Lester W. Milbrath, *Political Participation* (Chicago: Rand McNally and Company, 1965), p. 18.

[40] *Ibid.,* p. 19.

[41] Sidney Verba and Norman H. Nie, *Participation in America* (New York: Harper and Row, 1972), p. 47.

BOX 9.1 TYPES OF PARTICIPATORS: THEIR ORIENTATIONS TO POLITICS

Our orientational data clearly support our arguments that citizens differ not only in how much activity they engage in but also in the type of activity, and that this difference in type represents significant variations in the ways citizens attempt to influence government and the types of issues that lead them to become active.

The inactives are citizens who do not participate in politics and seem uninterested in participating. At the other extreme are the complete activists, whose orientations reflect their total involvement in politics. In between there are a variety of types of participants who perform different amounts and types of activities. There are the parochial participants, who perform the difficult act of contacting officials but confine the focus of their contacts to particularized problems. Their rather high levels of information provide them with the ability to use the government for private benefits while their preoccupation with this type of problem is reflected in their almost total lack of more general political involvement or sense of civic contribution.

The communalists are quite different, even though they often perform the same type of activity as the parochial activists—contacting. The communalists carry on numerous community and civic activities, but at the same time they avoid electoral politics. These citizens combine skill and competence with a strong commitment to politics and public affairs, a striking sense of civic-mindedness. The campaigners, in contrast, are heavily involved in conflict and cleavage, less concerned with the civic problems of the community than with the ongoing social policy debate and the electoral process. Finally, there are the voting specialists, whose peculiar pattern of political participation seems to emanate from their unusually strong attachments to political parties, which they maintain (unlike the partisans) without high levels of concern for politics or its issues.

It is clear from the data in this chapter that our various types of activists not only act differently, they think differently.

SOURCE: Sidney Verba and Norman H. Nie, *Participation in America* (New York: Harper and Row, Publishers, 1972), pp. 93-94.

suggest that there are different types of participators, who vary according to the form, as well as the amount, of their political participation. Box 9.1 details these types, which appear to specialize in various forms of participation.

Table 9.6 presents the six types of participators, their scores on the four participation scales, and their frequency in the U.S. By comparing each item in the table to the population average at the bottom of the table, the relative importance of each mode of activity to each type of participator is established. For instance, campaigners score high in campaign activity but low in group activities. Interestingly, those classified as "complete activists" score high in all modes except individualized contacts with officials. Such contacts are almost exclusively the domain of the 4 percent of the population labeled "parochial participants." These data indicate that political participation is a much more complex phenomenon than some of the literature suggests.

PARTICIPATION OTHER THAN VOTING

Table 9.7 lists the percentage of the population that reports having participated in specific activities. Only in voting, either local or national, does more than one third of the public participate. These data reinforce the importance of voting as the political act for most individuals. The most frequent types of activity other than voting are involvement in voluntary associations and working with others to solve community problems. Slightly less than one third participate in this manner.

Approximately one quarter of the population reports either persuading others to vote in a particular manner or actively working in a campaign. Fewer than 20 percent have contacted officials about an issue or problem, or have attended a political rally or meeting in the last three years. Similarly, only 13 percent have ever given money to a party or candidate, and only 8 percent are currently members of a political club or organization.[42] While these data are higher than comparable figures in a 1972 study, they reinforce the notion that Americans as a whole tend not to engage in political activities which require "more than trivial amounts of time or energy."[43]

PARTICIPATION: VOTING TURNOUT

For many Americans political participation is limited to voting. Although over 70 percent report having voted regularly in national elections, the actual

[42] *Ibid.*, p. 33.
[43] *Ibid.*, p. 32.

Table 9.6 Participatory Profiles of the American Citizenry

Groups produced by cluster analysis	Scores on participation scales for				Percent sample in type
	Voting	Campaign activity	Communal activity	Particularized contacting	
1. Inactive	37	9	3	0	22
2. Voting specialists	94	5	3	0	21
3. Parochial participants	73	13	3	100	4
4. Communalists	92	16	69	12	20
5. Campaigners	95	70	16	13	15
6. Complete activists	98	93	92	15	11
					93
Unclassifiable					7
					100%
Population means on the participation scale	76	29	28	14	

SOURCE: Sidney Verba and Norman H. Nie, *Participation in America* (New York: Harper and Row, Publishers, 1972), p. 79.

Table 9.7 Percentage Engaging in Twelve Different
Acts of Political Participation

Type of political participation	Percentage
1. Report regularly voting in Presidential elections	72
2. Report always voting in local elections	47
3. Active in at least one organization involved in community problems	32
4. Have worked with others in trying to solve some community problems	30
5. Have attempted to persuade others to vote as they were	28
6. Have ever actively worked for a party or candidate during an election	26
7. Have ever contacted a local government official about some issue or problem	20
8. Have attended at least one political meeting or rally in last three years	19
9. Have ever contacted a state or national government official about some issue or problem	18
10. Have ever formed a group or organization to attempt to solve some local community problem	14
11. Have ever given money to a party or candidate during an election campaign	13
12. Presently a member of political club or organization	8

SOURCE: Sidney Verba and Norman H. Nie, *Participation in America* (New York: Harper and Row, Publishers, 1972), p. 31.

voting data suggest that the proportion is closer to 55 percent.[44] Voting has been found to be influenced by the level or type of election, election laws (Chapter 4), and a series of personal orientations including interest in election, sense of citizen duty, and belief that the vote will make a difference.[45] Voting turnout is a central concept, since it is the most visible dimension of political participation.

It was noted in Chapter 4 that voting turnout is lowest in nonpartisan elections and for issue propositions, and highest for the presidential election. Generally, the more visible the election, the higher the turnout. Primary elections and for issue propositions, and highest for the presidential elections. general elections. In an examination of 72 presidential primaries from 1948-1968, the average statewide turnout was found to be 27 percent, compared with an average of 62 percent in the corresponding general elections in those

[44] One of the problems with surveys is that respondents tend to exaggerate their voting frequencies and their vote for the winning candidate.

[45] Milbrath, *Political Participation*, pp. 106-109.

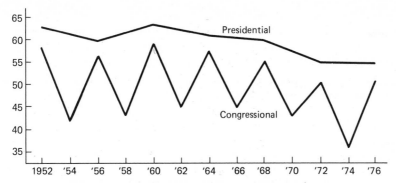

Figure 9.5   Voting Turnout for Presidential and
Congressional Elections, 1952-1976

SOURCE: U.S. Bureau of Census, *Statistical Abstract* (97th Edition) Washington, D.C.,
1976.

states.[46] As one moves from the state and local to the national elections, the
rates for both primaries and general elections increase, although the proportion between the two remains approximately the same.

Another major pattern of voting in the U.S. is that turnout rates during
presidential years are significantly higher than in off-years for all levels of
elections. Figure 9.5 demonstrates that turnout for presidential elections has
been consistently higher than for congressional. More interesting, however,
is the remarkably constant pattern of reduced turnout for congressional
elections in years when the presidency is not contested. There is a drop of
anywhere from 10-15 percent during these midterm elections. Although there
appear to be many reasons for this pattern, the most obvious is that the
highly salient presidential race brings out large numbers of voters who, under
other circumstances, would not vote. This reasoning has been used to explain
why the president's party invariably loses congressional seats in the midterm
election.[47] The marginal voters for the president fail to vote in the intervening election, thereby reducing support for the candidates of the president's
party.[48]

---

[46] Austin Ranney, "Turnout and Representation in Presidential Primary
Elections," *American Political Science Review,* 66 (March, 1972), 21-37.

[47] See Angus Campbell, "Voters and Elections: Past and Present,"
Journal of Politics, 26 (November, 1964), 745-57.

[48] Angus Campbell, "Surge and Decline: A Study of Electoral Change,"
in *Elections and the Political Order* (New York: John Wiley and Sons, 1966),
pp. 41-43. For a more complete analysis, see Edward R. Tufte, "Determi-
nants of the Outcomes of Midterm Congressional Elections," *American
Political Science Review,* 69 (September, 1975), 812-26.

Voting turnout varies by state, by level of election, and by the combination of offices contested in the election.[49] While voting in presidential elections varies between 55 and 60 percent, turnout for state and local offices might be as low as 10-20 percent. These differences, however, fail to explain why some people vote and others do not. The next question is: Who participates? What makes some people vote consistently, while others vote only in high visibility elections, and still others do not vote at all? While no in-depth analysis can be offered here, several of the major personal factors are examined.

PARTICIPATION RATES: WHO PARTICIPATES?

Some of the major characteristics of party activists were discussed in Chapter 5. It was demonstrated that high socioeconomic status (SES) groups predominated. Although there are a myriad of intervening factors such as place of residence, region, age, and race, that modify the basic impact of SES, the higher status categories are overrepresented in all types of political participation.

> The United States is often contrasted with other countries as being a society where class and status matter relatively little in political life. But in regard to the relationship between social status and political participation, the United States clearly has a class-biased pattern. Indeed . . . the U.S. pattern shows more class bias than almost all other countries for which comparative data exist.[50]

In all elections, the more frequent voters are those who have more education and are in the professions. Verba and Nie demonstrate that SES is crucial in explaining varying rates of political participation, especially campaign activity and group involvement.

The data in Table 9.8 illustrate this. The figures indicate the percentage of each participation category coming from each SES group. As expected, the upper SES individuals cluster in the high-participation categories, while the lower SES are concentrated in the low-participation categories. As usual in political analysis, however, there is substantial deviation from this general tendency. A small proportion (14 percent) of the highest participators come from low SES, while 10 percent of the lowest participators are from the

---

[49] Robert H. Blank, "Socio-economic Determinism of Voting Turnout: A Challenge," *Journal of Politics*, 36 (August, 1974), 731-52.

[50] Verba and Nie, *Participation in America*, pp. 132-33.

Table 9.8   Participation and Socioeconomic Status

	Socioeconomic Status			
Participation	*Upper*	*Middle*	*Low*	
Highest 1	57	29	14	100%
2	46	33	21	100%
3	38	38	24	100%
4	20	44	36	100%
5	18	36	46	100%
Lowest 6	10	32	59	100%

SOURCE: Sidney Verba and Norman H. Nie, *Participation in America* (New York: Harper and Row, Publishers, 1972), p. 131.

upper class. Overall, the relationship between SES and political participation remains strong. The higher status are more active at all levels.

ISSUE VOTING AND IDEOLOGY IN THE AMERICAN ELECTORATE

A major controversy in the study of American political behavior relates to the scope and role of issues and ideology in voting. According to Angus Campbell, issues play only a supporting role in voting. He suggests that three conditions must be met to have issue voting: (1) the voter must be aware of the issues, (2) the voter must care about the issue, and (3) the voter must perceive one party as closer to his position.[51] He found that only 18 to 36 percent of the electorate met these conditions on any specific issue.[52] When the attempt was made to see the extent to which attitudes are interrelated and organized around a liberal-conservative ideological continuum, Campbell found that less than 3 percent of the public made decisions on the basis of ideology. Another 9 percent of decisions were considered near-ideological. The remaining electoral decisions were made on the basis of perceptions of group benefits, candidate or party orientations, or simply on the nature of the times.[53]

In a follow-up study, Converse found that, at best, only half of his sample had even a reasonable comprehension of the terms "liberal" and "conservative." Approximately 17 percent had a broad understanding of

[51] Campbell, *American Voter,* pp. 169-171.

[52] *Ibid.,* p. 182.

[53] *Ibid.,* see table 10.1, p. 249.

liberal-conservative differences. Those with higher levels of ideology tended to be more educated and politically active.[54] In sum, Converse found no evidence of significant ideological organization in the public. For most citizens there exists no underlying organization of issues along a liberal-conservative dimension. Furthermore, there is little constraint among individual issues. Since constraint refers to the extent to which issues are interrelated, a lack of constraint means that changes in one aspect of a belief system can be made without affecting other elements.[55] It implies that each issue evokes a response independent of responses to other issues.

In another study, Converse demonstrates that individuals exhibit a high degree of instability in response to an identical set of issues over time.[56] Many assumed attitudes measured in sample surveys are probably nonattitudes. This means a person simply reacts to a survey question without any prior formulation of an opinion on that issue. On the basis of the presence of nonattitudes, Converse concludes that issue voting is even less prevalent than indicated by the surveys, since many of the so-called issue positions are in fact haphazard responses at a particular time. Again, the public is perceived as having little issue awareness.

In response to the conception of an electorate low in issue awareness and lacking in ideology, a series of studies were conducted which present a different perspective.[57] Several researchers suggest that the low level of issue awareness reported by Campbell and his associates in *The American Voter* was largely the result of the type of questions asked. By allowing the respondents to define the issues that are important to them, rather than simply presenting a predetermined list of issues, David RePass concludes that, contrary to SRC studies, "the public does perceive party differences on those issues that are salient to them."[58] By using different methods of collecting data, greater issue awareness has been demonstrated.

---

[54] Philip E. Converse, "The Nature of Belief Systems in Mass Publics," in *Public Opinion and Public Policy,* rev. ed., ed. Norman R. Luttbeg (Homewood, Ill.: The Dorsey Press, 1974), pp. 318-23.

[55] *Ibid.,* p. 302.

[56] Philip E. Converse, "Attitudes and Non-Attitudes: Continuation of a Dialogue," in *The Quantitative Analysis of Social Problems,* ed. Edward R. Tufte (Reading: Addison-Wesley Publishing Company, Inc., 1970), pp. 168-89. For a conflicting viewpoint, see John C. Pierce and Douglas D. Rose, "Non-Attitudes and American Public Opinion: The Examination of a Thesis," *American Political Science Review,* 68 (June, 1974), 626-49.

[57] For an excellent summary of this literature, see Richard G. Niemi and Herbert F. Weisberg, eds., *Controversies in American Voting Behavior* (San Francisco: W.H. Freeman and Company, 1976), pp. 67-84. Also see Nie, *The Changing American Voter,* especially pp. 110-73.

[58] David E. RePass, "Issue Salience and Party Choice," *American Political Science Review,* 65 (June, 1971), 394.

Others contend that SRC conclusions on ideology and issues are time-bound in the 1950s. Nie, for instance, argues that *The American Voter* is basically a book about the Eisenhower elections, and that the electorate, as well as the nature of issues, has changed since that time.[59] The new issues intrude more on personal lives than those of the Eisenhower era. Issues such as race, crime, drugs, and Vietnam in the late 1960s caught the attention of the public, with help from the media, and penetrated the citizens directly.[60] Issues today are not only more salient, but also more personal than those in the context of the SRC studies.

Gerald Pomper, using the same methodology as the SRC, concludes that perceived party differences along issue lines increased substantially during the 1960s.[61] The candidacy of Goldwater in 1964, especially, triggered increased levels of issue awareness and perception of distinctions between the parties on these issues. The McGovern candidacy in 1972 certainly extended this trend. The political context of each particular election is of crucial importance in defining awareness of issues, as well as perceptions of parties. Extending this, other authors have suggested that the respective position of the candidates on an issue is a central factor in determining its impact. If the candidates are perceived as offering little or no choice on an issue, it will have little impact on the vote, even though the voter might view it as an important issue.[62]

In addition to demonstrating increased levels of issue awareness, the studies cited have offered significant evidence of higher levels of ideological sophistication in the electorate. Field and Anderson find a substantial increase in the proportion of the public using some form of political ideology when evaluating candidates and parties. By using a somewhat different classification scheme, they conclude that 35 percent of citizens in 1964 were ideologues.[63] The corresponding figures for 1956 and 1960 are 21 percent

[59] Nie, *The Changing American Voter*, p. 8.

[60] *Ibid.*, p. 97.

[61] Gerald M. Pomper, "From Confusion to Clarity: Issues and American Voters, 1956-1968," *American Political Science Review*, 66 (June, 1972), 415-28. Also see Michael Margolis, "From Confusion to Confusion: Issues and the American Voter (1956-1972)," *American Political Science Review*, 71 (March, 1977), 31-43.

[62] Benjamin I. Page and Richard A. Brody, "Policy Voting and the Electoral Process: The Vietnam War Issue," *American Political Science Review*, 66 (September, 1971), 987-88.

[63] John O. Field and Ronald E. Anderson, "Ideology in The Public's Conception of the 1964 Election," *Public Opinion Quarterly*, 33 (Fall, 1969), 380-98. John Pierce, "Party Identification and the Changing Role of Ideology in American Politics," *Midwest Journal of Political Science*, 14 (February, 1970), 25-42, finds a doubling of the percentage of conceptual ideologues between 1956 and 1964.

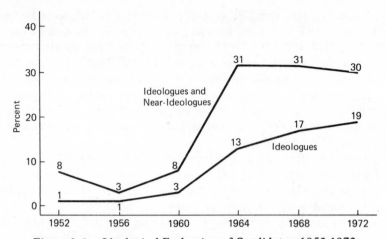

Figure 9.6   Ideological Evaluation of Candidates, 1952-1972

SOURCE: Norman H. Nie, *et al., The Changing American Voter* (Cambridge, Mass.: Harvard University Press, 1976), p. 113.

and 27 percent, respectively. Again, the political context emerges as an independent influence on ideological orientations in each election.

The graphs in Figure 9.6 illustrate the proportions of the American electorate that Nie considers ideologues, or near-ideologues, on the basis of the way they evaluate presidential candidates. They indicate that there is a sharp rise in 1964 of respondents who describe candidates using both general ideological terms (liberal-conservative) and issue references. By 1972, almost 20 percent of Americans, according to this data, could be characterized as ideologues. The near-ideologues, those who use ideological terms to describe candidates, increased dramatically in 1964, and have remained above 30 percent since. While the largest proportion of the electorate fails to see candidates and parties in liberal-conservative terms, the figures presented here suggest the proportion of ideologues is substantially higher than proposed in *The American Voter.*

Along with this support for ideological voting has come evidence of significant levels of belief system constraint. One study concluded that issues are more interrelated than suggested by the SRC.[64] They found the presence of a constraint across many issues fitting a liberal-conservative pattern. Not only has constraint of traditional issues increased, but also, as new issues have emerged, they have been incorporated into a broad liberal-conservative

---

[64] Norman H. Nie and Kristi Anderson, "Mass Belief Systems Revisited: Political Change and Attitude Structure," *The Journal of Politics,* 36 (August, 1974), 540-87.

ideology by a substantial proportion of the public.[65] Nie contends that the shape of attitudes of the American public as a whole has shifted from a centrist position toward the left and right extremes.[66]

In agreement with Nie, Stimson contends that changing times have resulted in a marked increase in belief constraint. At least half of the eligible voters display "evidence of belief structuring that is consistent with the standards established by Converse."[67] This is substantially in congruence with the Miller, *et al.* conclusion that ideology today is more relevant in influencing the vote, and that issues cluster more, than in the past. They attribute this to the clearer choices offered by the candidates as they respond to the issues of the day.[68]

While there is conflicting evidence concerning ideology and issues in American politics, the most recent research tends to imply that issue voting is becoming more predominant. Although a majority of the electorate continues to make decisions based on a combination of party, group, and candidate concerns, a growing minority has a more structured ideology with a relatively high degree of constraint across the major issues. Although party voting and issue voting are not necessarily incompatible, the issues of the 1960s and 70s have not coincided with the party alignments, and there is little indication that they soon will. While the public appears to be more issue-conscious and issue-consistent, the parties have been unable to adjust to the new voters. According to Nie, issue voting does not reinforce partisan commitments because: (1) fewer citizens have issue attitudes and party affiliations that are congruent, (2) more issue voters are independents, and (3) citizens experiencing cross-pressures between issue commitments and party identification vote more frequently on the issues than before 1964.[69]

Although political issues are given more weight in this issue-centered model, long-term party attachment is not negated, but rather, reacts with issues of the day.

> The evidence, as we shall see, strongly confirms the Michigan contention that party identification is a long-term commitment, established early in life and usually maintained after that. The fact that the

---

[65] Nie, *The Changing American Voter*, p. 123.

[66] *Ibid.*, p. 144.

[67] James A. Stimson, "Belief Systems: Constraint, Complexity, and the 1972 Election," *American Journal of Political Science*, 19 (August, 1975), 414.

[68] Arthur H. Miller, *et al.*, "A Majority Party in Disarray: Political Polarization in the 1972 Election," in *Controversies in American Voting Behavior*, ed Niemi and Weisberg, pp. 176-95.

[69] Nie, *The Changing American Voter*, p. 300.

number of citizens with no such commitment has risen substantially in recent years as more and more citizens identify themselves as independents, modifies but does not contradict that contention.[70]

In addition, personal evaluations of the candidates are still significant components of electoral decisions. Despite the increase in issue awareness and constraint, perceptions of the candidates are approximately as important as "issue evaluations even at the height of issue importance."[71] Candidates, issues, and parties all operate within the broader social and political context of each election to produce the vote.

PARTY AFFILIATION AND AMERICAN POLITICAL BEHAVIOR: A SUMMARY

Party affiliation is a central predisposition for many Americans. Although it seldom dominates political behavior, over 60 percent of the American electorate view parties within the context of their own party identification. While there has been a significant decrease in the proportion identifying with either party in recent decades, party identification is still the most stable political orientation. It tends to develop early in life and, more often than not, remains with the individual for life.

This chapter examined the social differentiation of Republican and Democratic identifiers. Despite differing proportions of support from certain social and economic groupings, neither party can assume consistently strong support from any one group. Both parties must continually attempt to widen their coalition or risk failure at the polls. Although Democrats tend to receive more support from the working class categories and Republicans do better among the more educated and established citizens, neither party is class based, and each receives substantial support from most groups.

Although party identification is related to voting behavior, it alone does not explain how a person votes. The increase in issue voting discussed here implies a weakening role of party affiliation in the American electorate. Chapter 10 examines the recent status of party as a psychological affiliation within the context of current trends in voting behavior, and outlines implications of these changes for the party organizations and the party system itself.

[70] *Ibid.*, p. 45.
[71] *Ibid.*, p. 319.

10

Voting Theories
and Voting Trends:
The Changing Role
of Party Affiliation

In Chapter 9 we saw how parties are composed of coalitions of various social groupings, from which support is expected from election to election. The political socialization process was summarized and party identification as a concept was examined. Chapter 9 also provided survey data to illustrate the social differention of the party electorates. In order to place voting in its proper context, the chapter ended by briefly summarizing the nature of political participation in the United States. It suggested that there is presently much controversy concerning the dimension of parties as psychological affiliations, and that political observers are divided in their interpretation of various trends in voting.

VOTING: THE THEORIES

This chapter will examine two major theories of voting in the United States: the normal vote (NV) model and the ticket-splitter (TS) model.[1] It will analyze the applicability of each model within the framework of current trends in the electorate. The implications of these shifts for the political parties will also be examined. Finally, several alternatives for the party coalitions are to be analyzed in light of current electoral trends.

[1] The terms theory and model are used interchangeably here, although those readers with methodology backgrounds are aware of the technical distinction. The issue-oriented model of Nie and Verba discussed in detail in Chapter 9 is intricately related to the Ticket-Splitter model.

For the last two decades the study of voting behavior in the U.S. has been dominated by a model introduced in *The American Voter*.[2] In this book, a group of Michigan Survey Research Center (SRC) authors presented a psychologically-based theory of voting which centered on the concept of party identification. Using 1952 and 1956 election data, it was demonstrated that party identification is the most basic and enduring attachment of Americans. As such, it serves a useful evaluative function for the individual. Not only is it the major determinant of voting behavior, but more importantly, it has been found to be very stable. This stability has meant that each major party could depend on party identification to provide a reliable source of support from election to election.

The American Voter concluded that party identification strengthens those attributes which are most associated with democratic citizens. Those with strong party identification displayed:

1. more interest in elections and their outcome;
2. increased exposure to politics;
3. more discussion with friends and attempts to persaude;
4. higher campaign activity
5. greater perception of policy difference between parties; and
6. more fully developed and cohesive stands on policy issues.

By emphasizing the heightened interest, involvement, and concern of party identifiers, these researchers deflated the image of the Independent. The early voting studies concluded that those self-classified as Independents, instead of being responsible citizens, making rational choices unbound by party loyalty, are the most uninformed, unconcerned, and unlikely to vote.

Throughout the 1950s and 60s, most campaigning was based on the assumption that the party loyalists were the key to success. Democratic candidates emphasized party loyalty, while Republicans generally attempted to minimize it. Both parties geared their campaigns to reinforce and stimulate their own identifiers, while appealing to enough Independents to win the election. Many candidates placed their trust in this assumption of the predominance of party identification.

Although this theory centers on the concept of party identification, never did the authors contend that it acted in isolation to determine the vote. Other factors which altered the final vote were present in each election. The

---

[2] Angus Campbell, *et al.*, *The American Voter* (New York: John Wiley and Sons, Inc., 1964).

authors termed these factors unique to each contest short term forces (STF). The STF are composed of candidates, issues, and events which combine in each election to influence the voters. Candidates, especially at the national level, are not evaluated fully in terms of party label. A candidate with attractive personal attributes, for instance, can draw party identifiers of the opposite party to defect for that one contest. Issues and events, likewise, can favor one party or a particular candidate, and at times may take precedence. According to the SRC, each election has a special of STF which operates on party identification to produce the vote (see Figure 10.1).

STF ⟶ Party ID ⟶ Vote

Figure 10.1 Simple Party ID Model

If strong enough, these STF can change the outcome from that expected solely on the basis of party identification.

In 1966, Philip Converse of the SRC modified the above model by adjusting party identification for turnout.[3] Since it is known that Democrats vote less often (see Chapter 9), their advantage is lessened, in terms of the normal vote expected, on the basis of their proportion in the electorate. It makes little difference whether all Democrats support their party's candidates, if only a small proportion turn out to vote. Therefore, the more complete normal vote model presently includes the elements found in Figure 10.2.

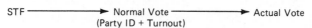

STF ⟶ Normal Vote ⟶ Actual Vote
(Party ID + Turnout)

Figure 10.2 Normal Vote Model

The "normal vote" is the vote expected in any election, based on the combination of the percentage in each category of party identification, adjusted for estimated turnout. This normal vote is influenced by STF to produce an actual vote (that is, percentage of Democrats and Republicans). The model implies that most cross-pressures between party identification and STF will be reduced in favor of long-term attachment to the party. It assumes that elections where STF overcome the normal vote are the exceptions.[4]

[3] Philip E. Converse, "The Concept of the Normal Vote," in Angus Campbell, et al., Elections and the Political Order (New York: John Wiley and Sons, Inc., 1966), pp. 9-39.

[4] These are termed "deviating" elections by the SRC as opposed to "maintaining" elections where the majority wins.

TICKET-SPLITTER MODEL

Recently there has been a challenge to several key assumptions of the normal vote model. DeVries and Tarrance have introduced the ticket-splitter model, which they contend better explains current voting behavior in the U.S.[5] Although they do not contend that party identification is a meaningless concept, they argue that it has become less relevant as an explanatory factor. Instead of concentration on long-term psychological attachment as a measure of party support, DeVries and Tarrance shift emphasis to actual voting behavior. They contend that recent trends toward dividing votes between the parties require a reexamination of party identification. Although party affiliation still plays a role in voting, it is not at the center of the TS model.

DeVries and Tarrance contend that the increase in splitting tickets has been accompanied by the estrangement of voters from strong affiliation with the parties. This shift in self-classification from the parties to the Independent category leads the authors to challenge the normal vote measure of Independents. The real test of independence is whether or not a voter splits his ticket. Actual voting behavior, not some attitudinal dimension of party attachment or lack of attachment, becomes the center of the ticket-splitter model.

In the process of shifting emphasis from attitude to behavior, DeVries and Tarrance find their Independents, the ticket-splitters, to be at least as informed, interested, and active as the strong party identifiers. In fact, the ticket-splitters are more likely to be Republican or Democratic identifiers than self-classified Independents. Ticket splitting is highest among the young, highly educated, suburban, white-collar voters. On many social measures, these behavioral Independents are the opposite of the attitudinal Independents of the SRC. They are heavy media users, play more active roles in persuasion attempts than straight Democratic voters, and have the highest turnout rates of all categories.

While shifting emphasis to behavioral patterns, DeVries and Tarrance argue that the basis for voting in the U.S. has changed. No longer is party ID most important. The dominance of the normal vote in the SRC model has evaporated.[6] As Table 10.1 indicates, the personalities and abilities of the candidates have replaced party affiliation as most important to the voters. Next in line come the issue stands of the candidates, and then the parties. In other words, short-term forces have become a more important single factor

[5] Walter DeVries and Lance Tarrance, Jr., *The Ticket-Splitter: A New Force in American Politics* (Grand Rapids, Mich.: William B. Eerdmans Publishing Co., 1972).

[6] *Ibid.*, p. 74.

Table 10.1   How Voters Make Up Their Minds

Currently	Prior to 1960
1. Candidate's personality and ability to handle job	1. Party
2. Issues: candidate's stands and ability to handle problems	2. Group Affiliations
3. Party: identification and membership	3. Candidates
4. Group affiliations: religious ethnic, occupational	4. Issues

SOURCE: Walter DeVries and Lance Tarrance, Jr., *The Ticket-Splitter: A New Force in American Politics* (Grand Rapids, Mich.: William Eerdmans Publishing Co. 1972), p. 74.

for many voters than long-term party attachment. Also, effective use of the news media is more crucial to success in this model, since the ticket-splitters are more attuned to and dependent on the media for information. They are less limited in their choices than strong identifiers in the normal vote model.

According to this more recent model of voting, the ticket-splitter has become a new force in American elections. He represents at least 25 percent of the electorate, and often is the balance of power in elections. In close elections, especially, the behavioral Independent holds the key to success. Campaign strategy must be revised to account for this new voter, according to DeVries and Tarrance. The ground rules underlying the ticket-splitter model are significantly different from those of the normal vote model. These two models offer competing explanations of voting based on different assumptions. In order to analyze them more completely, data on various voting trends are presented here.

VOTING TRENDS: THE DATA

Although the electorate has always been dynamic and fluid, the last decade has witnessed the emergence of several trends that threaten to alter both voting behavior and political party affiliation. Several of these trends are central to the ticket-splitter model, while others appear to be working independently. Much recent data is available to trace and analyze these emerging patterns of voting behavior. Each is discussed here in the context of the two theories of voting. Then conclusions will be drawn as to which theory is more accurate in terms of the data.

Table 10.2 Party Identification, 1952-1974, SRC

	1952	1956	1960	1962	1964	1966	1968	1970	1972	1974	Trend 1952-1974
Rep[a]	27	29	27	28	24	25	24	25	23	19	− 8
Dem[b]	47	44	46	46	51	45	45	43	40	41	− 6
Ind[c]	22	24	23	22	23	28	30	31	35	40	+18
DK	4	3	4	4	2	2	1	1	2		− 4

SOURCE: SRC, collected October or November of each year noted
a) Strong and weak Republicans
b) Strong and weak Democrats
c) Independents and leaders

LOOSENING OF PARTY ATTACHMENT

A very striking development since the mid-1960s has been weakening of party identification. "Perhaps the most dramatic political change in the American public over the past two decades has been the decline of partisanship."[7] This is most evident in the increase in the proportion of respondents who fail to identify with either party. Instead, they classify themselves as Independent. Table 10.2 demonstrates the magnitude of this shift. It has been estimated that between 1964 and 1970 alone there were ten million additional voters who considered themselves Independent. While the gap between the parties over the last two decades has remained quite constant, those classifying themselves as Independents have risen from 22 percent of the electorate to 40 percent, a jump of 18 percentage points. It is also suggested that the potential for further defections from the two parties is high. The Democratic party stands to lose support, especially from southerners, Catholics, and young voters. Republican defections are most likely to occur among the young, in the suburbs of the larger cities, and in the Northeast.[8]

More significant, perhaps, is the pattern of these defections. The greatest shifts towards independence have occurred among the younger voters. The data in Table 10.3 illustrate that in 1975 almost half of those between the

Table 10.3 Party Identification by Age, 1975

	18-24	25-29	30-49	50
Democrat	39	42	45	50
Republican	15	14	21	29
Independent	46	44	34	21

SOURCE: *Gallup Opinion Index*, #120 (June, 1975), p. 22.

ages of 18 and 24 considered themselves Independent. Although there have always been some generational differences, a discrepancy this large has additional dimensions. It reflects in part an inability of the parties to respond to the issues to which the young are especially sensitive. It is also easier for the young to defect because their party attachment is not as well established. Significant, too, is that among those who still identify with one of the parties, the ties have weakened. They do not tend to think of politics in terms of

[7] Norman H. Nie, Sidney Verba, and John R. Petrocik, *The Changing American Voter* (Cambridge, Mass.: Harvard University Press, 1976), p. 47.

[8] For an excellent discussion of this trend, see James L. Sundquist, *Dynamics of the Party System* (Washington, D.C.: The Brookings Institution, 1973), especially Chapter 16.

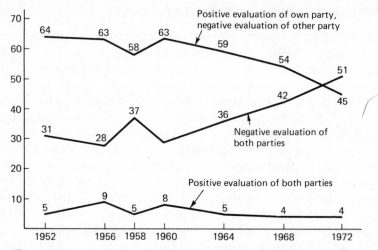

Figure 10.3 Decline in Positive Evaluation of Parties, 1952-1972

SOURCE: Norman H. Nie *et al., The Changing American Voter* (Cambridge, Mass.: Harvard University Press, 1976), p. 58.

political parties. Parties are less frequently used than in the 1950s as standards of evaluation or as guides to electoral choice.[9]

One obvious manifestation of this weakening of party attachment is the decline in the identification with the political parties. Figure 10.3 traces this decline over the last two decades. While the small proportion that is positive towards both parties has remained fairly constant since 1952, the percentage that evaluate their own party positively has decreased from 64 to 45 percent. Conversely, those considered non-supporters of the party system, that is, those with positive evaluations of neither party, have jumped from 31 to 51 percent of the population.[10] Less than half of all Americans feel positively about either party. This is not surprising, since all indicators examined here demonstrate a trend away from party affiliation.

INCREASED TICKET SPLITTING

In examining the concept of party identification, the data suggest that the normal vote model has been seriously weakened as an explanation of voting in the last decade. This weakening of party attachment is also manifested in the massive increase in ticket splitting in recent elections. Not only are more

[9] Nie and Verba, *Changing American Voter*, p. 48.
[10] *Ibid.*, p. 57.

people describing themselves as Independents, they are also voting for some candidates of one party and some of the other. It is estimated that, until the 1940s, over 80 percent of the electorate voted straight ticket in presidential elections.[11] By 1956 this figure had been reduced to approximately 60 percent. After the 1968 election, only 44 percent reported voting a straight ticket and by 1972 the corresponding figure was 38 percent. Almost two thirds of the electorate split their tickets in 1972.

Table 10.4   Proportion of Split Tickets, 1948-1972

	1948	1960	1964	1968	1972
U.S. Total	38	34	42	56	62
Northeast	27	23	45	54	60
Midwest	42	40	39	58	56
South	30	24	34	55	64
West	56	57	50	57	72

SOURCE: Everett Carll Ladd, Jr. and Charles D. Hadley, *Transformations of the American Party System,* 2nd ed. (New York: W.W. Norton and Company, 1978), p. 325.

As Table 10.4 indicates, the trend toward increased ticket splitting is not a regional phenomenon. The incidence is similar in all regions, including the West, which had a very early start in voting independently. Ticket splitting is, moreover, not limited to defections at the presidential level. The SRC has found a similar increase in ticket splitting in the votes for state and local offices below governor.[12] While 74 percent of the national electorate voted straight-party at the state and local level in 1952, only 33 percent did so in 1972 (see Figure 10.4).

The data on ticket splitting therefore support the model presented by DeVries and Tarrance. Behaviorally as well as psychologically, American voters are less likely to support either party completely. As noted by these authors, ticket splitting is certain to increase, since those most prone to such voting patterns are the young, better educated, and more media-conscious. This trend, along with the loosening of party attachment, supports the ticket-splitter model. It also minimizes the importance of political parties as affiliations.

[11] DeVries and Tarrance, *The Ticket-Splitter,* p. 22.

[12] Everett Carll Ladd, Jr. and Charles D. Hadley, *Transformations of the American Party System,* 2nd ed. (New York: W.W. Norton and Co., Inc., 1978), p. 326.

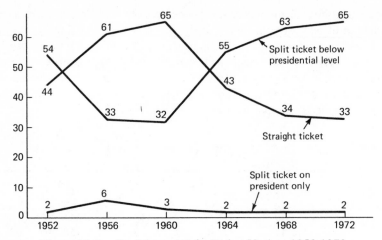

Figure 10.4   Straight and Split-Ticket Voting, 1952-1972

SOURCE: Norman H. Nie, *et al., The Changing American Voter,* (Cambridge, Mass.: Harvard University Press, 1976), p. 53.

PURPOSIVE NON-VOTING

Any act of voting is actually the result of two decisions: whom to vote for and whether to vote at all. Increasingly in the last decade, eligible voters have been saying "no" to the latter. Between 1968 and 1974, those not voting have increased by 18 million people. More importantly, those registered but not voting showed a 100 percent increase in the four years from 1968 to 1972. Although they invested time and energy in registering, 25 million people in 1974 failed to vote. All indicators portend additional increases in purposive nonvoting in the near future.

In the past, these non-voters have been explained away as the result of legal restrictions and lack of motivation. The contention was that, as legal barriers such as residency requirements were eliminated, education levels increased, and political information became more available, voting turnout would rise. The SRC theory of voting suggested that the non-voters were largely Independents with little motivation to vote. Although all of these factors shifted in the proposed directions, nonvoting has continued to increase, especially among younger citizens.

Although many reasons for this new surge of nonvoting have been expressed, Lance Tarrance sees this as one additional indication of independence from past behavior.[13] Although some of the nonvoting derives from

[13] V. Lance Tarrance, "The Vanishing Voter: A Look at Non-Voting as a Purposive Act," in *Voters, Primaries, and Parties* (Cambridge, Mass.: Harvard University Press, 1976), p. 10.

apathy, for an increasing number of persons it is a purposive expression of discontent with the conduct of elections. Nie agrees:

> The decline in interest appears to represent more a conscious rejection of politics than a withdrawal into more neutral apathy.[14]

George Gallup found "ample evidence of the public's distrust of politics and politicians" in the low turnout in 1974. A total of almost 40 percent sat out the election either because they were discouraged by the political process or because they did not like the candidates.[15]

Although related to the weakening of party identification and the increase in ticket splitting, purposive nonvoting appears to be the manifestation of an even deeper ambivalence toward parties and politicians. It might be seen as the ultimate symbol of distrust and resentment by an increasing proportion of the electorate. Although non-voters are similar to voters in terms of past behavior and party identification, they are better educated and younger than commonly assumed. It might be expected that a continued increase in nonvoting among the young, better educated electorate will contribute to even greater instability and polarization of policy preferences among the shrinking numbers who continue to vote.

EXPLANATION OF TRENDS TOWARD INDEPENDENT VOTING

Why this rather sudden increase in independence from political parties? Although there are a myriad of reasons for these patterns, several are most evident. First, the mass media have replaced the party as a major source of campaign information. Instead of having to rely on party identification as a cue or reference point for voting, the voters of the 1970s are more dependent on the mass media, especially television, for analysis of the candidates. Candidates now present their credentials directly to the electorate without utilization of the party structure. Party workers are displaced as sources of information about the candidates, because the viewers can assess them simply by turning on their television sets.

Second, and partly as a result of the mass media influence, campaigns have become more candidate-oriented. With attention focused on the style and personal attributes of the candidates, the role of party affiliation is minimized. Robert Teeter contends that Watergate provided the impetus by making voters more concerned with the personal qualities of each candidate,

---

[14] Nie and Verba, *Changing American Voter*, p. 280.
[15] *Gallup Opinion Index*, Report No. 118 (December, 1974), p. 24.

despite party label.[16] Certainly, the backgrounds of all candidates are now a public record within the context of increased investigative reporting and the new campaign disclosure laws. If neither candidate is successful in reassuring the voter, purposive nonvoting is an alternative.

Third, in addition to the new emphasis on candidates, issues have become more visible and central to voting decisions. It was demonstrated in Chapter 9 that these new issues are more personalized and less related to traditional party distinctions than issues of the past. The new concerns of the voters are not expressed through the parties, nor have the parties appeared capable of responding to these more complex value-laden issues. Issues such as abortion, school busing, ecology, crime, and the like, are not easily exploited or monopolized by either party. The awareness of the voters on the issues and the consistency of their positions have also increased, thereby minimizing the role played by party identification for many voters. They no longer need strong ties to a party since such attachments fail to help define the issues.

> It is a simple fact that Americans need parties much less now than in the past as intermediaries in shaping their electoral decisions. The electorate has become, for the long run, more issue oriented and more candidate oriented, and necessarily, then, less party oriented.[17]

ALTERATIONS IN THE PARTY ELECTORATES: PARTY REALIGNMENT

It has been suggested throughout the last two chapters that parties are flexible, loose coalitions of electoral supporters. It is expected, therefore, that changes in the composition of these coalitions will continue to occur. When the changes are of a magnitude sufficient to shift the balance of power between the parties, such alterations become critical to the political process. The trends in voting examined here imply that substantial alterations in voting are taking place with much potential impact on the parties. In order to analyze changes in the party electorates, political scientists study the concept of "party realignment," or the shift in voting blocs from one coalition to another. In realignment, the basic lines of cleavage in the electorate are altered, resulting in a rearrangement of the elements within each party. Certain blocs that supported one party prior to realignment now support either the

---

[16] Robert M. Teeter, "Recent Trends in Voting Behavior," in *Voters, Primaries, and Parties*, p. 5.

[17] Ladd and Hadley, *Transformations*, p. 332.

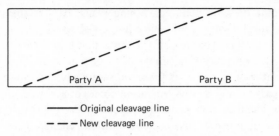

——— Original cleavage line
— — — New cleavage line

Figure 10.5   Hypothetical Shift in Basic Electorate Cleavages

opposite party or a totally new party. Figure 10.5 illustrates one possible alteration of basic cleavages and the resulting new pattern of support. If the whole rectangle represents the electorate, the original cleavage line defines the composition of the parties prior to realignment. The new cleavage line resulting from party realignment cuts into both original coalitions, resulting in shifts not only of individuals, but also of elements of the original coalitions. This example indicates that many elements in each coalition might not be affected by the realignment, or might themselves be divided and not easily placed in either coalition.

CHARACTERISTICS OF REALIGNMENT

Realignment, though having possible impact on the party electoral organization, is most related to party as a psychological affiliation. It has been argued that a realignment entails both short and long-term consequences which might arise from a single realigning force.[18] This process occurs over a period of decades, though it might be most clearly manifested in one or two critical elections. It is probably best to envision the electorate as dynamic and in a constant state of flux.[19] Although some observers have attempted to trace the "cutting points of transition" between two party systems, this becomes a difficult task. There is evidence that, despite identical party labels, there have been five party systems in our history. The transitions between systems are difficult to pinpoint. For instance, many observers suggest that the realignment attributed to the New Deal actually began prior to 1928, and was not complete until after 1936.[20]

[18] Sundquist, *Dynamics of the Party System,* p. 9.

[19] Gerald M. Pomper, *Elections in America* (New York: Dodd, Mead and Company, 1970), p. 123, argues that it is more accurate to talk about critical periods than critical elections.

[20] *Ibid.,* pp. 107-111. For a detailed account of the New Deal realignment see Sundquist, *Dynamics of the Party System,* Chapters 10-12.

One point of agreement concerning realignment is their periodicity. Fundamental turning points are generally agreed to have been 1800, 1828, 1860, 1896, and 1932. One reason for this is that it probably takes at least a generation to loosen party attachment of those who went through the original realignment. For instance, as those who were adults during the New Deal realignment pass on and a new generation comes of age, perhaps the weakening of party identification is to be expected. Party identification is not casually changed, however. As social conditions change, party attachment serves as a buffer for party action. Party coalitions at any one time probably reflect the social divisions of some earlier period. As the expectations of groups cease to be fulfilled by a party, group attachment becomes totally psychological. Such a group, without a material base for attachment, is very volatile, and its party is no longer assured of its support.[21]

SECULAR REALIGNMENT

Party realignment may come about in two distinct ways: through secular realignment and critical realignment. In practice, it probably results from some combination of both. Secular realignment is a gradual, long-term alteration in party attachment. It results from cumulative social trends occurring over a series of elections. Social mobility, urbanization, increased education, generational changes, and demographic modifications lead to shifting party attachments which over time modify the relative strengths of the parties. In secular realignment there is no sudden or sharp redistribution of party strength, although a crucial change in the composition of party support is occurring. The result of these incremental and often imperceptible processes is a new party alignment. Secular realignment usually includes countervailing movements across the cleavage lines, but only its cumulative effect is apparent. Figure 10.6 represents a hypothetical secular realignment of party strength.

CRITICAL REALIGNMENT

Realignment can also take place through a sharp and durable shift in the electoral strength of the parties. A critical election or series of critical elections can lead to a decisive alteration of electoral cleavages.[22] Large numbers

[21] Everett Carll Ladd, Jr., *American Political Parties: Social Change and Political Response* (New York: W.W. Norton and Co., Inc., 1970), pp. 308-9.

[22] Critical elections must be distinguished from the deviating election category where short-term factors have caused defections from the present party alignment. Although short-term forces may be present in critical elections, the major characteristic is an alteration in the composition of the coalition that breaks the current party alignment.

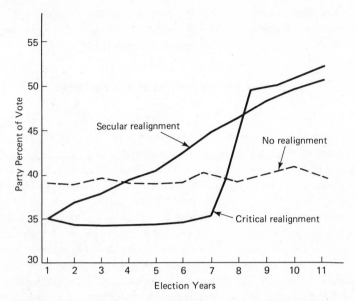

Figure 10.6 Hypothetical Secular and Critical Realignment

of identifiers with one or both parties might be shaken permanently from their attachment. In the past, critical elections have resulted from major economic and political upheavals such as the Great Depression or the Civil War. The critical election or elections are marked by depth and intensity of electoral involvement. The resulting realignment disclosed by the vote persists for at least several succeeding elections. Even in the most critical of these realignments, only a portion of the electorate is involved. Remnants of the original party alignment always survive.[23]

It is probable that there is no one critical election which results in party realignment. Secular realignment is more frequent than these isolated critical elections or political transformations. The most critical election probably represents a break in electoral continuity, but does not result in a complete establishment of a new, durable party alignment. Elections prior to the realignment are uneven and ambiguous, and generally blend together. Elections succeeding the critical election serve to assimilate the various elements into the new coalition. Once a stable and persistent coalition of voters is

[23] The most comprehensive book on critical elections basically from a historical viewpoint is Walter Dean Burnham, *Critical Elections and the Mainsprings of American Politics* (New York: W.W. Norton and Co., Inc., 1970). The impetus for interest in this concept is found in V.O. Key, Jr., "A Theory of Critical Elections" *Journal of Politics,* 17 (1955), 3-18. Much of this discussion on critical elections is based on these two works.

established, party support from the elements of the coalition will remain consistent for a number of elections. Minor fluctuations that occur are most likely attributable to short-term forces and demographic shifts.

PARTY REALIGNMENT POSSIBILITIES

One of the most popular diversions of political observers today is to suggest to what degree political parties are in a state of realignment. It has been over forty years since a major realignment occurred, and past realignments have come approximately once in a generation. Within the context of the attitudinal and behavioral changes in the electorate examined earlier, as well as demographic trends of the population, political commentators have offered many alternatives for describing current and future party coalitions. Several of the major realignment possibilities are discussed here within this broader context of change in the electorate. These alternatives include: (1) ideological realignment of the two parties, (2) emergence of a conservative third party, (3) creation of a majority Republican party, (4) strengthening of the New Deal Democratic majority, (5) decomposition or disintegration of the party system, and (6) maintenance of the status quo.

IDEOLOGICAL REALIGNMENT

In light of the new political awareness of the electorate and the increase in issue voting, some have argued that a vast ideological realignment is in order. Normally this is proposed for the party in government, although by inference it would necessitate a similar realignment of the party electorate. This approach implies that only by reordering politics in ideological terms can the parties really have a chance to govern and the electorate to make informed and rational decisions.

Generally, such proposals have recommended an electoral shift around a liberal-conservative dimension. Elements of the Republican party would join with the more conservative Democrats to form an ideologically conservative party. The liberal party would be composed of mostly liberal elements of the Democratic party, supplemented by liberal Republicans. Based on what is known about the electorate, such a realignment appears doubtful. Despite an increasingly ideological basis for voting decisions, most of the electorate makes decisions in a less structured manner. Also, such a realignment assumes that all issues can be easily distributed along one continuum (liberal-conservative). Research data indicate that American politics is much more complex.[24] Furthermore, recent attempts by two candidates to

---

[24] See Chapter 9 for a full discussion of the complexity of ideology and issue awareness in the United States.

purify the parties ideologically have failed. Goldwater and McGovern each received about 39 percent of the vote for their efforts.

Even if the limitations of the electorate can be overcome, there are forces operating within each party that counter such a realignment. Few officeholders and party leaders are willing to surrender or risk the relative comfort of their present positions for ideological reasons. Although party identification has been weakened, there appears to be very little impetus for such a massive restructuring. Despite a potential for shifts toward the right or left within each party, it appears unlikely that new parties will be formed along strictly ideological grounds. American politics is too complex for such a realignment to transpire, except perhaps in a very slow and imperceptible manner through the creation of intermediary third parties that absorb elements of the two present parties.

EMERGENCE OF A CONSERVATIVE THIRD PARTY [25]

Kevin Phillips contends that the possibility of a third party is now a probability.[26] He sees the American Party as a new conservative alternative. Phillips argues that the Democratic party is dominated irreversibly by the new bureaucratic elites and their client poor. The economic alliance between these groups is against the interests of the taxpaying middle class. This situation has led to a new populist taxpayer's revolt that can serve as the basis of a new majority coalition. The Republicans, he contends, are slated for extinction because of their failure to take advantage of this situation. William Rusher supports Phillips' analysis, and contends that the conservative majority already exists and is ready for appeals from a new political party.[27] The proponents of a new conservative party cite recent surveys which indicate that a clear majority of Americans classify themselves as conservatives.[28]

The optimism of Phillips and Rusher results in large part from the success of George Wallace in obtaining almost ten million votes in 1968. Until that election, minority parties had been declining in popularity as well as in number. The ability of Wallace to become a national candidate, coupled with the weakening of traditional party ties and the potential of electronic media,

---

[25] Attempts at creating viable third parties on the left have failed and are presently of minimal importance.

[26] Kevin P. Phillips, *Mediacracy* (Garden City, N.Y.: Doubleday and Co., Inc., 1975).

[27] William Rusher, *The Making of the New Majority Party* (Mission, Kans.: Sheed and Ward, 1975).

[28] In an April, 1974 Gallup Survey, 59 percent of the respondents who had an opinion classified themselves as conservative.

have led to the Phillips-Rusher speculation concerning the potential for third parties in the party system, or even the development of a multiparty system.

The strong Wallace showing is evidence to these authors that 1968 was a critical election, or one of a series of critical elections. The emergence of more ideological and issue-oriented voters and the volatile nature of the electorate, especially the youth, does suggest a possibility of third parties' becoming more crucial forces. Despite this greater potential for third party development, however, there is little evidence to suggest that the major parties are threatened by a new party coalition. The challenge to the two major parties is generally limited to a third party's potential deadlocking of the presidential race. No third party presently appears to be systematically developing viable continuing organizations. The American Independent Party, under which George Wallace ran in 1968 in most states, did poorly when Wallace was off the ticket in 1972 and 1976. Also, this party ran few candidates for other offices, even in 1968. The success of the Wallace movement was not extended to the party itself. Although there is some basis for the contentions of these conservative theorists in the current trends in the electorate, they tend to overlook the other two dimensions of political parties (see Box 10.1 for comments on this).

EMERGING REPUBLICAN MAJORITY

Prior to his conversion to the conservative party theory, Kevin Phillips was spokesman for the realignment theory which argued that the liberal Democratic coalition had given way to a new Republican majority.[29] This theory is based on the assumption that the fastest growing areas of the country are Republican, and will continue to be. The new popular majority is white and conservative, and Phillips placed much emphasis on the Southern Strategy. That initial stage was to be followed by the blue collar, ethnic, Roman Catholic phases in the North. Phillips argued that the Republicans benefited directly from the social issues.[30] Contrary to the trends toward independence, he assumed a continuation of ethnic and social bloc voting and the formation of strong new party attachments sympathetic to the Republican party.

[29] Kevin P. Phillips, *The Emerging Republican Majority* (Garden City, N.Y.: Doubleday and Company, Inc., 1970). Also see John S. Saloma III and Frederick H. Sontag, *Parties: The Real Opportunity for Effective Citizen Politics* (New York: Vintage Books, 1972), pp. 324-32, for an in-depth analysis of the emerging Republican majority.

[30] For a discussion of the "social issue" see Richard M. Scammon and Ben J. Wattenberg, *The Real Majority* (New York: Coward, McCann and Geoghegan, Inc., 1971), especially Chapters 3 and 20.

BOX 10.1 PROBLEMS WITH THIRD PARTY THEORIES

Q. Some people think that instead of a new two party system, we will have a disintegration of the parties with many more third and fourth party candidates bolting the two parties than there have been in the past.

A. We have had third, fourth, and fifth parties in most races, and they don't draw flies. The reason is that there is a dynamic working against them. First of all, candidates will be lured into running within their own party. If they win, they win. If they lose and bolt, they're considered sore losers. After the two parties pick the major candidates and then some rump convention picks a Reagan or whatever, unless the polls show them way up high right away, they have to face the whole he-can't-win syndrome.

The thing that usually prevents bolts is that all the bolters want to take over the parties. Once you bolt, it's hard to come back. Moreover, you just rule out, because of the seniority structure, any possibility of getting support from well known politicians. So there are a lot of strikes against them.

These grand theories are always being dreamed up, and the fact that they so rarely come about tells you something. There is something in the mechanism that tends to respond. Our political mechanism is cooptive and responsive.

If these ideas have crept up on us so silently, and there is something called conservatism that's so hot that it's got this majority, I will guarantee you that every liberal Democrat will be swiping some of that conservative rhetoric, just the way Nixon made some overtures to pick up the New Left rhetoric in 1968.

This is always going on, and it's the flaw in all of the mechanistic theories about politics, because they never understand how responsive and malleable and flexible the system is. As soon as they can put together a definable group of votes, somebody is going to steal them for the existing parties. These parties don't have written constitutions or written ideologies. They're a bunch of people who want to win elections. The mechanical view says that Ford is going to continue to play dumb, the Democrats are going to play dumb, everybody's going to play dumb.

SOURCE: Interview with Ben J. Wattenberg, *National Journal* (May 31, 1975), p. 811.

There appears to be little support in recent elections for an emerging Republican realignment. Even prior to the 1976 loss of the presidency by the Republicans, Congress and the state offices were dominated by Democrats, despite two presidential losses in a row (see Box 10.2). Also, although Democratic identifiers have been deserting or weakening their traditional ties,

---

BOX 10.2   CAN'T SELL WORD "REPUBLICAN"

We got wiped out in '58 because, some said, there was a recession, and '62 was the missile crisis, and '64 was Goldwater, and '70 was another recession, and '74 was Watergate. In the words of a client of mine "Somebody's trying to send us a message. . . ." People are not, for whatever reason, going to buy the word "Republican." The poll data shows that they are sympathetic to a lot of the issues of the Republican Party, but they're not voting Republican for some reason, whether it's a 1930's Depression on top of a recession now, with runaway inflation, or with Watergate and Nixon. I'm a marketing specialist. That's what I do in life, I guess, more than anything else. I'm concerned with getting people who are going in one direction to stop and move in a different direction. I'm very sure that in my lifetime I will not see anyone successfully market the word "Republican" year in and year out. You just can't do it. In '72 the Republicans got 62 percent of the vote for President and got wiped out in the House, the Senate, and state legislatures. What do the Republicans have to get? Eighty percent for President to get 51 percent of Congress? It's just not going to happen. So what we've got to do is get rid of the word "Republican" and come up with a new vehicle. I don't know the entire scenario. But I know you can't market the word "Republican." You just can't.

SOURCE: Richard Viguerie in *Voters, Primaries, and Parties,* eds. Jonathan Moore and Albert C. Pierce (Cambridge, Mass.: Harvard University Press, 1976), p. 51.

---

the Republican party has not been the beneficiary. Instead, these people have become independent of either party. In light of Watergate and related events, it appears unlikely that the law and order theme will benefit the Republican coalition, as Phillips assumed.

Revitalization of the New Deal coalition has been suggested as a possibility by some observers.[31] This renewal would result in a reordering of the Roosevelt coalition. It is suggested that the ethnic-labor-black coalition would be linked with the "new Democrats," the educated elite that leans toward the Democratic party on ideological grounds. A successful reconstitution of the Democratic party assumes many things. Among its assumptions are: (1) new Democrats are willing to link with old elements of the coalition and vice-versa; (2) the trend toward the weakening of party attachments is reversed in favor of the Democratic party; (3) blacks are satisfied with remaining solely in the Democratic coalition; and (4) the Democratic coalition can successfully integrate the more issue-oriented individuals and groups under one party label without the reinforcing social-economic division that existed in the 1930s.

There are some factors favoring a renewed Democratic coalition as a possible future alternative, despite the severe strain it presently faces.[32] First, when measured in races other than the presidency, Democratic strength is still impressive. The Democratic party still controls about the same proportion of the vote for Congress, for seats in state legislatures, and for statewide offices as it did ten years ago. Second, it has been suggested that much of the current dissatisfaction with the parties is short-term in nature, and will pass as leaders and policies change. James Sundquist sees a cycle back to the New Deal politics (see Box 10.3). Although a gradual decomposition of the two-party system might continue in the short run, it eventually will be checked and even reversed in favor of the Democratic Coalition. Strengthening of party attachment along party lines similar to the 1930s is not unlikely. Cross-cutting issues of the 1960s (especially Vietnam) will become coincident issues, basically economic and social. Old party attachments will be renewed, according to Sundquist.[33]

It is also suggested that the Democratic party has excelled in playing coalition politics. The ability of the Democratic leaders of the past to build coalitions is vital in linking together urban, southern, black, and liberal Democrats under one party label. Unlike the Republicans, the Democrats have maintained at least weak ties with many new independent forces, such as Common Cause and women's and black movements. Though presently, in in this period of confrontation politics, it appears that such groups are

---

[31] See especially, Sundquist, *Dynamics of the Party System.*

[32] Saloma and Sontag, *Parties,* pp. 321-24, discuss these problems more fully.

[33] Sundquist, *Dynamics of the Party System,* pp. 270-273.

BOX 10.3   WEAKENING OF PARTY TIES

My own view is that what has happened recently in the party system is much more the product of the peculiar events of the last decade than of any long term, secular, irreversible trends, I think we just have to pause for a moment and look at what happened in the last decade. We had the longest and most unpopular war in our history—so unpopular that eventually we withdrew from it without winning—and we suffered for the first defeat in our history. We had a civil rights revolution and some of the worst riots in the country's history, which increased social tension enormously. We had the worst peacetime inflation in history, followed by the deepest recession in 40 years. We had a President who was on the verge of impeachment and resigned—the first time that's happened—and a Vice-President who was forced out of office when he was exposed as a crook. Now, if you add all those things together you would expect a little rise in alienation, some increase in purposive non-voting, and a rise in ticket-splitting. But in order to project those trends in the future we have to project the proposition that the government is going to be as unsuccessful in the next few decades as it was in the last one. While we may all be a bit gloomy about the ability of our system to respond to public problems, even the law of averages tells us it's not likely to be that bad again. . . .

The weakening of party ties in the last ten years coincided once again with the rise of issues which cut across the existing alignment. Viet Nam, civil rights and race, and the so-called "social issue" all cut across the New Deal party system and that system was perceived not to have, and in fact did not have, much relevance. This applied particularly to the young people, who were the ones upset about Viet Nam and who saw that the party system was incapable of dealing with it.

If this interpretation is correct, then the importance of the party can be restored if either of two things happens. First, if the new issues persist and a new party system is formed that reflects the new polarization of the electorate. Second, if the new issues fade away and old issues reassert themselves that coincide with the existing line of party cleavage and thereby infuse the old party system with new meaning. The first of these does not seem likely to happen. What seems more likely is the second alternative: the reappearance of domestic economic issues on which the existing

302

parties will take clear and opposite stands. I would ask whether this in fact is not already happening. . . .

> SOURCE: James Sundquist in *Voters, Primaries, and Parties,* p. 37.

fragmenting the party, they might be broadening the base of a more loosely structured Democratic majority coalition. The reform movements within the Democratic party should lead to a more open party. If consensus on these procedures can be formed, possibilities of strengthening the coalition will be great, though not guaranteed within the context of a fluid and independent electorate.

DECOMPOSITION AND DISINTEGRATION OF THE PARTIES

In answering the question as to whether parties are presently in a period of realignment, political pollster Patrick Caddell stated:

> I don't think we are witnessing realignment as much as the death of the two party system. Realignment is less likely than the disintegration of both parties. Among voters you have movements that are not so much ideological as they are toward new faces. But inside the parties, the problem is that they are being fractured ideologically. The result of this is that you have both parties weakening internally, and a public that's moving away from both. . . . I'm not sure we'll ever see a reconstruction of the parties on the old style.[34]

An increasing number of political analysts are using terms like decomposition, disintegration, and dealignment, to describe the current state of the political parties. They point to the trends toward independent voting as indicators of a possible future pattern of politics without partisans. Several have argued that parties are past the stage of realignment and that the end of the party system is now imminent.

While many analysts, including DeVries, Tarrance, Caddell, and Teeter, see this disintegration as a recent development, Walter Burnham contends that the entire period since 1896 has been characterized by a decomposition and contraction of partisan structures and activities. The New Deal era is seen only as a temporary deviation from this trend toward gradual disappearance

[34] *National Journal* (May 31, 1975), p. 815.

of political parties in the United States.[35] The loosening of party attachments, increased ticket-splitting, and high rates of nonvoting are but current manifestations of this secular trend toward decomposition. According to Burnham, realignment as a concept is no longer appropriate, since it implies a continuation of the party system with different coalitions. He argues we may very well have moved beyond any possibility of realignment, due to the advanced state of party decomposition.

NO REALIGNMENT:
RETURN TO STATUS QUO

Not all observers are as pessimistic in interpreting the current voting trends as Burnham and Caddell. Ben Wattenberg contends that, despite these trends, the two-party system is in no immediate danger.[36] He sees the parties as more resilient than assumed by the decomposition theorists. Richard Scammon agrees that both the Democratic and Republican parties are capable of adjusting to new patterns.[37] At various times in our history, both parties have undergone great periods of stress, and have proved quite resistant. Scammon contends that, according to some observers, the Republican party has been "dying" for 120 years. Both Scammon and Wattenberg predict a two-party recovery from the current period of instability.

Arthur Miller of the Michigan Center for Political Studies argues that the current voting data suggest neither a major party realignment nor decomposition of the two-party system.[38] Although agreeing that we are presently in a period of electoral instability, he sees no evidence to suggest it is permanent. "Just because there is an extended period of chaos and a loosening of ties within the parties does not necessarily mean that there is going to be a realignment. . ."[39] Much of the increase in independence results from young voters' delaying their choice of a party. When they eventually identify, as Miller assumes they will, their choices may be similar to those of earlier periods. He also assumes that the cross-cutting issues of this decade will disappear, instead of having a realignment being built around them. Miller, along with Scammon, Wattenberg, and Sundquist, sees the current voting trends as the result of short-term fluctuations, not a long-term realignment or disintegration.

[35] Burnham, *Critical Elections*, pp. 132-33.
[36] *National Journal* (May 31, 1975), p. 811.
[37] *Ibid.*
[38] *Ibid.*, p. 803.
[39] *Ibid.*

CONCLUSIONS: VOTING TRENDS
AND THE POLITICAL PARTIES

Although the verdict on the political parties is not yet in, each observer has a prediction of the eventual outcome. As seen in this chapter, there are many disparate interpretations of the current voting data. While some analysts already have proclaimed the death of the two-party system, others have withheld final judgment for lack of concrete evidence. While agreeing that the system is in a state of flux, they argue that the data fail to confirm the demise of the parties or the party system.

It appears that the latter, more cautious approach is warranted. While the trends imply at least a severe weakening of the parties as psychological affiliations, the available data do not support the absolute decomposition theory. Although politics without partisans is a possible future alternative, it is based more on supposition than on substance. The weakening of party attachments and increased nonvoting are but two symptoms of a deeper alienation of the electorate from all aspects of politics. As support for political parties has lessened, so has support for all U.S. institutions. The alternatives to the present parties are quite limited at this time.

Also, U.S. parties and the party system have responded to reversals in the past. Although it would be foolhardy to minimize the current trends, it would also be a mistake to overemphasize the past few years at the expense of historical patterns of the last century. At present, both parties are attempting to recoup after the losses of the late 1960s and 1970s. Whether they succeed or not depends not only on their efforts at internal reform and attempts to broaden their electoral base. It also depends on whether the cross-cutting issues such as Vietnam, abortion, and busing give way to traditional economic and social issues.

It is obvious that the two parties will struggle to regain a stronger hold on the electorate. It is likely that they will be only partially successful. Although the data are inconclusive regarding the future of the political parties, they do corroborate the ticket-splitter model. No longer can the parties depend on the large, stable blocs of identifiers central to the normal vote model. The realities of a more independent electorate, both in attitude and behavior, must be faced. This task of the parties will be further complicated by the increased roles of the mass media and the independent candidate organizations. Unless the parties as organizations can cope with these changes, they may gradually die. It is too early, however, to write off the parties completely.

SECTION VI

THE ROLE OF
POLITICAL PARTIES
IN
U.S. ELECTORAL POLITICS

The first five sections of this book have discussed the characteristics and context of American political parties and examined each of the three dimensions of parties in the U.S. The decentralization of statutory party organizations, the failure of parties to govern, and the weakening of parties as psychological affiliation have been emphasized. The major conclusion so far is that U.S. political parties are almost exclusively limited to the electoral sphere of American politics.

The next four chapters examine the performance of political parties in the nomination and election of public officials. This is where all three dimensions of parties converge, and where interaction and influence should be maximized. Chapter 11 describes the means by which nonpresidential candidates are recruited and nominated for office, while Chapter 12 discusses the unique presidential nomination process. In both cases, the role of political parties in the selection of nominees for office is found to be limited severely.

The next two chapters examine the focus of party activity in American election campaigns. Chapter 13 describes the "new style of campaigning," with its emphasis on professional managers and the electronic media. It concludes that parties fail to dominate any aspect of campaigning and that the new style has reinforced the independence of candidates. Chapter 14 confirms that most campaign funding occurs outside the parties. In addition, recent financial reforms are analyzed as to their effectiveness, as well as their impact on political parties and American democracy.

11

Recruitment and Selection of Nonpresidential Candidates

One of the traditional functions of all political parties is to recruit candidates to run for elective office. Nomination of a candidate to represent the party in the general election is a crucial stage in the electoral process. It reduces the number of candidates and makes elections manageable. Theoretically, at least, the nomination process channels candidates into one of the two major parties, since party label is an important element in American elections. The frequent failure of Independent candidates, no matter how attractive personally, reiterates the importance of capturing a party nomination. This chapter will examine the recruitment and selection of party nominees for nonpresidential contests. Chapter 12 will focus on the nomination of presidential candidates.

The nomination of candidates for public office is one of the most important steps in the political process. The quality of candidates in the general election is dependent on the nomination stage. The openness of the nomination process determines the openness of the electoral process. If only a small elite is capable of being nominated, the entire electoral process remains closed to all but a few. On the other hand, an open nominating process will encourage more widespread participation at this stage, and make the system responsive to a variety of interests. This chapter first examines the formal/legal aspects of the nomination process and their impact on the recruitment and selection process. Then the informal elements of the process are discussed within this legal framework.

THE DIRECT PRIMARY SYSTEM

The nomination process in the United States is the most complex and intricate in any democracy. In an effort to include widespread participation, a highly involved set of procedures has been established to regulate the selection of the nominees of the two parties. A complicating factor, as with other electoral matters, is the variation of nomination procedures from state to state. The states write the laws that regulate the candidate-selection process. While they share certain common features, the details vary significantly. The most distinctive aspect of party candidate nomination in the United States is the pervasive influence of the direct primary system. No other single factor has had more impact on the political parties than that system.

ADOPTION OF DIRECT PRIMARY SYSTEM

The direct primary system, unique to the United States, is a relatively recent phenomenon in American politics. According to V.O. Key: "Throughout the history of American nominating practices runs a persistent attempt to make feasible popular participation in nominations and thereby to limit or to destroy the power of party oligarchies."[1] In each of several attempts to reform nomination of candidates over the last two centuries, the explicit objectives have been the weakening of party control and the increasing of citizen participation in the nomination process.

The most common type of nominating system early in the American Republic was the party caucus. Intitially, the caucus was a group of legislators who met and selected party nominees for the various offices. Prior to 1860, however, this legislative caucus was replaced in most states by an integrated party caucus, composed of local party activists in addition to the legislators. While this expansion resulted in more input into the selection process, most caucuses tended to represent a very narrow elite of party leaders in and out of the legislature, and membership in the caucus itself was very limited. The caucus came under increasing attack by Andrew Jackson and others as an aristocratic vestige of the past and an undemocratic means of nomination.

Although several states had held conventions earlier, the 1832 national Democratic convention set a precedent at the national level, and gave momentum to the adoption of state conventions. The state convention, it was argued, would democratize the nomination process by wresting power from the party leaders and giving it to a larger group of popularly elected delegates. The convention would serve as an indirect link between the rank-and-file members who were to be represented by the delegates and the nominees.

Despite the promises of these early party reformers, the convention itself soon came under attacks similar to those directed at the caucus 50

---

[1] V.O. Key, Jr., *Parties, Politics, and Pressure Groups,* 5th ed. (New York: Crowell, 1964), p. 371.

years earlier. By the end of the nineteenth century, conventions became identified with domination by special interests. Too often, selection of delegates and convention decisions were controlled by a small group of party bosses. Since many states during this period were dominated by one party, control of the nominations by party bosses all but eliminated any public voice in elections. The convention was, therefore, a vulnerable target for the progressives of the 1890-1910 period.

As an alternative, these reformers offered the direct primary to be a cure-all for all the ills of democracy. Again, party leaders became the scapegoats, the goals of the reforms were to reduce party control and increase participation of the electorate as a whole in the nomination process. Ironically, some of the earliest efforts at introduction of direct primaries were a result of the populist movement in the South, although it soon became a major tenet of the progressive movement in the northern states.

Despite predictable opposition from the party leaders, the time was ripe for the direct primary. The reformers' zeal was widespread, and its momentum led to a rapid adoption of primaries across the states. Although scattered primaries were held prior to 1900, the first comprehensive compulsory statewide primary law was adopted by Wisconsin in 1902, under the leadership of Robert LaFollette. Within 15 years, all but four states had adopted a direct primary system. As with other electoral reforms, the western states were first to adopt this new nomination system, while the eastern states, with strong party organizations and relatively balanced party competition, were the last. With the adoption of a limited form of primary by Connecticut in 1955, all 50 states were utilizing the direct primary for at least a portion of their elective offices. At present, most states utilize direct primaries for all state offices and for Congress.[2]

TYPES OF DIRECT PRIMARIES

Despite the widespread adoption of a direct primary system across the nation, there are many differences in state primary laws. The most obvious variation relates to the qualification of voters who can participate in the primary of a particular party. In some states, only those voters who have registered with a party can vote in that party's primary. Since voting is closed to all but stated members of the party this is called a *closed primary*. An *open primary*, conversely, is open to anyone qualified to vote in the general election.

Most states with a closed primary system require a person to register as

---

[2] Delaware uses conventions, not primaries, for statewide offices. Indiana had a similar system prior to 1976 and New York prior to 1970.

either a Republican or Democrat prior to voting. In order to obtain the primary ballot of a party, the voter's name must appear on the party registration list. A person registered as an Independent is not allowed to vote in the primary of either party. Most closed primary states set a deadline by which time a person who desires to switch registration from one party to another must do so. The lead time required varies significantly by state, although three months is most common. By requiring preregistration, closed primaries do place a limit on who may vote in a party primary. By definition the party primary is reserved for those who state that they are members of that party. Over two thirds of the states use a closed primary system.

The major characteristic of open primaries is that any registered voter can vote in the primary of either party. In a few states, a person must state his party preference at the polling place in order to get the ballot, but no record is kept. Under this system, there is no control over voting by party preference. In other words, a supporter of one party can legally vote for candidates of the opposite party. One reason for voting for candidates of the other party would be that the contests there were more exciting and competitive.

When a person registered in one party votes in the primary of the other party this is termed *crossing-over*. When there is an organized attempt by one party's supporters to support the weakest candidates in the opposition's primary, it is termed *raiding*. Little is known about the frequency or the success of raiding in open primary states, although crossing-over is common in such states, especially when there is minimal competition in one party and highly visible contests in the other party's primary.

> We do not have any accurate records of how much cross-over actually occurs, and whether a significant proportion of voters in open primary states frequently shifts from one primary to the other depending on candidates or issues that attract their interests.[3]

About one third of the states have open primary systems, to some degree. Most of these states are western or midwestern states such as Wisconsin, where the Progressive movement was most successful. Since voters in these states are free to vote in either primary, without demonstrating even minimal support for that party, open primaries most weaken party control. Obviously, party leaders favor the closed primary system, in which they maintain at least a modicum of control over who votes.

Most open primary states allow a person to vote in the primary of either party, but they do not allow the person to vote for candidates of both

[3] Malcolm E. Jewell and David M. Olson, *American State Political Parties and Elections* (Homewood, Ill.: The Dorsey Press, 1978), p. 141.

parties. Two states, however, Alaska and Washington, do have provisions for participation in both primaries in a single election. A voter in these states is given a combined ballot with the option of voting for the candidates of either party for any particular office. This *blanket* primary is least desired by the parties, since there is no demonstration of a commitment to the party by those participating in the selection of "party" nominees. The very presence of open and blanket primaries reflects the weakness of parties in maintaining control over the nomination process. Recent trends in primary laws have been in the direction of greater openness, not less.[4] The influence of political parties over the selection of their own candidates slipped badly as the direct primary became a central aspect of the nomination system. Certainly, the reformers succeeded in their aim of weakening party control, perhaps beyond their own intentions.

RUNOFF PRIMARY

The runoff primary is a device unique to the South, and reflects the long history of one-party domination. Since Democratic primaries tend to be more important than the general election, frequently there are many candidates for the Democratic nomination and few or none for the Republican. Therefore, it is unusual for any one candidate to garner a majority of the vote. In order to ensure a majority vote, the top two candidates in the primary must face each other in a runoff election, unless a candidate gets a majority vote in the primary. Ten of the Confederate states (all except Tennessee) plus Oklahoma utilize the runoff primary as a means of further narrowing down the Democratic party nomination. Bargaining among the two leading candidates for support of the losing candidates' support is not uncommon, and the first choices of many voters are eliminated in the process.

PREPRIMARY ENDORSEMENT

Some states offer the parties a means of control over primaries by allowing official party endorsement of a candidate or candidates prior to the primary election. Although there is much variation, a common method is to authorize endorsement by a state party convention or committee. As a minimum, this gives some candidates an advantage among party supporters, especially in those states where the endorsement appears on the ballot. Other provisions make it difficult for candidates not party-approved even to appear on the ballot. In some states, candidates receiving a certain proportion of

[4]*Ibid.*, p. 129.

convention votes are automatically placed on the ballot, while others must go through a difficult petition process. While preprimary endorsement is most common in closed primary states, at least five open primary states have provisions for either legal preprimary endorsements or informal endorsements by one or both parties.[5]

CROSS-FILING

While most states throughout the history of primaries have not allowed a candidate to run in the primaries of both parties simultaneously, there have been several exceptions. The provision which permits an individual to seek nominations from more than one party for the same office is termed *cross-filing*. California allowed cross-filing until 1946, when Earl Warren was successful in winning nominations for governor from both parties. His victories, and his decision to run as a Republican, meant that there was no Democratic candidate listed on the general election ballot. New York still permits cross-filing for candidates in its unique four-party configuration. If the other party agrees, Liberal and Conservative party candidates can cross-file as Democrats or Republicans. Under these conditions, unlike those of California, the concept of cross-filing seems reasonable.

NONPARTISAN PRIMARIES

Although all congressional and most statewide candidates are chosen through partisan primaries, many local officials, such as city councilmen, and most judges are selected in nonpartisan contests. The Nebraska legislature is presently the only state legislature selected on a nonpartisan ballot.[6] The nonpartisan ballots simply group all candidates for each office with no party designation. The two highest vote-getters in the primaries appear on the general election ballot, again without party designation. Despite the absence of party label on the ballot, in some cases the party organizations openly endorse and support candidates. Ironically, party endorsement in nonpartisan elections may be more easily accomplished than in many partisan primaries. Parties openly identify their choices in many nonpartisan elections, while in many partisan primaries they are legally barred from specifying their choice.

[5] See *Ibid.*, p. 130, for a summary of preprimary endorsement. These states include Utah, North Dakota, Minnesota, Illinois, and Wisconsin.

[6] Until 1973, Minnesota used nonpartisan ballots to elect all public officials except congressional and statewide candidates.

There is some evidence that the form of primary does have an impact on competition, participation, and results. Malcolm Jewell finds that state laws designed to strengthen party organizations by providing for closed primaries, or permitting organizational endorsements of candidates, do have the effect of reducing competition.[7] Also, in those states where party organization is strong and is able to reduce the level of primary competition, voting turnout in the primary drops considerably. The large variation in primary turnout among the states, then, is not unexpected. In some states, fewer than a quarter of the eligible voters turn out for primary contests, while in others the proportion approaches half. Although there is no one factor that explains this variation, states with open primary systems, hotly contested primaries, relatively weak party organizations, and high turnout in general elections tend to have higher levels of primary turnout.[8] Turnout might also be affected in any particular contest by specific factors such as the popularity of the candidate, the absence of any incumbent, or the presence of a highly visible and divisive issue.

In a study of four states with different forms of nominating systems, Richard Tobin examines the impact of various systems of party control on the recruitment process.[9] He contends that parties attempt to structure nominating procedures to give them the greatest possible control over "the gateways to public office." Restrictive nominating systems, such as the party convention or closed primary, are found to "generally circumscribe the conflict's extent, restrict public participation, strengthen a party's control over nominations and increase the power of the people who are already in the political arena."[10] Party convention and closed primary contests favor legislative nominees who are party regulars, while nonrestrictive systems such as open primaries encourage widespread participation and distribute control of nominations among a larger number of people, thereby reducing the party's role.[11] There is more opportunity for political novices and nonpartisans to win in the nonrestrictive systems. Prior political experience and a long career in public office are more important in states with closed primary systems

---

[7] Malcolm E. Jewell, "Voting Turnout in State Gubernatorial Primaries," *Western Political Quarterly,* 30 (June, 1977), 253.

[8] Jewell and Olson, *State Political Parties,* pp. 139-41.

[9] Richard J. Tobin, "The Influence of Nominating Systems on the Political Experience of State Legislators," *Western Political Quarterly,* 28 (September, 1975), 553-66.

[10] *Ibid.,* p. 554.

[11] *Ibid.,* p. 555.

than in those with nonpartisan or blanket primaries. In order to be given approval by the party organization, one must serve an apprenticeship in lower-level offices. Leo Snowiss concludes that, when party organization is highly structured and entrenched, candidates are recruited from among organization men with long party service. Under the opposite conditions, younger, less experienced candidates, with tenuous ties to organization are recruited.[12]

Due to the great variation in nominating procedures, as well as party organization by state, it is not possible to generalize a party role in nominating candidates for office. Certainly, parties seldom are the only factors involved. In some states they remain central to the nominating process, while in others their role is substantially limited. All one can do is look at specific cases. Frank Sorauf, for instance, concludes that parties in Pennsylvania can exclude outsiders from control of the party organization and participation in the primaries.[13] The parties have turned the primaries to their own account, by making them another hurdle the unannointed candidate must pass. Duane Lockard finds, similarly, that Connecticut parties dominate selection of party nominees and exclude nonparty groups from the nomination process.[14]

Conversely, the blanket primary of Washington apparently minimizes the influence of parties in the nomination process. Hugh Bone suggests that pressure groups actually might be more important than political parties in the recruitment and selection of candidates.[15] Other authors also have noted the wide variation of party involvement in the nomination process.[16] The type of nomination system, therefore, is viewed as a major influence in American politics. Nomination types make it easier or more difficult for various individuals and groups to gain access to the system. The nomination procedures expand or restrict the scope of the recruitment and selection process.

[12] Leo M. Snowiss, "Congressional Recruitment and Representation," *American Political Science Review,* 60 (September, 1966), 630-31.

[13] Frank J. Sorauf, *Party and Representation: Legislative Politics in Pennsylvania* (New York: Atherton Press, 1963), p. 153.

[14] Duane Lockard, *New England State Politics* (Princeton: Princeton University Press, 1959), p. 284.

[15] Hugh A. Bone, "Washington State: Free Style Politics," in Frank H. Jonas, ed. *Politics in the American West* (Salt Lake City: University of Utah Press, 1969), p. 412.

[16] For example, see Alan L. Clem, *The Making of Congressmen: Seven Campaigns of 1974* (North Scituate, Mass.: Duxbury Press, 1976), p. 243.

VOTING TURNOUT IN PRIMARY ELECTIONS

While the direct primary system has considerably weakened party control over nominations for most elected officials, the second goal of the primary advocates has met with much less success. Direct primaries have not led to the increased participation promised by the reformers. Certainly, a much wider spectrum of the public is involved in the primary system than in the convention or caucus nominating systems. However, voting turnout for primary elections outside the South is usually less than half of the turnout for the corresponding general election. Large numbers of potential voters fail to participate in primary elections. While some of this apathy is due to constraints on voting of Independents in closed primary states, it is largely the result of a lack of public interest in the low-visibility nomination process.

Jewell and Olson have found that, contrary to usual opinion, states with strong two-party competition do not have higher primary turnout than one-party dominated states.[17] They also demonstrate that primary turnout is highest in the South and among the border and western states, and lowest in the Midwest and Northeast, where party organizations are strongest. These regional distinctions tend to correspond somewhat to type of primary. The open and blanket primaries of the western states, especially, have high turnout rates. The closed primary states, especially those with long waiting periods for changing registration, generally have the lowest primary turnout.

Although primary turnout rates vary by state, in all cases outside the South they are substantially lower than in the general election. One question is: What type of person votes in primary elections? While the evidence is fragmentary at best, primary voters have been found to be unique in several ways. First, they tend to be of higher status, overrepresenting college graduates and professionals. Second, they are slightly older than those who vote only in general elections.[18] They also are more likely to be strong party identifiers rather than Independents or weak identifiers, although there are some variations by party under specific conditions.[19]

Not surprisingly, those party identifiers who play an active role in the party organization are most likely to participate in primaries. It is assumed that they are also most responsive to the desires of the party leaders. There-

[17] Jewell and Olson, *State Political Parties,* p. 144.

[18] See Austin Ranney and Leon D. Epstein, "The Two Electorates: Voters and Non-Voters in a Wisconsin Primary," *Journal of Politics,* 28 (August, 1966), 598-616.

[19] Austin Ranney, "The Representativeness of Primary Electorates," *Midwest Journal of Political Science,* 12 (May, 1968), 237.

fore, the larger the party organization, the greater its impact on the primary results. The influence of the party will be greatest where turnout is low, since those voting are most responsive to the leaders.[20] Increased participation dilutes the efforts of the party workers and weakens their influence. This is doubly true when the primary is open to members of the opposite party and to Independents, neither of which respond to the party leaders. While particular issues might draw out proportionally more conservative or liberal party supporters, there is little evidence of a consistent pattern.[21]

IMPACT OF DIRECT PRIMARY SYSTEM
ON PARTIES AND ELECTIONS

The widespread adoption of the direct primary system in twentieth century America has had a major impact on the conduct of elections. While the reformers were largely well intentioned and in part achieved their goals, several unexpected consequences have created problems. Not only have nominations been wrested from party control, but also the parties have been considerably weakened, to the point of losing all influence in some states. The direct primary has been the major procedural constraint on the development of strong party structures in many states. V.O. Key contends, however, that the primary is so firmly established that even if statutory mandates were abolished, direct primaries would be continued.[22] In the anti-party environment of the United States, the direct primary is a natural restriction on political parties. It is at the core of the nomination process, and, despite the problems it raises, it is expected to remain a central element.

CONTROL OVER CANDIDATES

The direct primary has affected parties adversely in many ways. By taking control over nominations away from the party organization, the primary has stripped the party of a powerful sanction over its officeholders. The weakness of party leaders in Congress is, in large part, a result of the lack of party control over nomination or renomination of congressmen. Candidates do not owe their nomination to the party leaders, especially in those states without

---

[20] Jewell and Olson, *State Political Parties*, p. 155.

[21] Ranney, "Representativeness of Primary Electorates".

[22] V.O. Key, Jr., "The Direct Primary and Party Structure: A Study of State Legislative Nominations," *American Political Science Review*, 48 (March, 1954), 1-26.

preprimary endorsement procedures. The primaries also reduce the ability of parties to reward faithful workers, and therefore eliminate a powerful incentive toward party activity.

CHANCES OF PARTY VICTORY

Direct primaries also affect the chances of party victory in the general election. Primary voters do not necessarily select the strongest candidate, especially when there are many vying for an office. Since voters in the primaries are not representative of the public at large, it is not surprising that their choice might not light on the candidate with the broadest appeal. In some cases, especially when primary turnout is low and influenced by ideological considerations, the candidate might not have broad support, even among party identifiers. In extreme cases, the person nominated might even be hostile to the party leadership and to the goals of the party organization. Furthermore, there is no guarantee that the interests of the party will be protected by the provision of a balanced slate of candidates. Minority candidates, whom the party leaders would include for balance in many urban areas, might be excluded in the primary.

DIVISIVE PRIMARIES

While the direct primary itself is a threat to party organization and usually produces divisions in the party, frequently these rifts are mended during the general election. Theoretically, however, a highly divisive primary could result in more lasting damage and cause a loss at the general election. This could happen if supporters of the losing candidate in the primary refused to vote for the winning primary candidate, or, even worse, voted for the nominee of the opposing party, in the general election.

The evidence of the impact of such divisive primaries, unfortunately, is mixed. Andrew Hacker, for instance, concludes that "a divisive primary in and by itself, bears little relation to a candidate's prospects at the general election."[23] Piereson and Smith, in a study of almost 1400 gubernatorial primaries, agree substantially with Hacker's findings, despite their shift in emphasis to the share of the vote won.

Thus, a candidate's primary election experience bears little relationship to his success in the general election. This finding holds true

---

[23] Andrew Hacker, "Does a Divisive Primary Harm a Candidate's Election Chances?" *American Political Science Review,* 59 (March, 1965), 110.

regardless of the candidate's party, his incumbency status, or the level of party competition in his state.[24]

In a more recent study, however, Robert Bernstein concludes that both incumbents and challengers do poorly when they have to face a divisive, hard-fought primary and their opponents do not. He finds a "consistently negative influence" of divisive primaries on the party in which they are held.[25] One result is to increase the number of office holders representing the weaker party, where primaries are less likely to be divisive.

A somewhat different aspect of the impact of divisive primaries is offered by Johnson and Gibson.[26] They examine the behavior of primary election activists in the general election, and find that party workers who supported the losing primary candidate are much less likely to work in the general campaign. Few of these activists can be remobilized to work for the party nominee who defeated their candidate in the primary. More significantly, about 20 percent of the primary supporters indicated that they planned to work for the opposition party candidate in the fall campaign. These authors conclude that divisive primaries are harmful because they weaken the organizational base of the party by discouraging potential workers.[27]

COST OF PRIMARIES

Certainly the expense of conducting primary elections is substantially greater than the cost of party conventions. According to Alexander Heard, "it seems likely that the use of the primary has . . . increased the costs of politics. Primary expenses easily rival those of general elections."[28] Candidates must wage two full-scale campaigns, and there is little evidence that primary expenditures reduce spending in the general election.[29] Studies in various

---

[24] James E. Piereson and Terry B. Smith, "Primary Divisiveness and General Election Success: A Re-examination," *Journal of Politics*, 37 (May, 1975), 562.

[25] Robert A. Bernstein, "Divisive Primaries Do Hurt: U.S. Senate Races, 1956-1972," *American Political Science Review*, 71 (June, 1977), 541.

[26] Donald Johnson and James Gibson, "The Divisive Primary Revisited," *American Political Science Review*, 68 (March, 1974), 67-77.

[27] *Ibid.*, p. 77.

[28] Alexander Heard, *The Costs of Democracy* (Chapel Hill, N.C.: University of North Carolina Press, 1960), pp. 321-22.

[29] David W. Adamany, *Campaign Finance in America* (North Scituate, Mass.: Duxbury Press, 1972), p. 70.

states confirm significant additional costs to candidates as well as to the political system.[30]

In addition to the monetary costs, primaries lengthen the campaign period and force candidates to expend their energies prior to the general election.

> Primaries suck up and waste large sums of money from contributors who might better be tapped for the November finals .. primary campaigns exhaust the candidate, use up his speech material, drain his vital energy, leave him limp before he clashes with the major enemy.[31]

Although there is no solid evidence that the primary campaign results in voter boredom, the combination of the primary and general campaigns makes for a long election year.

DIRECT PRIMARIES: A SUMMARY

On the one hand, direct primaries are praised as opening up the nomination process and widening participation overall. On the other, they are attacked as too expensive, divisive, and dangerous for democracy. Whatever one's viewpoint, it is obvious that the direct primary has had a major impact on the conduct of American politics. Although this impact has been blunted some-what by a lack of primary contests in many districts and the limited turnout in many that are contested, the direct primary has become imbedded deep in the heart of the recruitment and selection process. Despite the dangers they present, primaries are a major element of the electoral process and serve as a framework for informal interactions among the individual actors involved.

RECRUITMENT OF NONPRESIDENTIAL CANDIDATES

While most nominees in the states are selected through direct primaries, this does not explain why they were running for office in the first place. Prior to the primary, a decision must be made to enter the electoral arena. Although

---

[30] For example, see David W. Adamany, *Financing Politics* (Madison: University of Wisconsin Press, 1969), pp. 74-86, and Elston Roady and Carl D. McMurray, *Republican Campaign Finance in Florida, 1963-1967* (Princeton: Citizens' Research Foundation, 1969), p. 36.

[31] Theodore White, *The Making of the President,* 1960 (New York: Atheneum, 1961), p. 78.

the formal statutes define the boundaries of the selection process and present the procedures for attainment of the nomination, there are far more complex informal relationships which underly the recruitment process in any political setting. They determine not only who will run, but, at times, who will win. Unlike the legal prescriptions, these informal interactions vary from office to office and from one election to the next. In any particular contest, they represent the complex of relationships among candidates, their sponsors, and the electorate.[32]

FORMAL QUALIFICATIONS

The legal qualifications for running for office in the United States afford wide latitude. For many offices at the state and local level one need only be a registered voter. While many offices include a minimum age limit, for instance, 25 for U.S. congressmen and 30 for U.S. Senators, most of the electorate is legally eligible to run for most elective offices. The only other legal qualification in order to be placed on the primary ballot in most states is to file formally for office. Usually this entails obtaining a specified number of signatures to a nomination petition from registered voters in the district in question. The completed petition is then filed with the state Secretary of State or appropriate local election authority. The number of signatures required varies by state and by level of office, and might range from five for a local school board to some fixed percentage of the total vote in the last election for a given office. In some jurisdictions a filing fee is also required, although it is generally nominal. Most jurisidictions will waive the fee if the candidate is not able to pay. Once the petition and/or fee is filed and the signatures are certified as authentic, the person is placed on the ballot. Although cutoff dates for filing vary, by law they are generally advertised well in advance. The rationale for filing is to ensure that only serious candidates and not cranks be placed on the ballot.

RESOURCES AND POLITICAL OPPORTUNITY

Why then do only a handful of eligible citizens actually enter the electoral process? One obvious reason is that only a small proportion of the electorate have the resources necessary to run. They lack either monetary resources of their own or of someone willing to sponsor them. In addition to monetary support, a candidate needs certain skills and attributes to wage a successful

---

[32] Lester G. Seligman, et al., *Patterns of Recruitment: A State Chooses its Lawmakers* (Chicago: Rand McNally College Publishing Company, 1974), p. 2.

campaign. The ability to compete is also limited by social status, with the advantage going to those with higher education, more prestigious occupations, and supportive family status and backgrounds. Middle class lawyers and businessmen, for instance, are heavily overrepresented in politics. Access to news media is also an important asset, especially for statewide and congressional offices.

While the need for certain resources and talents might explain why many persons are eliminated from further consideration, it fails to explain why many who have the essential characteristics are not recruited into the electoral process. Out of all those with the qualifications to run, only a small percentage are sufficiently motivated to commit themselves to running for office. Social expectations concerning public officials might prevent many potential candidates from even considering entry, because they feel they do not have a chance of being elected. Many are deterred simply because of the press of day to day living and the fear of committing time, resources, and effort to what may be a losing cause.

RECRUITMENT RISK

Lester Seligman contends that it is a combination of motives and incentives that determines whether a person will become a candidate or not.[33] Recruitment risks must be balanced against the incentives, such as prestige, power, and self-fulfillment, which the office would bring. These risks involve three factors: (1) the cost of giving up a private job, income, and so forth, (2) the probability of winning or losing, and (3) the consequences of losing either the primary or general election. According to Seligman, the risk of recruitment in the U.S. generally is moderate.[34]

The process still favors those in certain professions such as law, where risks can be minimized. A lawyer running for office seldom incurs large expenses, due to the nature of his work, and commonly gains substantial benefits of publicity and status, even in a losing effort. On the other hand, an assembly line worker would very likely risk his job in any attempt at office and would receive few benefits, if any, in a losing effort. Not surprisingly, lawyers are more willing to run for office, since their recruitment risks are relatively low. While most individuals are unwilling to incur much risk to enter electoral politics, to some people politics is a way of life. These exceptions are the high rollers, who are willing to risk all for the chance of winning elective office. It is understandable that they represent a small proportion of the public when viewed in these terms. Only the most highly motivated or

[33] *Ibid.,* p. 25.
[34] *Ibid.,* p. 26.

those with unlimited resources tend to run for office. The breadth or narrowness of the recruitment process determines which individuals have the best and which the poorest chance, should they seek office.[35]

OPPORTUNITY STRUCTURE
IN THE UNITED STATES

Joseph Schlesinger offers an excellent summary of the opportunity structure in the United States.[36] First, he finds a proliferation of outlets for political ambition in the vast array of offices contested. Offices are held by fixed terms, which ensures a constant possibility of turnover. Second, the opportunity structure is primarily an open system. In other words, lines of advancement are not prescribed by law. Although there are patterns of succession from office to office in many states, legally there are few prerequisites for most offices, and competitors come from many sources. This relatively open access to political office in the U.S. broadens the chances of winning office.

A third characteristic of the structure of political opportunity is that, except for a few offices, especially those of congressmen and senators, public office is an avocation. Few state and local offices provide either the security or the monetary means needed to support the office holder. The same factors that open up the structure, such as fixed terms and limited tenure, create risks for the politician. These risks are most extreme when one must give up one office in order to seek a higher one.

Finally, the two-party system shapes political opportunity in the U.S. Most commonly, in order to have a reasonable chance to win one must be nominated as either a Democrat or Republican. This forces the ambitious person to weigh the competitive chances of each party. While the direct primary has weakened the role of the formal party organization, and allowed ambitious politicians to choose the party that gives them the best chance to win, the opportunity structure is intricately related to the realities of politics in any situation. These characteristics of the American opportunity structure serve as a framework for recruitment. Each potential candidate must work within this context. Although some flexibility is inherent in this structure, a single individual cannot alter its form. A prospective office holder must be continually aware that any decision made will affect his ability to advance, one way or the other.

[35] *Ibid.*, p. 5.

[36] Joseph A. Schlesinger, *Ambition and Politics: Political Careers in the United States* (Chicago: Rand McNally and Company, 1966), pp. 16-20.

While the nomination process is based on the formal statutory system as well as the opportunity structure unique to a particular office or district, at some point potential candidates must be persuaded to become candidates. This recruitment process has been viewed as "a chain of influence that selects some office seekers and transforms them into candidates and office holders and rejects the others,"[37] Schlesinger sees the drive for personal success as the major factor in determining the supply of candidates (see Box 11.1), while Seligman emphasizes the patterns of relationships between candidates and those who sponsor them. In each case, the focus is on personal expectations, desires, and motivations. The ultimate decision to run for office, then, is a complex interaction of many informal influences operating within the formal constraints of the nomination process.

Candidates are most easily categorized as either *self-starters* or *externally-instigated*. The self-starters are individuals who run without any apparent external encouragement from parties, interest groups, or individuals. Generally, they run to further their own political or professional ambitions or in response to particular issues or events. While the primary system allows a place for self-starters, the proportion of those who run for office without any external stimulation is probably quite small.

A majority of the candidates for office have been contacted prior to entering the contest. Seligman offers at least four forms of sponsorship of potential nominees.[38] *Conscripted* candidates consent to run out of loyalty to the party. Many times a minority party utilizes conscription to get a candidate on the ballot when none would run on his own. Other individuals might be *coopted* or persuaded to run in order to strengthen the ticket. Political groups are expected to encourage attractive candidates to run for office, as well as to discourage those who they feel would hurt the ticket. An *agent* is a person who represents an interest group. Obviously, viable interest groups will benefit if a person sympathetic to their cause is nominated, and they will attempt to persuade such people to run for office. Finally, there are many people who run for office because of *instigation* from friends and relatives who feel they would make a good candidate. While lacking the support of the party organization or interest groups, they are motivated to become a candidate because of the support and commitment of those closest to them.

---

[37] Seligman, *Patterns to Recruitment*, p. 5.
[38] For a summary, see *Ibid.*, pp. 29-32.

BOX 11.1   THE DIRECTION OF AMBITION

One of the most important ways in which office ambitions vary is in their direction. The office structure of the United States, for example, provides a variety of outlets for office goals, including the opportunity to leave public office. Each direction has its own constituency, and it is, therefore, essential to define the ambition before inferring its impact. Failure to consider more than one direction for ambition is the major weakness of party theory, which assumes a horizontal direction—to govern.

I would suggest that there are three directions which office ambitions may take. Ambitions may be *discrete:* The politician wants the particular office for its specified term and then chooses to withdraw from public office. If he is a candidate, the political tensions he experiences are simply those caused by the immediate objectives. If he is an office holder, he has no political tensions (i.e., office ambitions). This type of ambition is certainly not uncommon for many lesser local offices, for the state legislature, and for higher offices as well. Indeed, the Twenty-Second Amendment prescribes this ambition for American Presidents once they have been re-elected.

Ambitions may also be *static:* the politician seeks to make a longrun carrer out of a particular office. In this case the tensions he experiences derive primarily from his constituency. How widespread such ambitions are we cannot tell, for the possibilities of making a career of one office are varied. Nevertheless, it is certainly a marked goal of many American congressmen and senators.

Finally ambitions may be *progressive:* The politician aspires to attain an office more important than the one he now seeks or is holding. Here, at the least, he is under tension not only from his current constituency but also from that of the office to which he aspires. A likely assumption is that progressive ambitions dominate and are suppressed only when they appear unreasonable in terms of the chances.

We can also assume that one type of ambition is unlikely to remain constant for any one politician over his lifetime. A city councillor may start with discrete ambitions but find politics so exciting that he develops static or progressive goals. Later failure may temper his expectations. Many a congressman retires voluntarily after a lengthy term of office. In his last term his ambitions have shifted from static to discrete. A theory of ambitions, however, is not so much concerned with predicting what a man's ambitions will be over his entire career, but rather with taking a man's current ambitions and predicting from them his political behavior. A legislator's votes and a governor's policies are therefore a consequence of current rather than possible future ambitions. This does not mean that a politician's ambitions may not combine both short- and long-run goals. It is a matter of assigning relative weights to each type of ambition.

SOURCE: Joseph A. Schlesinger, *Ambition and Politics* (Chicago: Rand McNally and Company, 1966), pp. 9-10.

PARTIES AND POLITICAL RECRUITMENT

It was stated earlier in this chapter that recruitment of candidates is generally defined as one of the primary functions of political parties. That being the case, we should expect party leaders to take an active role in recruiting and sponsoring candidates. Although the complexity of the opportunity structure would provide competition from other sponsors, parties should be at the center. However, the role of parties in the recruitment process actually varies considerably from state to state. For instance, while 69 percent of the state legislative candidacies in New Jersey are instigated by the party leaders, it is only 20 percent in California and 21 percent in Wisconsin.[39]

Several major studies demonstrate that the influence of party organizations on recruitment is limited. Samuel Patterson, however, finds that two thirds of the party leaders report that they urged candidates to run for office and about three quarters had talked with "several" or "many" candidates prior to their announcements of candidacy.

The legislative function in Iowa is by no means the sole domain of party leaders; it is shared with other members of the politically active subculture.[40]

The legislators themselves usually reported more frequent contracts from businessmen than from party leaders, though recruitment efforts of party

[39] *Ibid.,* p. 4.
[40] Samuel C. Patterson, Ronald D. Hedlund, and G. Robert Boynton, *Representatives and Represented: Bases of Public Support for the American Legislatures* (New York: John Wiley and Sons, 1975), p. 88.

331

leaders were more frequent among Democrats and in urban districts. In the entire recruitment process, however, at least as much contact came from activists as from party leaders.[41]

Lester Seligman is even more emphatic in noting the minimal recruitment activity of the parties in Oregon:

> Among the variety of groups and individuals that sponsor legislative candidates, political parties are neither the most important, nor are they even first among equals.[42]

While he agrees that the direct primary system prevents parties from officially endorsing particular candidates, he finds very little informal influence in instigation of candidates exercised by the parties. Also, once the primary is completed and official party nominees are designated, the candidates generally campaign independently of the party. Seligman demonstrates that as the direct primary has fragmented political parties and diluted their influence in the recruitment process, interest groups have become more salient. "Time and time again, the candidates referred to interest groups and their importance in the recruitment process . . . ."[43] In Oregon, at least, interest groups perform many of the functions that parties are expected to monopolize.

Due to these limitations, any examination of political opportunity and recruitment that focuses on parties is incomplete. Joseph Schlesinger argues that the opportunity structure operates independently of the party system and might instead have an impact upon the party system.[44] The party system is a product, at least in part, of the manner in which political opportunities are ordered, and must be discussed within that context.

> At the very least, then, these data allow us to deny the party system a dominant role in determining political opportunity in the United States.[45]

While parties, to be sure, play a role in the recruitment process, it is a limited role. Even the central function of political parties, to recruit and nominate candidates for office, has to be shared with a variety of other organizations and individuals. While parties in some areas consciously seek

[41] *Ibid.,* p. 89.
[42] Seligman, *Patterns of Recruitment,* p. 185.
[43] *Ibid.,* p. 186.
[44] Schlesinger, *Ambition and Politics,* p. 197.
[45] *Ibid.,* p. 64.

out individuals and encourage them to be candidates, those in other areas
have little or no influence over the selection process.

RECRUITMENT AND NOMINATION:
A SUMMARY

The United States has a more complex and intricate process for selection of
party candidates than any other western democracy. The direct primary
system, as the reformers desired, has effectively stripped the parties of control over the nomination of their own candidates. Under the direct primary
provisions, party leaders cannot block the candidacy of any legally qualified
candidate. The electorate, not the party organization leaders, selects the
nominee. While the role of parties in the nomination process varies from
state to state, depending on the legal framework and the means by which
politics is conducted, in general the introduction of the direct primary has
weakened parties considerably.

Several characteristics of the primaries, however, grant ambitious
parties more influence than might be expected on the surface. Since nominations for many offices are not contested, political leaders can influence the
selection. Potentially, they have informal influence if they can encourage
the candidacy of acceptable candidates and discourage outsiders, or those
deemed unresponsive to party demands. While such influence is possible in
some situations, limited evidence suggests it is by no means universal.

A second characteristic of primary elections which offers the parties
some control over nominations is that turnout for primaries is low. Generally,
the lower the voting turnout, the greater the influence of the party leaders.
This is true not only because those who do vote tend to be more responsive
to party influence, but also because they are a more manageable number to
be contacted by the party. Some states further facilitate party influence by
provision of preprimary endorsement of candidates, utilization of conventions for particular offices, and use of closed primaries.

It is argued in this chapter that the scope of the nomination process
goes well beyond the formal/legal framework of the direct primary system.
The opportunity structure, which is independent of the party system, determines who will run and who will not. While the formal qualifications eliminate a small proportion of the electorate from seeking office, the structure of
opportunity determines who may run and those who do. A person must not
only weigh the risks inherent in running against the rewards of office, but
must also analyze the opportunity structure for any particular office. At least
several authors contend that there are patterns of recruitment for particular

offices. Potential candidates must be aware of the expectations of the public with regard to the office, as well as of their own ambitions and motivation in seeking the office. The resulting recruitment process is a combination of candidates and sponsors, each desiring some gain from their efforts. While politicial parties traditionally have been expected to be active in initiating and sponsoring candidates, especially for state and local office, they are constrained not only by the formal statutory restrictions but also by competition from an array of nonparty sources and individual candidate organizations.

12

Presidential Nominations:
The Summit
of National Party Politics

While most candidates in the United States are nominated through the direct primary system, presidential nomination continues to be the product of conventions. While popular selection of nominees has been highly successful at every other level, candidates for the highest office continue to be selected, at least formally, through conventions. The coalitional nature of the national parties and the highly complex and diversified nature of presidential nominations have strengthened the tradition of conventions. Despite this, however, much of the actual decision making of the convention has been usurped by prior activities, most notably the presidential primaries.

We have seen in earlier chapters the limited role of American parties in governing and in the organization of most elections. If there is any one area of American politics that is within the realm of a national party organization, it should be the selection and nomination of that party's standardbearer. As with other functions discussed, the parties are no longer, if they ever were, dominant in this nominating process. Restricted by a multiplicity of state laws, they also compete as an electoral organization with many other forces. The national committees rely on the separate state organizations for support of the system, and are clearly seen as coalitions of such organizations. Even in the presidential nominations, the party electoral organizations must share the selecting of a candidate.

The presidential nomination process is here seen as a series of events that officially begin with the first delegate selected. In recent years this process has begun much earlier, as candidates have attempted to build their names and attain national stature on a broad range of issues. Traces of this preliminary stage of presidential nominations can be seen as early as the previous convention. By the beginning of the election year, many candidates have wide experience on the campaign trail. This chapter examines not only the formal nomination process, but also the preliminary stages which lead up to the selection of delegates for the national convention.

INFORMAL PRELIMINARIES

This discussion of presidential nominating procedures centers on the excellent framework provided by Donald Matthews.[1] The nominating process is divided into three stages: the emergence of "presidential possibilities," the definition of the competitive situation (preconvention strategy and the setting for competition), and the formal/legal nominating machinery. The first two stages extend back as far as the previous election and are presented here as "informal preliminaries." They have become critical stages in the nominating process. By the time the formal processes begin, about six to eight months before the election, the party's nominee frequently is apparent.

> Officially, presidential nominees are selected by delegates to the national convention but the convention decision is usually a symbolic culmination of a process that began much earlier and whose decisive stages occurred long before.[2]

In other words, the decisions made at the convention seldom result in a reversal of earlier decisions. In many recent conventions there has been little doubt as to who the nominee would be, even prior to the formal delegate-selection process.

PRESIDENTIAL POSSIBILITIES EMERGE

Although the nomination process is useful in narrowing the field of contenders, the formal procedures generally eliminate few, since only a handful are considered at this stage. A vast proportion of the population, although legally eligible to run, are not considered presidential possibilities.[3] Since 1936, this has commonly meant that they had no support in the national public opinion polls. Matthews finds that all nominees since 1936 have shown up in the Gallup polls before their nomination, and most have had substantial support as reflected in the polls. If "reasonable chance" is defined as a 1 percent showing in Gallup polls, there have been very few individuals with a "reasonable chance" over the last four decades. Only 62 Democrats and 47 Republi-

---

[1] Donald R. Matthews, "Presidential Nominations: Process and Outcomes," in *Choosing The President,* ed. James David Barber (Englewood Cliffs, N.J.: Prentice-Hall, Inc., 1974), pp. 35-70.

[2] *Ibid.,* p. 39.

[3] For a discussion of George McGovern's presidential image problem see John G. Stewart, *One Last Chance: The Democratic Party, 1974-76* (New York: Praeger Publishers, 1974).

cans have shared this honor over these years, many repeating year after year. At times the field has been very narrow (that is, 1948 Democrats whom Eisenhower refused really had no one left but Truman).

How do people become presidential possibilities? Although there are many factors extending far beyond any particular election period, a major element is nationwide publicity through the news media. Once an individual becomes a personage in the regular news and editorials of the mass media, he or she has made a start. As the individual becomes molded in a presidential context, the image of a presidential contender is born. The role of the press in the nomination process has become crucial, not so much in its evaluation of candidates as in the amount of its attention paid to each candidate. The press has great influence over which individuals are considered serious candidates and which are not. This entire process tends to benefit those already ranking high in public opinion polls, because they receive the most attention. And, without national coverage, the unknowns continue to draw little support in the polls. Impressive wins in primaries, as demonstrated by George McGovern and Jimmy Carter, are one means of increasing press coverage and standings in the polls, although such wins are difficult without publicity, poll support, and money.

Another factor important in determining potential candidates concerns the accepted routes to the presidency. The structure of opportunities tends to be dominated by three offices, the vice presidency, senatorships, and governorships. Although the vice presidency is by far the most advantageous position from which to run for the nomination, recently it appears to be a liability in the general election. Also, the limited number and availability of vice presidents in recent elections has resulted in the success of senators in gaining nominations. The opportunity structure tends to focus on those offices from which past presidential possibilities have emerged. "The political opportunity structure probably has more impact on nomination outcomes than the legal machinery of the formal nomination process itself."[4]

Closely related to the opportunity structure, to press coverage, and to standing in the polls, is the availability of money. Potential candidates for the presidency must be able to raise millions of dollars in order to be taken seriously. The new federal financing of primaries (Chapter 14) requires candidates to have a broad base of financial support in order to qualify for matching funds. Here again, the advantage rests with those who are already established. Money naturally flows most easily to individuals who appear to be popular. Since few people are willing to risk much money in backing unknowns, many hopefuls are eliminated very early at this stage. If funds can be raised that result in several strong showings in early primaries or caucuses,

[4] Matthews, "Presidential Nominations," p. 51.

BOX 12.1 CARTER COASTS TO NOMINATION IN 30 PRIMARIES

There were three distinct phases to the presidential primary season that lifted Jimmy Carter from obscurity to the Democratic nomination.

The first began in New Hampshire, February 24, and extended through Carter's landslide win in Pennsylvania, April 27. During this period, Carter established himself as the clear front-runner with a broad national base, and effectively eliminated opposing candidates Jackson, Bayh, Shriver, Harris, Shapp, and Wallace. He also managed to survive the brief but worrisome "ethnic purity" controversy.

Then came a brief transition period in late April and early May, in which Humphrey decided not to run, and Udall appeared to offer the only active opposition to a Carter sweep.

This phase ended with Church's surprising win over Carter in Nebraska, May 11. The Nebraska result marked the start of a new period, in which Carter faced more intense public scrutiny, and a second line of primary challengers—Church and Brown—probed for his weaknesses.

Between May 11 and June 8, Carter's momentum faded visibly with defeats in Maryland, Idaho, Nevada, Oregon, Montana, Rhode Island, California and New Jersey, and a near-loss to Udall in Michigan. But Carter continued to gain delegates, until victory in Ohio unleashed a stampede of party elders into his camp, destroying the credibility of Brown and Church overnight despite impressive primary victories for each.

Carter was not seriously hurt by his poor showing in the late primaries for two reasons. First, his regional base in the South provided a cushion strong enough to absorb the cascade of defeats elsewhere. He had victories May 25 in Arkansas, Kentucky and Tennessee to counterbalance simultaneous losses to Church and Brown in small western states.

Second, the proportional division of delegates in most primaries allowed Carter to continue accumulating them even in states where he was beaten.

Momentum lost by defeat in the popular vote in these states was more than compensated for by a delegate count that rose steadily toward the 1,505 required for the nomination. In most southern states Carter lost little in the proportional division because his popular majorities were overwhelming enough to garner almost all of the delegates.

Carter's losses thus had minimal impact. Brown's Maryland triumph did not prevent Carter from receiving a majority of that state's delegates, and Church's near-sweep in the Pacific Northwest did not produce enough delegates to make him look like a contender nationally. Ohio, which led to the slew of Carter endorsements, appeared decisive not so much for the size of his victory—which was impressive—but because it was the last primary and guaranteed that there would be no more opportunities to damage him.

SOURCE: *Congressional Quarterly Weekly Report* (July 10, 1976), 1806.

it may be possible to generate more resources through increased publicity and higher standings in the polls. In 1976, Carter was able to translate several key victories into increased support in the public opinion polls and substantial increases in contributions to expand his campaign (see Box 12.1).

THE COMPETITIVE SITUATION

Another informal influence in the early stages of the nomination process is the development of the competitive situation. Although most political scientists and politicians agree that the formal campaign period is too long, the extension of the informal campaigning back to the previous election has become commonplace in the outparty. Matthews contends that tentative agreement is generally reached before the formal nominating process begins as to who ought to be the party's nominee. Only under unusual circumstances, such as Edmund Muskie encountered in 1972, does this "man to beat" actually lose the nomination. Although it is more common for the party of the president to have a single frontrunner for the nomination, the normal competitive situation in the outparty is similar.[5] Generally, one or two potential nominees are seen as far ahead and attention is focused on

[5] Prior to 1976, when Gerald Ford faced a stiff challenge for the nomination, it was commonplace to suggest that the outcome was predetermined if an incumbent desired renomination. Perhaps Ford's position as an unelected or "accidental" president made the difference, or perhaps the incumbency has become less dominant a factor in the nomination process.

them. The central question in such a case is whether or not the front-runner can survive the various pitfalls that must be faced. A candidate's preconvention strategy will depend on his position in the contest at any given time.

Many presidential hopefuls, then, are eliminated before the formal selection process begins. The number still running at the time of the first primary is small, considering the number of individuals eligible to run. The emergence of presidential possibilities is determined by a series of limiting factors such as the opportunity structure, public opinion polls, media exposure and coverage, and the scarcity of political resources. Although the competition is more open in the outparty, it tends to be quite well defined. By the time the elaborate formal nominating machinery gets underway, the field has been narrowed to presidential possibilities. The formal procedures pare this figure down to two: one Democrat and one Republican.

FORMAL NOMINATING PROCESS:
PRE-CONVENTION

Of all the nations that elect chief executives, the United States has devised the most complex nominating process. Although this process culminates in the national party convention, it is based on a series of fragmented and confusing decisions made prior to that traditional meeting. This convention process has been criticized as undemocratic, undignified, and unfair since its inception in the 1830s, but it has survived the tests it has encountered.

Recent debate has centered on specific aspects of the nominating process. Although most observers accept the national convention as a legitimate nominating device for presidential candidates, there is much concern over the representativeness and fairness of present convention procedures.[6] Recent reform efforts by both parties to democratize conventions have resulted in major changes in delegate selection, as well as convention rules. Although the impact of such changes on the selection of specific candidates may be minor, their implications for the overall process are great. The following sections examine specific elements in the nomination process. Where appropriate, they include discussions of the immediate and possible long-range consequences of both actuated and potential reforms. This formal/legal nomination process is examined within its broader political and nonpolitical contexts.

---

[6] Much of the following discussion is based on Judith H. Parris, *The Convention Problem* (Washington, D.C.: The Brookings Institution, 1972).

APPORTIONMENT OF DELEGATES
AND VOTES

A crucial step in the convention procedure is the apportionment of votes to the states by each national party organization. Although this appears to be an easy task, it is not, since any system of distribution benefits certain elements and deprives others. Although devising apportionment formulas is a mathematical procedure, any distribution method is highly political in nature. The entire question of representation centers here. For instance, if the convention is to be representative of those who support the party at the polls, then the apportionment formula should be built around party support in each state. If, however, the convention is to represent the whole electorate, then total population is the most appropriate basis for allocating votes. It might be argued that the convention is a meeting of party leaders. In that case, votes should be apportioned directly to constituent party organizations. Over the years, apportionment of convention votes has been a problem for both parties, especially the Democrats.

Republican Apportionment of Delegates. The Republican apportionment system has changed little since 1952, and is adopted explicitly at each successive national convention. As of 1972, convention votes were distributed to each state based on the following criteria:

1. Four delegates at large.
2. Two additional delegates at large for each congressman.
3. Six additional delegates to each state that in the last election (a) cast its electoral votes for the Republican presidential candidate, or (b) elected a Republican senator, or (c) elected a Republican governor, or (d) had a congressional delegation that was at least half Republican any time during the previous 4 years.
4. One district delegate to each congressional district that cast at least 4,000 votes for the Republican presidential ticket in the previous election or for the Republican congressional nominee in the preceding congressional election.
5. One additional district delegate to those congressional districts that cast at least 12,500 votes for Republican president or congressional nominee in the last election.
6. Nine delegates for D.C., 5 for Puerto Rico, 3 for Virgin Islands, and 3 for Guam.

343

Although categories 4 and 5 were originally designed to reward party voting, the number of popular votes necessary to receive bonus delegate votes has not increased rapidly enough to keep up with population growth. Only two districts in 1968 failed to meet the more stringent requirement, number 5. Essentially, this bonus formula rewards population size (that is, the number of congressional districts in a state) and not partisan support. Only item 3 rewards party voting. This Republican apportionment formula heavily emphasizes population of states without much regard to the party strength in any given state.[7] This has most benefited the southern states, where party support, other than in several presidential elections, has been minimal. Under a stricter party support formula, the South would have far fewer delegates to Republican conventions.

Democratic Apportionment of Delegates. In December, 1974, the Democratic Party Charter, adopted at the "mini-convention," specified that delegates should be allocated to the states

> consistent with a formula giving equal weight to population, which may be measured by electoral vote, and to the Democratic vote in elections for the office of President.[8]

Until the adoption of this provision, apportionment procedures of the Democrats were less organized than those of the Republicans. Instead of the previous national convention's deciding on the apportionment criteria, the Democratic National Committee made the apportionment rules for a convention about a year in advance. This produced serious political repercussions. Representatives of the various states were in a good position to see what their state would gain or lose by the alternatives, since they knew the outcome of the last election. Those states which had demonstrated strong Democratic support in the previous election naturally desired party support to be the most important criterion in apportionment. This lack of a structured formula has led to substantial fluctuations in the Democratic delegate apportionment over the last two decades. The Charter formula reduced the conflict surrounding apportionment. It also increased the proportion of delegates held by northern industrial states. As the majority party, the Democrats give substantially more weight to the strength of the party vote in previous elections, while Republicans emphasize state population.[9]

[7]*Ibid.*, p. 26. Also see Paul T. David, *Party Strength in the United States* (Charlottesville, Va.: University Press of Virginia, 1972), for data concerning the measurement of party strength in the states from 1872-1970.

[8]"Charter of the Democratic Party of the United States," *Congressional Record*, December 20, 1974, p. H12737.

[9]See Parris, *The Convention Problem*, pp. 36-49, for data concerning various apportionment alternatives.

SELECTION OF DELEGATES:
INTERNAL PARTY CHOICE

Once each state is assigned a specific number of votes, it is the responsibility of that state, within national party rules, to select the actual delegates to attend the national convention. If the convention is to be representative of the party electorate, these selection procedures must guarantee as broad a participation as possible. Since delegates are the only link party members have with the national convention, it is imperative that they be representative. It is vital to each party to obtain broad participation in the selection process, because, in the long run, the party will need a candidate acceptable to the entire electorate. Therefore, the recent trend has been for both parties to open their delegate selection process to include larger segments of the party identifiers (see Box 12.2).

There are three basic means by which delegates to the national convention can be selected. The first two are internal party selection techniques: (1) selection by party leaders or committees; and (2) choice of delegates at state or substate conventions. The third means of choosing delegates is the presidential primary. Although there are only three major methods of selection, the process is more complex because some states use a combination of methods. Also, the rules and procedures for each of these methods vary by state.

The most centralized means of selecting delegates is the party committee. Generally, these committees are dominated by state party leaders or strong county leaders. As recently as 1968, twelve Democratic and four Republican state parties used this method of selection. Generally, the party committee system benefits presidential candidates supported by those in power. Even when primaries are used to elect members of the state party committee, the rank-and-file party members are several steps removed from the actual choice of delegates. The voters seldom understand what they are voting for, and turnout is very low in such contests. Both parties have rejected party committee appointments as an ineffective means of selecting delegates.

The federal nature of our nomination process is reflected in the numerous variations on the state convention method of selecting delegates to the national convention. There are state conventions, congressional district conventions, county conventions, and various combinations of these. The convention delegates themselves might have been selected by local party leaders, in open caucuses attended by party members, or in precinct primaries. The apportionment of votes for state conventions also varies, and may be based on population, party strength, or political boundaries. Despite these differences, all internal party methods of selecting delegates have been criticized as undemocratic.

345

BOX 12.2   REFORM EFFORTS IN
DELEGATE SELECTION

Both political parties have attempted to strengthen and open the delegate selection process by instituting a series of reforms. After the 1968 convention, the Democrats established the Committee on Party Structure and Delegate Selection, which came to be called the McGovern-Fraser Commission. Similarly, the Republicans established a Delegate and Organization (DO) Committee. Although their purpose was similar, the Democratic group worked under more immediate pressure in the public limelight, while the Republican effort received little attention and produced less controversial and sweeping reforms.

The McGovern-Fraser Commission created 18 guidelines, which, although more wide-ranging, focused mainly on nonprimary states.[10] The Commission required that at least 75 percent of the delegates in nonprimary states be elected in open caucuses at the precinct, district, or other regional level and not at the state convention. All such meetings for the party were to be scheduled well in advance, held in easily accessible locations, and well publicized. These Democratic reforms also banned the proxy, the automatic delegate, and the unit rule. The guidelines also facilitated the inclusion of various minorities in the nomination process by guaranteeing adequate representation of their political views. This provision was interpreted as a quota system by many of the party regulars.

The battle over minority representation came to a head in August, 1974, at the final session of the Democratic Charter Commission, when the women's caucus, blacks and liberal reformers walked out to protest the tactics of the AFL-CIO and the party regulars' caucus. The Democratic Charter adopted several months later in Kansas City served as a compromise of sorts. Direct or indirect imposition of mandatory quotas by either state or national party organizations was banned, and emphasis was shifted to affirmative action. Although what constituted an approved affirmative action program was not specified, the goal was to encourage minority group participation at all stages of the delegate selection process. The delegates were to be chosen through processes which

[10] See *Mandate for Reform* (Washington, D.C.: Democratic National Committee, 1970, especially pp. 33-48.

1. assure all Democratic voters full, timely, and equal opportunity to participate and include affirmative action programs toward that end
2. assure that delegations fairly reflect the division of preferences expressed by those who participate in the Presidential nominating process
3. exclude the use of the unit rule at any level
4. do not deny participation for failure to pay a cost, fee, or poll tax
5. restrict participation to Democrats only, and begin within the calendar year of the Convention . . . .[11]

Until the 1970s, a majority of the delegates were selected through party committees or conventions. By 1976, however, only 27.4 percent of the Democratic delegates, and 32.1 percent of the Republicans, were so chosen. It is expected that the proportion will continue to decrease as more states adopt a primary system. Generally, those participating in internal party affairs are more committed to particular candidates than are primary voters. Although presidential candidates with a strong appeal to party regulars normally have an advantage, a candidate who is able to arouse intense feelings in a small following may succeed in winning many delegates in nonprimary states. George McGovern and George Wallace were both able to arouse much enthusiasm among well-organized supporters, resulting in impressive victories over the "regulars" in Democratic party state conventions. Despite the increased emphasis on presidential primaries, delegates selected through the state convention process are essential to a winning campaign. Seldom will a candidate mobilize primary delegates to the extent of not requiring broad support in the convention states as well. This is increasingly true as the proportional distribution of delegates becomes more universal in primaries.

SELECTION OF DELEGATES: PRESIDENTIAL PRIMARIES

In 1976, 29 states plus the District of Columbia held some form of primary election, one function of which was to choose delegates to the national conventions. These primaries extended over almost four months, cost over $72 million,[12] and were entered by 15 presidential candidates. This formal

[11] "Charter of the Democratic Party," p. H12737.
[12] *Congressional Quarterly Weekly*, September 25, 1976, p. 2606.

347

Table 12.1   Major Presidential Candidates' Pre-Nomination
Finances (in millions of dollars)

	Receipts	Expenditures	Matching Funds Received
Ronald Reagan	$18.0	$16.1	$5.1
Gerald R. Ford	14.4	13.8	4.7
Jimmy Carter	13.8	12.8	3.5
George C. Wallace	7.7	7.6	3.3
Henry M. Jackson	5.5	6.3	2.0
Morris K. Udall	4.4	4.3	1.8
Lloyd Bentsen	1.7	2.3	.5
Edmund G. Brown, Jr.	2.0	2.0	.5
Frank Church	1.6	1.6	.6
Fred Harris	1.5	1.4	.6
Birch Bayh	1.0	1.1	.5
Milton J. Shapp	.9	.9	.3
Terry Sanford	.6	.6	.2
R. Sargent Shriver	.6	.6	.3
Ellen McCormack	.5	.5	.2

SOURCE: Federal Election Commission

process of determining delegates was almost twice as long as the general election campaign, and at least as physically exhausting for the presidential candidates. For the first time in history, federal monies were given to the candidates on a complicated matching basis (see Table 12.1).

Besides the money, time, and energy consumed in the primaries, the lack of uniform timing is confusing, and contradictory rules and procedures cause problems in interpreting the primaries' meaning. It is very easy to overestimate the importance of any one primary, or of all the primaries together. Candidates can generally choose the primaries they enter, and seldom does one candidate receive a majority of votes in a primary.

Primaries continue to be popular, however, and serve as a growing source of delegates.[13] The number of primaries has more than doubled since 1968, when 15 states held such contests. As a result of the McGovern-Fraser Commission's reform rules, this figure expanded to 26 in 1972 and 30 in 1976. This outcome is ironic, since the intention of that commission was

[13] The most complete source on the presidential primary is James W. Davis, *Presidential Primaries: Road to the White House* (New York: Thomas V. Crowell Company, 1967). For a critical analysis of primaries see Austin Ranney, "Turnout and Representation in Presidential Primary Elections," *American Political Science Review*, 66 (March, 1972), 21-37.

to minimize the number of state presidential primaries. The rationale behind reforming the delegate-selection rules of the nonprimary processes was to prevent the development of more primaries. Increased participation according to the guidelines was intended to reduce the need for primaries. The result, however, was the opposite of what was desired by the commission, since it was easier to switch to a primary system in many cases than to revise the customary ways of conducting caucuses and conventions.

Variation of Primaries by State. No two presidential primaries are identical. One major difference which characterizes primaries is that between preference polls and the election of delegates. In a straight preference poll, the voters indicate a choice for presidential nominee from a list of contenders, while delegates are chosen separately. The delegates may or may not be bound by the results of the preference poll. Some states' presidential primaries are means of selecting delegates directly. Instead of listing the presidential candidates, a list of delegates is provided and voters make their choice of delegates, with no indication on the ballot of which presidential candidate each delegate supports. In New York in 1972, McGovern was able to capitalize on this system by organizing slates of delegates committed to himself, and getting them elected.

More common than either of these clearcut types are various combinations of delegate selection and presidential preference on the same ballot. Although each primary is different, most states, using a combination form, list delegates who are pledged to specific candidates. California lists only the names of the presidential candidates, each of whom in turn selects a slate of delegates pledged to him. Still other states include both elements on the ballot, but physically separate them. The voters must not only indicate their presidential preference, but in a separate section must select delegates from a list. The format of these separated ballots is not consistent from state to state, but in each case the voter must make several decisions. Conflicting advice is not unusual, and some delegates might find themselves bound to a candidate other than the one to whom they are personally committed.

To complicate the primary selection process further, states differ by the commitment of delegates to candidates. Some states require a pledge of loyalty to a candidate, though in many states this pledge to vote for a particular candidate is not legally binding. In those states with presidential preference polls, some delegates are bound to vote for the candidate for one or several ballots, while in other states the preference poll is simply advisory in nature.

There are also variations in states concerning the size of the voting constituency. In some states, convention delegates are elected on a statewide basis, while in others they are selected on a congressional-district basis. Most states include both district delegates and state delegates-at-large. Within these combination states there is further diversity. In Indiana for instance, district delegates are bound by the district results and the state delegates-at-large are bound by the statewide figures. The congressional-district constituencies, especially in the larger states, tend to result in fragmented state delegations at the convention.

Other variables in the conduct of presidential primaries relate to the freedom to form slates of delegates, the need for the consent of the candidate to be put on the ballot, and the composition of the eligible electorate. Providing slates of candidates simplifies the voting decision, especially when the list of delegates is long. Most states, Oregon being the most notable exception, allow the candidate to decide whether or not his name will appear on the ballot. Since 1965, at least five other states have placed all candidates' names on the ballots. Only by formally submitting a sworn affidavit disclaiming all interest in the party nomination can the name be removed.

Impact and Problems of Presidential Primaries.   These variations by state in presidential primaries, along with the length and costs of the primaries, have led to much criticism, and even more confusion. Voters have a difficult time understanding the procedures in their states, and potential candidates have an even more difficult time in sorting through the various state laws in order to arrive at a realistic preconvention strategy. Decisions must be made as to which primaries should be entered, how much time should be alloted to each state, and what issues should be raised in each primary campaign. Strategy will in part be defined by the relative position of the candidate at the start of the formal nomination process.

Donald Matthews found that despite the long duration of the primaries and the attention focused on the primary states, the overall impact of primaries on the nomination outcome has been minimal since 1936. For the inparty, the primaries seldom provide a serious challenge to the president. In 1952 and 1968, two unpopular presidents did face a challenge in the polls and voluntarily withdrew from the race. In both cases, the most the challengers (Kefauver in 1952 and McCarthy in 1968) accomplished was to throw the nomination to some other inside candidate. The primaries did not offer these challengers a strong possibility of gaining the nomination.[14] The success of Ronald Reagan in winning 50.7 percent of the vote in the Republican primaries in 1976, of course, almost offered an exception to this rule, though he narrowly lost the nomination to incumbent President Ford.

The impact of primaries on the outparty has not been much greater when there has been a strong frontrunner prior to the primaries. Edmund

[14] Matthews, "Presidential Nomination," p. 57.

Muskie is perhaps the only clearcut frontrunner to be destroyed in the primaries since 1936. If the outparty has one strong contender before the primaries, the primaries seldom alter the situation. When they do change the situation, it is generally to strengthen the initial leader. When the competitive situation is more complex before the primaries, the primaries might facilitate the emergence of a leader, or confuse the competitive situation even more. The basic function of the primaries tends to be one of eliminating those candidates who had little chance of capturing the nomination in the first place.

This is not to suggest that primaries have no place in the nomination process, nor does it mean that the entire formal nomination process is a sham. It does suggest, however, that much thought must go into analyzing the performance of presidential primaries. Modifications in the nomination process are needed to make up for the limitations of the present system.

NATIONAL OR REGIONAL PRIMARIES: PROPOSED CHANGES IN DELEGATE SELECTION

Recently there has been renewed emphasis on several alternatives to the present haphazard and long primary system. Although the provisions of specific proposals vary, there are two basic designs: the national primary or a series of regional primaries. Each of these alternatives has advantages and disadvantages which are summarized here.

National Primary. There are many proposals for a national primary which would be held on the same day in every state across the nation.[15] Although not a new idea (Woodrow Wilson proposed it first in 1913), it has lately received much support, because of the current proliferation of primaries. Although national primary proposals differ in detail, they generally call for a constitutional amendment requiring the states to hold a primary on a particular date. Provisions are included for a runoff primary to be held if no candidate receives at least 40 percent of the vote. In order to be placed on a ballot, candidates would have to file petitions in a certain number of states, although some plans allow for "recognized candidates" to be placed on the ballot automatically. The primaries would be closed in all states. The actual conduct of the primaries would remain under the jurisdiction of the states, within the broad context of the amendment. Under all but the most radical national primary proposals, the national convention would be retained to

---

[15] For a summary of national and regional proposals see *Current American Government* (Washington, D.C.: Congressional Quarterly, Inc., 1972), pp. 29-33.

write the platform, select a vice presidential nominee, and serve the traditional symbolic unifying functions. Only the selection of the presidential nominee would be formally eliminated.

These proposals for a national primary have several major advantages and several serious drawbacks. The advantages are simplicity and directness. Proponents argue that people could easily understand the process, and that it would expose all candidates to the people at one time. In other words, candidates would not be allowed to enter only their strong states to build up momentum. It is also contended that the national primary would shorten the primary campaign period. Several proposals contain specific limits on campaigning prior to the primary. Another point the proponents stress is that the public strongly supports such a reform. Since the 1950s, the Gallup polls consistently have registered about 75 percent support for a national primary.[16] The case for the national primary rests on its directness, its popular support, and the contention that it is more democratic.

Opponents see dangers inherent in the national primary (see Box 12.3 for critical comments). Less recognized candidates would find it difficult to participate in a single primary and would be at a great disadvantage. It would be difficult, if not impossible, to set campaigning limits, and more stress would be put on mass media advertising, polling, and the like. Also, critics argue that candidates might win the nomination with a very narrow distribution of support in the electorate, since primaries give an advantage to more extreme candidates. This would increase the chance of selecting a nominee unacceptable to a majority of the party. Theoretically, with a runoff situation, the two candidates might be representative of a very small portion of the party electorate. Even if a candidate receives 40 percent of the vote in the national primary, there is no assurance that he will be acceptable to the other 60 percent. Moderates might be eliminated in the national primary and the convention could do nothing about it. The national primary with a runoff might deepen party conflict and result in a divided party. It would also restrict most citizens to one form of participation in the nominating process.[17] Disadvantages of the national primary proposal are mainly the weakening of party structure and the unpredictable choice of nominees.

Regional Primaries. The regional primary system is a more recent proposal which attempts to minimize the disadvantages of both the present

---

[16] A poll conducted by the American Institute of Public Opinion in May, 1972, showed 72 percent in favor of a national primary, 18 percent opposed, and 10 percent uncertain.

[17] Austin Ranney, "Changing the Rules of the Nominating Game," in *Choosing the President*, ed. James David Barber, (Englewood Cliffs, N.J.: Prentice-Hall, Inc., 1974), p. 78, sees this as most unhealthy for the nation.

system and the national primary. Again, there have been a series of proposals, some of which vary greatly. The Packwood Plan (Robert W. Packwood, R-Oregon) would establish five regional primaries to be held once a month from March through July. A five-member federal elections commission would be established and would select by lot the order of primaries and judge which individuals should be placed on the ballot as serious contenders. Additional candidates could be added to the ballots by petitions and filing fees. All candidates receiving at least 5 percent of the vote in any state in a region could appoint delegates to the national convention. Delegates would be committed for two convention ballots, or until released. Under the Packwood Plan, states would be required to participate in the regional primaries. The plan would prohibit them from choosing delegates through any other method. The national convention would be retained in its present form and only the delegate-selection process would be altered.

The major concern with regional primaries is the increased possibility of having deadlocked conventions. Since delegates are appointed proportionately to the votes accumulated in individual states across five regional primaries, there is an excellent chance of four or five-way splits. The decision of the convention in such a case would be difficult, and conflict within the party would be increased. Other problems with the various regional primary proposals center on the technical aspects of making such proposals workable.

Prospects for Change.   Although lately there has been more impetus for alternative plans such as national or regional primaries,[18] the chances of any radical changes being made in the delegate-selection process in the near future appear minimal. Although there are many advantages to these proposals, they are fraught with uncertainty and danger. As mentioned earlier, it is very difficult to predict the consequences of any reform on the entire electoral system and on the political parties. In discussing such proposals, one is limited to theoretical possibilities and projections. Despite the strong public support for a national primary and the general discontent with the present fragmented primary system, the delegate-selection phase of the nomination process will continue to be a major problem area. There is no easy and comprehensive solution to such a complex and controversial matter.

THE NATIONAL CONVENTION

The culmination of all previous stages in the presidential nomination process is the national convention. Of all political events in the U.S., none is more publicized or has more media exposure than the national party convention.[19] Once every four years, the fifty state parties gather to imitate a national organization, and for that short period, the illusion seems very real. In addition to legitimizing a national ticket, compiling a general document of party priorities and programs, and providing a forum for party leaders, the conventions attempt to demonstrate unity behind their choices. If successful, a convention will create enthusiasm for the candidates, not only among

[18] There has been, for instance, voluntary state coordination in several regions. For example, Oregon, Idaho, Nevada, and Wyoming held their presidential primaries on the same date in 1976. A similar attempt in Washington was vetoed by the governor.

[19] The most comprehensive book written specifically on the national conventions is Paul T. David, Ralph M. Goldman, and Richard C. Bain, *The Politics of National Party Conventions* (Washington, D.C.: The Brookings Institution, 1960). Although dated in terms of examples, its scope is not rivaled in more recent books. It is well supplemented by Parris, *The Convention Problem.*

delegates, but also throughout the vast audience watching the spectacle on television.

PLANNING THE CONVENTION: NATIONAL PARTY HEADQUARTERS

Of the many stages in the formal nominating process, only the convention is solely a party matter. No state laws or federal statutes interfere with the actual conduct of the convention. The responsibility for planning rests with the national committees, although, as was seen in Chapter 6, the national headquarters staff does the actual work. At times a strong incumbent president, such as Johnson in 1964 or Nixon in 1972, can have a commanding influence through his control of the national committee and his role as party leader.

Time and Place. Since organizing the convention is the major function of the national committee, planning begins at least two years prior to the event. Due to the size of the conventions there are two decisions which must be made early: the time and place of the convention. Adequate convention sites are becoming more difficult to obtain, not only because of the vast facilities needed, but also because of an increasing unwillingness by some cities to host the convention. Although cities may no longer offer cash to the parties, they still must provide services. It is estimated that New York spent $3.5 million in 1976 to host the Democrats, while Kansas City had $500,000 budgeted for the Republican Convention.[20]

In addition to selecting a convention site, it is necessary to plan well in advance.[21] While early planning is necessary to ensure adequate hotel and convention facilities and adequate arrangements for media coverage, the dates also serve a strategic importance. Although conventions have always been held during July or August, the scheduling has varied. Timing of the convention might be crucial, and depends mainly on the party situation at the time. Parties with popular incumbents generally plan a late convention. In a highly competitive situation, it makes sense to have the convention earlier. This gives the winning candidate time before the formal campaign period to mend party rifts and gain momentum. After holding a late convention in 1968 and viewing its adverse affect on Hubert Humphrey's campaign, the Democrats in 1972 planned an early convention in July. Unfortunately, other problems

---

[20] *Congressional Quarterly Weekly*, April 3, 1976, p. 784.

[21] For more details on the logistic problems of national conventions, see Cornelius P. Cotter and Bernard C. Hennessy, *Politics Without Power* (New York: Atherton Press, 1964), pp. 107-27.

developed which did not facilitate consensus building or provide any momentum for McGovern. Timing of the convention, however, continues to be a major practical and strategic decision.

Financing the Convention.   Until 1976, party organizations paid the costs of the conventions by negotiating with potential host cities for payments, selling expensive advertisements in their programs, and using their own funds. With the implementation of the 1974 Campaign Finance Law in 1976, a significant change in financing conventions was begun. Under this law, each national committee received over $2 million in public funds from the income tax checkoff. In order to receive these public funds, however, no private funds may be used. This restriction includes cash bids by host cities and private contributions for ads in the convention programs.

Standing Committees.   Each national party has four standing committees, which are supplemented by ad hoc or special committees when necessary.[22] The functions and responsibilities of the standing committees are clearly defined and their decisions are recommendations to the full convention body. The national committees are responsible for, though they seldom actually choose, the chairmen of these committees. National party officials appoint the committee members after consultation with state organizations, and according to rather narrowly defined guidelines. These committees meet prior to the convention, so that by the time it opens they will be able to present their recommendations to the full convention for approval. As a rule, committee recommendations are approved. When they are not, a major floor fight may occur.

> *Permanent Organization Committee*—The permanent organization committee is the least controversial committee. It is responsible for selecting the permanent officials of the convention. These include the permanent chairman or co-chairmen, the secretary, and the sergeant-at-arms, all of which are generally confirmed with little discussion.
>
> *Rules Committee*—The rules committee establishes the rules for the convention within the bounds of the formal parliamentary rules.[23] It is most specifically concerned with procedures of selecting the presidential and vice presidential nominees.

[22] The Democratic Charter established three councils in addition to the standing committees of the convention. They include the Judicial Council, the National Finance Council, and the Education and Training Council.

[23] In 1968, the Republicans adopted Robert's *Rules of Order Revised* as their official procedures. The Democrats utilize more complex rules similar to those of the U.S. House of Representatives.

This committee makes recommendations for rules governing the length and number of nominating speeches, the nominating procedures, the method of polling state delegations, and the extent of demonstrations that are allowed in support of candidates nominated. In several recent conventions, rules concerning the right of challenged delegates to vote have been very crucial and hotly contested on the floor. Most rule committee recommendations are accepted on the convention floor, however.

Credentials Committee— The credentials committee accepts or rejects the credentials of the delegates and alternates and draws up the official delegate list of the convention. Seating of delegates has been a problem at recent conventions, especially for the Democrats. The most difficult tasks of the credentials committee are to decide contests between two delegates or slates of delegates claiming the same seats, and to judge the qualifications of any challenged delegate. In 1972, the Democratic credentials committee opened its deliberations over two weeks before the convention opening. They faced 82 challenges, representing 30 states and over 40 percent of the delegates. Their major concern focused on the Illinois challenge, in which the Daley delegates were replaced, and the California challenge, in which they decided to award delegates on the basis of proportion of popular votes rather than winner-take-all. The reversal of this recommendation on the convention floor assured George McGovern of the nomination and resolved perhaps the most emotional contest of the entire convention.

Resolutions Committee— The resolutions committee is responsible for drafting the party's platform, later approved by the convention. In order to accomplish this, the committee holds open hearings in advance of the convention. The Democratic rules require the committee to hold at least eight regional hearings before writing the platform. In conjunction with the hearings, a series of planning groups are set up to consider specific issues, hold pre-platform hearings, and write reports. Following the hearings, which are more symbolic than effective, executive sessions are held to draft the actual planks. The platform is then presented to the convention for its approval. Seldom is this document rejected, or even extensively amended. The last major contest over a platform proposal concerned the minority report on Vietnam in Chicago in 1968. In an emotional battle, the minority report was defeated.

THE GRAND ILLUSION:
CONVENTION PROCEEDINGS

Although details of each convention differ, the general timetable is remarkably consistent and predictable. After months and years of planning, the convention meets for less than a week. In recent years, most conventions of both parties have lasted only four days.[24] Within that four-day period, most of the work of the national parties is conducted. Almost without exception, opening ceremonies are held in the afternoon or evening of the first day. Traditional rituals provide a parade-like atmosphere. An invocation and welcoming speeches by the host mayor and governor are common. A keynote speech is the first major appeal to delegates and public. Generally this is one long address by a party notable, although the Republicans in 1972 broke with tradition and had three shorter speeches. Usually, the credentials committee report is also presented the first night, so that delegates can be seated. At times, (among the 1952 Republicans and 1972 Democrats, for instance), the battle over the credentials report has been emotional and crucial to the nomination.

The rule committee's report is generally adopted on the second afternoon or evening, and the permanent convention chairperson is elected and installed. Then the platform committee report is filed. Debate over this report varies greatly from convention to convention, depending on whether or not an incumbent president is running for reelection. For instance, in 1972 the Republican platform, written under the direction of the White House, was adopted with few changes and little debate. That same year, the Democratic platform debate continued long past midnight, while delegates considered 20 minority reports on platform planks. The result, however, was general acceptance of the original committee report.[25]

The third evening brings what is considered by many to be the central event of the national convention, the nomination of the party's presidential candidate. Though the choice is seldom in question by the time of the balloting, symbolically there is little else in American politics so dramatic.[26] As the roll call of the states begins, the end of the long nomination process is near. Nominating and seconding speeches have been planned well ahead of time. In recent years, both parties have attempted to limit the number of candidates nominated, as well as the length of nominating speeches. Favorite-son candi-

[24] The well-orchestrated 1972 Republican convention required only three days.

[25] Only two minority planks out of twenty were accepted. All other committee planks were ratified.

[26] It is unlikely that American politics will ever again witness anything close to the 103-ballot marathon the Democrats put on in nominating John W. Davis in 1924. The Democratic convention in 1952 was the last to require more than one ballot in nominating a presidential candidate. Richard C. Bain and Judith H. Parris, *Convention Decisions and Voting Records* (Washington, D.C.: The Brookings Institution, 1973), not only summarizes the proceedings of all major party conventions since 1832, but also provides the voting records by state and by ballot.

dates must demonstrate a wider base of support than one state if they hope to be nominated. All nominations must be cleared with the convention officials prior to the roll call and speeches. Demonstrations in support of candidates, though subdued in recent years, are a tradition which is difficult to eliminate. The duration and scope of such demonstrations, however, are regulated by both parties.

Several items must be completed on the last day of the convention before adjournment. Following a tradition that is likely to be modified in the near future, the presidential nominee announces his choice of a running mate. That evening, in the last session of the convention, nomination of the vice presidential designate is conducted. Procedures for selecting the vice presidential nominee are similar to those for the presidential nominee, although competition, in deference to the presidential candidate, is minimal. The call of the states, nominating and seconding speeches, and the actual balloting ratify the choice announced earlier that day.

The final stage in the convention includes acceptance speeches by both the presidential and vice-presidential candidates. It also includes a symbolic closing of the ranks, a demonstration of party unity, and an enthusiastic and optimistic launching of the campaign. The convention, if successful, is adjourned on the fourth night in an atmosphere of unity and optimism concerning the upcoming elections. More than a few of the recent conventions have fallen short of expressing such a united front, but the effort is always there.

FORCES OF CHANGE: DELEGATES
AND MEDIA COVERAGE

While the planning for and proceedings of national conventions remain outwardly unchanged, there are strong forces at work altering the nature of the conventions. Since conventions are central to the party organization, these forces have a direct influence on the parties themselves. These forces of change revolve around two major social trends: the infusion of amateurs into the political process and the increased influence of the mass media, especially television. The second of these, because it is less complex, is discussed first.

DOMINANT ROLE OF ELECTRONIC MEDIA

Since the advent of television coverage in 1952, convention managers have been well aware of the media presence. Tons of television equipment, thousands of technicians, and hundreds of reporters and commentators are hard

BOX 12.4   PROJECTING THE IMAGES

The Democrats want their 1976 convention to play to a prime-time television audience, not to the insomniacs and political buffs who watched 3 a.m. platform debates and acceptance speeches in 1972.

With this in mind, the Democratic National Committee has hired a television consultant. He is Al Vecchione, 44, who has taken a six-month leave of absence as director of public affairs programming for the National Public Affairs Center for Television (NPACT) in Washington, D.C.

"I came to the job with the conviction, after 16 years of doing these things, that during those four fateful days in July you not only nominate a candidate, you elect a President," said Vecchione. The convention, he continued, leaves an indelible impression on the voters. "The basic impression they carry away has a very strong effect on what they end up doing four months later when they go into the voting booth."

Vecchione cited as negative examples the 1964 Republican convention, which nominated Barry Goldwater, and the 1968 Democratic convention, which nominated Hubert H. Humphrey. A positive example, he said was the 1960 Democratic convention, which nominated John F. Kennedy.

Vecchione expects to advise this year's convention speakers "to see that they get projected in the best possible way. This is a year when rhetoric should be reduced and candor should be emphasized."

One certainty is that the Democratic presidential nominee will make his acceptance speech during the prime evening hours of Thursday, July 15. Vecchione has recommended the shortening of platform debate by postponing time-consuming roll-call votes until the end of the debate and by having speakers make their arguments from convention-floor microphones instead of the podium.

The podium itself can be designed to add a functional but homey touch to the proceedings, Vecchione believes. "All I'm trying to do," he said, "is create an atmosphere where the politicians coming there to do some serious work can do so in the best possible atmosphere."

Republicans

The Republican convention has a different kind of television problem. In 1972, the party was criticized for the split-second timing

360

that left some viewers with the impression that the convention was little more than a stage-managed spectacular.

Iantha LeVander of South St. Paul, Minn., chairman of the Republican Program Planning Subcommittee for the 1976 convention, is not worried about a repeat performance. The party's national committee will have direct responsibility for this year's convention, she noted. In 1972, President Nixon's re-election committee went its own way, with little influence from the national committee.

Nate Halpern of New York City will be the Republicans' television consultant this year, as he has been in the past. Assisting again with the convention program will be former movie actor and California Senator George Murphy (R 1964-71).

SOURCE: *Congressional Quarterly Weekly Report* (April 3, 1976), 785.

to ignore. The impact of such media exposure is also prevalent in the thoughts of the convention officials. Not only are they conscious of the constant exposure to a broad public audience, but also they are extremely sensitive to the image of the convention operations this audience is receiving.

The reaction of the party leaders to media presence has led to well-organized conventions, specifically designed for television coverage. Prime time is exploited by scheduling major events, such as acceptance speeches, during the early evening hours. The time allotted to speeches, roll calls, and polling of state delegations is reduced to provide a more fast-moving and entertaining show. The movies shown at recent conventions to glorify the parties and honor their heroes have reinforced this aura of an entertainment spectacular. At the same time, delegates have been urged to look attentive and serious in order to impress the television audience. Finally, the conventions themselves have been shortened to sustain the interest and attention of this outside audience. The impact of the media coverage on convention operations is substantial, because the politicians have consciously attempted to arrange the convention to present their party in a most favorable manner.[27] In many ways, the conventions have become slaves of the medium and its audience (See Box 12.4).

[27]Parris, *The Convention Problem*, p. 149. Also see Paul Tillet, "The National Conventions," in *The Presidential Election and Transition 1960-1961*, ed. Paul T. David (Washington, D.C.: The Brookings Institution, 1961), pp. 54-55.

The officials of both parties realize how vital a good public image is. They also are aware that media coverage can influence that image greatly. Unfortunately, media publicity is not always favorable, nor can the convention managers control it. The 1968 Democratic party image suffered greatly due to the immediate, sensational, and somewhat misleading television coverage. On the other hand, it appears that the 1972 Republican convention, though staid and lacking in dramatic appeal, presented the image of an organized and unified party, in contrast to the more wide-open Democratic convention.

In their quest for favorable publicity, convention officials have sacrificed much freedom and privacy. As the press and television cameras have invaded not only the convention floor but also the committee rooms and state caucuses, the tendency has been for actual decisions to be made in private meetings behind the scenes. The now-public forums serve only to confirm what has already been decided previously in closed meetings. This has resulted not because secrecy is desirable, but because some privacy is needed as protection from one's political opponents.

FORCES OF CHANGE ON THE DELEGATES

A less evident but more important change in the conduct of conventions has been in the nature of the delegates. This change actually has three dimensions which must be examined: (1) the rise in the status of amateur delegates, (2) the greater representativeness of delegates, and (3) their increased numbers.

Amateur Activists: A New Breed of Delegate. A major change in delegates was first apparent in 1960, when strong personal supporters of Kennedy were much in evidence. The percentage of delegates committed to a candidate has sharply increased since that convention, most obviously since 1968. According to Sullivan, the decline in the power of party leaders in presidential politics has been accelerated by three factors: (1) the increase in amateur activists, (2) the flow of money to candidate organizations, and (3) the atrophy of state and local party organizations in recent years.[28] Activists are drawn into presidential politics not by party loyalty, but by participation in candidate organizations. Once at the convention, their commitment to the candidate organization or an issue group is strong, while their ties to state and local parties are correspondingly weaker (see Chapter 5 for more details on this subject).

[28] Dennis G. Sullivan, Jeffrey L. Pressman, and F. Christopher Atherton, *Explorations in Convention Decision-Making: The Democratic Party in the 1970's* (San Francisco: W.H. Freeman and Co., 1976), pp. 20-21.

This increasing presence of amateurs, as opposed to professionals who are oriented towards the formal party organization, has been due in part to the rapid increase in the percent of delegates selected in presidential primaries. More and more delegates owe little to the party organization, since state and local leaders no longer handpick the delegates. Complementing the weakening of party leaders' role in selecting delegates is the emphasis on candidate-oriented campaigns. In order to participate effectively in the primaries, a candidate must have a strong personal organization. The new federal finance law further encourages early organization across many states to collect money and qualify for matching funds. By the time of the convention, many delegates have been actively working for a candidate for six months or more. They are at the convention primarily to support their candidate, and their perceptions of the convention roles they play are at variance with those of the party professionals (see Box 12.5).

A by-product of the shift toward amateur delegates is that most delegates are inexperienced, not having attended previous conventions. At the 1972 Democratic Convention, for instance, only 16 percent of the delegates had attended at least one previous convention.[29] This high turnover rate leads to more dependence upon leaders of candidate organizations, caucuses, and in some cases, state delegations. High turnover might also be viewed as increasing the legitimacy of candidate selection by demonstrating that access to the convention is open.

The traditional leadership of the national conventions, therefore, has lost much of its leverage in running the show. Even in the outparty, candidate organizations have chopped away at the already eroded power base of state and local party leaders. At this pinnacle of national party activity, the move toward amateur, candidate or issue-oriented delegates threatens even the minimal centralized control necessary to ensure the selection of candidates. Supplementing this trend in delegates have been two other trends related to the structure of the convention.

More Representative Delegates. Delegates to both party conventions in the past have in no way represented a cross-section of the electorate. They have been overwhelmingly middle-aged, white males with relatively high education and income levels. Republican delegates are predominantly businessmen, public officials, or lawyers, while Democrats lean more toward labor and to a lesser extent academe. Only small proportions of delegates for either party through 1968 were composed of women, blacks, and youths. In 1968, for instance, only 2 percent of the Republican delegates and 6 percent of the Democratic delegates were black.

[29] Dennis G. Sullivan, et al., *The Politics of Representation: The Democratic Convention 1972* (New York: St. Martin's Press, 1974), p. 24.

BOX 12.5   PURIST AND PROFESSIONAL
ATTITUDES ON CONVENTION FUNCTIONS

If we compare the attitudes of the purists and professional politicians toward the major functions of nominating conventions—the selection of a candidate, the writing of a party platform, and the resolution of political differences—we can gain a clearer perspective on the distinction between purists and professionals. Purists pledge themselves to a candidate on the basis of his stand on the issues; professionals justify their commitment in terms of the candidate's capacity to unify the party and win elections. For professionals, issue preferences are relevant but secondary. Concerning the writing of a platform—the second major function of nominating conventions—the purist arrives at a platform that is correct according to some conception of the public interest or good; for the professional a platform is correct if it placates the losers without alienating the winners and, at the same time, offers a good chance of winning the general election.

Finally, for the purists, the resolution of issue differences ought to occur through open discussion and debate in which each participant has an equal weight; for the professional, issue differences are resolved through bargaining and compromises in which the outcome is determined (and should be) by the relative power of contending groups. For the purists, intra-party democracy is highly valued; for the professionals it is not.

SOURCE: *Explorations in Convention Decision-Making: The Democratic Party in the 1970's* by Dennis G. Sullivan, Jeffrey L. Pressman and F. Christopher Atherton. (San Francisco: W.H. Freeman and Company, 1976), p. 23.

The delegate-selection reforms in the early 1970s resulted in a more representative cross-section of the electorate, at least as defined by the presence of minority group members and women. Conscientious efforts were made by Republicans to include higher proportions of women and youth as well as minority groups. Under the impetus of the McGovern-Fraser guidelines, a significant change was made in the demographic characteristics of the 1972 convention. Table 12.2 illustrates this clearly. Whereas only 5 percent

Table 12.2   Minority Representation of Democratic Conventions
1968 and 1972

Demographic Categories	General Population (1970)	Convention Delegates 1968	Convention Delegates 1972
Blacks	11	5	15
Women	51	13	40
Ages 18-30	27	4	21

SOURCE: Austin Ranney, *Curing the Mischiefs of Faction* (Berkeley: University of California Press, 1975), p. 155.

of the 1968 delegates were black, 15 percent were black in 1972. Corresponding figures for women were 13 and 40 percent, and for those under 30, 4 and 21 percent, respectively. Although not conforming to the general population characteristics, the shift over these four years was remarkable.

By their very presence at a national convention, most delegates have exhibited more commitment and interest in politics than average citizens. Delegates are also more ideological and better aware of the issue distinctions between the parties than simple party identifiers. Despite the infusion of blacks, women, and young into the 1972 Democratic Convention, the delegates remained predominantly upper-middle class.[30] Democratic delegates are more liberal than Democratic identifiers, and Republican delegates are more conservative, generally, than rank-and-file Republicans.[31] The Goldwater and McGovern nominations probably derived more support from party activists than from party identifiers, in part because of their ideological appeals.

Increased Number of Delegates.   While reform efforts of the last decade have been moderately successful in producing delegates more reflective of the electorates, they also have contributed to increased numbers. While there has always been pressure from state parties for additional delegates, this has now been extended to various nonformal party organizations

[30] Austin Ranney, *Curing the Mischiefs of Faction: Party Reform in America* (Berkeley: University of California Press, 1975), p. 156, states that while 23 percent of the general population had annual incomes of over $15,000, 62 percent of the 1972 Democratic delegates did. Corresponding figures of those holding postgraduate college degrees were 4 percent in the general population and 39 percent at the Democratic convention.

[31] John W. Soule and James W. Clarke, "Issue Conflict and Consensus: A Comparative Study of Democratic and Republican Delegates to the 1968 National Conventions," *Journal of Politics*, 33 (February, 1971), pp. 72-91.

such as caucuses and issue-oriented groups. There has been a tendency to equate increased representativeness with increased numbers, and each group desires their proportion. Because of these pressures, the 1976 Republican Convention had a total of 4,518 delegates and alternates, while the Democrats had 4,944. The corresponding figures for 1952 were Republicans 2,412 and Democrats 2,256. Although the Democrats still have more delegates than the Republicans, in 1976 they slightly reduced their 1972 figure, while the Republicans registered a 63 percent increase from 1972 to 1976.

The increased number of delegates has led to a problem. Although it is rare when a convention as a whole makes a decision, the size of the present conventions makes realistic deliberation very unlikely. Four thousand individuals can not effectively participate in making decisions. The result has been to place more power in the hands of committee leaders, caucus leaders, candidates' strategists, and state delegation leaders. As with all large groups, the real decisions are made by subgroups, while the convention as a whole simply ratifies or, more rarely, rejects these decisions.

In examining the more traditional standing committees and state delegations, it is evident that they also are too large. Currently, standing committees in both parties exceed 150, with many being 200. State delegations and caucus groups have also grown as the convention size has increased. The average state delegation of Republicans in 1972 was 20 delegates and 20 alternates. Corresponding figures for the Democrats were 35 and 28, with the New York delegation totalling 398. It is not surprising that these large delegations and committees negate effective deliberation and are of necessity controlled by a handful of leaders.

The increase in size of committees and delegations reflects the inherent conflict between the principles of representativeness and effective deliberation. In order to make such groups more representative, the reform elements in each party have mistakenly assumed that size must be increased. In the process, they have reduced these groups' capacity for decision making. Although there is general agreement on the need for reduction in size, few groups are willing to reduce their numbers. State delegations are fearful of losing one of the few patronage rewards they still control. Substantial reductions in the number of delegates at either the full convention or the subgroup level appear unlikely, especially while pressures continue to expand participation. Ultimately, a decision must be made to limit the number in attendance to a level below that now allowed. Most moves in this direction have been attempts to reduce the number of nonparticipants on the floor, especially the media. Although such moves are probably justified, they still do not solve many of the long run problems of the representativeness-deliberation conflict.

NATIONAL CONVENTIONS:
SUCCESS OR FAILURE?

Once every four years the two major parties of the United States hold conventions. They attempt to nominate their presidential and vice presidential candidates, draw up a platform that appeals to various segments of the party, and through it all, unify the diverse interests behind the candidates and platform. They conduct this business in a production-like atmosphere, with a body of delegates too large and often too confused to make meaningful decisions. A question which must now be asked is: How successful are national conventions in achieving their narrow but vital goals? To answer this question, it is best to examine each of the three major convention objectives in turn.

SELECTION OF THE PRESIDENTIAL TICKET

The principal task of the convention is to choose a presidential candidate. As was mentioned earlier, this task has been minimized in recent years because the decision has generally been made before the convention. Not since 1952 has a convention gone beyond the first ballot in choosing a candidate. Even in those years when a concerted effort was made to stop the frontrunner (that is, Democrats, 1960 and 1968; Republicans, 1964) the number of committed delegates was too great to overcome. As the impact of the media, polls, and money before and during the primaries increases, it is unlikely that many conventions in the future will actually select the candidate. It is more probable that conventions will serve to ratify the decision made prior to the formal meeting of the delegates.

The data in Table 12.3 demonstrate the wide variation still possible, however. Although Carter received only 39.9 percent of the primary vote in a crowded field, the momentum he took with him to the convention enabled him to take 75 percent of the votes. There was no doubt about the outcome and attention centered on whom Carter would select as a running mate. Conversely, the Republican decision was in doubt until the vote was taken. While it was presumed that Ford would withstand the Reagan challenge, the results were close, with Ford taking less than 53 percent of the delegates. While the challenge of the incumbent was unsuccessful, this example shows that generalizations about party nominations are less than reliable.[32]

[32] For more details on the 1976 conventions, see Gerald M. Pomper, "The Nominating Contests and Conventions," in *The Election of 1976*, ed. Gerald M. Pomper (New York: Longman, Inc., 1977), pp. 1-34.

Table 12.3   Convention Results, 1976

Candidate	Vote Total	Vote Percentage
Democrats		
Carter	2238.50	74.5
Udall	329.50	11.0
Brown	300.50	10.0
Wallace	57.00	1.9
Others	79.50	2.6
Republicans		
Ford	1187.00	52.6
Reagan	1070.00	47.4

SOURCE: *Congressional Quarterly Weekly Report*, (July 7, 1976), 1873 and (August 21, 1976), 2313.

While the suspense surrounding presidential nominations is commonly minimal, uncertainty has shifted toward the vice presidential choice. The custom of allowing the presidential candidate, in consultation with other party leaders, to make the choice on the afternoon after he is nominated has resulted in some surprises. The drama is usually limited to the announcement of the presidential candidate's choice, however, since convention ratification of his choice is almost certain.

This is not to suggest that the presidential candidate is entirely free in his choice. His range of selection may be limited by such concerns as ideological or factional balance, party unity, and geographical constraints. Certain candidates might be vetoed by sectional factions, making a compromise candidate necessary. Such was the case with Spiro Agnew in 1968. He was one of the few candidates who was acceptable to both northern liberals and the southerners led by Strom Thurmond. It mattered little that Ted Agnew was not a household word.

The dangers inherent in choosing the vice presidential nominee in this haphazard manner are evident from recent selections. Some of these candidates have seldom faced close scrutiny by the public, the delegates, or most party leaders. The fate of two contemporary products of this sytem indicates that more deliberation is necessary. Spiro Agnew was forced to resign from office after being "only a heartbeat away" from the presidency for five years. Thomas Eagleton, the choice of George McGovern in 1972, resigned before the formal campaign period began. Careful screening by a wider range of persons might not have averted these situations, but at least the decision would have been made in open competition, with more time to scrutinize the contenders. The attempt by Jimmy Carter to screen a list of at least a dozen prospective nominees was the most deliberate, in-depth selection process on record.

> Like all presidential candidates, Carter claimed that competence would be the guiding criterion in selection of his running mate. Like other candidates, however, he also kept political considerations in mind, seeking a candidate who would help bring some geographical balance to the ticket and help to unify the party. Mondale, the preference of labor and ideological liberals, met these needs. The deliberate pattern of selection further aided Carter's election effort, by presenting a public image of a careful but decisive leader.[33]

In an era when vice presidents frequently become presidents, many observers feel that the entire selection process needs a major overhauling. Unfortunately, there is a lack of agreement on what form this change should take.[34] One proposal for eliminating pressure from the presidential candidate is to nominate the vice president first. This proposal would achieve its objective only when the presidential contest was in doubt, and then would limit the field to candidates with no hope of winning the top spot. Another proposed reform would restrict eligibility for running mate to the top three contenders for the presidential nomination. This might eliminate selection of the strongest ticket for the party, since there is no guarantee that any of the runners-up would make suitable candidates. A third proposed method would have the presidential and vice presidential candidates run as a team.[35] Although feasible, this plan gives the presidential nominee even more latitude in his choice, especially if he is the frontrunner all the way. It also eliminates the runners-up in the presidential competition from consideration. Each of these proposals sets restrictions on vice presidential selection that, if rigidly enforced, might be counter-productive.[36]

[33] *Ibid.*, p. 28.

[34] For more details on these alternatives, see *Congressional Quarterly Guide to American Government,* Spring, 1977 (Washington, D.C.: Congressional Quarterly Service, 1977), pp. 35-38.

[35] Ronald Reagan's designation of the liberal Senator, Richard Schweiker, three weeks before the 1976 Republican Convention was a calculated risk to balance his ticket and win the nomination. There is no evidence that it succeeded in winning liberal support, and it probably damaged Reagan's conservative ideological credentials.

[36] See Gerald Pomper, *Nominating the President* (New York: W.W. Norton and Co., Inc., 1966), especially pages 174-80, for more details on these various proposals.

WRITING THE PLATFORM

A second major task of the convention is to adopt a platform that not only reflects the party's views and intentions, but also helps unite the various interests and factions. Party platforms have often been criticized as meaningless and evasive. Recent research has demonstrated, to the contrary, that platforms are meaningful guides to party action. Although not officially binding, they do contain commitments and appeals of the parties and are taken seriously by most politicians.[37]

In his analysis of party platforms from 1944 to 1964, Gerald Pomper found much evidence to indicate that they are meaningful, especially to their drafters. Pomper studied the content of the platforms and the degree to which they were carried out by politicians, once in office. He first dispelled the myth that platforms are vague and ambiguous. Through content analysis he found that almost 50 percent of the platforms from 1952-68 were specific pledges of future policy. Less than 20 percent were rhetoric, while the remaining portions were evaluations of party records.

Pomper also found significant differences between the platforms, especially in emphasis. This is to be expected, since the parties are appealing to different constituencies, though the usual criticisms of platforms ignore this. The platform fights reinforce the belief that these are not meaningless documents, but highly controversial issues at times. Some aspects of both parties' platforms, to be sure, are similar rhetoric, but a greater portion reflects real differences between the parties. Platform pledges also are fulfilled to a much greater degree than they are usually given credit for. Of the pledges supported in the platforms of both parties from 1944 to 1966, 85 percent were adopted. Adoption is defined as some substantial governmental action of the kind and in the direction promised.[38] In addition, 79 percent of the inparty pledges were fulfilled, and 53 percent of the outparty pledges were adopted.[39]

---

[37] There are three major works on party platforms. The most detailed study is that of Gerald M. Pomper, *Elections in America* (New York: Dodd, Mead, and Company, 1970), pp. 149-203. Also see, Paul T. David, "Party Platforms as National Plans," *Public Administration Review*, 31 (May-June, 1971), pp. 305-15 and James L. Sundquist, *Politics and Policy* (Washington, D.C.: The Brookings Institution, 1968), pp. 389-415.

[38] Pomper, *Elections in America*, p. 183.

[39] Robert S. Erikson and Norman R. Luttbeg, *American Public Opinion: Its Origin, Content, and Impact* (New York: John Wiley and Sons, 1973) p. 301, however, express caution with the Pomper data. They note that policy pledges constitute only 27 percent of the platform statements and that the parties take alternative stands on only about 10 percent of these. Despite

Platforms are more meaningful than is commonly believed, and they do distinguish between the parties. The more critical views of these documents are rejected in the data available. Paul David has argued that platforms have become important as "alternative and partly overlapping national plans" that are usually executed to a substantial degree.[40] In the process, parties generally are successful in appealing to most elements of their coalition through the platform.

UNIFYING THE PARTY

Another major goal of the convention is to unify the disparate factions and interests of the party behind the candidate and, to a lesser degree, the platform. The entire convention builds toward the drama of the acceptance speeches and the symbolic demonstration of unity prior to the adjournment of the convention. Although the convention meets for only a few days, its momentum is expected to continue for months. It is hoped that the convention will not only activate the party workers but also serve as a major reinforcement of party affiliation. Workers from the nuclear organizations of the primaries are called to the aid of the winning candidate.

In addition to facilitating unity among the delegates and other convention participants, the national conventions also seek to create a highly favorable party image in the mass media audience. For that reason, many of the convention events and appeals are aimed not at the delegates but at the television cameras. A successful convention will end on a note of optimism, which will be translated into active, enthusiastic support for the party and its candidates. As long as there are elements in the party that do not share in the enthusiasm, the convention has not been a total success. The greater the degree of frustration and division remaining at the close, the more the convention has failed in achieving the major goal of unification.

It has been argued by some that the ability of traditional party leaders to unify all factions behind a candidate can no longer be assumed.[41] The increased role of amateurs, combined with the growth of various caucuses and issue groupings, makes it more difficult to achieve even a facade of unity. Several recent conventions have signally failed in unifying these various elements. In 1968 and 1972, the Democratic party came out of the conven-

---

general fulfillment of platform pledges, therefore, only about 3 percent of the platform content gives the electorate a choice of policy alternatives between the parties.

[40] David, "Party Platforms."

[41] Sullivan, *Explorations in Convention Decision-Making,* p. 124.

tion in a more weakened and divided state than when it began. In 1968 those most frustrated were McCarthy supporters, who felt that the convention had been rigged by the party regulars. In 1972 those alienated were the more traditional elements of the Democratic coalition, who resented the tactics and issue-orientation of George McGovern. These groups were defined generally as labor and ethnics.[42] The platforms, instead of uniting factions, created disarray. The candidates, especially McGovern, left major elements of the party disenchanted and bitter.

Although other recent conventions have been less than total successes in this regard, most have concluded in an enthusiastic or at least cordial atmosphere. Candidates have faced the formal campaign period with the support of the party regulars and most of their party's identifiers. Even Goldwater in 1964 retained the enthusiastic support of the party actives and strong identifiers, though not of all Republican affiliates. Most conventions, especially those renominating an incumbent, are rated as successful in unification. With a popular candidate and a moderate platform, parties are almost guaranteed to enter the campaign in as strong a position as possible.

CONVENTIONS AND THE PARTY ORGANIZATION

In addition to choosing a presidential ticket, drafting a party platform, and unifying party members behind a candidate, national conventions (1) create some semblance of a national party, (2) serve as a symbol of democracy in action, and (3) provide a means of rewarding party faithful. Only during the convention is there a meaningful national party structure. Delegates selected at state level join at the convention to perform certain tasks. In an era of increased centralization and nationalization of politics, this is the only time the parties can function as national organizations. The convention serves as a necessary organizational link between the individual and autonomous state parties. For this brief moment the numerous state and local organizations become united under a common set of goals.

Many textbooks emphasize the symbolic function the conventions perform in reinforcing the concept of democracy. Surely the national conventions provide a more impressive image of democracy than the party caucus. The conventions also emphasize certain traditional values, such as patriotism and fair play (the losers are expected to be good losers). The symbol of conventions as democracy, however, has been tarnished for many years, and it is questionable whether conventions have the impact expected.

[42] Andrew M. Greeley, *Building Coalitions: American Politics in the 1970's* (New York: New Viewpoints, 1974), especially pages 354-79.

A final by-product of the convention which, more than anything else, ensures its continuance despite changes in the presidential selection process, is the reward it provides for good party work. One of the few incentives state party organizations have retained is the honor of attending the national convention. Although the delegate-selection reforms will minimize such rewards to party leaders, attending a party convention will continue to be a reward for political activity at some level. Any shift that occurs will tend to favor the nuclear or candidate-centered organizations.

THE PRESIDENTIAL NOMINATING
PROCESS: PROSPECTS FOR CHANGE

Prospects for the replacement of national conventions with another method of presidential candidate selection are dim, because of the many other tasks conventions perform. Most major proposals for nomination reform still retain a convention to perform attendant functions, including a symbolic approval of the nomination. All but the most extreme proposals for a national primary are limited to selection of delegates to the national convention. In most proposals, the multifaceted convention would remain. It serves too many interests to be eliminated.

Most of the recently accepted reforms in the presidential nominating process have been related to delegate apportionment and selection. Both parties have instituted new rules to expand the base and representativeness of the selection of convention delegates. Although conflict will continue over these changes, there appears to be general acceptance of the basic principles of such reform.[43]

Change has also been instituted in the rules and procedures of the national conventions themselves. Although limited to detail, several of these recent changes, such as the elimination of the unit rule by Democrats in 1968, have had substantial impact on the conduct of a convention by reducing the importance of state delegation leaders. The controversial midterm convention of the Democrats in late 1974 was a major departure, although its influence on party structure remains to be seen. In general, the proposed reforms and recent changes have aimed at facilitating a more open and democratic convention process, not at altering its basic structure.

[43] The most recent of the Democratic reform efforts is the result of almost two years' work of the Democratic Party Commission on Presidential Nomination and Party Structure (The Winograd Commission). Their recommendations are presented in *Openness, Participation and Party Building: Reforms for a Stronger Democratic Party* (Washington, D.C.: Democratic National Committee, 1978).

It should be evident from this chapter that the most substantial changes in the presidential nomination process have resulted not from internal party reforms, but from broader social forces. The increase in number of presidential primaries and the emphasis on candidate organizations has resulted in a massive shift of power from the party professionals to the more amorphous and transient amateur activists. Similarly, the impact of television has transformed the convention, as almost every stage is opened to public scrutiny. The combined effect of these and other social changes on presidential nominations has been to reduce further the role of party leaders in the one arena where, until recently, they were dominant.

13

The New Style
of Campaigning:
The Minimal Role
of Parties

This chapter examines campaign organization and strategy as related to party organizations. It notes the shifts in campaigning from a party-dominated to a media-oriented and professionally mediated activity. While various aspects of the "new style" of campaigning are discussed in detail in order to demonstrate the forces of change, emphasis is placed on the weakening role of political parties in campaigns, especially statewide and national. For those interested in more practically oriented books on campaign organization and activity, many recent works are available.[1]

Campaigns must be viewed in the uniquely American historical, institutional, and cultural context emphasized in this book. The conduct of American campaigns is based on the electoral system. The decentralized and federal nature of the party system naturally has led to a dispersed and fragmented campaign system. It is futile to argue whether: (1) weak parties led to candidate-centered organizations or (2) candidate-centered organizations resulted in weak parties, although most evidence favors the first hypothesis. What is important is that parties play a minimal role in most campaigns, especially at the national level. It is a most unusual situation when a candidate can depend solely on the formal party organization to run his campaign. More commonly, candidates are forced to build their own personal campaign organizations. This tendency has accelerated as campaigns have become increasingly technical. The parties simply do not have the necessary resources.

[1] For instance, Edward Schwartzman, *Campaign Craftmanship* (New York: Universe Books, 1973); Daniel M. Gaby and Merle H. Treusch, *Election Campaign Handbook* (Englewood Cliffs, N.J.: Prentice-Hall, Inc., 1976); James Brown and Philip M. Seib, *The Art of Politics* (Port Washington, N.Y.: Alfred Publishing Company, 1976); Xandra Kayden, *Campaign Organization* (Lexington, Mass.: D.C. Heath and Company, 1978).

Furthermore, even if willing to perform campaign services it is not clear whether political parties, as they are now constituted, are able to fully assist candidates in campaigns. At a time when campaigns rely increasingly on systematic vote analysis, polls, advertising, and print and broadcast media, political parties do not have all the important skills to offer the candidate.[2]

Campaign organizations in the U.S. tend to be as decentralized as all other components of American electoral politics. This both reinforces and reflects the weakness of American political parties in the electoral process.

CAMPAIGN STRATEGY

While the scope and the form of political campaigning have changed dramatically over the last five decades, the major goal has remained constant: to win the election by influencing the electorate. Candidates for office at all levels, from the local school board to the presidency, expend much energy planning their strategy to achieve this goal. Increasingly, they hire professional campaigners to develop a winning strategy for their particular campaigns. Obviously, fewer than half the candidates are successful in their quest for victory, while the remainder are not. Few candidates ignore or minimize the importance of an all-out campaign effort. Three major objectives appear to be central to campaign strategy: (1) getting the candidate's propaganda to the voters, (2) producing attitudes favorable to the candidate, and (3) getting his supporters out to vote on election day.[3] Failure in any of these might cost a candidate the election.

GET PROPAGANDA TO THE VOTERS

In order to obtain votes, it is obvious that the candidate must be known to the voters. Much effort, therefore, must be directed toward making the candidate known to the electorate. This creates difficulties for challengers, since incumbents commonly enjoy relatively high visibility and name identification vis-a-vis those on the outside. Also, due to their official positions, incumbents normally have easier access to the media and, thereby, to their

---

[2] Robert Agranoff, *The Management of Election Campaigns* (Boston: Holbrook Press, 1976), p. 17.

[3] For more details see Dan Nimmo, *The Political Persuaders: The Techniques of Modern Election Campaigns* (Englewood Cliffs, N.J.: Prentice-Hall, Inc., 1970).

constituents. In either case, all media communications are exploited by candidates in order to get their messages to the potential voters.

Whereas in the 1800s such communications might have been limited to the printed media, personal contacts, and gatherings such as the torchlight parade, at present they are a multimedia effort. Public relations experts make use of the newest electronic techniques as well as the well-tested mass mailings, personal solicitations, and direct contacts, in order to establish a candidate's name in the minds of the electorate. Although there is little evidence that the money spent on getting the message to the voters is always well-spent or that it actually alters the outcome, a candidate is unlikely to win an election without it.

PRODUCE FAVORABLE ATTITUDES

Simply becoming known to the voters and identified as a valid candidate, although necessary to a winning effort, is not in itself sufficient. Exposure to the candidate and the candidate's propaganda will do little good if the attitudes toward the candidate produced by such communications are negative. Much emphasis currently is placed on projecting a favorable image to the public (see Box 13.1). Nimmo sees a shifting of the electorate's perception of the candidates.[4] Often the shift requires stressing the style and form of campaigning rather than content. The latest mass persuasion methods are utilized to produce favorable responses to the candidates. At times such methods might include a minimization of party when its popularity is low. In most cases, a favorable image is a moderate or centrist one.

GET SUPPORTERS OUT TO VOTE

The first two objectives of campaigning, though crucial, are meaningless unless the third goal is achieved. A successful candidate must be able to motivate supporters to vote on election day. Favorable attitudes and good intentions alone are of little help to a candidate. Therefore, it is important to use all resources to stimulate supporters to vote.

There is much evidence to suggest that the major effect of campaigns on the electorate is to alter the intensity of voter attitudes without changing their direction. Most commonly, this takes the form of (1) *reinforcement* of

---

[4]*Ibid.*, pp. 179-93. For an examination of the role of images in political campaigns, see Dan Nimmo and Robert L. Savage, *Candidates and Their Images: Concepts, Methods, and Findings* (Pacific Palisades, Calif.: Goodyear Publishing Company, 1976).

BOX 13.1 SELLING 'EM JIMMY
AND JERRY

The TV commercial's sprightly jingle accompanies handsome footage of people working, playing, relaxing and flashing warm all-American smiles. Coca-Cola? McDonald's? Nope. The next face on the screen belongs to a nice, reliable, fatherly type who looks very much like—in fact, who is Gerald R. Ford. No name is mentioned; there is no appeal for votes. "Peace with freedom," intones an announcer as the minute draws to a close. "Is there anything more important than that?"

Not really. But to Gerald Ford, Jimmy Carter and many other candidates, winning elections seems to come in a close second, and hiring the right advertising agency is considered one sure way of getting more votes. Indeed, results of campaign commercials have been mixed, but political accounts are a significant part of the advertising business—more for the prestige than the billings they bring. Yet for the industry the billings are nothing to sneeze at; the Ford and Carter campaigns have advertising budgets that total at least $18.5 million (about $10 million of that for Ford). Perhaps in an effort to keep their small-town, mainstream images unsullied, both candidates have avoided the sophisticated agencies of Madison Avenue. Carter's ad man is Atlanta-based Gerald Rafshoon, while the Ford campaign is being handled by Bostonian Malcolm Mac-Dougall . . . .

MacDougall was recruited by a fellow Harvardman, Washington Campaign Consultant John Deardourff. With his partner Douglas Bailey, Deardourff is co-chairman of Campaign '76, the advertising arm of the President Ford Committee. The three men, closeted in a Kansas City hotel during the Republican Convention, drafted a thick tome they called simply The Plan. Its broad strategic aim: to focus attention on Ford's openness and his healing effect on the country, rather than on details of his positions on the issues . . . .

MacDougall is delighted that Ford chose Robert Dole. Reason: Ford-Dole neatly fits most designs. Says MacDougall: "If Ruckelshaus had been the nominee, we would have been dead—in terms of design."

Getting Jimmy Carter elected is the grand design of Gerald Rafshoon, 42, the New York-born head of the Atlanta shop bearing his name. A University of Texas graduate, he cut his teeth doing publicity for 20th Century-Fox and founded his own shoestring

380

those already predisposed toward voting for the candidate or (2) *activation* of those leaning toward the candidate but unlikely to vote without stimulation received during the campaign. In both cases, the emphasis is on strengthening the intensity of the individual's initial choice. Prior to the advent of TV, Lazarsfeld and associates found that 53 percent of the citizens were reinforced by campaigns and 14 percent stimulated to vote. The campaign had no effect on 22 percent of the citizens.[5]

While most of the emphasis in campaigns appears to be on arousing interest in the candidate in an attempt to maintain initial support and motivate supporters to vote, the *conversion* effect of most campaigns is severely limited. It is most unusual for a person to switch during the campaign from active support of one candidate to a vote for the opposing candidate. Obviously, the weaker an individual's preconceptions prior to the campaign, the more "convertible" he is.[6] Also, some independents might "shop around" for the most attractive candidate, or the candidate most appealing on the issues. Lazarsfeld estimated that less than 10 percent are converted during the campaign period.[7]

One of the primary reasons for the emphasis of campaigns on reinforcement and activation rather than conversion is the large proportion of voters who make their voting decision early. Table 13.1 illustrates this. Consistently, over the last three decades, approximately 60-65 percent of the voters have made their decision prior to the start of the general election campaign. Accordingly, about one third of the voters make their decision during the campaign. These provide a target group for those interested in converting voters.

[5] Paul F. Lazarsfeld, Bernard Berelson, and Hazel Gaudit, *The Peoples' Choice* (New York: Duell, Sloan and Pearce, 1944), p. 103.

[6] Agranoff, *Management of Election Campaigns*, p. 75.

[7] Lazarsfeld, *The Peoples' Choice*, p. 103.

Table 13.1   Timing of Vote Decision in Presidential Elections, 1948-1972

	1948	1952	1956	1960	1964	1968	1972	Mean
Decided								
before conventions	37%	34%	57%	30%	40%	33%	43%	39.1%
during conventions	28	31	18	30	25	22	17	24.4
during campaign	25	31	21	36	33	38	35	31.3
don't remember	10	4	4	4	3	7	4	5.1
(N)	424	1251	1285	1445	1126	1039	1119	

SOURCE: William Flanigan, *Political Behavior of the American Electorate*, 3rd ed. (Boston: Allyn and Bacon, 1975), p. 158. All data made available from Michigan Survey Research Center.

Stephen Shaddeg divides the electorate into the committed, the undecided, and the indifferent, depending on the timing of their final decision.[8] According to this theory, the committed must be reinforced, the indifferent must be activated, and the undecided must be converted. Even a highly efficient campaign will be limited largely to strengthening the committed and stimulating the indifferent.

PHASES OF CAMPAIGNS

Although campaigns can be parceled into many stages, a most appropriate distinction is made among three phases: organizing, adapting, and closing.[9] While all three overlap and are mutually dependent, effort at various times before and during the campaign must be directed toward specific goals. The *organizing* phase begins prior to the decision to enter the race and centers on the creation of the campaign organization and establishment of the overall campaign strategy. The *adapting* phase involves alteration of the original strategy during the campaign in order to meet changing situations, while the *closing* stage relates to the final thrust designed to close the campaign at the peak of support. Failure to adjust one's strategy throughout the campaign can be disastrous to an otherwise well-planned operation. Depletion of resources prior to the closing stage, in the final weeks of the campaign, can be equally calamitous.

[8] Stephen C. Shaddeg, *The New How to Win an Election* (New York: Taplinger, 1972) pp. 120-21.

[9] Nimmo, *The Political Persuaders*, p. 18.

ASSESSING ONE'S RESOURCES

Although the goal is seldom fully achieved, it is helpful if, before entering the campaign for office, a potential candidate carefully appraises available resources as well as the context of the particular election contest. As seen in Chapter 11, the resources necessary will vary substantially with the opportunity structure and expectations unique to each office. Certainly, a person contemplating entrance into a local contest must evaluate his resources differently than a candidate for Congress. In no case can one's resources or lack of resources be ignored. David Leuthold contends that "from the standpoint of the candidates, an election campaign can be considered as the process of acquiring and using the political resources that can secure votes."[10] While some resources are readily available and easily controlled by a campaigner, others are more elusive and difficult to control.

Although monetary resources are the most visible assets required, many other considerations must be assessed. Money in itself does not ensure a successful candidacy, although all candidates must be able to raise funds sufficient for the contest at hand. Personal skills and knowledge of the candidate must also be appraised, as well as his/her personal background, including the length of his/her residency in the district. His/her public record and experience may be an asset or a liability, as may his/her relationship with the press. As the electronic medium becomes more central in campaigns, personal attractiveness and speaking ability may become more crucial than in the past. Any and all of these personal factors may become a campaign liability. Therefore, their potential impact must be evaluated at this early organizational stage.

Other assets to be analyzed include the amount of group support which might be mobilized during the campaign. Lewis Froman contends that candidates for all offices must depend to some extent on an already committed pool of voters.[11] A lack of such organizational support is a significant liability. In those rare instances where party organizations are active, party support will be crucial. The lack of active party support in such instances must be considered in the early planning stages. One study demonstrated that 64 percent of the candidates who lost in marginal congressional districts cited the lack of local party support as a major factor in their defeats.[12] Most candi-

---

[10] David A. Leuthold, *Electioneering in a Democracy* (New York: John Wiley and Sons, 1968), p. 1.

[11] Lewis A. Froman, Jr. "A Realistic Approach to Campaign Strategies and Tactics," in *The Electoral Process*, eds. M. Kent Jennings and Harmon Zeigler. (Englewood Cliffs, N.J.: Prentice-Hall, Inc., 1966), pp. 4-5.

[12] Robert J. Huckshorn and Robert C. Spencer, *The Politics of Defeat* (Amherst: University of Massachusetts Press, 1971), pp. 150-51.

dates discover very early that the party organization is ineffective, and establish their own personal organization. Failure to make an early appraisal of party support, and overdependence on the party organization, may result in a disastrous misinterpretation of the available resources.

In addition to weighing his personal assets and liabilities, a candidate must also appraise the situational factors unique to each contest. How many candidates are running, what is the party balance in the district, and how strong is the opposition? These are obvious questions that each potential candidate must consider. Also, the expectations of the electorate are critical factors which cannot be controlled, although one might be able to adjust campaign strategy to minimize discrepancies.

Perhaps the most important contextual factor for most offices is the presence or absence of an incumbent in the contest. As seen earlier, incumbency is most commonly an advantage, but not always.

> Perhaps the major advantage the challenger possesses is his ability to criticize politics freely and sometimes in exaggerated terms, whereas the incumbent is often restrained by his current official responsibilities from talking too much about them.[13]

In addition to more familiar names and greater newsworthiness, incumbents generally have many perquisites which, if used effectively, can be quite important. Finally, incumbents often have an ongoing organization which has proven itself in at least one prior test. Such an organization offers the candidate an important psychological as well as material advantage. The decision to challenge an incumbent under normal circumstances requires a greater commitment than entering a race with no incumbent running.

ESTABLISHING THE ORGANIZATION

Once the resources and situational factors have been appraised and the decision has been made to enter the campaign, an organization must be established. While the form and extent of campaign organizations vary by office and locale, most organizations designate key campaign officers, including at least a campaign manager and a treasurer. Communication lines among the candidate, the campaign officials, and the workers must be established without delay. Many campaign efforts have been dashed by a failure of the many participants to coordinate their efforts. Unfortunately, most campaigns suffer from lack of planning, organization, and sound information (see Box 13.2).

---

[13] Nelson W. Polsby and Aaron Wildavsky, *Presidential Elections*, 4th ed. (New York: Charles Scribner's Sons, 1976), p. 165.

BOX 13.2　CAMPAIGN PLANNING

To those who follow politics and campaigns, one of the most striking phenomena is that in a society priding itself on efficient management of enterprises, most American campaigns are poorly run. They lack managerial experience and ability, with low levels of reason or little application of a body of knowledge. Candidates and campaigners rush into their campaigns, trying to duplicate activities they have observed, without the slightest knowledge of why or how it should be done. One political consultant calls this the "why don't we" mode of planning. If victory is achieved it is assumed that those activities contributed to victory.

Campaigns very often are so void of reasonable planning, management, and coordination that they would have to be ranked below family financial management in efficiency. That is, the average family probably does a better job of managing its financial affairs than the average campaign manager does managing a campaign. When the family embarks on a major financial undertaking—going into a small business, the purchase of stocks or insurance, the purchase of real estate, or the purchase of a major appliance—one tries to avoid impulse buying by consulting consumer information and considering alternatives. For example, think of the questions buyers must consider when purchasing a home. (Can we afford it? How much are the mortgage payments? What will these payments do to our budget? Is the title clear? How much insurance will we need? How much will the insurance cost? What are the hidden costs beyond the purchase price? How much additional money will we have to spend for improvements? What are our financing options? How much interest will we be paying? How much are the property taxes? Will this be offset by tax deduction?) In other words, the purchasers chart a path by bringing premises into a "field" that blends information assessment, resource assessment, and alternatives into a plan. Campaigns are generally devoid of such activities; they are too frequently characterized by "impulse buying."

SOURCE: Robert Agranoff, *The Management of Election Campaigns*, (Boston: Holbrook Press, 1976), pp. 12-13.

Early in the organizing phase, much planning must also be directed toward issues to be emphasized or deemphasized. If possible, public opinion polls should be conducted to discover what the public wants and what issues they perceive as most important. Preliminary decisions must also be made as to where and when resources should be expended. Responsibilities of each person involved in the campaign must be clarified before the inevitable frictions develop among the various officials. Campaign slogans and the theme of the campaign should be carefully planned before they are used. Pretesting the theme among selected groups is a necessary precaution and might save future embarrassment. Basically, then, the organizing stage results in a well-planned, comprehensive campaign strategy as well as a solid organizational framework. Everyone clearly understands his/her own duties and knows the overall objectives and direction of the campaign. While this scenario is most unusual, it is attainable.

Increasingly, candidates have turned to professional campaign managers or campaign management firms to coordinate and implement their campaigns. The campaign manager, whether a professional or volunteer, relieves the candidate of time-consuming routine campaign details and is generally responsible for the overall conduct of campaign strategy.

> When I first got here, Milt Shapp was running around worrying about the size of lettering on bumper stickers and getting typewriter ribbons for secretaries. I had the job of convincing him to forget that stuff because I'd been hired to do it.[14]

The need for professionals has arisen out of the increased specialization of campaigning, the need for technical experts, and the self-actualizing perception of the need for professionals. Candidates afraid of falling behind their opponents in professional staffing are bound to hire professionals themselves, and this pattern continues indefinitely.[15] One can either hire a full-service firm to handle the entire campaign or rely on consultants trained in specific tasks such as polling, campaign research, publicity, direct mail solicitation, documentaries, advertising, and speech training. Add to these the more traditional campaign staff positions such as press secretary, advance man, speech writer, and finance chairman, and the campaign structure takes on a very complex appearance. It is not surprising that coordination of such

[14] Joseph Napolitan commenting on his involvement in Milton Shapp's Campaign for governor, quoted in *Wall Street Journal*, September 15, 1966, p. 1.

[15] Huckshorn and Spencer, *Politics of Defeat*, p. 95, found that over 90 percent of the losing congressional candidates they studied had nonprofessional managers.

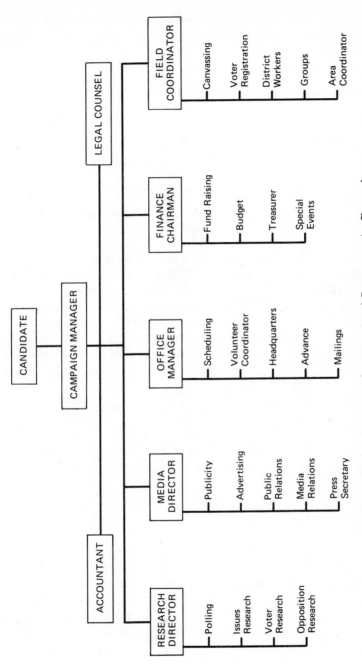

Figure 13.1 Campaign Organizational Structure: An Example

organizations frequently disintegrates and factions develop. It also seems understandable that candidates sometimes may become slaves to their own organizational structure.

ADAPTING TO CHANGING SITUATIONS

Once the organization has been established and the strategy devised, candidates must constantly be aware of events and circumstances which require a modification of their original plans.

> The contents of election campaigns appear to be largely opportunistic. The swiftly changing nature of events makes it unwise for candidates to lay down all-embracing rules for campaigning which cannot meet special situations as they arise.[16]

Therefore, as the campaign progresses the candidates take soundings and attempt to modify their tactics to take fullest advantage of opportunities as they arise. A drop in the economic indicators or a social upheaval might necessitate a shift in strategy. The complexion of campaigns can change dramatically in response to changing conditions. Gerald Ford's contention that Eastern Europe was not under Russian domination, and Jimmy Carter's *Playboy* interview immediately put each candidate on the defensive, and shifted what momentum there was in an otherwise unexciting campaign to the other candidate.

In many campaigns, with crucial issues lacking, there is an effort to manufacture drama for the campaign. Dan Nimmo suggests that "psuedo-events" are often contrived to appear spontaneous.[17] While this is certainly not a new tactic (all political rallys and events are contrived to some extent), the dependence on electronic media has extended the possibilities for producing the desired effect.

CLOSING STAGE OF CAMPAIGN

In addition to adjusting to changing conditions throughout the campaign, candidates must plan carefully the closing phase of their many months of campaigning. In close elections, especially, the last week of the campaign may make the difference between victory and defeat. If resources are exhausted prior to the closing phase, the candidate might lose by default. Therefore, most campaign managers plan for an all-out effort during the last days preceding the election. They hope the momentum built during this

---

[16] Polsby and Wildavsky, *Presidential Elections*, p. 164.
[17] Nimmo, *The Political Persuaders*, pp. 26-27.

Table 13.2 Network Spending by Nixon
and Humphrey, 1968

Dates	Nixon	Humphrey
July 30-Aug 12	65,000	45,000
Aug 13-Aug 26	410,000	276,000
Aug 27-Sep 9	165,000	000
Sep 10-Sep 23	360,000	000
Sep 24-Oct 7	535,000	380,000
Oct 8-Oct 21	910,000	570,000
Oct 22-Nov 4	1,540,000	1,625,000

SOURCE: Extracted from Figure 5 of *Voters' Time*, Report of
the 20th Century Fund Commission on Campaigning Costs In ·
the Electronic Era. Copyright © 1969 by the Twentieth Century
Fund, Inc., New York.

concentrated period is enough to ensure that their candidate is at peak
strength on election day.

In order to accomplish this objective, campaign resources, including
the energies of the candidate, are "paced" so that the candidate does not
"peak" too early.[18] Timing is especially crucial during these last critical days.
Attempts are made to maximize media exposure by reserving blocs of media
time well in advance. The electorate is saturated immediately prior to the
election with the last-minute appeals of candidates for support. Table 13.2
illustrates the last-minute increase in network spending by Nixon and
Humphrey in 1968. Efforts also are made to increase personal contacts
through door-to-door canvassing by volunteers. Similarly, telephone calls are
made to those earlier identified as supporters or leaners. They are urged to
turn out and vote for the candidate, and are offered transportation to the
polls or other election day services. Since most candidates, no matter how
large their presumed lead, fear a last-minute loss, the closing phase of the
campaign usually results in the pulling out of all stops. Few candidates are
willing to sit on their lead or admit defeat during this critical period of the
campaign.

PROFESSIONAL CAMPAIGN MANAGEMENT:
THE NEW STYLE

As party organizers have yielded to professional managers, the professional
campaign managers have come to play a major policy-making role. No longer
are they limited to an occasional consultant status. "The key decision makers

[18] *Ibid.*, pp. 29-30.

in most contemporary major-office campaigns are no longer party chieftains but political consultants."[19] It is estimated that in 1972 there were approximately 100 public relations firms that offered full management services and about 200 other companies offering specialized campaign services.[20] While some firms offer their wares to Republican or Democrat candidates only, many sell their services to any candidate of any party or ideological persuasion who has sufficient funds.

THE POLITICAL CONSULTANT

As political consultants have become more visible, the use of such consultants by candidates at all levels has increased rapidly. For instance, in 1970, of 67 Senatorial candidates with some opposition, all but five used professional consultants of some type. Sixty-two employed advertising firms, 30 hired media consultants, and 24 utilized national polling firms.[21] Many others employed the services of state polling organizations. While the large majority of congressional and gubernatorial candidates already utilize professional campaign managers, an increasing proportion of those running for lower-level offices are also entering the new style of campaigning. Robert Agranoff estimates that by the end of the 1970s virtually all candidates for statewide or national office will employ the services of professional political consultants.[22]

One result of this alteration in campaigning is an increased dependence on specialists. (See Box 13.3 for a defense of the political consultants.) Whereas the old-style campaigns were based on permanent party organizations that transcended single elections and depended on the long-term loyalties of party workers, the professionally mediated campaigns are organized on an ad hoc basis, predominantly with the short-term goal of victory in a

[19] Robert Agranoff, ed., *The New Style in Election Campaigns*, 2nd ed. (Boston: Holbrook Press, Inc., 1976), p. 49. For a discussion of how public relations techniques were first applied to political campaigns, see Stanley Kelly, Jr., *Professional Public Relations and Political Power* (Baltimore: Johns Hopkins Press, 1956). Also see Louis Maisel, ed., *Changing Campaign Techniques* (Beverly Hills, Cal.: Sage Publications, Inc., 1976), which has several interesting articles on various aspects about campaigns.

[20] David L. Rosenbloom, *The Election Men* (New York: Quadrangle Books, 1973), p. 50. For a comprehensive listing of campaign management firms and political consultants see David L. Rosenbloom, *The Political Marketplace* (New York: Quadrangle Books, 1972), especially pp. 807-948.

[21] See "Professional Managers, Consultants Play Major Roles in 1970 Political Races," *National Journal* 2 (September 26, 1970), 2084-85.

[22] Agranoff, *New Style in Election Campaigns*, p. 50.

specific election.[23] While the politician of past campaigns relied on personal power and the application of patronage and other preferments to motivate volunteers, the management firms rely on paid staff members hired to perform specific functions. Obviously, this has contributed significantly to the rapid increase in campaign costs.[24]

SPECIALIZED DATA COLLECTION AND ANALYSIS

A by-product of this shift away from party involvement in campaigns has been the substitution of sophisticated means of collecting information to replace the intuition and personal knowledge of local party leaders. Information specialists have brought with them the latest in technical developments of data collection and analysis. Voting profiles of specific political units are created and fed into computers, and campaign efforts are directed at those areas with the highest potential. Public opinion polls are conducted frequently to ascertain the attitudes of specially selected "target" audiences and campaign appeals are adjusted accordingly.[25] Computer-printed letters are sent to lists of voters in predetermined categories. Armed with past voting records, data on key issues, demographic characteristics of the electorate, and numerous statistical indices, the processional specialists map out campaign strategy.[26] A major difference of contemporary from past campaigns, according to Agranoff, "is a greater emphasis on systematically examining a range of factors affecting the setting on a more comprehensive basis."[27]

USE OF PUBLIC OPINION POLLS

Of all the information specialists employed in campaigns, none has become as influential as the pollster. While most candidates utilize polls to estimate their relative standing within the electorate, DeVries and Tarrance use polls to

[23] For discussion of related distinctions, see Robert J. Pitchell, "The Influence of Professional Campaign Management Firms in Partisan Elections in California," *Western Political Quarterly*, 11 (June, 1958).

[24] See Agranoff, *New Style in Election Campaigns*, pp. 28-35. Also, see Chapter 14 this book.

[25] See Gaby and Treusch, *Election Campaign Handbook*, Chapter 4 for a discussion of targeting the voters.

[26] For an in-depth analysis of this, see Agranoff, *Management of Election Campaigns*, especially Chapters 4 and 5.

[27] Agranoff, *New Style in Election Campaigns*, p. 37.

BOX 13.3   THE POLITICAL CONSULTANT

I am a political consultant. My business is helping elect candidates to high public office. I don't see anything particularly sinister about that, but some people do.

It's always been difficult for me to understand why the press and other observers, inside and outside of this country, believe that people like me pose a threat to our political system.

Politics is big business in this country—and in most countries that have free elections. In the United States the major parties spend anywhere from ten to twenty million dollars every four years, trying to elect a President. In the larger states it costs a million or more to run a respectable campaign for governor or United States senator or mayor of a large city, and I'm not even considering here the extraordinary expenditures of a Nelson Rockefeller.

If someone were going to erect a building that cost a million dollars, he'd undoubtedly hire an architect to help him design the building, or at least a skilled contractor to build it. State and local regulations wouldn't even allow him to proceed unless the blueprints were prepared by a competent engineer . . . .

Even if you were moving from one house to another you'd probably want an experienced mover to do the job, rather than two husky fellows with a pickup truck.

Why, then, is it so unusual for a political candidate who is spending several hundred thousand dollars, or a million or more, to want to hire the best talents available to help him achieve that office? Damned if I know. But there is reluctance, even resentment, about this emerging business . . . .

Questions often are raised concerning the ethics of political consultants. I can't speak for everyone, but the people I know in this business have high ethical standards—higher than those of most businessmen, doctors, or academicians. If they are going to continue in business, they have to.

If we were to work on just one campaign for just one candidate and felt very strongly about it, we might be more tempted to pull out all the stops and win at any cost. But when you know that you've got to come back the next year, and the years after that, you know that you must survive on your reputation, and if the reputation stinks you're not likely to get clients, or at least the kind of clients you want.

I happen to be a Democrat. In the United States I work only

for Democratic candidates I like, and the last part of that description is as important as the first part. Life is too short to work for candidates whom you don't like, or with those whose political philosophies you strongly disagree. This isn't to say that other consultants may not strike a rapport with candidates whom they have no feeling for and do a superb job for them, but I can't work that way.

SOURCE: Excerpt from *The Election Game: And How to Win It,* by Joseph Napolitan. Copyright ©1972 by Joseph Napolitan. Used by permission of Doubleday and Company, Inc.

monitor shifts in opinions on issues throughout the campaign period.[28] They recommend the continuous use of extremely localized polls in target precincts to identify the concerns of potential ticket splitters. These almost daily measurements are computerized, and overnight analysis is conducted. While the use of such a concentrated polling technique is still uncommon, the employment of professional (and sometimes not so professional) polling experts is widespread. It is almost universal among senators and governors and prevails among over half of the congressional candidates.[29] Recent presidential candidates have employed up to six pollsters simultaneously.[30]

This demand has rapidly expanded the number of polling firms since the early 1960s, when only a handful of pollsters were active. It is estimated that there are now over 200 polling firms operating in the U.S., ranging in scope from multiclient firms such as the Opinion Research Corporation and Oliver A. Quale and Company, to one-man operations in some areas.[31] In addition, some candidates rely on polling operations organized specifically for them, occasionally headed by political scientists.

In addition to providing polling services, some private pollsters have become "highly valued members of the campaign team—an advisor, a chief strategist, and sometimes a defacto campaign manager."[32] Patrick Caddell,

[28] Walter De Vries and Lance Tarrance, Jr., *The Ticket-Splitter* (Grand Rapids, Mich.: William B. Eerdmans Publishing Company, 1972), pp. 116-17.

[29] Robert King and Martin Schnitzer, "Contemporary Use of Private Polling," *Public Opinion Quarterly*, 32 (Fall, 1968), 433-35.

[30] Agranoff, *New Style in Election Campaigns*, p. 147.

[31] Andrew J. Glass, "Pollsters Prowl Nation as Candidates Use Opinion Surveys to Plan '72 Campaign," *National Journal*, 3 (August 14, 1971), 1693-1705.

[32] Agranoff, *New Style in Election Campaigns*, p. 145.

who also served as McGovern's pollster in the 1972 fiasco, had much influence on campaign strategy as Jimmy Carter's major pollster in 1976. After the election, he continued to advise Carter, not only on public attitudes, but also on political questions and on means of strengthening public support while in office. Hubert Humphrey and Nelson Rockefeller, among others, depended heavily on private polls throughout their various attempts to achieve the presidency. Some candidates have been dissuaded from running on the basis of the results of private polls:

> George Romney withdrew from his 1968 Presidential bid before a single primary vote was cast because his pollster, Fred Currier, reported to him on the eve of the New Hampshire primary that he could expect no more than 10 or 12 percent of the vote.[33]

Although much has been written about the influence of publicly released polls on voting, there is little substantial evidence that poll results consistently and substantially give an advantage to the leader or the underdog. The *bandwagon theory* suggests that the candidate leading in the polls will gain support of those interested in voting for a winner; that is, they will "jump on the bandwagon." However, many examples, such as Harry Truman's comeback from far behind in the polls in 1948, and Hubert Humphrey's near-victory in 1968 despite being 15 percentage points behind early in the campaign, refute this theory. While poll results certainly have some influence on voting, "mere poll results are insufficient to impel would-be bandwagon or underdog identifiers to switch their votes."[34] It is more likely that a wide gap in the polls between the candidates might lead to voter apathy and reduce turnout. The leading candidate's supporters become overconfident and abstain from voting, while the less interested supporters of the lagging candidate write the election off as a lost cause. Both Nixon and McGovern were concerned about this problem during the last several weeks of the 1972 campaign.[35]

Poll results do seem to have a direct influence on the acquisition of key campaign resources, especially money and workers. A candidate far behind in the polls, like George McGovern in 1972, has a difficult time raising large contributions and maintaining worker morale. Not surprisingly,

---

[33] *Ibid.* From Stephen C. Shaddeg, *Winning's A Lot More Fun* (New York: Macmillan and Company, 1969), p. 132.

[34] Daniel W. Fleitas, "Bandwagon and Underdog Effects in Minimal Information Elections," *American Political Science Review*, 65 (June, 1971), 434-38.

[35] Robert H. Blank, "Published Opinion Polls and the Conduct of the 1972 Presidential Campaign," paper delivered at Western Political Science Association Meeting, San Diego, April 7, 1973.

candidates at times "leak" polls that are favorable, in an effort to reinforce and activate convention delegates and voters.[36] Despite contentions to the contrary, campaign strategy is influenced by private as well as public polls, and candidates are aware of poll results.[37] While there is no evidence that polls themselves have directly affected the results of an election, they are a major factor in the new style of campaign. More than any other technical innovation, due to their visibility and saliency to the candidates, polls are central to most campaign efforts.

DEPENDENCE ON MASS MEDIA

The demise of the old-style politicians has also increased dependence on the mass media. No longer is personal contact and the distribution of political favors enough to provide blocs of party volunteers to do the leaders' bidding. Increasingly, emphasis is on the electronic media, especially television. Although the expenditure of $120,000 by Calvin Coolidge in 1924 for radio time was a significant departure from past campaigning practices, it pales by comparison with recent expenditures on radio and TV.[38] Expenditures for electronic media for all candidates in 1972 were estimated to be approximately $60 million, with George McGovern alone spending $9.6 million. Before media spending limits were imposed on presidential candidates, spending on media was even higher. For instance, in 1968 Richard Nixon put $12 million into radio and television. With the shift in emphasis to the mass media, the party organization has lost its advantage in the campaign communications process. Candidates now appeal directly to the voters, without the parties as intermediaries. This has resulted in devising campaign strategy that conforms to the demands of the electronic media.

It is understandable that the professional campaigners would turn to TV as the central aspect of disseminating information and selling the candidate.[39] Most homes in the U.S. are equipped with one or more television sets, which are used on an average of over five hours per day. In addition,

---

[36] Leo Bogart, *Silent Politics: Polls and the Awareness of Public Opinion* (New York: John Wiley and Sons, 1972), pp. 25-41.

[37] See Blank, "Published Opinion Polls."

[38] According to Richard L. Worsnop, "Television and Politics," *Editorial Research Reports*, 54 (May 15, 1968), 369, Coolidge spent this money for a series of radio addresses over 500 stations across the country.

[39] See Joe McGinniss, *The Selling of the President 1968* (New York: Trident Press, 1969); Sig Mickelson, *The Electric Mirror: Politics in an Age of Television* (New York: Dodd, Mead and Company, 1972); and Theodore White *The Making of the President* (1960, 1964, 1968, 1972), (New York: Atheneum Publishers), for discussions of the dominance of the mass media in current campaigns.

research indicates that television is the most important source of campaign information in national elections, at least. While 50 to 60 percent of the electorate depend primarily on TV, only about one fifth depend on the newspapers.[40] The most efficient and practical way of contacting large electorates is through electronic media. While many local campaigns cannot effectively be conducted through normal TV channels, cable television (CATV) offers potential for more flexible and less expensive coverage of concentrated or limited electorates. The radio also provides a crucial supplementary medium for the new campaigners.

The increased organization of campaigns around the electronic media has produced substantial alterations in the overall campaign process, according to Robert Agranoff.[41] Obviously, the high salience and use of the broadcast media has attracted larger numbers of people, especially the more passive and uninterested who find it difficult to follow campaigns in newspapers and magazines. Also, all voters are exposed to opposition candidates to a greater degree than ever before. Because of the use of repetition and spot commercials, it is difficult to escape completely the messages of the opposition. While the influence of the electronic media should not be overemphasized, it has become more difficult to selectively tune out certain candidates' appeals. In addition, TV has shifted emphasis to the personal image of the candidate as projected on the screen. Greater emphasis is placed on the "production and merchandising of talent," with a corresponding deemphasis on substantive political issues.

Certainly, the presence of the electronic media has dramatized the campaign to an extent not possible in the printed media. The immediate presence of the TV viewer at the various campaign stops has produced a carnival-like atmosphere. Media events, designed to provide specific viewer reactions, can be staged for maximum impact. This has given the media a major influence in setting the agenda of a campaign, scheduling candidate appearances, and allocating resources. The candidate has become, in effect, a superstar who performs on the road for the television audience, or at least networks. A successful candidate is one who is able to adjust to the new demands.

IMAGE MAKING

The image of the candidate has become central to presidential campaigns, but is also very important for other national and state offices. Large amounts of time and resources are spent in an attempt to project the image of the candi-

---

[40] This is a consistent finding by the Survey Research Center, University of Michigan, 1960-1974 Election Studies. Made available through the Inter-University Consortium Political and Social Research.

[41] Agranoff, *New Style in Election Campaigns*, pp. 261-64.

date to the electorate. Negative aspects of the candidate are minimized, while the positive attributes are emphasized. The camera angle, timing, and symbolic effects of setting, clothes, hairstyle, and so forth, have become integral aspects of modern or "new style" campaigns. Personal characteristics are crucial to the election of a candidate, but the public never knows whether it is viewing the genuine article or a packaged image, predesigned to ensure maximum voter acceptance. In 1960, for instance, Kennedy restyled his hair to look older while Nixon thinned his eyebrows to look less threatening.[42] Was the new Nixon in 1968 actually a new person or simply a new package, was the famous Carter smile of 1976 genuine or not, was Gerald Ford really able to overcome his earlier tendency to stumble? These may not have been the most important aspects of each campaign, but they certainly had much to do with the images of these three candidates in the eyes of the electorate.

The candidate need not be experienced, or even well versed in politics, to elicit enthusiasm from the viewing electorate. Unknowns can be and have been thrust into prominence in short periods of time through the electronic media. Certainly, Jimmy Carter, George McGovern, and Barry Goldwater had television to thank for their rise to national recognition as genuine candidates. No longer is it necessary to work through the party for many years through lower-level offices. It is now possible, with adequate resources, to use the media to bypass these intermediate stages.

PRESIDENTIAL DEBATES

The prevalence of the electronic media has produced, among other things, the advent of the televised debate as a factor in presidential campaigns. The Kennedy-Nixon debates of 1960 "contributed a new avenue for image exposure."[43] National surveys indicated that about 65 percent of American adults saw the first debate and only slightly fewer watched the remaining two.[44] Over 85 million potential voters were exposed to both candidates through the debates. Although the debates added little to the rational discussion of issues, it has been estimated that they provided Kennedy with a net gain of approximately 5 percent by producing the image of a viable and mature candidate.[45]

Due in part to the potential advantage gained by the lesser-known

---

[42] Polsby and Wildavsky, *Presidential Elections*, p. 175.

[43] Nimmo, *The Political Persuaders*, p. 159.

[44] Delmer D. Dunn, *Financing Presidential Campaigns* (Washington, D.C.: The Brookings Institution, 1972), p. 95.

[45] Paul J. Deutschmann, "Viewing, Conversation, and Voting Intentions," in *The Great Debates*, ed. Sidney Kraus (Gloucester, Mass: Peter Smith, 1968), p. 247.

candidate, no debates were held at the presidential level again until 1976, when the incumbent, Gerald Ford, far behind in the public opinion polls, challenged Jimmy Carter to a debate. After settlement of legal and logistical problems, three nationally televised debates were sponsored by the League of Women Voters. According to the Institute for Social Research, 83 percent of the electorate viewed at least one of the debates.[46] In addition, the debates become a major media event in their own right and dominated campaign attention. While there is little solid evidence that the debates, in themselves, influenced the outcome of the election, they were an integral part of the 1976 presidential campaign. Most observers agree that in a close election, events such as debates might swing the victory toward one candidate.[47]

What does the future hold for presidential debates? Some advocates favor passing a law requiring debates so as to "remove the decisions from politics and make it a permanent part of presidential campaign dialogue."[48] Conversely, opponents such as Sander Vanocur suggest future debates be banned by Congress.

> Failing that . . . lovers of the American political system should take the issue to the courts in an effort to forever proscribe two consenting candidates from committing unnatural acts in public.
>
> The televised confrontations are unnatural because they are replacing the political process of electing a President. They have become the campaign itself.[49]

While neither of these possibilities seems desirable, the Federal Election Commission proposed new regulations that would ease financing of the debates by permitting nonprofit organizations with a history of nonpartisan activity to accept contributions from corporations or unions to help defray the expense of sponsoring debates.[50] Televised debates are a part of presidential campaigning, at least, and must be considered as part of a candidate's overall strategy.

---

[46] "Debates Increased Awareness," Institute for Social Research *Newsletter*, 6, 1978.

[47] See Donald T. Cundy and John J. Havick, "Impact of the 1976 Presidential Debates: A Preliminary Analysis," paper delivered at Western Political Science Association Meeting, Los Angeles, March 17, 1978, for more discussion of the 1976 debates.

[48] *Guide to American Politics,* (Washington, D.C.: Congressional Quarterly Service, Spring, 1977), p. 23.

[49] *Ibid.,* pp. 22-23.

[50] *Congressional Quarterly Weekly Report,* (December 17, 1977), p. 2616.

FROM PARTIES TO CANDIDATES

The shift to professional management of campaigns, with its attendant emphasis on political specialists, polling, and the mass media, has further weakened the party organizations. The new techniques largely depend on individualistic appeals, further eroding already sagging party loyalty. According to Agranoff, "Candidates seem disinclined to sell party, as well as themselves, through the new channels."[51] Parties, as such, are emphasized only when to do so serves the needs of the candidates. Current campaign strategy generally dictates the inclusion of party appeals simply as one means of solidifying support for the candidate.

The complete separation of candidate organization and formal party organization is exemplified in Richard Nixon's successful reelection attempt in 1972.[52] The Committee to Re-Elect the President (CRP) was deliberately designed to bypass the Republican National Committee. Entirely independent of the Republican party, CRP supported a headquarters staff of 355 fulltime employees, plus over 300 regular volunteers. In addition, the White House Staff members and regional and state directors of the Finance Committee for the Re-Election of the President further differentiated the Nixon organization from the Republican party committees. Nixon's appeal to many conservative Democrats disenchanted with McGovern (Democrats for Nixon) underscored the personal nature of his campaign effort. In addition, the fundraising tactics of CRP drained much traditional Republican support from other Republican candidates and weakened their positions considerably. It is important to note that while this case represents an extreme, many statewide and national campaigns are similarly individual-oriented, thereby virtually eliminating a meaningful role for the party organization.

FACTORS LIMITING THE DIRECT EFFECTS
OF MASS MEDIA

Even with all the emphasis on mass persuasion techniques in American campaigns, it would be wrong to conclude that the techniques are highly successful in achieving their goals. Actually, there are many factors working to constrain or limit media influence. As seen in Chapter 9, all individuals are predisposed to accept messages that are psychologically satisfying, and to reject those which contradict their already held beliefs. These predispositions

[51] Agranoff, *New Style in Election Campaigns,* p. 23.

[52] For more details see *National Journal,* 4 (May 27, 1972), 882-90; *National Journal,* 4 (September 2, 1972), 1381-93; and *National Journal,* 4 (October 14, 1972), 1607-16.

are durable and quite resistant to change. Psychological "defense mechanisms," such as selective attention, selective perception, and selective retention, enable the voter to notice only those messages which are satisfying. It is difficult to penetrate these perceptual screens if the purpose is to change a person's attitude or behavior. Inattention, distortion, or misinterpretation of the message, and purposive lack of retention, among other mechanisms, function as a "protective net in the service of existing dispositions," according to Joseph Klapper.[53]

In addition to internal personal limitations on mass persuasion, there are social restraints. Voters are not isolated individuals, but rather elements in intricate interpersonal relations with others. Much research has been conducted to demonstrate the important influence of group norms on individual attitudes and behavior. Each group affiliation contains cues which guide members to select messages in keeping with group norms and goals. Furthermore, research indicates that personal influence intervenes between the mass media and the public. Katz and Lazarsfeld found opinion leaders in all social strata for particular subjects.[54] One theory suggests that groups and opinion leaders serve to interpret and screen media messages for their followers. The mass persuasion appeals seldom impinge directly upon the target audience, but rather appear to be filtered by groups for the consumption of their membership. Since a large proportion of Americans affiliate with social groups, it seems likely that mass persuasion techniques must be combined with group appeals, through which the public might ultimately be reached. The flow of information is much more complex than a direct media model suggests. In situations where there are *cross-pressures* among two or more affiliations of an individual, there is a greater tendency either to delay the voting choice or to refrain from voting at all.

In addition to personal and social factors which limit mass persuasion attempts, there are variables relating to the specific persuasive attempt. The reputation of the message source might be crucial to acceptance by the voters. Although it has been demonstrated that the credibility advantage tends to disappear over time as people disassociate the source from the message (sleeper effect), much emphasis is placed on trust and confidence in candidates. The rise of frequent spot commercials, rather than long paid political programs, has the double advantage of minimizing the possibility of selective attention (by turning off the program), and overcoming the credibility problem through repetition. DeVries and Tarrance contend that the most effective media exposure comes through regularly scheduled news programs,

[53] Joseph T. Klapper, *The Effects of Mass Communication* (Glencoe, Ill.: The Free Fress, 1960), p. 25.

[54] Elihu Katz and Paul F. Lazarsfeld, *Personal Influence* (New York: The Free Press, 1964).

not paid political announcements against which defense mechanisms operate most effectively.[55] Due to such findings, consultants have minimized hard sell campaign advertisements and opted for news style approaches such as panel discussions, documentaries, and talk shows.[56]

Due to the intrusion of these forces in campaigns, Nimmo argues that the purpose of persuasion is not to change attitudes of the committed, but rather to shift the perceptions of the least involved voters.

> The more highly involved or committed he is to his stand (the greater the intensity of his attitude), the more likely he is to reject all alternative views; conversely the lower his involvement, the more noncommittal he is toward other positions.[57]

Campaigns, therefore, are probably most effective with the least involved elements of the electorate, that is, those with least-structured political beliefs and those with fewer and weaker group affiliations (including, of course, political party affiliation). By stressing the form of the message over its content, the use of imagery and vague themes and slogans, and through constant repetition, campaigns may shift individuals' perceptions of the candidates without causing attendant shifts in underlying attitudes. The primary targets of professional campaigners, then, are the marginally involved elements of the electorate with relatively unstable attitudes of low intensity. Their low involvement weakens their perceptual screens and exposes them to the professional campaigner who "contrives the campaign stage to his own advantage, employs the appropriate media, and endeavors to teach by example."[58] While the impact of campaigns is limited significantly, effective use of the resources at hand might be crucial, especially in close elections.

IMPLICATIONS OF THE
NEW STYLE OF CAMPAIGNS

What meaning does all this emphasis on professionally mediated campaigns have for political parties? Certainly, the massive shift from locally organized and primarily volunteer-oriented campaigns to the present emphasis on

[55] DeVries and Tarrance, *The Ticket-Splitter*, pp. 75-86. However, Thomas E. Patterson and Robert D. McClure, *Political Advertising: Voter Reaction to Televised Political Commercials* (Princeton: Citizens Research Foundation, 1973), pp. 10-35, found a much more substantial role for controlled media and less for the uncontrolled media.

[56] "Political Advertising: Making it Look Like News," *Congressional Quarterly Weekly Report*, 30 (November 4, 1972), 2900-2003.

[57] Nimmo, The *Political Persuaders*, p. 180.

[58] *Ibid.*, p. 193.

public relations experts, campaign management firms, and the vast array of mass persuasion technicians, has taken its toll on party organizations. To a large extent, the professional managers (pros) have replaced the politicians and party workers (pols) in directing and carrying out the campaign. Volunteers (vols) are more likely accountable to paid professionals than to the traditional party leaders. No longer is the party assured a central place in the campaign, especially at the state and national levels. Not only must parties compete for influence with independent candidate organizations and ad hoc personal campaigns, but also they face substantial and increasing friction from the professional managers. Ironically, as party organizations have become infused with more amateur-oriented strains, campaigns have become overwhelmingly the realm of professionals.

DECLINE OF PARTY ORGANIZATION IN CAMPAIGN

The movement toward the new style of campaign has been greeted with antagonism by many of the party pros. The emphasis on public opinion polls and media experts has been met with suspicion and hostility by many party organization leaders, resulting not in maintenance of party control, but in greater isolation of these leaders from the campaign process. The power of the social forces leading to media-oriented professional campaigns is simply too strong for the parties to oppose. As a result, the party leaders have been unprepared and unable to control campaign activities for all but a handful of offices, generally at the local level where funds are limited for waging personal campaigns.

Paul Allen Beck suggests one reason for the parties' apparent lack of effectiveness in the new media-oriented campaigns. He contends that the new style of campaigning, with its emphasis on the marketing of candidates through the mass media, puts a premium on *persuasion*. However, it appears (Chapter 5) that party organizations are better suited for *service* and *mobilization* activities than for persuasion. The changing nature of the electorate, along with a retreat from traditional methods of mobilization and continuous party service, has shifted emphasis toward mass persuasion, a task in which the party organizations are unable to compete successfully.[59]

Not only are party organizations no longer dominant during the campaign; they also have a difficult time maintaining the loyalty of the candidates when the election is over. The lack of party discipline was the most

[59] Paul Allen Beck, "Environment and Party: The Impact of Political and Demographic County Characteristics on Party Behavior," *American Political Science Review*, 68 (September, 1974), 1243.

obvious characteristic of parties in government discussed in Chapters 7 and 8. The emphasis on candidate organizations and campaign managers to the exclusion of the parties results in independent candidates with little obligation to the party organization. Unlike the parties of decades ago, current parties fail to monopolize the campaign workers, finances, and other resources. While volunteers are still relied upon for crucial personal contact, they are most frequently committed to candidates, not parties. Also, since professionals have become central to most campaigns, volunteers, hence party resources, are not of major importance. Most candidates cannot rely on the parties for the resources they need, since the parties are commonly years behind the times. The basic conflict between long-term party commitments to the political system and immediate election concerns of the campaign management firms accentuates the antagonism. As control continues to slip away from the party leaders, their frustration intensifies and they become even more isolated.

Similarly, the new campaign techniques have facilitated the independent voting patterns which are becoming increasingly common (Chapters 9 and 10). The primary tie is now between the candidate and the voter, not between the party and the voter. The media image is sent directly to the voter, and while the party still serves as a major voting cue, it must now compete with candidate images implanted directly in the voter's mind. While the new campaigning has not caused the trend toward independent voting patterns in the electorate, without doubt it has contributed to it. The voting cues available to a voter now include direct references in the media and efforts by ad hoc candidate organizations, in addition to the work of the parties themselves.

NEW CAMPAIGNING AND DEMOCRACY

In addition to the severe weakening of political parties, observers perceive several additional dangers in the media-oriented campaigns. Dan Nimmo foresees the "likelihood of systematic deception" arising out of these new techniques.[60] The emphasis on manufactured, contrived personalities certainly offers a prime opportunity for electronic deception, as well as old-fashioned rhetorical deception. The problem becomes graver when one realizes that those professionals running the campaigns have no general code of ethics to guide their actions.

---

[60] Nimmo, *The Political Persuaders*, p. 195. Also see Dan Nimmo, *Popular Images of Politics* (Englewood Cliffs, N.J.: Prentice-Hall, Inc., 1974), and Murray Edelman, *The Symbolic Uses of Politics* (Urbana, Ill.: The University of Illinois Press, 1964).

Cases of deception may be isolated, but we would be naive to believe that deception will not occur. Campaign management is a competitive enterprise. To make a profit each agency must accumulate accounts. To entice prospective clients each agency must distinguish itself from its competitors. In the beginning this means a desperation for victory that would systematically mislead the electorate.[61]

It is not unreasonable to expect that some firms will employ questionable practices in order to achieve success in their business of winning elections.

Not only is there the selling of the president, but also of the senator, congressman, governor, and so forth, at least in the sense of the creation of images. As the packaging and selling of candidates becomes more common, the danger arises that electoral decisions may be somehow reduced to a choice, not between candidates, but between the sophisticated engineers they employ for the sole purpose of getting themselves elected. To this extent, the professional campaigners have become independent factors in the campaign, with potential for intrusion into election results. Although the professional managers have not yet entered the area of candidate recruitment on a large scale, they tend to be selective in choosing clients who should win and avoiding losers. Indirectly, then, they might influence the selection process. Also, there have been notable incursions of professional campaigners into candidate recruitment. For instance, Richard Nixon was recruited in 1946 by a committee searching for a congressional candidate when he answered one of their newspaper ads.

Nixon responded, appeared before the committee, was selected to make the race, and ultimately became a force in American politics for the next quarter of a century.[62]

Concurrently, the emphasis on mass persuasion techniques, and the corresponding reduction in direct personal contact, has tended to insulate candidates from the electorate. Increasing amounts of candidates' time are spent in taping sessions, media events, and the like.

Finally, the new style of campaigning has added substantially to the sky-rocketing costs of campaigns. When campaigning was largely a matter of organizing volunteers to distribute brochures and bumper stickers, the costs were limited. The current emphasis on highly paid professionals has altered costs dramatically. The result is that many potential candidates are unable to finance the expensive campaigns. The entire election process becomes

[61] *Ibid.*, p. 195.
[62] *Ibid.*, p. 43.

constrained, and the less well-to-do candidates are eliminated for lack of funds. Chapter 14 examines the question of campaign finance and the spiraling costs of American elections.

THE NEW STYLE OF CAMPAIGNING
AND POLITICAL PARTIES: A SUMMARY

In past years, one could imagine (although rarely with complete accuracy) a highly loyal band of party workers combing the streets and successfully persuading the community to support the party ticket. One could also expect that many of the residents would be waiting for, or at least anticipating, this communication. At least the campaigning prior to the advent of the "new campaigning" gave the parties a chance to have an influence, whether they were successful or not. Also, in that era, party organization was the only organization available in election campaigns. Money, workers, and communication resources were primarily from the party. Although party organization rarely achieved the cohesiveness and unity exemplified by the big city machines, it had little competition during the campaign.

All this has changed. The role of the political party organizations in most election campaigns is minimal. Although the statutory party organizations survive, they are generally understaffed, underfinanced, and ineffective. Candidates depend not on the party, but on their own organizations. In each county or state, there are now independent candidate organizations for each candidate running for office. For local offices the "organization" might include a campaign manager (usually unpaid and a friend or relative of the candidate), a treasurer (many states' sunshine laws require a treasurer), and a handful of volunteers to do the legwork. As one moves from local offices to state and, finally, national offices, these organizations become: (1) more structured, (2) more elaborate, (3) more expensive, and (4) more professional. The campaign manager and staff commonly are professionals, hired by the candidate at very high fees to plan and execute the campaign. Specialists in public opinion polls, advertising, fund raising, public relations, speech writing, and so forth, are hired, depending on the amount of money available. Volunteers are organized not by the political party leaders, but by the professionals. There is less dependence on volunteers than in the past. The professionals direct the campaign, and at times control the actions of the candidate.

14

Financing
the Campaigns

It was stated in Chapter 13 that the new style of campaigning, with its emphasis on professional mediators and the electronic media, has contributed to the escalating cost of elections. This chapter examines the cost of recent election campaigns in the United States, the means by which money is collected, and the ways in which it is spent. Central to this discussion is the idea that party organizations normally perform a minor role in the funding of campaigns. Fundraising and campaign spending are more commonly the domain of independent candidate organizations, not the parties. This chapter also describes various attempts to regulate campaign finance. The major reforms of the 1970s are discussed, and their impact on political parties, as well as the conduct of American campaigns, is analyzed.

MONEY AND POLITICAL CAMPAIGNS

While much public attention recently has focused on financing campaigns, concern over the use of money in campaigns is not new. Money has always played a central role in American election campaigns, as it has in those of most representative democracies.

> In a town meeting democracy, the question of political finance has little significance. Issues are defined in common, and the voters and candidates know and have equal access to each other . . . . In a modern mass society, in which democracy must be representative rather than direct, the question of political finance can be of decisive importance.[1]

[1] David W. Adamany and George E. Agree, *Political Money: A Strategy for Campaign Finance in America* (Baltimore: Johns Hopkins Press, 1975), p. 2.

Interestingly, campaign expenditures in the United States are relatively low compared to those in nations such as Germany, Japan, and Israel.[2] One of the costs of democracy is payment for the selection of representatives through democratic elections. Someone has to pay these costs.

In the United States, political activity traditionally has been financed through voluntary contributions to parties and candidates. An assumption of this private funding system is that, since all citizens have an equal right to participate, all interests will receive financial support in proportion to their support in the electorate. This system of private funding has been defended as one means of freedom of expression, and attempts to eliminate all vestiges of private contribution have been declared unconstitutional on that ground. Unfortunately, this basic assumption of equal resources is erroneous. Since not all persons have equal financial resources, there are major inequities in the ability to contribute to political campaigns. While there certainly is a maldistribution of all resources, including skills, knowledge, interest and motivation, inequalities of wealth are probably greater than any others.[3] Therefore, the views and interests of the wealthy are vastly overrepresented in privately-funded campaigns.

It is no surprise, then, that few subjects have evoked as much controversy, or caused as many problems for candidates, as the financing of campaigns. The great imbalance in campaign resources available to various candidates and parties is of concern to political observers. In addition, there is a fear that those elected are not free agents if they are dependent on large private contributions for their victory. The assumption is that large contributors expect, and receive, something in return for their contribution once their candidate is elected. A contingent area of concern relates to the diversion of campaign funds for personal use, and the illegal use of pressure to coerce individuals into contributing. According to Herbert Alexander, "a fine line separates contributions and bribes."[4] He contends that political financing in the United States has long been undemocratic because of its reliance on large contributions and its strong tendency toward corruption. The question of corruption in the raising and spending of large sums of money contributed as an expression of support for a candidate is a continuing one in American electoral politics, as evidenced by Watergate.

[2] See David W. Adamany, *Financing Politics* (Madison, Wis.: University of Wisconsin Press, 1969), pp. 52-55.

[3] Adamany and Agree, *Political Money*, p. 3.

[4] Herbert E. Alexander, *Financing the 1972 Election* (Lexington, Mass.: D.C. Heath and Company, 1976), p. 3.

MONEY: HOW IMPORTANT?

Is money really as important to campaigning as all this concern would seem to show? Certainly, money is but one of many resources essential to any campaign. The skills and reputation of the candidate, incumbency or non-incumbency, amount of organizational support, number of volunteers, and access to the mass media are among many interrelated resources other than financial. However, while no single resource is likely to determine the outcome of an election, money is commonly indispensable to the success of a campaign. While it seldom guarantees victory, it is generally required.

David Adamany contends that money has two unique characteristics which set it apart from other campaign resources.[5] First, it is the most easily *convertible* of resources. In other words, it can be readily exchanged for other resources. Money can purchase workers in the absence of volunteers, it can pay professionals in the absence of party organization support, and it can buy media exposure. While monetary resources are not equivalent to incumbency, they can offset some of its impact. Likewise, while money cannot drastically alter the personal attributes of a weak candidate, it can provide professional voice coaches, makeup men, issue specialists, and film editors, who accentuate the positive and minimize the negative characteristics of the candidate. Because money is easily convertible, it is an essential resource, especially when needed to offset specific liabilities.

Second, money is a crucial resource because it is readily *transferable* from one locale to another. At many times it is difficult to move volunteers from one area to another, and impossible to translate other nonmonetary resources, such as good press relationships, into other resources of equal value. Conversely, money is easily transferred anywhere in the nation, because it is liquid. It is legal tender anywhere. Also, unlike other resources, it moves silently, which allows it to be "laundered" or passed through intermediaries, so that the source can remain anonymous.

> Transfer payments among committees can obscure the original source of funds, whereas the citizen who serves on a political committee, canvasses his neighbors, posts a sign on his car or lawn, attends a caucus, or in other ways uses his time, energy, and skills can hardly conceal his attempt to influence politics.[6]

Certainly, the transferability of money makes it the most flexible of the many resources used in American campaigns.

---

[5] Adamany, *Financing Politics*, pp. 8-9.

[6] Adamany and Agree, *Political Money*, p. 3.

While money has advantages over other campaign resources, and might be a crucial factor in some elections, too often it is singled out as the one resource which can assure victory. This approach is misleading.

> Certainly money is a key campaign resource, and a paucity of funds can be a critical disadvantage, especially when one's opponent has an abundance. But, money is only one among many resources in a campaign.[7]

In certain elections, party membership and incumbency can offset the large monetary advantages of an opponent. In some cases, no amount of money spent by a candidate could produce a victory, while in other cases a small advantage in financial resources might be decisive. The importance of money, then, depends on a complex set of factors which are unique to each campaign. The situation is more confusing because resources tend to reinforce each other, and seldom act in isolation. For instance, money tends to flow toward candidates who are well-known, with established credentials; in many cases, the incumbents. Large contributors are unwilling to gamble on candidates with little else but candidacy in their favor. Instead, the big money tends to flow toward those candidates who already hold the advantage in other respects. It is very difficult, therefore, to specify exactly how important money is in each election. Overall, however, money continues to be a major campaign resource and a crucial commodity in American electoral politics.

MONEY: HOW MUCH?

It is extremely difficult to estimate, with any high degree of accuracy, the actual cost of U.S. elections. While recent federal and state campaign disclosure laws have made reporting of expenditures more reliable, the large number of elected offices in the U.S. and the variation in reporting laws make any estimates shaky at best. Also, many nonmonetary goods and services which are not reported change hands during the campaign. Finally, many individuals and groups expend money on "political education" activities which are not overtly "campaign" expenditures. Obviously, millions of dollars in expenditures for campaign purposes go unreported, and are not included in the data presented here.

[7] Robert Agranoff, *The Management of Election Campaigns* (Boston: Holbrook Press, Inc., 1976), p. 226. Also see, Alexander Heard, *The Costs of Democracy* (Chapel Hill, N.C.: University of North Carolina Press, 1960), for a discussion of the importance of money.

Table 14.1   Estimated Expenditures for All Partisan Campaigns, 1952-1972

Year	Total Spending	Cost/Eligible Voter	Cost/Vote Cast
1952	$140 million	$1.40	$2.27
1956	155 million	1.52	2.50
1960	175 million	1.60	2.57
1964	200 million	1.75	2.83
1968	300 million	2.49	4.10
1972	425 million	3.04	5.66

The data in Table 14.1 illustrate the rapid increase, both in total campaign spending and cost per voter, between the 1952 and 1972 elections. Total spending tripled during these 20 years, while the amount spent per actual voter doubled. Despite a probable decline in 1976, due to strict expenditure restrictions in presidential and congressional contests, the costs of elections are bound to remain high in relation to past decades. Also, these figures do not include the costs of primaries, which are substantial, or any nonmonetary expenditures in the general elections.

While these costs are impressive and the spending increase is substantial, when one puts the costs in a broader perspective, they do not appear to be too high a price to pay for democratic elections. As stated earlier, campaign costs in most other democracies are relatively higher. Also, the $425 million price tag of the 1972 election represents a mere .037 percent of the 1972 Gross National Product, and only .045 percent of the total 1972 Personal Income for the nation. When analyzed from this perspective, the increase in expenditures from previous elections is minimal. Also, the record $425 million expenditure for campaigns in 1972 was less than the total advertising budgets for that year of the two largest corporate advertisers, Procter and Gamble and General Motors, and less than 1 percent of the amount spent by the various levels of government in the U.S. that year.[8]

> Although the dollar costs of politics stagger the individual citizen, from a national perspective campaign expenditures are quite modest ... Nor are campaign costs rising inordinately. Personal Income and government spending have both increased more rapidly.[9]

[8] Herbert E. Alexander, *Financing Politics: Money, Elections and Political Reform* (Washington, D.C.: Congressional Quarterly, 1976), p. 43.
[9] Adamany and Agree, *Political Money*, p. 27.

When put in perspective, the overall cost of campaigns does not appear too high. The distribution and use of the available money, perhaps, is a greater concern than the number of dollars expended.

RISING COSTS: THE NEW STYLE
OF CAMPAIGN

There is no single explanation for the rapid increase in the costs of campaigns in the last several decades. Rather, it results from a combination of many factors, some totally beyond the control of the candidates. Obviously, costs rise as the electorate expands. The combination of general population increase and the lowering of the voting age from 21 to 18 has added approximately 40 million more qualified voters since 1960. Inflation also has contributed to rising costs since the staples of campaigning—postage, airline fares, printing, and media time—have increased in price more rapidly than prices in general. Also, as more candidates contest more elected offices, total costs naturally rise. All these factors, however, still fail to explain the rapid cost increase since the 1960s.

The basis for these increases is the change in style of campaigning that has emerged in recent elections. Chapter 13 discussed the shift from party-oriented campaigns to professionally mediated campaigns, and suggested that one product of this shift has been more expensive campaigns. Several observers contend that the decline of the party organization has eliminated a "reliable system of precinct workers who both took the public pulse and tried to regulate it."[10] Tasks that earlier were performed without cost by volunteers now are performed by paid campaign workers. Canvassing of precinct voters by party workers has been largely replaced by public opinion polls conducted by high-priced professionals. Computerized letters and telephone banks replace personal contacts by precinct workers, and continually drive up the costs of campaigning.

While it might be argued that these new, expensive technologies would be used even if the work were still performed by the party organization, it is the heavy reliance on technology which has accelerated the costs. Since candidates no longer can turn to their traditional source of campaign support, the party, they must rely on professionals and their high technology. Obviously, the scarcity of campaign support pushes up the cost of these services substantially.

The absence of party organization involvement in campaigns, combined

---

[10] Adamany and Agree, *Political Money*, p. 22.

with the decentralizing influence of the direct primary system, also force most candidates to build their own campaign organizations.

> The reliable, year-in year-out ward organization got voters registered, tallied their pre-election preferences, and took them to the polls. Now candidates must painstakingly and expensively build citizen organizations for each campaign, or they must pay workers to get these tasks done.[11]

This results in much duplication among independent organizations and further diminishes the possibility of dependence on volunteers. Instead of the party organization's coordinating and managing a slate of candidates, each candidate organization must compete for volunteers against other candidates of the same party.

DISPARITIES IN DISTRIBUTION
OF RESOURCES

The competition among autonomous candidate organizations within each party also results in major disparities in the distribution of money and other campaign resources. Table 14.2 illustrates how money flows to the more

Table 14.2   Expenditures and Competition, House, 1972

Winning Percentage	Average Winners' Expend.	Average Losers' Expend.	Average Expenditure
70% to 90%	$ 38,729	$ 7,479	$ 46,208
65% to 70%	42,212	16,060	58,272
60% to 65%	55,065	30,483	85,548
55% to 60%	73,616	54,600	128,216
up to 55%	107,378	101,166	208,544

SOURCE: Campaign Finance Monitoring Process, Common Cause, September 1973.

competitive races.[12] The average total campaign expenditure for 1972 House races in which the winner had less than 55 percent of the vote was $208,544. The corresponding average for races in which the winner received over 70

[11] *Ibid.*, p. 23.

[12] See David A. Leuthold, *Electioneering in a Democracy* (New York: John Wiley and Sons, 1968), p. 80, and David W. Adamany, *Campaign Finance in America* (North Scituate, Mass.: Duxbury Press, 1972), pp. 65-69.

Table 14.3   Expenditures and Incumbency,
House and Senate, 1972

Category	Mean Total Spending
House: With Incumbent	
Incumbent	$ 50,900
Challenger	$ 30,300
House: No Incumbent	
Democrat	$ 89,400
Republican	$ 88,400
Senate: With Incumbent	
Incumbent	$495,400
Challenger	$244,100
Senate: No Incumbent	
Democrat	$496,300
Republican	$495,300

SOURCE: David Adamany and George Agree, *Political Money: A Strategy for Campaign Finance in America* (Baltimore: The Johns Hopkins University Press, 1975), p. 25.

percent of the vote was $46,204, less than a fourth of that for competitive races. The data further demonstrate that the discrepency between expenditures of winning and losing candidates in noncompetitive districts is substantially higher than in the more competitive districts. The danger here is that this pattern may reinforce already secure office holders and minimize their accountability to the electorate. As incumbents become more secure in their positions, challengers have an even more difficult time, and thus the cycle continues. The very candidates who need most support get the least.

The advantage given funding of competitive races is related to the clearest spending disparity of all, that between incumbents and challengers. The data in Table 14.3 illustrate the scope of this discrepancy. Incumbent senators in 1972 enjoyed on an average, a two-to-one advantage in spending. House incumbents averaged $50,900, while their opponents only managed to raise an average of $32,100. In an examination of House spending in 1976, Rhodes Cook concludes that "most money went to incumbents and nearly all the incumbents won."[13] In that year, incumbents outspent challengers by $12.3 million, a margin of 1.7 to 1. Not surprisingly, only 13 incumbents

[13] Rhodes Cook, "Congressional Campaign Spending," *Practical Politics* 1 (December 1977/January 1978), 12.

lost in the general election. Furthermore, their ability to raise more funds is supplemented by all the perquisites of their office, which more than double any monetary advantage they have.

A 1975 study by the liberal Americans for Democratic Action calculated that an incumbent congressman has a $488,505 edge on his challenger. This figure takes into account the value of salaries and office space, communications, and travel allowances and other benefits that members receive and that help them stay in office.[14]

The disparity in spending by incumbents and challengers reduces meaningful competition in congressional campaigns, and facilitates the monopolization of a majority of the districts by one party.

PRESIDENTIAL SPENDING

Without a doubt, most attention is focused on that single contest which is most visible and expensive, the presidency. As a result, in-depth studies of presidential expenditures are available which detail all aspects of the campaign.[15] In addition, the excesses of Richard Nixon, as well as of other candidates seeking the presidency, have sparked reforms which resulted in public financing of presidential elections within strict spending limits. Because of the attention paid to presidential campaigns, and the vast amounts of money spent on them, there has been an erroneous tendency to extrapolate presidential data to other contests. Any such comparisons are bound to err, since the presidential contest is unique.

The data in Table 14.4 demonstrate the increase in presidential general election spending until 1976, when, in part as a reaction to the high-cost election of 1972, public financing greatly restricted expenditures. Herbert Alexander estimates that the 1972 election actually cost $137.9 million, if primary expenditures are included.[16] The Committee to Re-Elect the President alone spent close to $62 million on Nixon, with another $6 million coming from the Republican National Committee. The 1968 primary and

[14] Alexander, *Financing Politics*, p. 55.

[15] In addition to his detailed volume on the 1972 election, Herbert Alexander has similar books on the 1960, 1964, and 1968 presidential elections: *Financing the 1960 Election* (Princeton: Citizens' Research Foundation, 1962); *Financing the 1964 Election* (Princeton: Citizens' Research Foundation, 1966); *Financing the 1968 Election* (Boston: D.C. Heath and Company, 1971). Also, Delmer D. Dunn, *Financing Presidential Campaigns* (Washington, D.C.: The Brookings Institution, 1972).

[16] Alexander, *Financing the 1972 Election*, p. 79.

Table 14.4 Direct Expenditures for All Presidential
Candidates, General Elections, 1912-1976

1912	$ 2.9 million	1948	$ 6.2 million
1916	4.7	1952	11.6
1920	6.9	1956	12.9
1924	5.4	1960	19.9
1928	11.6	1964	24.8
1932	5.1	1968	44.2
1936	14.1	1972	103.7
1940	6.2	1976	50.0
1944	5.0		

SOURCE: Citizens' Research Foundation

general election total is estimated at $100 million, including about $33 million spent during the Democratic primaries.

In 1976, each presidential candidate spent most of the $21.8 million received under public financing.[17] Also, each party could spend an additional $3.2 million on behalf of its candidate. If candidates accepted public funds, they were barred from accepting private contributions. Under these conditions, expenditures in the general election were restricted. At the same time, however, the availability of federal matching funds during the primaries accelerated spending during that period. Preliminary estimates indicate that about $64 million of private and public money was spent in the 1976 primaries, $38 million by the Democrats and $26 million by the Republicans. Of this, approximately $24 million was provided by public matching funds.

CONGRESSIONAL SPENDING

The large amounts of money expended on the presidential campaign should not lead to the conclusion that all campaigns are equally well funded. Despite a record outlay for House candidates of $60.9 million in 1976, compared to $40 million in 1972, many congressional campaigns continue to be "mom and pop" operations, low on both money and professionalism.[18] The average total cost of House campaigns in 1976 was approximately $140,000, but the variation among the 435 districts was substantial. The total expenditure for Senate candidates in 1976 was $38.1 million, for an average of slightly over $1 million per contest. Figure 14.1 presents a comparison of expendi-

[17] See later section this chapter on public financing.

[18] Cook, "Congressional Campaign Spending," p. 13. Many reports on congressional campaign spending are published by Congressional Quarterly, Inc. See *Dollar Politics: The Issue of Campaign Spending*, vol. 1, 1971 and vol. 2, 1974, for a summary of their coverage through 1974.

Table 14.5   FEC Matching Funds for
Presidential Candidates,
1976 Primaries

Candidate	Amount
Birch Bayh	$ 460,973.54
Lloyd Bentsen	511,022.61
Edmund Brown, Jr.	491,001.89
Jimmy Carter	3,465,584.89
Frank Church	615,126.68
Gerald Ford	4,657,007.82
Fred Harris	633,099.05
Henry Jackson	1,980,554.95
Ellen Mc Cormack	244,125.40
Ronald Reagan	5,088,910.66
Terry Sanford	246,388.32
Milton Shapp	299,066.21
Sargent Shriver	285,069.74
Morris Udall	1,831,058.55
George Wallace	3,291,308.81
Total Democrat	14,454,380.64
Total Republican	9,745,918.48
Total	$24,100,299.12

SOURCE: Federal Election Commission

Figure 14.1   Campaign Spending: President, House, and Senate;
1972 and 1976

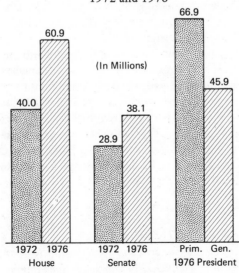

SOURCE: Federal Election Commission

tures for President, House and Senate in 1972 and 1976. While congressional spending in 1976 rivaled the total cost of presidential spending, it must be noted that there were approximately 470 congressional contests in each election year.

Out of the 435 House contests in 1976, 63 races cost more than $250,000 apiece. In 1972 the corresponding figure was 24 contests. Five contests in 1976 topped the previous record of $537,474 set in 1974. The highest total expenditure for a House race in 1976 was that for California's 27th Congressional District, where two candidates spent a total of $1,040,755. One of these candidates, Gary Familian, set the single candidate record by spending $637,080 in a losing effort. An additional 14 candidates spent more than $250,000 each in their primary and general election campaigns. Despite these few expensive campaigns, one survey of candidates found that 43 percent of the 1976 congressional candidates spent less than $15,000.[19] Fifty percent of the campaign money was concentrated among 10 percent of the candidates. Contrary to popular belief, therefore, most congressional campaigns are low-budget operations.

STATE AND LOCAL CAMPAIGN SPENDING

As one shifts from presidential to congressional to state and local elections, spending decreases rapidly. For instance, it is estimated that of the $425 million spent in 1972, $138 million went into electing a president and $98 million toward congressional campaigns. The remaining $190 million was split fairly evenly between the cost of state elections (such as governors, other statewide offices, state legislators, and ballot issues) and the costs of selecting hundreds of thousands of local public officials.[20] This reduces to an average total expenditure of approximately $400 for each of the 500,000 or so offices in the United States.

No attempt is made here to summarize such spending except to note that many thousands of campaigns, especially in the smaller state and local constituencies, are conducted with relatively small sums of money. While the expenditures for high visibility campaigns, such as Hugh Carey's $5 million effort to win the 1974 New York gubernatorial election, are well publicized, they are the exception. Most expenditures, even for statewide campaigns, are more modest. Although a few state legislative races might cost over $100,000, many more, even in the large states, are conducted with budgets of only a few thousand dollars.[21] In smaller constituencies, the entire cam-

---

[19] *Ibid.*

[20] Alexander, *Financing Politics*, pp. 16-17.

[21] See Herbert E. Alexander, *Campaign Money: Reform and Reality in the States* (New York: The Free Press, 1976), for case studies of spending in specific state elections.

paign budget might be substantially less than a thousand dollars, most of which is contributed by the candidate and a few close friends and family members.[22] As in all aspects of comparing state elections, expenditures for the same offices in different states vary considerably. For this reason, presidential and congressional campaigning is emphasized in this chapter.

SPENDING PATTERNS: WHERE DOES THE MONEY GO?

The largest single increase in campaign spending during the 1950s and 1960s is attributable to television. By 1952, the number of Americans with TV sets reached a point where TV was considered an essential element of campaigning, at least at the presidential level. Since the Federal Communications Commission requires detailed reports on all media advertising, the data on campaign spending for the broadcast media are most accurate.

No matter how it is measured, the cost of broadcasting is high, with the most growth appearing in the late 1960s. The total of $58.9 million spent for radio and TV in 1968 was 70 percent above the 1964 total of $34.6 million. While the 1972 total of $59.6 million represented a smaller proportion of overall campaign expenditures than in 1968 (14 percent instead of 20 percent), it was still the largest single identifiable cost in political campaigns."[23] This relative decrease resulted from a combination of the broadcasting limits established in 1971 and the emergence of direct mail as a means of communication. Table 14.6 demonstrates the relative cost of broadcasting for the Nixon Campaign in 1972.

The broadcast expenditure figures in Table 14.7 represent only network and station costs, and do not include costs of production and promotion. Herbert Alexander states that 20 to 50 percent production costs are not uncommon in campaign advertising. He estimates that the comprehensive cost for broadcasting in 1972 could approach $90 million.[24] One interesting aspect of 1972 broadcast spending was that McGovern spent more than Nixon. This reflected a major shift in strategy by Nixon, since the much heralded "selling of the president" by TV had done little to help his 1968 campaign. Also, the unknown McGovern had to depend on television for the needed exposure. In 1976, Ronald Reagan used TV appeals quite successfully

---

[22] Robert J. Huckshorn and Robert C. Spencer, *The Politics of Defeat* (Amherst: University of Massachusetts Press, 1971), pp. 127-28. Also see Donald G. Balmer, *Financing State Senate Campaigns* (Princeton: Citizens' Research Foundation, 1966), pp. 37-38.

[23] Alexander, *Financing Politics*, p. 29.

[24] *Ibid.*

Table 14.6   1971-72 Republican Presidential Expenditures of
CRP and Related Organizations

Expense Category	$ Millions
Advertising (broadcast, including production costs and fees)	$ 7.0
Direct mail to voters (not including fund raising)	5.8
Mass telephoning to voters	1.3
State organizations (primary elections, personnel, storefronts, locations, travel, voter contact, etc.)	15.9
Campaign materials	2.7
Press relations, publications, and literature	2.6
Headquarters (campaign, personnel, rent, telephone, travel, legal, etc.)	4.7
Travel and other expenses of President, Vice-President, surrogates, and advance men	3.9
Citizen group activities	1.9
Youth activities	1.0
Polling (including White House-directed surveys)	1.6
Convention expenses	.6
Election night	.2
Fund raising (direct mail—$4 million, and major events—$1 million)	5.0
Fund raising (national administration and gifts for contributors)	1.9
Legal fees	2.0
Democratic settlement	.8
Democrats for Nixon	2.4
Total[a]	$61.4

[a]Does not include $1.4 million in miscellaneous cash, some used for dirty tricks or hush-money in 1972-73, and some used for political or other purposes in 1969-70-71, not directly related to the 1972 presidential election.

SOURCE: Reprinted by permission of the publisher from *Financing the 1972 Election* by Herbert E. Alexander (Lexington, Mass.: Lexington Books, D.C. Heath and Company, Copyright 1976, D.C. Heath and Company).

Table 14.7   Radio and Television Expenditures
Presidential General Elections 1952-1972

Year	Republican	Democrat
1952	$2,046,000	$1,530,000
1956	2,886,000	1,763,000
1960	1,865,000	1,142,000
1964	6,370,000	4,674,000
1968	12,598,000	6,143,000
1972	4,300,000	6,200,000

SOURCE: Herbert E. Alexander, *Financing Politics: Money, Elections and Political Reform* (Washington, D.C.: Congressional Quarterly, Inc., 1976), p. 28.

during the primaries to raise funds. Jimmy Carter also depended heavily on media expenditures during the general campaign to establish himself as a national candidate. He devoted 40 percent of his general budget to TV and radio, mostly for five minute and 60 second spot announcements.

There has been a resurgence of spending for radio in the 1970s, leading to a more rapid increase in radio costs than TV costs since 1968. One advantage of radio is that it is much less expensive per message. Another is that it can be directed more easily to target audiences. Many candidates interested in appeals to specific ethnic groups find radio well suited to their purpose. Although it is not yet clear how much cable television (CATV) will cut into radio expenditures, it is expected that candidates, especially at the state or congressional levels, will continue to depend heavily on the radio.

In addition to the increased spending for broadcast media, payments for campaign consultants, polling firms, computerized mailings, and other specialized services have added to the accelerated spending pattern. Also, recent legislation requires that a substantial proportion of funds raised be used to keep records. Legal consultants and accountants are fast becoming integral parts of the campaign team. Also, despite the emphasis on the broadcast media in recent years, large sums continue to be expended on printed campaign materials. Table 14.8 represents only part of the costs of supplies for the 1968 and 1972 campaigns. It is estimated that production costs, warehousing, and distribution of campaign materials raised the total bill for Nixon to $2.7 million in 1972.[25]

In part a response to the unbridled media expenditures of 1968, the Federal Election Campaign Act of 1971 went into effect on April 7, 1972. A major provision of this Act was to limit mass media expenditures for radio, television, and newspaper advertising, as well as for billboards, other display facilities, and telephone banks. Candidates could spend a total of either (1) ten cents times the number of eligible voters in their constituencies, or (2) $50,000, whichever was greater, in each of the primary and general elections. Of this total, only 60 percent could be used for Radio-TV advertising.[26] The statute further required the media to sell time and space to all candidates at their lowest per unit cost. Communications media could not accept advertising without the authorization of the candidate or his agent, who was then responsible for staying within the statutory limits. According to David W. Adamany and George Agree, the Act fell short of the reformers' expectations and represented an "inadequate response to the problem of campaign finance in American democracy."[27] Perhaps as a consequence,

---

[25] Alexander, *Financing the 1972 Election*, p. 338.

[26] For presidential candidates, this ceiling was computed by state so that a candidate would not concentrate funds in certain states.

[27] Adamany and Agree, *Political Money*, p. 82.

Table 14.8   Campaign Supply Costs, 1968 and 1972

Item	Nixon			McGovern	
	1972 Quantity	*1972 Cost*	*1968 Cost*	*Quantity*	*Cost*
Buttons and tabs	25,000,000	$ 400,000	$ 300,000	10,804,100	$ 82,419
Bumper strips	16,000,000	$ 450,000	$ 300,000	5,320,000	$ 77,140
Posters	100,000	$ 100,000	$ 70,000	1,000,000	$ 46,000
Brochures	40,000,000	$ 300,000	$ 500,000	26,975,000	$161,694
T-shirts	10,000	$ 20,000	—		
Jewelry	10,000	$ 25,000	$ 50,000	Total	$367,253
Strawskimmers	40,000	$ 25,000	$ 30,000		
Balloons	300,000	$ 7,000	$ 70,000		
Floppy hats	10,000	$ 20,000	—		
Totals		$1,347,000	$1,320,000		

SOURCE: Herbert E. Alexander, *Financing the 1972 Election* (Lexington, Mass.: Lexington Books, D.C. Heath and Company, 1976), p. 339.

the spending limits imposed by this law were repealed by the 1974 Campaign Act.

RAISING CAMPAIGN FUNDS

As seen in Chapter 13, one of the first steps in organizing a campaign for any office is the selection of a finance chairperson and creation of a fund-raising committee. Although money is not the only resource, fund-raising is central to most campaign efforts. Unfortunately for many candidates, it is difficult to raise adequate funds, since the parties no longer can be depended upon to provide funding for most candidates. For maximum success, the candidate must enlist the aid of a finance chairman who both knows the potential sources of funds and is well-known in the community. The goal of the fund-raising committee is to gain access to various segments of the community and open as many financial doors as possible.

Normally, fund-raising activities in lower-level campaigns are not well organized and seldom achieve full potential. The result is a relatively narrow base of contributors, commonly composed of family, friends, and a handful of active partisans and group contributors. Due to a lack of planning, many candidates must spend much of their valuable and limited campaign time personally soliciting funds. Although the use of professional fund-raising firms has lagged behind the use of professionals in other areas of campaigning, the larger campaigns hire full-time fund-raising firms or consultants to plan and administer efforts to raise funds. Despite this, Robert Agranoff concludes that fund-raising efforts are "often undertaken unrealistically, too late, with little planning, and they consume other valuable campaign resources."[28] Although the means of collecting funds varies, certain patterns of raising campaign monies appear to be deeply ingrained in U.S. politics.

DIRECT PERSONAL SOLICITATION

The single largest source of campaign funds continues to be direct solicitation of potential individual contributors. Normally, this is accomplished by personal contact with the contributor, either in person or by telephone. While there is some evidence that much potential is unrealized, since many unsolicited persons would contribute if contacted, it has been noted that, "Expanded solicitations and greater attention to money in politics have

[28] Agranoff, *Management of Election Campaigns*, p. 244.

Table 14.9 Percent of U.S. Adult Population Solicited and Making Contributions

Year	Organization	Solicited by: Rep	Dem	Total	Contributed to: Rep	Dem	Total	Percent Solicited Who Gave
1952	SRC				3	1	4	
1956	Gallup	8	11	19	3	6	9	50
1956	SRC				5	5	10	
1960	Gallup	9	8	15	4	4	9	70
1960	SRC				7	4	11	
1964	Gallup				6	4	12	
1964	SRC	8	4	15	6	4	11	77
1968	SRC	8	6	20	3	3	8	40
1972	SRC	9	13	30	4	5	10	33

SOURCE: Survey Research Center, University of Michigan and American Institute of Public Opinion.

not yet broadened participation in campaign finance."[29] The data in Table 14.9 suggest that although solicitation increased from 15 percent in 1964 to 30 percent in 1972, the number of those contributing has remained virtually stable at about 10 percent of the population. It is imperative, therefore, that campaign finance committees target in on the most likely prospects. Generally, this entails compiling priority lists of potential contributors from lists of party contributors, previous campaign donors, and contributors to other candidates. While this procedure is necessary to maximize return on fund-raising effort, it results in dependence on a rather narrow base of perennial contributors.

DIRECT MAIL SOLICITATION

As direct personal contact has lessened in recent years due to the decline in available volunteers, efforts to solicit contributions of many individuals through the mails have increased. The increase in solicitations reflected in the 1972 figures of Table 14.9 are the result of substantial attempts at mail solicitation by both presidential candidates. The McGovern campaign sent out 15 million pieces of mail at a cost of $3.5 million. This direct mail effort was central to McGovern's campaign and raised over $12 million from nearly 700,000 contributors. Although direct mail was a less important element of the 1972 Nixon campaign, 30 million pieces were sent, bringing in about

[29] Adamany and Agree, *Political Money*, p. 28.

426

$9 million. Ideological candidates such as George Wallace and Barry Gold-water have been successful in using this method to collect large numbers of small contributions.

While the scope of direct mail solicitation is narrower for other offices, most state and congressional campaigns utilize it to some extent. This normally entails selecting a list of those most likely to contribute. Attempts at utilizing general population lists generally are not highly successful, since it costs between 20 and 25 cents for each letter sent. If computer-printed letters specifically aimed at target audiences are utilized, the costs can go even higher. Often incentives are offered for contributions of various amounts. In 1972 the Nixon Campaign offered a Nixon coin for a gift of $15 or more, an RN pin with a diamond chip for a contribution of $5,000 or more, a pen and pencil set with the presidential seal and Nixon's embossed signature for $12,000 or more, and a White House invitation for $25,000. A $10,000 gift to McGovern was rewarded by membership in the Woonsocket Club and an 18 carat gold lapel pin. To be successful, a campaign must reduce the odds by soliciting from already proven contributors. Professionals are available, at a high price, who specialize in direct mail drives. They either run the entire direct mail fund-raising portion or sell lists of potential contributors to the candidates. Although direct mail solicitation has many advantages, candidates must use it with caution, since success or failure will depend on the selectiveness of the lists.

POLITICAL EVENTS

Another device for soliciting individual contributions is the staged political event. Although the political dinner is the most common fund-raising event, yard sales, cocktail parties, auctions, dances, or any other conceivable situation will do. These events serve to reinforce the faithful as well as raise money. But their effectiveness as fund-raising methods is limited by the overhead costs and the costs of the goods used. For instance, even though most political dinners unite candidate supporters, the cost of the food and entertainment often dilutes the contributions substantially. Even if the goods are donated, the organizational costs in the use of scarce campaign-worker resources might be high. "By contrast, the harvest from direct solicitation is nearly free, with the exception of the time of solicitors who would often do little else in the campaign anyway."[30] Seldom do fundraisers attract large numbers of new supporters. More often they are a gathering of those already contributing in other ways. Therefore, any attempts to raise money through

[30] Agranoff, *Management of Election Campaigns*, p. 246.

political events must be carefully analyzed. If the benefits in money and campaign support do not offset the overhead and organizational costs, other more direct fund-raising appeals should be used.

POLITICAL TELETHONS

One special type of political event, the telethon, staged by the Democrats in the early 1970s and previously used as a fundraiser for various charities, is designed to appeal directly to wide television audiences. The telethon as a political fund-raising event was initiated by a Democratic party deeply in debt on the day before their 1972 national convention. The 19-hour extravaganza netted about $2 million and advertised the party at the same time. Similar telethons were conducted in the three succeeding years. In 1976, Democratic National Chairman Robert Strauss bought $250,000 worth of television time during the convention, mostly for short 30 or 60 second spots. These advertisements were designed to appeal for contributions as well as to advertise the party and its candidates. Obviously, the potential uses of the broadcast media in raising funds are far from being exhausted.

GROUP CONTRIBUTIONS

The amount of money raised by appealing to groups for support varies significantly by locale and by office. Seldom, however, is the amount contributed by interest groups as large as commonly assumed. In 1972, only 14 percent of the total funds contributed to congressional candidates came from registered interest groups. Although this proportion increased to 22 percent in 1976, the role of interest groups in campaigns commonly is overestimated. The bulk of interest group contributions nationwide comes from union auxiliary groups such as the AFL-CIO's Committee on Political Education (COPE), and campaign units of business or trade associations.[31] While both unions and corporations are barred by law from contributing directly to political campaigns, they have circumvented the law by channeling funds indirectly to political committees.

The proliferation of political "education" or action committees over several decades created about 150-200 groups registered for national campaigns and numerous others registered for particular states. Not surprisingly, incumbents have a large lead in contributions from interest groups. A portion of what is termed "private" contributions, then, is institutional, not individual.

---

[31] See Alexander, *Financing the 1972 Election*, pp. 457-511, for a comprehensive examination of business and labor in campaign finance.

Table 14.10 Interest Group Contributions to Congressional
Campaigns, 1974 and 1976

Interest Group Category	1974	1976
Agriculture	$ 361,040	$ 1,534,447
Business	2,506,946	7,091,375
Health	1,936,487	2,694,910
Lawyers	–	241,280
Labor	6,315,488	8,206,578
Miscellaneous	682,215	1,299,928
Ideological	723,410	1,503,394
Total	$12,525,586	$22,571,912

SOURCE: Common Cause

Financially powerful labor and business, though without official standing as part of the electorate, "have acquired, by deploying money, a kind of corporate citizenship."[32]

PATTERNS OF INDIVIDUAL GIVING

Contributions from individuals, raised by direct contact, mail solicitation, or fundraising events, constitute the largest proportion of campaign funds. Table 14.11 illustrates the estimated number of contributors in U.S. elections between 1952 and 1972. After the advent of mass mailing techniques and increased efforts to broaden the base of campaign funding during the 1950s, the number of contributors more than doubled between 1952 and 1956. Since that time, however, the number of contributions has leveled off, despite increased solicitation by a larger number of primary and general election candidates.

Despite the outpouring of small contributions to a few candidates such as George Wallace, Eugene McCarthy, and Barry Goldwater, national politics is dominated by large contributors. Table 14.12 demonstrates the scope of large contributions and the dramatic increase in the number of individuals contributing over $10,000 in the 1968 and 1972 presidential elections. The sharp acceleration of the big-giver pattern came to a peak in the reelection effort of Richard Nixon, which in turn led to public financing of presidential elections two years later.

[32] Adamany and Agree, *Political Money,* p. 4.

Table 14.11   Number of Individual
Contributors to
All Campaigns, 1952-1972

Year	Number of Contributors
1952	3.0 million
1956	8.0 million
1960	10.0 million
1964	12.0 million
1968	8.7 million
1972	11.7 million

SOURCE: Herbert E. Alexander, *Financing the 1972 Election* (Lexington, Mass.: Lexington Books, D.C. Heath and Company, 1976), p. 367.

Table 14.12   Large Contributions in Presidential Campaigns
1952-1972

Year	No. of Indiv. Contributing $500 or More	No. of Indiv. Contributing $10,000 or More	Amounts Given by Contributors Giving $10,000 or More
1952	9,500	110	$ 1,936,870
1956	8,100	110	2,300,000
1960	5,300	95	1,552,009
1964	10,000	130	2,161,905
1968	15,000	424	12,187,863
1972	51,230	1254	51,320,154

SOURCE: Herbert E. Alexander, *Financing the 1972 Election* (Lexington, Mass.: Lexington Books, D.C. Heath and Company, 1976), p. 372.

While the Committee to Re-Elect the President depended heavily on contributions in excess of $200,000 each, George McGovern also depended, though to a lesser extent, on large contributions.[33] (Table 14.13). Nixon received over $19 million, or 33 percent, of his entire contributions from 153 contributors, each of whom made a contribution of $50,000 or more. McGovern received over $7 million, or 25 percent of his campaign total, from 41 contributors in that category. W. Clement Stone's contribution of over $2 million to Richard Nixon in 1972 is by far the largest sum ever contributed by one person to a single candidate in one election year.

[33] See Alexander, *Financing the 1972 Election*, especially Chapter 10 and selected appendices for a complete discussion of 1972 finance.

Table 14.13 Top Twelve Contributors to Nixon and McGovern

Nixon	Amount	McGovern	Amount
W. Clement Stone	$2,051,643.45	Stewart R. Mott	$407,747.50
Richard Mellon Scaife	1,000,000.00	Max Palevsky	319,365.00
John A. Mulcahy	624,558.97	Anne and Martin Peretz	275,016.44
Arthur Watson	303,000.00	Alejandro Zaffaroni	206,752.76
Ruth and George Farkas	300,000.00	Nicholas Noyes	205,000.00
John J. Louis, Jr.	283,360.22	Daniel Noyes	199,317.11
John Rollins	265,523.50	Alan and Shane Davis	158,872.25
Roy Carver	263,323.77	Richard Saloman	137,752.02
Sam Schulman	262,574.56	Joan Palevsky	118,616.86
Daniel Terra	255,000.00	Miles Rubin	108,000.00
Walter Annenberg	254,000.00	Bruce Allen	100,000.00
John Safer	251,000.00	John Lewis	100,000.00

SOURCE: Herbert E. Alexander, *Financing the 1972 Election* (Lexington, Mass.: Lexington Books, D.C. Heath and Company, 1976), p. 377.

Why the emphasis on big contributors in American elections in recent years? One answer is that the rapid growth in campaign costs has forced candidates to raise large sums of money in the easiest way possible. Obviously, if big givers are available, it is most efficient to collect large contributions. If given a choice between soliciting 25,000 ten dollar contributions or one $250,000 contribution, finance chairmen will opt for the latter. This pattern of contributions creates two major political dilemmas noted earlier. First, it gives a great advantage to wealthy candidates, or those who can attract large contributors. This bars potential candidates with fewer resources from even running for office, resulting in a campaign process dominated by the upper class. As Representative Podell of New York stated:

> When I ran for Congress, the first question asked me was whether I could finance my own campaign. If I had said, "No, I cannot," I would not have been a candidate. When you mention candidates for public office, you are only mentioning men of affluence.[34]

Second, this pattern of contributions raises the basic question of influence for money. Given the realities of politics, it is likely that most large contributors expect something in return. How much influence does a $250,000 contribution buy? While there is no clear answer, there are data to suggest that rewards are available. While not all large contributors receive or desire key positions as rewards, there is an association between large contributions and political appointments. Federal district judges, federal attorneys, and key administrative posts are often given to long-time financial supporters of winning candidates. "The reward of ambassadorial posts to large contributors has been a common practice in U.S. politics."[35] Certain more prestigious ambassadorial posts require larger contributions for consideration of appointment than other, less prestigious posts. For instance, when offered the ambassadorship to Costa Rica in 1973, Dr. Ruth Farkas balked, saying that she was interested in a European post and "isn't $250,000 an awful lot of money for Costa Rica."[36] She was subsequently appointed ambassador to Luxembourg, traditionally a political post. As long as large contributions are necessary, the possibility of direct or indirect influence is significant.[37] Therefore, attempts have been made to regulate campaign finance.

[34] Joseph R. Biden, Jr. "Public Financing of Elections: Legislative Proposals and Constitutional Questions," *Northwestern University Law Review*, 69 (March, 1974), 6.

[35] Alexander, *Financing Politics*, p. 86.

[36] *Ibid.*, p. 89.

[37] For a listing of contributions among selected Nixon appointees, see Alexander, *Financing the 1972 Election*, pp. 711-15.

CAMPAIGN FINANCE REFORM EFFORTS

The history of campaign finance reform efforts is a long one, although only recently has comprehensive finance legislation been attempted. Most legislation prior to the 1970s was piecemeal, generally imposing negative controls and spending limits on the candidates. "One after another, traditional sources of political funds were cut down without provision for new sources of supply."[38] One of the earliest finance statutes, the Federal Corrupt Practices Act of 1925, banned contributions from corporations. The Hatch Acts of 1939 and 1940 limited individual contributions to $5000, set a $3 million limit on spending by political committees, and barred federal employees from specified partisan activities. Another piece of finance legislation, a provision in the Taft-Hartley Act of 1947, prohibited contributions from labor unions.

Despite the intentions of reformers, each of these efforts to limit contributions and spending was circumvented. "Bonuses" were given to corporate executives and then "contributed" to the parties. Contributions were split into $5000 parcels by all conceivable family members and distributed to a multitude of ad hoc political committees designed specifically to evade the spending limits of the Hatch Act. Finally, unions created political action or "education" committees funded by "voluntary" union member contributions. Not only were the reform acts consciously evaded, they were seldom enforced, even if enforcement had been possible. Also, all of these reform efforts were directed solely at federal elections, not state or local. The history of campaign finance reform until 1970, then, is one of failure.

While the verdict is not yet in on the reforms of the 1970s, never before have so many fundamental changes been made in the conduct of campaigns in one decade. Within the context of the rapidly expanding costs, the increased role of the mass media, and the many excesses and illegal activities conducted in the "Watergate" era, the rules of the game were altered substantially in a series of unprecedented federal and state actions. The regulations enacted during the 1970s took four basic forms: (1) public disclosure requirements, (2) contribution restrictions, (3) spending limits, and (4) public financing provisions.

PUBLIC DISCLOSURE AND REPORTING PROCEDURES

The purpose of public disclosure is to provide the public with information concerning monetary influences on elected officials and, hopefully, curb excesses and abuses by requiring full public reporting of campaign finance

[38] *Ibid.*, p. 4.

data. One of the major provisions of the Federal Election Campaign Act of 1971 was to tighten requirements for reporting contributions and expenditures. House, Senate and presidential candidates were required to file reports at specified intervals with the Clerk of the House, the Secretary of the Senate, or the Comptroller General of the U.S., respectively. With the creation of the Federal Election Commission (FEC) in 1974, reinforced by subsequent legislation in 1976, enforcement provisions were strengthened and the Commission was given exclusive authority to prosecute both civil violations of the finance law and violations formerly covered in the criminal code. Fines of up to $25,000, or three times the amount of the contribution or expenditure in the violation, plus jail terms of up to one year, were provided for knowingly committing a finance law violation involving more than $1000. As of June, 1977, the major regulations regarding public disclosure and reporting stipulate that:

1. An individual can undertake an exploratory effort, such as taking a poll, without having to report contributions and expenditures.

2. Once an individual has declared his candidacy, however, within 30 days he must file a statement designating a principal campaign committee.

3. A quarterly financial report must be filed in any quarter of an election year during which a candidate or political committee receives or spends more than $1000.

4. Contributions of more than $100 must be itemized in the quarterly report.

5. Labor unions, corporations, and membership organizations must report expenditures of over $2000 per election for communications to their stockholders or members in which they advocate the election or defeat of a clearly identified candidate.

CONTRIBUTION RESTRICTIONS

Attempts to limit contributions have long been central to efforts to minimize obligations of candidates to large contributors or special interests. In the past, however, most attempts to place a limit on contributions have failed. The comprehensive Campaign Finance Act of 1974, however, set strict limitations on contributions to counter the big-money trend in the 1972 election. One of its provisions, that limiting independent expenditures on behalf of a candidate by an individual citizen, has been ruled unconstitutional by the Supreme Court in *Buckley v. Valeo* (1976) as an infringement of freedom of expression. While the 1976 amendments to this act eliminated that provision, they did retain limitations on contributions to candidates or committees. The major rules regulating contributions as of June, 1977 were:

1. Individuals are limited to contributions of $1000 per candidate per election, with a total contribution not to exceed $25,000 to all federal candidates each year.
2. Individuals are limited to contributions of $20,000 to a national committee of a political party and $5000 to other political committees annually.
3. Multicandidate committees are restricted to a $5000 contribution per candidate per year.
4. Democratic and Republican campaign committees can give up to $17,500 a year to a candidate.
5. Corporations and unions are barred from contributing to campaigns.
6. Anonymous contributions of over $50 cannot be used in federal elections.

SPENDING LIMITS

In order to balance the vast inequities in the monetary resources of candidates, restrictions have been placed on campaign spending as a reform effort. These may take the form of limits on certain types of expenditures, such as the 1971 restriction on broadcast spending discussed earlier, or limits on the total spending by a candidate. While the 1974 Campaign Finance Act set rigid spending limits on all federal elections, using formulas based on the office contested and number of eligible voters in the constituency, the Supreme Court ruled (*Buckley v. Valeo*) that the ceilings imposed were unconstitutional. It argued that a law which prohibits a person from using funds in excess of some arbitrary figure to bring his or her views before the electorate is in clear violation of the First Amendment. If, however, restrictions on spending are prerequisites for obtaining federal dollars for purposes such as presidential campaigns, the Court ruled that such restrictions are valid. In such cases, the candidate has the choice of accepting public funds or relying totally on personal wealth or private contributions and forfeiting the public monies. Only if the same principle were applied to congressional elections could spending be limited, according to the Court.

PUBLIC FUNDING

The most dramatic change in campaign financing was effected by the Federal Election Campaign Act of 1974, in which public funding of presidential campaigns was mandated. As a result, three types of government funding became available for the 1976 presidential campaign. First, the Act gave each major party candidate a flat grant of $20 million.[39] Smaller amounts were available for qualifying minor party candidates, although none met the rather stringent qualifications. In addition, each major party received about $2.2 million in 1976 to arrange and run its national convention. And finally, this act provided matching funds to qualified candidates seeking presidential nominations.[40]

No longer are presidential candidates dependent on large private contributions. Instead, public funds are provided through an income tax check-off system initiated in the Revenue Act of 1971. Under this system, each taxpayer can stipulate that one dollar of his taxes goes toward financing the presidential campaign. The program operates on a four-year cycle, accumulating funds each tax year to be paid out during presidential years. During the four years 1972-1975, for instance, a total of $94.1 million was raised from the tax plan. The payout in 1976 was:

Prenomination matching funds	$24.1 million
National Conventions	$ 4.4 million
General election grants	$43.6 million
Total	$72.1 million

The excess of approximately $20 million could revert to the national treasury or be held for the next election. Although the proportion of taxpayers participating in 1972 was only 3 percent, by including a check-off box on the tax return itself, the proportion in recent years has been increased to about 25 percent (See Table 14.14). It now appears that about $30 million per year will be collected by this means.

Public financing, being a radical change in the rules, naturally led to controversy. In January, 1975, only three months after passage of the Cam-

---

[39] This allotment is adjusted for increases in the Consumer Price Index. In 1976, each candidate received $21.8 million on that basis.

[40] A candidate might receive up to $5 million in federal matching funds. In order to initially qualify, the candidate must raise $100,000 in amounts of at least $5000 in each of 20 states or more. Only the first $250 of any individual private contribution is matched. The 1976 Amendments cut off federal subsidies to presidential candidates who receive less than 10 percent of the vote in two consecutive presidential primaries in which they run.

Table 14.14 Federal Income Tax Checkoff Response 1972-1975

Year	Percent of Taxpayers	Amount Checked Off
1972	3.0%	$ 4.0
1972 (retroactive)	–	8.9
1973	13.6%	17.3
1974	24.2%	31.9
1975	25.8%	33.0
Total		$94.1

Federal Election Commission

paign Finance Act, a suit was filed in federal court challenging the constitutionality of the statute. Among a vast array of opponents were Senator James Buckley of the Conservative Party of New York and liberal Independent presidential candidate Eugene McCarthy. They argued that the federal government should not intervene in the traditionally private arena of campaign financing, and that this act specifically favored major parties over minor ones by making it difficult for any candidates other than Republicans and Democrats to qualify for federal funding.

In the landmark *Buckley v. Valeo* decision, the Supreme Court upheld public financing of presidential campaigns. This ruling did, however, strike down individual spending limitations and absolute ceilings on campaign spending as violations of the First Amendment. Individuals who spent money directly on behalf of a candidate could not be restricted in this variety of free expression. Also, presidential candidates still could raise money through private means, although, if they did, they would have to forfeit the public funds. Not surprisingly, neither presidential candidate in 1976 chose to turn down the public money. While upholding the creation of the Federal Election Commission and its investigative and enforcement powers over the execution of the 1974 Campaign Act, the Court ruled that the means of selecting commission members violated the Constitution. Instead of half of the members being appointed by Congress and half by the president, all members would have to be appointed by the executive branch. As a response to this decision came the 1976 Amendments to the Campaign Finance Act. Intact, however, was the principle of public finance for presidential elections.

While reformers in Congress have attempted to include public funding of Senate and House Campaigns, they have been unsuccessful in applying this principle to their own elections. Opposition comes from several quarters. Republican legislators on the whole tend to oppose public funding, because normally they are better able to obtain private financing, especially from the party committees. The situation is more complex than a simple party line vote, however. Many incumbents fear public financing with strict limits on

437

private contributions, because incumbents have a much easier time raising funds than challengers. Some incumbents see public financing as encouraging potential challengers for their position. "Congress apparently affirms this wisdom by its willingness to authorize public financing of presidential but not congressional campaigns."[41]

One of the factors contributing to the acceptance of public financing, at least at the presidential level, is the dramatic shift in the public attitude toward public financing. In 1964 Americans rejected public financing of presidential campaigns by a 71 to 11 percent margin. Perhaps out of disgust with the excesses of the 1972 campaign, especially those of the Committee to Re-Elect the President, and by other revelations of campaign corruption, the 1977 electorate was much more receptive. In fact, it would go beyond even pending legislation dealing with federal funding of congressional elections. A majority of 57 percent agreed that "the federal government provide a fixed amount of money for election campaigns of candidates for Congress and that all private contributions from other sources be prohibited."[42] Thirty-two percent disagreed while 11 percent were uncertain.

As it stands at this time, the presidential campaign is unique in that private funds are prohibited if the candidate accepts federal funding. Depending on inflation rates, presidential candidates of the major parties can expect approximately $25 or $26 million dollars from the F.E.C. in 1980. In addition, each national party committee will be allowed to spend approximately $4 million on behalf of its nominee (this figure was $3.2 million in 1976), although that spending cannot be directly controlled by the candidate. Unless the law is altered again, each candidate in 1980 is expected to have about $30 million. While some observers contend that this is insufficient for a candidate to reach the voters effectively,[43] no longer is the price tag of presidential elections expected to run rampant, as in 1972.

STATE EFFORTS AT FINANCE REFORM

While the states vary in the direction and scope of their regulation of political finance, this issue has attracted attention in all states since the early 1970s.[44] Between 1972 and 1976, 49 states revised their laws regulating campaign finance. Despite the lack of uniformity, several generalizations are warranted

[41] Adamany and Agree, *Political Money*, p. 6.

[42] The Gallup Poll, March 25-28, 1977.

[43] See "Tight Budget for Presidential Candidates," *Congressional Quarterly Weekly Report* (July 31, 1976), 2036-37.

[44] For discussions of state action, see Alexander, *Financing Politics*, pp. 169-91, and "Campaign Finance: The States Push for Reform," *Congressional Quarterly Weekly Report* (August 31, 1974), pp. 2360-65.

from the data in Table 14.15. Approximately half of the states have established independent bipartisan commissions to oversee campaigns and elections. In most cases, these commissions replace the secretary of state, who is usually an elected official subject to attendant political pressures. Although some states have given these commissions enforcement powers, such as issuing subpoenas and assessing fines, few have evolved into truly autonomous administrative agencies like the Federal Election Commission.

Virtually all the states now require disclosure of political funds. This is the most obvious result of the "sunshine" laws introduced in the early 1970's, designed to make public information about influences on the political process. Forty-three states require disclosure both before and after the election, thereby giving the public insight prior to voting.

> Full disclosure of political income and disbursement is widely recognized as a basic requirement in eliminating campaign abuses. Full and frequent disclosure is a keystone of regulation.[45]

Public disclosure laws are designed to give the public full and accurate information on how much candidates are spending and where the money is coming from. Sunshine laws (1) provide a means of financial accountability, (2) curb excesses and abuses by increasing the risk for those engaged in illegal campaign activities, and, hopefully, (3) increase public confidence in the electoral process. "Publicity has a unique cleansing power which tends to reduce the potential influence of financial pressure on the electoral process."[46]

Full disclosure laws have been attacked as an invasion of privacy. It is argued that contributions to candidates should be as secret as the vote. Minor parties see disclosure as a deterrent to potential contributors, especially in those states where place of employment of contributors is part of the public record. Despite the problem of invasion of privacy, the Supreme Court has supported disclosure laws of those states. Another controversial area of regulation is the imposition of limits on contributions. Twenty-two states limit individual contributions, while others limit corporate and/or union contributions. Again, the constitutional question of contributing as a free expression of support has been decided in favor of reasonable contribution limits.

A final area where some states have made innovations is that of public subsidies to the parties. At least ten states have income tax check-offs, while at least three others have a voluntary surcharge of one or two dollars which a person may check on his or her tax return. Six states (Idaho, Iowa, Kentucky, Oregon, Rhode Island, and Utah) distribute money collected from the tax

---

[45] Alexander, *Financing Politics*, p. 171.
[46] *Ibid.*

Table 14.15 State Political Finance Provisions

State	Election Commission	Disclosure Before & After[a]	Individual Contribution Limits	Public Subsidy	Credit	Deduction	Checkoff
Ala.	X						
Alaska		X	X		X		
Ariz.	X	X					
Ark.		X	X				
Calif.	X	X				X	
Colo.		X				X	
Conn.	X	X	X				
Del.		X	X				
Fla.	X	X	X				
Ga.	X	X					
Hawaii		X				X	X
Idaho		X		X			
Ill.	X	X					
Ind.		X					
Iowa	X	X	X	X		X	X
Kan.	X	X	X				X
Ky.	X	X	X			X	
La.		X					
Maine	X	X	X	X			X
Md.	X	X	X	X			X
Mass.		X	X	X			X
Mich.	X	X	X	X		X	
Minn.	X	X		X	X	X	X
Miss.		X				X	
Mo.	X	X	X			X	X
Mont.		X	X	X		X	
Neb.		X					X

Table 14.15   State Political Finance Provisions (continued)

State	Election Commission	Disclosure Before & After[a]	Individual Contribution Limits	Public Subsidy	Tax Provisions Credit	Deduction	Checkoff
Nev.							
N.H.		X	X				
N.J.	X	X		X			X
N.M.			X				
N.Y.	X	X	X				
N.C.	X	X	X	X			X
N.D.							
Ohio	X	X					
Okla.	X	X	X			X	
Ore.		X		X	X	X	X
Pa.							
R.I.	X	X		X			X
S.C.	X	X					
S.D.	X	X	X				
Tenn.		X					
Texas		X					
Utah		X		X		X	X
Vt.		X	X				
Va.		X					
Wash.	X	X					
W. Va.		X	X				
Wis.	X	X	X				
Wyo.			X		X		
D.C.	X	X	X				

[a]Only North Dakota requires no disclosure at all.

SOURCES: Based on data as of May 1, 1977, from *Analysis of Federal and State Finance Law: Summaries* and *Analysis of Federal and State Finance Law: Charts*, prepared for the Federal Election Commission by the Congressional Research Service, Library of Congress, Washington, D.C. (December 1975); *The Book of the States, 1978-79* (Lexington, Kentucky: The Council of State Governments, 1978), XXII, pp. 250-59; and conversations with secretary of state offices in several states.

check-off directly to the parties, without restrictions on its use. Although suits have been filed claiming this tax distribution to be discriminatory against certain parties, until now it has been upheld. In addition to direct public financing, about one quarter of the states provide indirect public support through tax deductions or tax credits for political donations. Other states indirectly subsidize parties by assuming greater responsibilities for voter registration, distribution of campaign materials, and election day activities.[47]

CAMPAIGN FINANCE AND
POLITICAL PARTIES

Throughout this discussion of campaign finance, political parties have been relegated to the background. While parties potentially are central elements in financing political campaigns, seldom are they major participants, and even less frequently do they play a dominant role. As in the nomination process and the organization of campaigns, parties have surrendered most of their influence to autonomous candidate-oriented organizations. American campaigns are characterized by candidate, as opposed to party, spending. Ad hoc candidate organizations raise the funds and spend the money, with little party involvement, if any. Although party committees occasionally supplement candidate organizations and continue to be important in some states and localities, overall, their influence in campaign finance is minimal, especially for national elections. While party activists often are called upon to work and contribute money to candidates, they are solicited as potential contributors, not in their capacity of party members.

Continued emphasis on private financing of American campaigns, deepened by the rapid increase in campaign costs, has pitted candidates within the same party against each other in competition for limited funds. It is not unusual to hear the complaint that a national or gubernatorial candidate has drained off funds from lower-level contestants of the same party. While some candidates might consolidate their efforts and resources with a party ticket, few candidates can afford to tie their fates to other candidates in this manner. The new style of campaigning generally precludes such cooperation among candidates, since most are hard-pressed enough to raise adequate funds for their own efforts.

Ironically, many of the reforms initiated to overcome problems inherent in political finance have further weakened the party organization as a viable funding device. Many of the public disclosure laws, for instance, require that each candidate designate a finance chairman or committee upon becoming

[47] *Ibid.*, p. 188.

a primary candidate. Some of these laws specify that the candidate's finance representative must be independent of any other committee affiliations. Also, multicandidate organizations often are discouraged by contribution and spending limitations which include party expenditures in the totals that candidate can spend or raise.

While the current conduct of campaign financing in the U.S. appears to weaken party influence in elections, it may increase party control in the future. As noted earlier, a handful of states currently distribute funds collected from income tax check-offs to parties instead of candidates. The state party organization then apportions this money to candidates as it sees fit. Obviously, this gives the party leaders considerable leverage over the candidates as the amount of available funds rises. At least that portion of the funds which is public becomes centralized in the party. While dependence on private finance strengthens independent candidate committees, public finance, if funnelled through the political parties, has the opposite effect. There is little evidence that Congress is sympathetic toward centralization of federal campaign finance in the parties, however, since it would be counter to their individual interests and reduce their own independence. This again demonstrates the friction and competition which have developed between the party organization and the party office holders in government.

Campaign finance clearly reflects and reinforces the basic characteristics of the electoral system. Just as all other aspects are decentralized and fragmented, so the funding of campaigns revolves around candidates, not parties. Despite many attempts at reforming campaign finance, it must be realized that all changes will be made within the context of American politics. Past reforms have failed to alter substantially the conduct of election campaigns. Finance reform will not solve any problems unless momentum exists to carry it into practice. The parties cannot be saved by financial reforms alone; it will take major alterations in the fabric of American politics. Campaign finance is but one aspect in the electoral process, although certainly an important one. It is likely that parties will continue to play a minor supporting role in campaigns. While alterations in financing campaigns might shift this role slightly, there is little hope that parties soon will regain a central role in the campaign process.

SECTION VII

THE PARTIES:
HOPE
OR DESPAIR?

This last chapter offers suggestions as to the future of the American party system based on the framework developed within the earlier chapters. After briefly summarizing the weakened status of the political parties, consequences for the political system are discussed. An increased role for interest groups and the rise of the non-politician as a major political force are viewed as products of weakened parties. Most importantly, the deliberative foundation of politics is shaken considerably when parties are unable to sustain their role as broker or mediator of the various competing interests. Without the majority-building capability of parties, more fragmented and unstable politics might follow.

The chapter ends by examining the extent to which parties might be able to regroup and reverse the trends now working toward their demise. Some argue that the level of public support is crucial to the success or failure of the parties' reemergence as a positive force in American electoral politics. While many political observers disagree about the future of U.S. parties and some contend that they are already dead, the conclusion here is that it is too early to count them out. The future of parties depends largely on the willingness and ability of party leaders to adapt to changes in the electorate and to revitalize the parties from within. No longer can leaders depend on the voters to come to them and obediently accept the party line. Instead, leaders must provide an environment for meaningful change within the party and again instill a need for the parties within the electorate, especially among the young and educated segments of society. Although this will not guarantee party survival, it certainly is a necessary condition for it.

447

15

The Future
of Political Parties
in America

This chapter is an attempt to summarize briefly some of the major aspects of American political parties discussed in earlier chapters, and to offer suggestions of what the future may hold. It emphasizes the weakening of all three dimensions of parties and the consequences for parties and the party system. Because it is assumed that the future of the parties is dependent on public support, recent behavioral and attitudinal reactions to the parties are summarized and their impact is evaluated. Tentative conclusions are offered as to the possibility of a revitalization and renewal of the parties in the future.

THE WEAKENED STATE OF
POLITICAL PARTIES

This book started with the assumption that U.S. political parties have evolved through a combination of cultural and social forces unique to the United States. The development of political parties has paralleled that of other political institutions. Alterations in other aspects of American politics are expected, therefore, to influence the shape and characteristics of the parties. Throughout this book, American parties have been examined as multidimensional and complex organisms which react to outside pressures. Much emphasis has been placed on the weakening of each dimension of parties and the growth of organizations which compete with the parties. Extra-party organizations, ad hoc candidate and issue-oriented groups, and the mass media have all been found to provide alternatives to party control. Some of the major factors altering the role of parties in American politics are summarized here for each dimension.

PARTY ORGANIZATION

Although party organizations were rarely as centralized or powerful as a few big city machines, changes in perceptions of democracy over the last century have substantially reduced their influence over the nomination and election process. Reform efforts, designed specifically to weaken party organization control, have been largely successful. Nonpartisan elections have taken the parties out of politics. Welfare reforms and the civil service system have eliminated incentives crucial to ongoing organizations. Most importantly, the virtually universal use of the direct primary to nominate party candidates has resulted in the loss of control by party leaders over candidates. Most campaigns are now organized and financed by autonomous candidate organizations, independent of the party.

Other social forces have also weakened political parties. Among these is the growing proportion of party purists who reject the pragmatism and accommodation central to traditional party politics. As party organizations have lost their ability to provide patronage and other material incentives to recruit party workers, more issue-oriented and ideological activists have come to predominate. As these better educated and more affluent "amateurs" have replaced the full-time party workers, the composition of party organizations has become less stable, since many of the issue or candidate-oriented activists will work within the party only so long as it serves their goals. If their personal goals are not satisfied in the party, they have no long-term loyalty to bind them to it. The increased tendency of political activists to work outside the formal party organization and to establish groups which challenge the supremacy of parties has furthered this decline.

The shift in campaigning from dependence on volunteers and personal contacts to paid professionals and the electronic media has also contributed to the loss of party control. The party organizations have little to offer candidates who require polling services, media specialists, and other technical expertise. As a result, candidates must organize autonomous campaign units, staffed not with party workers but with their own personal supporters. Despite the efforts of some state parties, and to some extent the national committees, to modernize their operations and meet the needs of the candidates, most party organizations have been less than successful in maintaining a central role in campaigns.

PARTIES AS GOVERNING ORGANIZATIONS

The weakness of the formal party organizations in the nomination process has contributed significantly to the lack of party discipline in government. Since party leaders are unable to influence consistently nomination and renomination of party candidates for office, they have no effective sanction over those elected on their party label. No longer do candidates rely on the party organization for crucial campaign support, nor do they utilize the official organization. The independence of candidates in the nomination process and the election campaigns results in office holders independent of the party leaders. Although many elected officials display allegiance to their party, the present system does not guarantee a party influence.

While there is a tendency in much literature to minimize party control of government, several chapters here have demonstrated that party label continues to be a major component in legislative bodies. Despite competition from constituency, personal background of the candidate, and interest groups, the parties are much in evidence in Congress, and to a greater degree in many states. However, it is crucial that the distinction between the statutory party leaders and the legislative leaders be explained. Due to the reasons stated above, there is little coordination and cooperation among office holders and the formal/legal party leaders. Once elected, the party members have no accountability to the national, state, or local party organizations. While party is still the single best indicator of voting in Congress, especially on economic and social welfare issues, this is more the result of members with similar perspectives, or constituencies with particular characteristics, than of control exercised by the official party leaders.

The party as a governing organization also is characterized by a decentralization of party leadership. While the president is nominal leader of the national committee, congressional parties are largely independent. Within Congress, power is widely diffused among committees, subcommittees, and individual members and their staffs. The institutional context of federalism and separation of powers further fragments power among the branches of government and between the nation and the states. It is not surprising that the governing dimension of political parties in the United States consistently has been the weakest link. It must be noted again, however, that the weak state of the statutory parties has led inevitably to this minimal governing role. Both dimensions reflect and are reinforced by the context of American politics. Although it is not unreasonable to perceive future governing parties as more responsible, it appears quite unlikely, given this context and the trends toward a weakening, not a strengthening, of parties.

PSYCHOLOGICAL AFFILIATION

As the trends in party organization and party governing are far from hopeful for the political parties, the trends in the electorate are not favorable. Although evidence is mixed, there are indications that the electorate is becoming more issue-oriented. On the surface, this would tend to buoy the hopes of the responsible party advocates, since it implies a potential division of the electorate on the basis of issues or perhaps even ideologies. In order for this trend to benefit parties, however, the issue divisions must take place along party lines. However, the nature of the issues of the last decade has not been amenable to exploitation by the parties. Neither party has been able to mobilize the electorate on the major issues. Vietnam, crime in the streets, abortion, and even the economy have proven elusive for both the Democrats and Republicans. The issues of the future do not appear to be any more party-oriented than recent concerns of the electorate.

Contributing to this lack of ability of either party to mobilize the electorate on the issues is the increased complexity of the issues themselves, and the tendency of many individuals and groups to demand compliance of candidates on a single issue. The traditional ability of parties to aggregate and articulate policy concerns on a wide range of issues has been strained. Despite the increased issue-awareness of many voters, the parties have not benefited. Also, it must be noted that the majority of voters continue to be candidate-oriented, not issue-oriented.

Other trends in the electorate appear to be in direct conflict with strengthening the psychological dimension of parties in the electorate. The data presented in Chapter 10 illustrated a clear behavioral trend away from parties. The unquestioned weakening of party identification in the electorate, coupled with the large increase in self-identified Independents, has been substantial since 1960. The rapid increase in split-ticket voting by a majority of voters, including those strongly identified with one party or the other, is further evidence of the weakened state of party affiliation. Purposive non-voting, although less well researched, is another indication of the tendency toward independence from party identification.

While these overall trends away from party loyalty are, in themselves, disheartening to party advocates, the specific patterns are even less encouraging. Data demonstrate that it is the young voters who are most prone to exhibit independent attitudes and behavior. Although young voters traditionally have had the lowest levels of party affiliation, the magnitude of the gap between young and old is increasing. Also, the young voters are remaining independent of parties longer than past generations, leading to the possibility that this pattern is more durable than in the past.

As reflected in the electoral and governing dimensions of political party, intensity and scope of party affiliation have diminished in recent years. Obviously, the change in voting is related to alterations in the other party dimensions. The weakness of the statutory party organizations and the lack of centralized party control over government result in a lower profile for the parties. Conversely, independent candidates and the emphasis on media campaigns have worked to the detriment of mobilized party support in the electorate. As candidates downplay parties, it is natural to expect a similar reaction in the electorate. On the other hand, as party affiliation becomes weaker, independent minded candidates can be expected to proliferate, since party effectiveness is checked. The trend toward weakened parties is consistent across all three of the party dimensions discussed in this book.

CONSEQUENCES OF WEAKENED PARTIES

While the public continues to be indifferent, at best, to political parties, and the long-term consequence of many reform efforts has been to weaken parties further, there is much danger in the breakdown of traditional party roles. Political parties have served as a moderating influence during most of U.S. history, and have accommodated a wide variety of conflicting interests in this heterogeneous society. While parties have largely failed as governing organizations, until lately they have served as brokers for the many competing interests in American politics. Walter Burnham sees parties as the only effective devices for generating countervailing collective power on behalf of singularly powerless individuals, and views the effect of party decomposition as profound.[1] David Broder goes further and states that the "government system is not working because the political parties are not working."[2] Party affiliation has stabilized voting and moderated shifts in the electorate. The weakened party organizations and the decreased importance of party identification for many Americans threaten to minimize these contributions of political parties to the maintenance of the U.S. electoral process.

ALTERNATIVE ELECTORAL GROUPS

One result of the weakening of parties will be to increase further the importance of other elements of the political system at the expense of the parties. Special interest groups have always been powerful in specific policy areas. Their impact on electoral politics at times when political parties were strong, however, has been limited, since it has been the parties, not the interest groups, that have had the votes needed to win elections. As parties' domina-

[1] Walter Dean Burnham, *Critical Elections and the Mainsprings of American Politics* (New York: W.W. Norton and Company, Inc., 1970), p. 133.
[2] David S. Broder, *The Party's Over: The Failure of Politics in America* (New York: Harper and Row, Publishers, 1971), p. xxiii.

tion of the electorate, and their role in the nomination and election process have dissipated, however, interest groups have begun to fill the vacuums in sponsoring candidates, financing elections, and providing reference points for voters. The advent of ad hoc issue-oriented groups as electoral forces has followed in the parties' wake, as candidates strive to gain their support. General purpose interest groups such as Common Cause, the League of Women Voters, and electoral extensions of Ralph Nader-type consumer advocates might conceivably provide long-term affiliations if the parties abdicate their role.

The strengthened position of special interest groups vis-à-vis political parties further fragments and disperses electoral power. This is reinforced by the tendency of the electronic media to serve as a forum for various group appeals. While this trend is not necessarily dysfunctional, it leads to a lack of direction, since the issue- and candidate-oriented groups tend to be most concerned with short-term goals, whereas parties largely are concerned with long-term survival. Restraints on party action are broader, since parties must be responsive to varied demands, while special interests can afford to concentrate their efforts on a narrow range of issues.

Jack Dennis sees an increase in nonpartisan elections as another product of the breakdown of parties.[3] The data presented in Chapter 4 indicate that elections without parties are no panacea for democracy, and that normally turnout for nonpartisan elections is considerably lower than in partisan contests. It would be expected that various citizen groups would be created to support slates of nonpartisan candidates, should nonpartisan elections become widespread for higher offices. Obviously, the importance of independent candidate organizations increases as party influence decreases. If alternative electoral groups fail to surface in the event of political party disappearance, mass confusion at the polls is a very real possibility as tens of millions of voters lose their primary voting cue. While it is certainly too early to assume that contingency electoral mechanisms are necessary, a future without parties would be anything but idyllic.

RISE OF THE NONPOLITICIANS

Also emanating in part from the decline of parties has been the emergence of the nonpolitician. Candidates of the late 1970s have exploited their lack of experience in party politics, quite successfully in many cases. Since the parties have few sanctions over candidates, there is nothing to lose by

---

[3]Jack Dennis, "Trends in Public Support of the American Party System," *British Journal of Political Science*, 5 (April, 1975), p. 230.

denouncing politics. The direct primary system reinforces the candidates' ability to run for office without working up through the party ranks. Furthermore, the weakened party affiliation frees many voters to support the nonpoliticians, and thereby encourages them to do so. Although the present pattern of running against politics may simply reflect the immediate political mood of the country, weak parties and Independent candidates augur well for its continuance.

LOSS OF DELIBERATIVE ROLE

Several authors see the American party system as shifting toward policy advocacy.[4] Due to the impossibility of determining policy implications of election results in the U.S., however, parties have difficulty emphasizing policy functions. A major evidence of the shift from parties as agents of consensus to agents of policy government is the shift in type of party activitists from politicians whose major concern is the good of the party, to "purists," who take rigid views of candidate orientations.

According to Nelson Polsby and Aaron Wildavsky, "purists . . . are favored as never before by the rules of the game and politicians disfavored."[5] This advantage exists since purists tend to be involved earlier, and the rules, including federal subsidies for primaries, encourage early activity. Party regulars, conversely, prefer to wait until a consensus develops. Under the current rules, by the time the politicians are ready to apply their skills at majority-building, it is too late to enter the nomination process. Not surprisingly, an increasing number of convention delegates are candidate activists. While this encourages advocacy politics,

> What is lost . . . is the capacity to deliberate, to weigh competing demands, and to compromise so that a variety of differing interests each gain a little.[6]

As political parties have come to emphasize advocacy of policy, the crucial function of mediation has been reduced substantially. Under the circumstances, candidates have little need of state and local party leaders or of traditional interest groups. The primary system penalizes moderate, compromise candidates while rewarding those with narrow but intense followings.

---

[4] Nelson W. Polsby and Aaron Wildavsky, *Presidential Elections: Strategies of American Electoral Politics*, 4th ed. (New York: Charles Scribner's Sons, 1976).

[5] *Ibid.*, p. 277.

[6] *Ibid.*, p. 278.

Easy access to the mass media by those with adequate resources further reinforces advocacy politics. Ironically, the participatory democracy of the 1970s appears to be "inimical" to deliberative democracy.

> As more (and different) people have won the right to participate in the nomination process, the kinds of communication they have been able to send one another have become impoverished. They can vote, but they cannot bargain. They can make speeches, but they cannot deliberate.[7]

The results of recent presidential conventions, especially those of the 1968 and 1972 Democrats, are evidence of the need for consensus-building within political parties. The heterogeneous nature of the American electorate works against purism in electoral politics. Polsby and Wildavsky "prefer politicians to purists and parties of intermediation to parties of advocacy," and contend that the motive of winning elections must be central to party activity.[8] This desire to win tends to moderate appeals to diverse groups in the electorate and brings a multitude of varying interests together. Certainly, the new style of campaigning and the direct primary system diminish the possibility of consensus-building and deliberation.

PUBLIC SUPPORT:
THE CRITICAL ELEMENT

After all these trends and possible alternatives for political parties have been examined, two questions remain central to the future of political parties: (1) are the parties in their weakened state capable of regrouping and adjusting to changing conditions, and (2) to what extent are Americans, especially the politically active, willing to support rejuvenated political parties? There currently is much concern about the low level of support for political parties, which has led some observers to forecast the disappearance of parties as a major political institution in the United States. One of the future alternatives examined in Chapter 10 was politics without parties. Walter Burnham, for one, argues that parties are in such an advanced stage of decomposition that they are incapable of regrouping.[9]

[7]*Ibid.*, p. 279.

[8]*Ibid.*, p. 283.

[9]Burnham, *Critical Elections.* Also see Burnham, "American Politics in the 1970's: Beyond Party?" in *The American Party Systems: Stages of Political Development*, 2nd. ed., ed. William Nisbet Chambers and Walter Dean Burnham (New York: Oxford University Press, 1975), pp. 308-57.

In his comprehensive examination of party support in the U.S., Jack Dennis concludes that:

> Taken as a whole, these items on public perception of the performance of the parties, compared both across time and across institutions, show a low and declining level of support. The decline in positive sentiment has been especially marked in the past few years.[10]

Although support for all political institutions has declined in the last decade, the low levels of support for parties at the start guarantees them the lowest overall rating. In addition to weakened party identification and other manifestations of independence such as ticket splitting, Dennis demonstrates a "fairly sharp decline" in support for keeping party labels on the ballot and continued low support in other attitudes toward the role and the legitimacy of political parties.[11] He finds a decline in the public's perception of the capacity of parties to make the government attentive and a growing tendency to feel that parties confuse issues and create conflict.

Despite the decline in support of political parties by the mass public, party membership has remained constant at around 7-8 percent. Actually, the volunteer activity for parties has increased slightly in the last decade. Additionally, there is a trend toward increased financial support for parties.[12] While Dennis suggests that the institution of party is far from dead as long as it continues to attract a substantial degree of elite and activist support, there is a danger here that parties might become an increasingly elite phenomenon with little mass appeal.

Although there is much discontent with political parties, the changes supported by the public would do little to strengthen them. For instance, there is overwhelming public support for the national primary to replace the convention. This, however, would remove the one major function of the national parties, reinforce the fragmentation of the party system, and place even more power in the states and localities.

Also, despite the low levels of support for political parties in the U.S., the present two-party system and current form of two-party competition are still favored by the public. Dennis finds that a "strong majority" favor status quo, although they tend to see little difference between the parties.[13]

---

[10] Dennis, "Trends in Public Support," pp. 208-9.

[11] *Ibid.*, pp. 200-202.

[12] This is reflected in an increase from 28 percent in 1948 to 43 percent in 1968 of those willing to contribute $5.00 or more to a party.

[13] Dennis, "Trends in Public Support," p. 217.

In this data there is little support for making parties more responsible. Dennis finds minimal public support for ideologically pure parties, and a favorable response to divided government. "People are clearly unwilling to reorient the present parties to make them more ideologically pure."[14] This attitude would seem to negate realignment of parties along strict ideological lines.

On the basis of similar data, some observers contend that the most effective means of reinforcing public confidence in the parties is to avoid extremist candidates and work for consensus through a deliberative process.[15] They argue that most people do not want parties with extreme policy appeals, but are satisfied with the present policy and ideological composition of the parties. They note that alienation and nonvoting increase when parties nominate extreme candidates. According to Polsby and Wildavsky, policy-oriented, responsible parties reflect the tastes of the purists, not the general public. At least part of the decreased levels of public support for the parties in this decade is the result of their attempts to placate the purists.

FUTURE OF PARTIES: HOPE OR DESPAIR

In Chapter 10 various realignment possibilities were discussed within the context of current trends in voting behavior. If nothing else, that discussion demonstrated the depth of disagreement among observers of political parties. Some political scientists predict a realignment of the parties along either traditional or new ideological lines, an evolving multiparty system, an emergence of a Republican majority, or creation of a new conservative coalition. Others, such as James Sundquist, contend that current shifts are temporary adjustments to contemporary issues, and that the Democratic New Deal coalition will again be strengthened.[16] Still other observers speculate on the disintegration or decomposition of political parties, and see the trends in voting as one manifestation of a future politics without parties as we know them. A final perspective is that politics will continue on largely as usual. It has been argued that the parties have been in serious trouble before but have, nevertheless, persisted.

While it is seldom virtuous to take a cautious stand in analyzing trends, the substantial differences among political "experts" suggest caution in this case. The basic problem here relates to the complexity and interrelatedness

---

[14] *Ibid.*, p. 218.

[15] Polsby and Wildavsky, *Presidential Elections*, p. 280.

[16] James L. Sundquist, *Dynamics of the Party System* (Washington, D.C.: The Brookings Institution, 1973).

of the many elements which constitute politics in the U.S. We simply cannot at this time be certain whether the current patterns represent a long-term shift in voting, or whether they are simply responses to short-term conditions. Therefore, while Walter Burnham sees the present patterns of voting behavior as part of an obvious long-term trend toward party decomposition, Jack Dennis concludes that there has not yet occurred a massive shift from the parties:

> We should probably await further evidence before deciding that the drift away from identifying with one or the other of the two major parties is more than a temporary public reaction to recent experience with particular leaders and polities.[17]

In a recent work, Warren Miller and Teresa Levitin agree that the "party system remains largely intact" and that there is no "conclusive evidence of the decay of popular support for American political institutions."[18] Despite the evidence presented throughout this book, one cannot say with assurance that the parties have become or are destined to become a phenomenon of the past.

Arthur Miller of the Michigan Survey Research Center, for instance, casts some doubt on those who interpret the weakening of party identification in the late 1960s and early 1970s as evidence of an end to the parties. He contends that party identification as a determinant of voting hit a low in 1972, and that by 1976,

> The growth of Independents appeared to have levelled off at 36 percent and party identification had resurfaced as a major explanation of the vote decision.[19]

While there continue to be notable degrees of defection from parties and a deterioration of the public's ties to the party system, the parties are far from dead. However, competition from ideological orientations, as well as evaluations of candidate performance on the basis of which candidate would provide the most competent leadership, threaten to displace parties if they fail to respond to these current needs of the voters.

[17]Dennis, "Trends in Public Support," p. 193.

[18]Warren E. Miller and Teresa E. Levitin, *Leadership and Change: The New Politics and the American Electorate* (Cambridge: Winthrop Publishers, Inc., 1976), pp. 225 and 227.

[19]Arthur H. Miller, "Partisanship Reinstated? A Comparison of the 1972 and 1976 U.S. Presidential Elections," *British Journal of Political Science*, 8 (April, 1978), 130.

To some extent these conflicting conclusions can be attributed to the use of different data and different methods with which to interpret the data. While much of the research on party realignment is based on voting for president, there is much evidence that presidential voting is, by any standard, the least adequate measure of party voting. Voting in congressional and state elections demonstrates much higher degrees of partisan stability than the more media-oriented and candidate-centered presidential contests. Although Jack Dennis found a decline in the importance of party identification for higher-level offices, that pattern was reversed for state elections below governor and for local elections. "In contests for lower offices, the importance of party seems to be increasing, if marginally."[20] This suggests the possibility that parties might be substantially more important at the state and local levels, if indeed they have failed at the national level. Given the decentralized nature of the party system, this should not be surprising.

In the first chapter it was suggested that political parties must be perceived as but one element in a highly complex political reality. It was argued that both overemphasis on the role of political parties and underestimation of their effectiveness are misleading and unfair to parties. In such a complex system, it is unrealistic to establish stringent criteria by which to judge the success or failure of parties. On the other hand, just because parties demonstrate a limited influence over the political process, they should not be ignored or dismissed as irrelevant. Therefore, expectations of party potential must be tempered with the realization that numerous other political and nonpolitical elements also have major roles in American politics. We study political parties as one element of American political existence, not as the sole or dominant element. Despite a decline in the influence of political parties in recent years, they continue to be the most persistent of U.S. political institutions.

While an exhaustive and vigorous effort to adjust will be required to maintain even the admittedly weak parties of the 1970s in the future, it is expected that American political parties will adapt to the changing circumstances much as they have to other challenges over the last century and a half. Throughout their existence, American political parties have faced almost insurmountable odds. While they seldom have overcome these obstacles, parties have survived. Although this book has summarized many trends that appear to be debilitating to political parties, they are expected to outlast these threats, albeit in an even less dominant form. The party transformation thesis of Ladd and Hadley largely supports this conclusion. They suggest that while less stable electoral politics, with alternating presidential landslides

[20] Dennis, "Trends in Public Support," p. 198.

such as 1964 and 1972 and a more transient electorate, will emerge from the current transformation of parties, the demise of parties will not follow.[21]

While the death of parties suggested by some observers is a possibility, and a probability if parties fail to adapt, the theory assumes that the parties are unable or unwilling to adjust to recent changes in the electorate and electoral context. Certainly, most state and national party leaders are now willing to restructure and revitalize the parties. Whether they are able to do so is, of course, the major question. While it is dangerous to predict anything in politics, and the odds certainly do not favor the parties, the feeling of this author is that the parties will continue, although in a diminished state. While the future of parties is not one of great hope, neither is it one of total despair. Political parties still have a major place in American electoral politics. It is up to party leaders to provide a context for reasonable and meaningful change. Ultimately, however, the future of the parties will depend on the support of the public, especially the younger electorate which holds the key to the continuance or demise of these unique political institutions.

[21] Everett Carll Ladd, Jr. and Charles D. Hadley, *Transformations of the American Party System*, 2nd ed. (New York: W.W. Norton and Company, Inc., 1978). See especially Chapter 7.

Index

JK   Blank, Robert H.
2261
B64   Political parties

DATE